The Science of the Mind:
2001 and Beyond

The Science of the Mind: 2001 and Beyond

EDITED BY

Robert L. Solso
University of Nevada, Reno

Dominic W. Massaro
University of California, Santa Cruz

New York   Oxford   OXFORD UNIVERSITY PRESS   1995

Oxford University Press

Oxford   New York
Athens   Auckland   Bangkok   Bombay
Calcutta   Cape Town   Dar es Salaam   Delhi
Florence   Hong Kong   Istanbul   Karachi
Kuala Lumpur   Madras   Madrid   Melbourne
Mexico City   Nairobi   Paris   Singapore
Taipei   Tokyo   Toronto

and associated companies in
Berlin   Ibadan

Published by Oxford University Press, Inc.,
200 Madison Avenue, New York, New York 10016

Library of Congress Cataloging-in-Publication Data
The science of the mind : 2001 and beyond / edited by
Robert L. Solso, Dominic W. Massaro.
p.   cm.   Includes bibliographical references.
ISBN 0-19-508064-5
1. Psychology.
2. Twenty-first century—Forecasts.
I. Solso, Robert L., 1933-   .
II. Massaro, Dominic W.
BF149.S347   1995
150'.09'0501—dc20   94-24537

1 3 5 7 9   8 6 4 2

Printed in the United States of America
on acid-free paper

We dedicate this book

to the twentieth century scholars

who envisioned the science of the mind

and the twenty-first century scholars

who may make our dreams come true

PREFACE

As we are about to witness the close of the twentieth century, it seemed appropriate to ask some of the most thoughtful people in psychology to address an age-old question: Where have we been, where are we, and where are we going?

One hundred years ago, psychology coalesced around a small group of unusual men and women whose thoughts defined the science of the mind as practiced throughout the twentieth century. Those early pioneers, working with modest equipment by today's standards, commenced a century-long experiment which involved measuring behavior, analyzing brain processes, and developing models of mind. When people look back over the last hundred years of progress in psychology (as well as all science and technology), the enormity of what our forebears wrought is manifest in the proliferation of types of psychologists, diversity of laboratories, and fantastic array of apparatuses. Did these early pioneers foresee the future? What would the likes of Francis Galton, William James, Lloyd Morgan, James McKeen Cattell, Sigmund Freud, Wilhelm Wundt, Mary Calkins, G. Stanley Hall, Margaret Washburn, Ivan Pavlov, Hermann Ebbinghaus, Edward Titchener, or F. C. Donders write about "the science of the mind: 1901 and beyond"? (And isn't it regrettable that they didn't!) Would any of these scholars envision the developments of the twentieth century, or would they see only solutions to nineteenth-century problems, not new models of the mind? Would they have foreseen the expansion of psychological organizations, the commercialization of psychology, the impressive impact of computers on psychology, the rise and fall of psychoanalysis, Gestalt psychology, behaviorism, cybernetics, learning theories, and all the diversity that is psychology today?

When looking back on this remarkable twentieth century, it is easy to believe that the science of the mind has progressed magnificently. Although scientific historians may debate the relative value of certain specialties (e.g., "Was it really necessary to study, in detail, the behavior and physiology of the Norway rat? Did psychoanalysis prove to be a comprehensive theory of the human mind? Were early tests of intelligence and abilities beneficial or harmful?"), the consensus is that the last hundred years have seen unprecedented technological and scientific progress in the science of the mind. Will the vector of unusual development continue throughout the twenty-first century?

It is within this context that the present book was planned. The editors were interested in what the leading scholars of today thought about the future of the science of the mind. And with that simple objective, we invited papers from a cross section of distinguished scholars. We were delighted with the overwhelming support for the idea of pulling together ideas from contemporary scholars on their vision for the future. While a few people we contacted could not write a chapter because of their schedule ("I'm committed to writing projects up to 2001!" one wrote) and others because of modesty ("I'm afraid I can't even figure out what tomorrow will bring, let alone what the next century will be like," another wrote), all endorsed the idea of a book in this area and many promised to be eager readers.

The reader will find that the contributors to this book are among the most distinguished assemblage of scholars in psychology; yes, even equal to the illustrious group mentioned above. The present group, however, has an historical advantage in that we *know* what the last hundred years have produced. Also, we have exceptionally fancy tools not even imagined by our intellectual ancestors.

In an initial letter of invitation the editors suggested that a book dealing with the future of the science of the mind might "serve as an opportunity . . . to express your expectations for the future and, by so doing, influence the destiny of the field. Only recently, American psychology celebrated its centennial and, with the turn of the century only a few years away, many people will be anxiously looking forward to the next 100 years. If the past is any indication of the future, then the next century is likely to produce profound changes. It seems to us that we should record the collective wisdom of twentieth-century scientists at this time as they look forward to the future."

Authors were encouraged to write pieces for enlightened lay readers, who would appreciate well-written, carefully reasoned, interesting, and informative chapters; colleagues, who might be looking for critical insights into the future of their field; and students who may search for a glimpse of the future which, ultimately, they, not we, will be a part. Readers will find in the chapters a fanciful blueprint for the future written by wise people of the twentieth century. And, as heady as our ideals are, most authors modestly agree that the way our blueprint for the future plays out will undoubtedly be modified by the next breed of scientist, just as the plans made 100 years ago did not materialize exactly as their authors had envisioned they might. The study of the science of the mind is dynamic, and we would not wish a different fate (although most of us, with some trepidation, hope that our ideas will not look too wacky 100 years from now!).

The Science of the Mind: 2001 and Beyond is organized around five parts, followed by a final chapter by the editors. We had in mind a gentle structure, not a strict taxonomy, since we asked the contributors to cut loose and follow their muse. We begin with four general overviews by Robert Solso, Gordon Bower, the late Roger Sperry, and Roger Shepard of not only how the science of the mind will unfold, but also how science and society in general might evolve. The second part covers specialized topics in developmental psychology and neurocognition and includes chapters by Howard Gardner, Jean Mandler, and Stephen Kosslyn. The third part, consisting of chapters on memory, perception, and ecological considerations by Bennet Murdock, Robert Sternberg, Richard Gregory, and Michael Turvey and Robert Shaw, is followed by a section on language and categorization by James Jenkins, Willem Levelt, Dominic Massaro, and George Lakoff. Our fifth and final part, with chapters by Donald Norman, Earl Hunt, Robert Sommer, and John Pittenger, deals with some of the ways our scientific knowledge might be applied. In the final chapter, the editors give an overview of all of the essays.

Sadly, before this project was completed, Roger Sperry died. Professor Sperry personified the best of twentieth-century science, and we respectfully pay homage to his scientific work, and to this, his final chapter.

We also wish to acknowledge the authors who have dedicated themselves to this project with unusual energy and wisdom. They have won our gratitude and the coming appreciation of countless scientists of the future.

December 1994
Lake Tahoe, Nevada   R.L.S.
Santa Cruz, California   D.W.M.

CONTENTS

I

INTRODUCTORY COMMENTS AND GENERAL THEORIES

In this part, chapters by Robert Solso, Gordon Bower, Roger Sperry, and Roger Shepard present general theories of the state of the "science of the mind" as might be realized in the next century. The ideas expressed in this first part range from ecological–humanistic concerns (Solso), to designing a friendly technology (Bower), to a call for a new way of thinking about survival (Sperry), to a theory of mental universals (Shepard).

1

Turning the Corner

ROBERT L. SOLSO

The science of the mind in 2001 and beyond can be forecasted paradoxically by taking a look backward in time. And the further we look back, the clearer will be the view of the future. In this retrograde approach to the future science of the mind, two historical periods can be considered—the twentieth century and the entire history of the universe that preceded it. That ought to cover just about everything important.

Predicting the Future

The assortment of people who have trod this earth are a curious lot, but we have at least one thing in common: We humans have a penchant for trying to figure out how things work and what the future holds. So prevalent is this trait among our species, that it is likely that individual and collective survival is linked with accurate anticipation of the unknown. Reliable prediction of what might lie around the next corner, or bush, probably saved our ancestors from getting killed before they had a chance to reach maturity. Anticipating the fall harvest from seeds planted in the spring not only provided sustenance but also was the source of civilization. Those who possessed prophetic powers, either real or imaginary, became the most highly esteemed members of their community. Throughout history, medicine men, prophets, seerers, soothsayers, and priests have always stood close to the center of authority.

While some predictions about the future of the world are based on pragmatic considerations—like the popular *Wall $treet Week,* in which modern soothsayers divine the direction of the stock market, attesting to the profit motive of the prophet motive—others appear to be mostly whimsical, like the person who predicted that by the year 2010 the world would see a Jewish-African Pope who would move the Vatican to Jerusalem, or the loonies who predict that a subterranean culture will surface and make slaves of humans.

3

"I shot an arrow into the air . . ."

Other (more credible) predictions simply extrapolate the vector of a trend, as in the case of medical research, to a point sometime in the future, and infer a logical conclusion—that a cure for Alzheimer's disease will be found in the twenty-first century, for example. The accuracy of the latter type of prediction, which I shall call the "vector extrapolation hypothesis" (VEH), is determined by the strength of the vector, and the distance, in time, from the date of the prediction, not to mention the perspicacity of the prophet.[1] This technique is based on looking back (to find a vector) to predict the future, and it is generally quite accurate,[2] especially for short-term trends.

"It fell to earth, I knew not where"

The antithesis of the VEH is the "contrarian" reaction (CR), which is well known among Wall Street investors and which, in its unpretentious form, suggests that if most people believe a trend will continue, then it will not. These people are heard to say such things as, "What goes up, must come down," or " 'Red' has not been hit on the roulette wheel for a long time, so it's 'due' "; or "The Cubs will win the World's Series." Looking back over the twentieth century, it is unlikely that early "VEHers" would have predicted that a movie actor from California would become president, that the Berlin Wall would be torn down, or that the Soviet Union would fail to exist. The "CRers," on the other hand, might have predicted these things—plus a whole lot of crazy things that didn't happen. In fact, none of the VEH tea leaves I studied predicted these things—but then, perhaps, I was reading the wrong vectors. Sometimes the vector extrapolation hypothesis works; sometimes the contrarian theory works. Such is the fickle state of prognostication at the close of the twentieth century.

A third related technique for predicting the future, which we shall call a "multiple influence model" (MIM), is to look at a wide range of critical variables, such as natural resources, food supply, pollution, gross national products, and population, and predict their interaction over a certain time period as projected by a mathematical formula. Unlike the VEH model which assumes that an arrow shot into the air will continue to fly along its course, or the CR model that holds that an arrow shot into the air is *not* likely to maintain its course and will fall to the earth, the MIM suggests that an arrow's course may be influenced in meaningful ways by other forces, such as a strong cross current and gravity. Many scholarly financial planners, as well as futurists involved in governmental and social planning, have used this approach in their projections. But the best known association using this approach is the group of thirty individuals from ten countries representing diverse backgrounds—teachers, economists, industrialists, scientists, and so on—who first met in 1968 at the Accademia dei Lincei in Rome and became known as "The Club of Rome."[3] A fundamental concern of the club was to identify the salient forces that influence the future of civilizations; to define what the important tea leaves are and how they interact. This august group considered the economic, political, natural, and social components whose interrelationships comprise the global system in which we all live—with particular attention to understanding the consequences of contemporary policies on the future of the world.

Since the formation of the "Club," many other organizations have sprung up and countless people have become professional futurists. Many use an interdisciplinary approach in which sophisticated models of the world's future are played out on computers. While the models seem to be getting more precise in predicting the future, they are obviously not perfect. If they were, you would not be reading this book.

Change

The reason predictions are made is that the world, more or less, is changing. Some things change so imperceptibly that we plan our lives in the belief that they are immutable. Here I am thinking of the physical laws of the universe that were created immediately after the "big bang." Shortly after that cataclysmic event, all the original hydrogen and helium were created, the laws of gravity established, and elements formed. These things haven't changed, and I confidently predict they will remain the same for (at least) the next millennium.

"The more things change . . ."

The things that do change, which makes the predicting game interesting, are the seemingly capricious ways in which these invariable elements interact. Of course, much of modern science is predicated on the assumption that the laws of interaction are *not* unpredictable, but lawful, and, that when all relevant facts are known, the subsequent interactions are as predictable as that night will follow day—chaos theory withstanding. Prediction of an event whose antecedents are known is not so much a statement of probabilities of occurrence as an accurate conclusion. Predicting the acceleration of falling objects is certain, within very narrow tolerances. Predicting the way a human will react to a specific set of environmental circumstances remains vague at best, largely, I suspect, owing to the diverse and ill-defined causes of human behavior.

Billions of years after the "big bang," some 3.5 billion years ago, the basic elements of the universe combined to form complex biochemical molecular structures. Life began. Ancient life was little more than a complex molecular chain able to reproduce itself and produce energy. During the Paleozoic Era, animals with hard shells and skeletons evolved in the milieu of an ever-changing environment governed by stable physical laws. Primitive sensing receptors became increasingly complex in reaction to the basic laws of nature and a changing environment. In time, a collection of nerve cells was organized into a central nervous system capable of executing a wide range of actions. Thought, the process of the brain, accompanied the development.

These evolutionary changes occurred over such vast periods that, as far as any living creature was concerned, the changes did not have any importance for day-to-day life: It was much more important for our distant ancestors to find food and build shelters. The subtle changes of biological evolution were invisible to our antediluvian forebears, as they are to most of us. Yet, most scientists are convinced that biological mutations occurred throughout the history of life on earth and that those creatures who demonstrated more adaptability to their environment, survived; those who demonstrated less, perished.

While many anthropologists place the time the first humanoid species appeared at about 3.5 million years ago, the first stone tools about 2.5 million years ago, the use of fire about 700,000, and the cave paintings in Lascaux in the Vézère Valley in what is now the south of France about 17,000 years ago, the "blueprint" for the human sensory and cognitive system emerged eons before—when primitive creatures first developed sensorimotor structures designed to enable them to find food and escape danger. These elementary sensorimotor connections became organized in ever more complex networks that have been formalized only recently in modern theories of neural networks and parallel distributed processing. *These* systems developed to "see" and respond to the environment. It is with the more recent model of these primitive sensorimotor systems that we see, think, and respond to the vicissitudes of the modern world. By studying the primitive systems, we modern scientists may see what ancient creatures saw, but—more important for our immediate concerns—we may "see" into the future.

A central thesis of this essay is that the forces that shaped the evolution of living creatures were the invariant elements and their complex products. This position presupposes that the environment formed the conditions under which evolution was allowed—a kind of stage upon which human behavior could be played out. The set changed locally, but there were underlying invariant physical rules. It was under these conditions that living organisms evolved the attributes—physical, genetic, and intellectual—that made them better equipped to survive and procreate. These attributes were passed on to future generations genetically. In the beginning were the elements and the laws that governed their interaction; now, in addition, there is the brain and its unique capacity to understand its past, its present environment, and its future.

The human brain and sensory systems were forged through eons of interaction with an omnipresent and omnipowerful physical and social environment. Now, the palpable changes in the physical and social environment experienced during the "civilized" part of life are sensed and comprehended by a creature whose entire sensory/cognitive purpose was spawned to apprehend portentous cues that were related to its survival. To suggest that our sensory/cognitive system was designed to appreciate a fine wine, a beautiful picture, or enjoyable music, is to reverse the logic of these pleasures. The sensory/cognitive system existed long before these civilized artifacts were created. The artificial things of this world are, generally, contrived to stimulate human brains and senses, both of which have remained essentially unchanged over millennia and whose function evolved for the processing of natural, not synthetic, information.

While the world will change radically beyond the year 2001, human cognition will not. As the twentieth century was radically different from the nineteenth century, the twenty-first century will be radically different from the twentieth. Yet, only about twelve generations separate the woman who was born when Jefferson was president from her great, great, great . . . grandson, who will see the close of the *twenty-first* century when, perhaps, legislatures may be comprised of a complex computer program, rather than a body of persons. During these three centuries, no changes in the mind of humans will have taken place (unless genetic tinkering becomes commonplace), and grandmother and grandson will still be able to sit down together, enjoy a pot of tea, and, after comparing the different gadgets of their ages, will soon find that they share a great deal after all. Although the twenty-first century will produce many technological advances that will undoubtedly tell us about the brain and its workings, the understanding of that information will be processed by a mind no finer (or worse) than the one being used to process this thought.

The "important" discernible changes for humans are environmental, cultural, and intellectual. Should we know, precisely, the laws that govern these important phenomena, then knowing what is "around the corner" would be a matter of science, not rank speculation. And, it is my second (brazen) prediction that the next century will bring us far closer to that realization than we are now.

". . . the more they are the same"

Whereas other futurists will point out that the vector of change created in the twentieth century portends revolutionary changes for the twenty-first century, I suggest that the basic nature of the universe—our cosmology—and humans have, up to now, changed very little over the past hundreds of thousands of years. The laws of the cosmos, as far as we can tell, have been consistent for billions of years. Also, we humans still "see" the world with the same visual apparatus that ancient people used to distinguish edible berries and swiftly moving game. We still cogitate with the same brain our forebears used to imagine and design baskets from reeds, and tools from stone and sticks; and we use the same motor skills to execute these plans in weaving and fabricating implements. The agile algorithms for survival and adaptation are now being applied in wondrous ways. All human attributes, from intelligence, to imagery, to memory, to artistic ability, to the inventiveness behind calculus and Boolean algebra, have their unarticulated counterparts in the minds of our primeval ancestors.

The great trap futurists fall into is the false notion that because the technological products of the world change radically, that the human mind changes correspondingly. Were that true, then we should all be daffy over "heavy-metal" music and eschew Mozart (and especially Palestrina), and prefer Christo over Raphael and Camus over Plato. These intellectual preferences are not universally shared. Indeed, as many of my undergraduate students have discovered, "There is brilliance among our intellectual forbearers"! As far back as we can trace the intellectual history of our species, humans not only were "brilliant," but also discovered many of the universal properties of the mind—through art, literature, philosophy, and living compatibly with nature and other peoples—well before we were dazzled by the technological revolutions of our own century. Accordingly, thinking men and women in the twenty-first century will attend to the "classic" products in art, philosophy, music, dance, humanities, recreation and sports, literature, interpersonal relations, and the natural environment, as well as science, that have been created over thousands of years—because they sound internal repercussions among fundamental structures of the archetypal mind. These things may ultimately tell us as much of the "true" nature of the human mind as will any technical advance, which will (unquestionably) yield reliable descriptions of the brain and its processes. It is likely that along with these technological advances, new knowledge will accrue that may allow humans to tinker with their own body and brain, changing cognition in fundamental ways. However, whether these new ways will be more enlightening, adaptive, or useful is doubtful. What the twentieth century has produced is a description of "how" things work, such as how the brain works and how much information can be processed in a short time. And, I hasten to add the (unnecessary) caveat that our description is not yet perfect. We still haven't answered the question of "why" things work as they do—but some problems must wait for the next century to be solved.

Twentieth-century Vectors

No other century in the history of the world has produced more technological and environmental changes than the one we are about to close. In transportation we have gone from the horse and buggy to space shuttles; in calculation, from the abacus to the computer; in medicine, from care and comfort to laser surgery and organ transplants; in communication, from limited personal conversations geographically restrained to audiovisual communication in which events happening almost anywhere on the globe can be shown immediately in distant lands, from a planet with boundless clean air and waters to one plagued by smog and polluted waters, and in leisure from the phonograph and home piano to the television and rock concerts, to mention only a few changes.

During this revolutionary century, the study of psychology has also changed— with the greatest changes happening during the last part of the century. These changes occurred when serious models of cognition were proposed and validated experimentally.

Presently, it appears that we are experiencing another paradigm shift in which greater attention is being given to the physiological structure of psychological processes, as seen in the many neural theories of mind. These current models of mind which simulate future neural or mental events (like those now being used in diagnostic medicine and in predicting the future performance of securities) may turn out to be the most accurate models for predicting the future. Recent developments in neural network models are also more compatible with developments in visual imaging technology. Yet, twentieth-century psychology has sent other arrows in the air—including the limited capacity model.

Limited Capacity Models

Among the most important discoveries made by psychologists in the twentieth century are those that relate to the limited capacity of the human brain. These well-known studies will not be discussed in detail here, except to emphasize that the immediate environment is teeming with information, whereas our capacity to process stimuli is limited. Quantification of human information capacity (by Bartlett, Broadbent, G. Miller, Peterson & Peterson, among others) have led to important theories of schema and prototypes that help account for the sophisticated performance of humans—despite our limited processing capacity.

We know far more about the capacity and structure of memory at the close of this century than we did at its beginning. These attributes of human memory and thought are unlikely to be altered in the next century. What is anticipated is the visualization of these structures and processes, followed, perhaps, by their manipulation. While it is now impossible to locate the engram responsible for a debilitating memory (resulting from a traumatic episode, for example) and surgically alter it, or to increase the span of apprehension by humans, recent experiments by Richard Thompson *have* successfully located the site of a conditioned response (in a rabbit), surgically excised it, and permanently eradicated the conditioned response. Using the VEH, my crystal ball foretells that microlaser surgery (or some other technique such as cryosurgery, modification of neurotransmitters, or one not thought of yet) will be used on humans to alter memories, sometime before 2020.

Computers

Few futurists fail to mention the impact computers have had on cognitive science and the whole of society, and that the trend will continue beyond 2001. Although I do not deny that computers have had a monumental effect on twentieth-century life—they are as ubiquitous as paperclips and far more versatile—it seems that the next century will see a far greater integration of computers with "natural" cognition. Already we see this trend. In the early days, computers worked only for a smattering of "grunts" who laboriously wrote Fortran programs to crunch a few numbers. Now, computers are "user friendly" and have become almost intimate.

I remember about 25 years ago I had to write a computer program to analyze the data for my dissertation. As I recall, it took me about a week to write the program. When I tried to debug it, it had an error and it took another few days to rewrite the program. Today the same data could be entered into any of the numerous "canned" programs available and the results obtained in seconds. Future computers will take over many laborious cognitive tasks and execute somewhat complicated assignments with ease. It is likely that a business executive will say to her voice-responsive computer something like, "E-mail Mr. Quackenbush and tell him to cancel my reservations to Fredonia. I want to go to Malaysia on June 3 instead. Program the usual syrupy material about his family, cocktail parties, and the state of the economy."

The role computers will play in the future will likely be more "interactive" in the sense that they will provide users with an overview—far more capacious than is now possible—of past research data and a digest of these data with an aim of diminishing redundant research and directing future research. Such "friendly" devices will surely win the affection of graduate students in all disciplines, including cognitive psychology, for not only might the programs review the literature, identify pertinent problems, and design experiments, but also advanced computers may actually collect data, compute a myriad of statistical calculations, write a cogent discussion, and, with little effort, draft a copy of your acceptance speech when you win the Nobel Prize!

Futurists will prize such devices as they can play out billions and billions of scenarios in which the parameters of change are tweaked a bit here and another bit there. Musicians will be able to command their computer to score an opera in the style of Donizetti, with lyrics in the mode of Pushkin, and sung with the voices like those of Sutherland and Pavarotti. . . . Ah, I can hear it now! Translation devices will make international travel much easier and, perhaps, a type of prosthetic can be built into one's ear so that conversations between you, speaking in your native language, and another person, using any of the world's languages, can take place simultaneously.

As remarkable as these devices might be, nothing described thus far will change the basic nature of human cognition. We shall still be galumphing along with the same old brain born and bred during the halcyon days of the early Pleistocene Epoch.

The genie out of the bottle

One change that would affect the basic nature of human cognition, as well as the casing in which it resides, is human genetic engineering. We have seen experiments in this century (and to a limited extent in previous centuries) designed to enhance the genetic predisposition of creatures through selective breeding; indeed, our common propensity to mate with fit partners enhances the survival of the species. However, we well remember the arrogance of Nazi leaders who promised to create a "master race" through "purification" of the blood lines. America's own KKK had similar ideas. At present, a woman can choose to be impregnated by "superior" sperm. The practice was advocated by a Nobel laureate in science. Cattle breeders have used artificial insemination to strengthen their herds for many decades.

Such embryonic practices are child's play as compared to the generic engineering in recombinant DNA that is underway in today's laboratories. The efforts are well financed and sumptuously rewarded. Further developments are likely to yield techniques that, when applied, will identify the most minute of physical and psychological attributes. The next logical step is to synthetically restructure genes so that desired traits are preserved or constructed and undesirable ones eradicated.

The promise of producing a healthier, smarter breed of humans appears to be a panacea for the world's problems and has great intuitive appeal. Who would argue that people would not be better off if parents could be assured, through genetic engineering, that their baby will be healthy and intelligent rather than born without a cerebral cortex? Furthermore, overzealous parents might insist on bearing intelligent children rich in musical talent, athletic ability, and leadership skills, whereas another might opt for physically beautiful children. Some might decide that the world would be well served if their genetic mutates (dare we label them "genmutts?") had the body of Arnold Schwarzenegger and the brain of a Rottweiler, whereas others would have the combination reversed.

Yet the prospect of assembling human genmutts represents a significant departure from the vector of modern science and psychology. So different is genetic engineering of humans that, I believe, it should be treated as a separate class of scientific inquiry rather than the logical extension of cellular biology research. Several dangers accompany the field of gene splicing generally and human genetic engineering specifically. Most apparent is the danger of creating an avaricious new virus, impervious to known antidotes, which could destroy life on the planet.

While it is important to recognize the potential peril involved in biological engineering, it is also necessary to note that our knowledge of the basic nature of life will be advanced during the next century. The "secret of life" (whatever that means) may be discovered.

We see signs of fundamental discoveries being made today by computational biologists interested in such esoteric topics as artificial life. Furthermore, it is anticipated that biological research on protein synthesis, the chemistry of neural transmission, the physical structure of cell, the relationship between neural transmitters and thought, and so on, will see the emergence of "bio-physio-chemico-psychology" (BPCP) specialists, whose intradisciplinary approach to human life will acknowledge the interdependency of biological components. Psychologists, who throughout the nineteenth and twentieth centuries sought hard empirical validation for their diaphanous theories, will undoubtedly embrace this "neo-biology," append the prefix "psycho-," and call it their own. From this union more and more basic issues of life will be addressed and organized in more and more complex ways. These developments in BPCP will also have profound social and psychological effects, including the clinical application of newly developed psychoactive drugs and chemicals which may cure many of the age-old forms of mental illness, notably Alzheimer's disease, chronic depression, autism, and the like.

"No man is an island"

Because widespread human genetic engineering could affect all humanity in profound and potentially deleterious ways, I suggest that applications in this area be made with the greatest care and that "fail safe" controls be standard fare in all research projects. Although research and understanding of the social consequences must move forward, my basic concern in this area is based on our ability (or lack thereof) to play the role of the Creator, especially when very tangible rewards entice people to create radically new life forms and permanently eradicate old forms. Our engineering of the world's ecology throughout the twentieth century has been so shameful that we turn the corner astride a badly bruised planet. For all the great achievements, we twentieth-century scientists crow about, I suspect, that in the long history of humankind, we shall be remembered as the "great rapers of the planet."

We should modestly acknowledge that the human animal was forged over the past millennia and that it is unlikely we shall be able to improve on the design, especially after only half-century of genetic spicing research. Although some might suggest that my caution is no more than a restatement of the anti-intellectual credo—"If God had wanted man to fly, He would have given him wings"—I argue that rampant creation of genetically perfect, or even genetically correct, humans may violate a poorly understood "balance of nature," which may have catastrophic consequences for the species. At present, we have found that most naturally developed and artificial mutates produce nonadaptive creatures.

I am also troubled by the molecular genocide of "genetically flawed" people for two reasons: First, the definition of "flawed" is subjective (should Beethoven's birth have been prevented because he was destined to become deaf?) and susceptible to malevolent application. Second, I suspect that because "abnormal creatures" have survived for millions of generations, they serve some function in the overall scheme of the human family. Before we permanently remove these people from our care and concern, we need to have a clear idea of their function (and utility) in the society of humankind. Finally, my apprehension in these matters is *not* an appeal for a reduction in genetic research—quite the opposite is demanded—but a cry for restraint in the premature *application* of knowledge, especially in regard to the permanent creation or destruction of life forms.

Predictions from the Past

If we use past predictions by thinking men and women as a gauge for the occurrence of future events, we find that, in general, they anticipated technical changes far earlier than they actually happened. Take two cases from the twentieth century as examples: space exploration and computer science. In the decades of the 1960s and 1970s, when the American and Soviet space programs were attaining unprecedented achievements, projections about future programs foretold of lunar colonies, deep space exploration, and widespread space travel (PanAm airlines, now defunct, even offered advanced tickets for space travel). The timetable for these events was set to occur before the end of the twentieth century. They haven't, and it may be that further space exploration will be an uninteresting "moondoggle" to our grandchildren.

Similarly, advances in computer technology, and especially artificial intelligence, produced wide speculation by scientists and futurists alike that robots capable of advanced thought and emotions were just around the corner. Yet, in spite of the fantastic capabilities of these devices, the most advanced computer is still dumb as a brick when it comes to imitating human cognition. These errors in projecting future technological events are classic flaws of the VEH. The shape of the trajectory for space and computer development turned out, at least in the latter part of the twentieth century, to be more like a negatively accelerating curve than a positively accelerating one. The lesson to be learned by those who optimistically predict technological changes before their time is not that the future will bring considerable change, but that these changes may require many years to cultivate.

On the other hand, changes in the political and social arena seem to take place earlier than many experts have anticipated. To cite examples drawn from the twentieth century, consider first the widespread conflict and wars between nations that have blemished our past. In at least some cases, these conflicts have been the result of misjudgments made by one nation about the rate of political or social change in another. Or consider the remarkable changes in the Soviet Union at the close of this century. Although many Soviet scholars in the 1980s thought that the Soviet Union would eventually lose control over its satellite countries and republics (those of us who traveled during that time to Estonia, Georgia [USSR], and Poland, among other Soviet block territories, saw the seeds of discontent), the sage advice suggested that such changes might appear around 2020. Virtually everyone believed in the steady-state vector of Soviet rule. Virtually everyone was wrong. The vector took off.

Models of the anticipated rate of change within technical and social arenas may prove to be imperfect; however, the salient point is that predictions about the future that affect our lives in important ways (e.g., technical developments and political and social developments) are frequently wrong: Some events appear later than anticipated, some earlier. For these reasons, it behooves us to exercise the greatest of caution before setting in motion changes to our world (e.g., through global warming) and ourselves (e.g., through genetic engineering) that may be irreversible.

Around the Corner, or "The Sky Is Falling!"

Although I haven't (yet) taken to marching around Hyde Park with a sandwich board announcing "The end is near!" my crystal ball shows clearly that unwonted dangers lurk just around the corner. The vectors of self-destruction are strong, and the more we learn about the flight pattern of the arrows launched during the twentieth century, the more ominous the pattern appears. If we continue along the same direction, then the science of the mind much beyond 2001 will be a moot question. It is just possible that Henny Penny could be right.

Self-annihilation could result if any one of many devastating vectors continues its lethal trajectory. These include the population explosion, irreparable damage to the atmosphere through manmade pollutants, exhaustion of essential natural resources, widespread disease or plague, the proliferation of nuclear and biochemical weapons, the eradication of life forms that may irreparably decompose the chain of life, political unrest through disparate distribution of wealth, nonsustainable practices in agriculture and mining, inept or shortsighted decisionmaking in genetic engineering, and—a final catch-all topic—"screwing up the world in some other unforeseen way so that we all get killed." Let's hope that "destiny is *not* a crap shoot."

I fear all of these, but the unrelenting growth of the world's population presents the most appalling statistics. In the first three million years our numbers grew from a few to two billion. Then, in 45 years, we added a second two billion; and at present, a third two billion increase will require only 22 years. The vast and exponentially growing number of people tax the natural resources in extraordinary ways. In addition, civilizations, communities, families, and people have already

World Population 1000 AD to 2025 AD

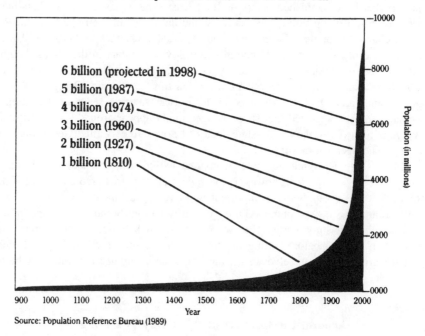

Source: Population Reference Bureau (1989)

changed remarkably. And yet, if the trend continues, future changes will be beyond our imagination.

If you are still reading this, then you know that these pernicious arrows have not hit their mortal target and we still may have time to deflect their awful course. What we know of the flight pattern, however, indicates that nothing short of draconian measures will be required to rescue the planet and its inhabitants, and it is probable that the human condition will become tragically worse during the first half of the next century: It is even possible that the species will come to the edge of extinction. The old canard "Man can fix what he has ruined" may prove to be seriously tested.

The Science of the Mind: 2001 and Beyond

The future of the science of the mind will bring enormous technological change. Yet, unlike some of my prophetic colleagues, I believe the nature of the mind will not change at all; in other words, we shall understand the workings of the mind better, but change it little. The human brain, wrought over millions of years living in exquisite symmetry with nature, is unlikely to profit from experimental change (at least in the next century) before the consequences of these changes are correctly anticipated. Whereas futurists have typically been captivated with technological and scientific advances—the term "sci-fi" implies the future—I have a slightly different view. The twenty-first century is bound to bring dazzling new scientific gadgets that will enhance our knowledge of the human animal, both psychological and physical. These advancements are sure to attract attention, being the first things we Earth people will display to our fellow humanoids and, should the circumstances prevail, to alien correspondents.

A Postmodern Earthy Renaissance

Should we survive another millennium, I believe that the close of the twenty-first century—about a century from now—will spawn a reawakening of interest in the arts, literature, humanities, and natural environment. This "postmodern" earthy Renaissance will be a reaction to the technological revolution which developed rapidly throughout the twentieth century and, along with its accomplishments, brought the near destruction of our ecology. The effects of the scientific revolution and ecological insult, when carried forward into the twenty-first century, will leave people feeling empty, sterile, mechanical, and homeless—conditions we know to be associated with pathological feelings of worthlessness. The arts and literature have characteristically portrayed man as majestic, complex, and self-determined, with feelings of being valued. Romantic idealism dies hard, and it will undoubtedly survive the next hundred years. People will rediscover their roots in the soil of earth. While the pattern of the twentieth century has been to remove humans from their natural, and sometimes harsh environment ("civilization" has become synonymous with "artificial," "development" with "destruction," and "natural" with "underdeveloped") by the close of the twenty-first century, life, families, homes, society, and civilizations are likely to be much closer to "nature." Not only will our grandchildren enjoy rustic pleasures of the planet, but also their psychology will be more earthy, realistic, and unaffected.

So, I believe these things will happen: The arts and humanities will experience a revivification, not only in the development of important new forms, but also in the attention paid to "the meaning of life," as portrayed throughout history. We shall also learn much more about the brain—its functions, capacities, workings, and physical attributes.

The window to the mind

Only within the past few years have we been able to "see" the workings of the brain through magnetic resonance imaging (MRI) and positron emission tomography (PET), among other imaging techniques. Yet, during that time, some vexing problems of human cognition have been better understood (see especially the work of Petersen, Posner, Raichle, and Tulving). The "enchanted loom" is yielding secrets not dreamed of years ago, and the future of this technology is sure to tell us more, not only about the anatomy of thought but also about the relationships among thoughts, a topic close to the heart of early associationist psychologists.

Furthermore, these imaging techniques will surely become integrated into the darling topic of cognitive scientists as we close this century: parallel distributed processing, or connectionism. The growth of a more refined technology for viewing mental processes will result in further developments of the model, and the model will further assist neurocognitive researchers in their search for illuminating structures. Advancements in this area promise to be so successful that much of conventional experimental psychology—the type practiced throughout most of this century—will be abandoned in favor of neurocognitive research, or "psycho-neurobiology."

The window to knowledge

While the "window to the brain" might look like a CAT scan in the future, the window to knowledge will be a computer screen supported by a mega-computer with "good international connections." Shared knowledge (read "shared technology") will proliferate throughout the twenty-first century. Humans have never been able to keep a secret, and useful information—be it the bow and arrow, new medicines, or atomic power—somehow gets around. Technical information has traditionally spread rapidly, and today it is being transmitted worldwide in seconds through e-mail channels in labs and homes and hospitals and universities throughout the globe. At present, we see the wholesale absorption of any information by countries previously isolated within the Soviet block. The network of information transmission will unite all scientists.

So copious will be the facts, theories, and discoveries, that no human (working with his or her clunky Pleistocene brain of limited information processing capacity) will be able to absorb all of them. But, the ingenious, imaginative human mind will write programs designed to "understand" the profusion of information. These "information processing" programs will sort out truly new research findings from the glut of research findings that simply "replow old fields." But more exciting are the prospects of organizing the world's technical and theoretical knowledge in a type of giant three-dimensional matrix composed of knowledge "cells" where known elements are located and "empty cells" may be identified.

Thus, the cell of knowledge on paired-associate learning of nonsense syllables may well be bursting (some cynics may suggest we know too much about the topic), whereas the cell on emotions and cerebral brain flow may be virtually empty. Furthermore, in the logical extension of this vector (another VEH), the program could suggest other forms of research, as chess programs now suggest alternative moves. Of course, the logical extrapolation of this fantasy would have the computer identify the holes in knowledge, suggest research alternatives, design and carry out the research, and fill the vacant cell with knowledge. All that is left for us humans to do, then, is to try to understand it all with our old-fashioned brains and eat a few sweet berries in the fleeting moment between birth and death.

Acknowledgment

I wish to express my thanks to Rich Bissett for his helpful remarks on an earlier version of this paper.

Notes

1. Using the "vector extrapolation hypothesis," it is likely that during the early part of the twenty-first century the world will see a palpable increase in population, a greater number of deaths through starvation and infectious disease, more pollution, and a diminution in the number of animal species.

2. Recently, a well-known financial magazine reported that at the beginning of each year if an investor reinvested assets in the mutual fund that had accrued the greatest gain *for the previous year* and continued to use that strategy over the past two decades, the final amount would be considerably greater than that accrued by almost any other type of investment policy.

3. See *The Limits to Growth: A Report for the Club of Rome's Project on the Predicament of Mankind,* by D. H. Meadows, D. L. Meadows, J. Randers, and W. W. Behrens III (1972), New York: Universe Books.

2

Empowering People Through Friendly Technology: Psychology in the Twenty-first Century

GORDON H. BOWER

In this chapter I present some speculations regarding what people in Western civilization might be like a hundred years from now. This is a matter of some curiosity to contemporary psychologists as well as of great concern to those future psychologists who will study these people and treat them for their psychological problems. Although people are assuredly limited by their biology and brain in what they can do, I believe that technological innovations of the coming century will greatly expand the power of individuals to control their environment, to control themselves and guide their children, and thereby to better direct their own destiny. As a consequence of this greater power, people will be better able to improve the quality of their lives, and increase the intelligence, creativity, and humanity of themselves and their children. It is my contention that psychologists will play a pivotal role in helping design such technologies to be "user-friendly," in field-testing their efficacy, and in refining the technological designs until they achieve a proper fit to the capabilities and talents of individual users. That, at least, is the hope that I express in the following pages.

Pitfalls in Predicting the Future

If any profession knows the hazards and pitfalls of predicting people's moment-to-moment behavior, it is assuredly experimental psychologists. Even in their closely controlled laboratory experiments, psychologists are continually frustrated by their failed predictions about human behavior. Therefore, it borders on some unholy perversion of our professional upbringing to try to predict what people will be like a hundred years from now. The request to speculate upon the distant future is like receiving a license to write science fiction and fantasy. The challenge is also a bit intimidating because gazing into a crystal ball to forecast the future is a bit like

18

taking a Rorschach projective test. There are so many trends to extrapolate, so many things to see out there, that whatever one selects to discuss reveals a lot about the concerns and values of the writer.

In writing of the future, authors can either extrapolate current trends to their likely conclusion, whether or not the outcome is desirable, or they can commingle their forecasts with their wishes and value judgments, suggesting changes they would like to see come about. Because people differ considerably regarding the ideal state they would have humankind strive to achieve, it is fitting that some of the values of psychologists be stated at the outset.

Psychologists' Values

By professional selection and trained indoctrination, psychologists, when viewed as political animals, are basically social liberals, reformers, and caregivers. We see lots of suffering people with lots of problems in living. As a group we are trained to help the sufferers with their problems so they can lead happier, more fulfilling lives. Our collective urge to help people resolve personal and social problems stems from a utilitarian moral base—namely, that one's actions are to be judged according to whether they increase the welfare of the general population. But the notion that psychologists can often ameliorate people's behavioral problems is founded on the belief that humankind—or at least humankind's behavior—is changeable, malleable, and improvable. While we view the individual human life as precious, we also value individuals as members of a universal human culture and civilization that is worth preserving.

Universal Laws of Human Nature?

Psychologists hold nearly contradictory beliefs about people. On the one hand, we recognize the nearly infinite diversity of individual personalities; on the other hand, we believe in certain behavioral constraints and "laws of human nature" (regarding perception, memory, reasoning, etc.) that apply universally, regardless of the gender, ethnic background, or nationality into which one is accidently born.

Social Differentiation

Infants the world over are born with gene combinations and uterine environments that provide tremendous diversity in their propensities for developing differing cognitive abilities and personality traits. The infant's caregivers and early trainers produce a continual bombardment of cultural experiences that assail and buffet the infant through a process of profound social and individual differentiation. This sociocultural environment produces vastly different experiences during children's most impressionable ages of development, resulting in vast differences in personal learning, knowledge, habits, skills, values, and personality traits. The social culture determines the "content" or substance of what is learned, and thereby determines which emotional adjustments, perceptual–motor skills, and cognitive abilities are emphasized for training.

Universal Constraints on Human Behavior

While recognizing the diversity of human personalities, psychologists also persist in the belief that certain universal constraints or limits on behavioral and cognitive capacities exist and that certain invariant "laws of human nature" apply to nearly everybody.

Many of these universal laws characterize *Homo sapiens* as an intact species produced by biological evolution. For example, because humans share similar bodies and physiology, they all need to maintain their body temperature within a narrow range, and they need to breathe oxygen, ingest nutrients, eliminate bodily wastes, and so on. But exactly what nutrients are ingested—when, where, how prepared, and with what rituals—varies enormously according to one's culture. Thus, whereas physiology determines general needs, the way in which those needs are satisfied varies with environmental and cultural factors. For example, local climates and cultural customs dictate the kind of clothing we wear or the shelters we live in.

Similarly, biological needs such as securing food, shelter, and protection from predators were probably the original bases for many of our social customs, such as the formation of families, clans, and communities, the division of labor, and the specialization of skills of production (into hunters, farmers, builders, warriors, etc.). Because people living in groups often need to coordinate work and social activities, systems of speech communication have developed; and fluency in speaking is acquired according to more or less the same timetable by all children throughout the world. I believe that these universal facts about behavior are not going to be altered by technological innovations of the future.

Universal Limits on Cognitive Capabilities

Just as our shared biological makeup imposes certain requirements on our bodily functions and limits our physical achievements (we can't run 10 miles in 15 minutes or lift 2000 pounds), so also do our nervous systems and brains impose limits on us. Theories about the "architecture of cognition" attempt to describe some of these limitations and constraints (Anderson, 1983; Newell, 1990). For example, psychologists believe that people have a short-term memory of limited capacity which serves as a small workspace (also called "working memory") for storing information and for carrying out the cognitive operations required by mental problem-solving sequences (e.g., adding several two-digit numbers in your head). This working memory has access (through content-addressable associations) to a vast collection of personal knowledge stored in a large, passive, long-term memory. Relevant knowledge in long-term memory can be "activated" and brought into working memory as it is required. For example, in the middle of some mental calculation you may activate the retrieval query, "What's the sum of 8 + 7?" and your memory answers "15."

Because short-term memory has a very limited capacity, we are practically forced to carry through most complex mental calculations or problem-solving sequences one step at a time in serial order. Although our sensory receptors (ears, eyes, etc.) can take in large amounts of sensory information at once through parallel processing, that overload is of little use because it fades away very rapidly unless it is attended to and recoded into something memorable. And our attention span is severely limited, perhaps to only one or two "items" at any given moment. People can appear to attend to several sensory channels at once only by rapidly switching attention among the sensory images residing briefly in a sensory memory. This happens, for example, when we listen in on several conversations at once.

The capacity limitation on attention appears to be structural (hardwired into the mammalian brain) and is rarely modified by extensive training. Rather, through training, people can learn how to better reduce distractions and better concentrate on relevant information; they can learn how to repackage lots of information into single "chunks" that take up less space in working memory but nonetheless serve as "proxies" that point to large collections of information in long-term memory.

Constraints in Cognitive Architectures

I mention such structural features of cognitive architectures to point out that most cognitive psychologists would maintain that these kinds of capacity limitations within working memory are nearly universal and invariant across cultures and across centuries. Although the capacity varies somewhat across individuals (and correlates with reading comprehension and reasoning ability), it probably exhibits similar ranges across cultures and across time. Brain injuries, strokes, and some degenerative brain diseases often reduce working memory capacity, resulting in a variety of related deficits in carrying out everyday cognitive tasks such as keeping oriented in time and space, tracking conversational topics, and speaking coherently.

The built-in constraints on cognitive architecture limit what people can or cannot do. Let us consider just a few of these limitations. For example, people can take in and store new information at only a certain, relatively slow rate, and attempts to speed up that intake, say, by computer-compressed speech, have had only limited success. We suffer interference and forgetting of information briefly attended to, and we have only limited means to overcome that inexorable process. We can usually think of just one "thing" at a time, and we are unable to hold in mind a lengthy chain of reasoning. When making a complex decision about which house or car to buy, which job to take, we are usually frustrated because we cannot keep in mind all the relevant factors to be considered for all the possible options. Instead, we fall back on a few factors in determining our decisions. Consequently, our decisions are much affected by irrelevant factors such as the salience or availability of particular kinds of biasing information. As a final example, our moods and emotions color our thinking, our ways of interpreting the social world, ourselves, and our own actions, biasing the kinds of memories and interpretive categories that come to mind as we canvas the library of our mind for an opinion; and these biases often arise in subtle, unconscious ways.

These kinds of influences and constraints are universal, shared by all people, and presumably have been present since time immemorial. They are likely to continue as mental governors constraining the thought processes of our distant descendants well beyond the twenty-first century.

Technologies To Overcome Constraints

Despite the kinds of constraints enumerated here, I nevertheless still believe that in the coming century, clever inventors will fabricate technological protheses (extra "cognitive hands") that will help humankind overcome at least some of the limitations imposed by our biology.

Consider just one example. Hitherto, a person's intelligence was considered to be a stable ability residing "in" him or her; but increasingly, we are coming to view intelligence as partly residing in the environment—or, rather, in the way people arrange the environment around themselves to promote and support intelligent actions. In the future, a larger part of that intellectual environment will be technological and probably machine-based.

Just as the invention of the automobile helped humans move faster over longer distances, so has the invention of computers enabled us to think faster and more accurately over longer chains of reasonings. Just as paper and pencil enabled the architectural designer to draw different plans for a building, so have computer-assisted video displays enabled modern designers to visualize buildings in three dimensions, to see through structural barriers, to rotate the angle of viewing, to alter a few parts to examine quickly their widespread effects throughout the entire building, and so on. Such computer graphic displays illustrate the power of a technology that allows people to externalize the products of their thought processes, to build visual displays that model some reality, to display symbolic models which they can manipulate and judge on the graphics terminal. In this manner, thinkers can use the power of visual pattern recognition to enhance their otherwise limited ability to reason with words and symbols.

Reshaping Humankind

One can look upon the history of science as our species' attempt to predict and control nature; for psychologists and social scientists, this includes most especially human nature. Technology holds out the prospect of enabling people to control better their physical and cognitive environment and to solve more easily the problems it poses. In this manner, people should be able to follow a better planned life and attain more predictable outcomes. Of course, all this requires that we in some way "reshape" human behaviors, which is my next topic.

There are four primary ways to reshape human actions: (1) alter their genetic makeup; (2) change their technological environment; (3) change their learning environment and learning experiences; and (4) change their motivations. I shall first discuss the reshaping of humankind's genetic makeup before moving on to the last three topics, which might be thought of as a reshaping or engineering of people's behavioral environment. In most cases, I shall simply be extrapolating some likely future consequences of the current direction of research knowledge, and I do so without gainsaying whether certain changes would be ethically acceptable, politically correct, or politically feasible during the next century.

The Eugenics Program

The idea of improving humans through genetic engineering is the program of *eugenics,* an ancient idea that was suggested by the success of animal husbandry. The scientific underpinnings of the eugenics thesis have been known for centuries, ever since herdsmen selectively bred cattle, camels, horses, and domesticated fowl to maximize properties in the offspring. The scientific basis is now understood in even greater detail owing to major advances in molecular genetics over the past thirty years.

Eugenics is the geneticists' contribution to social reform. The problems with the eugenics programs have always been moral and political, and only secondarily scientific. Eugenics got a bad reputation from association with the Nazis and other fascists who wanted to impose their view of human genetic perfection (i.e., the Aryan race) upon the rest of the world, and in the process "cleanse" the rest of us.

We strongly and rightly reject the idea that some central governmental agency should be given the power to decide for all of us what human qualities should be fostered. However, the possibility of such governmental abuses does not mean that prospective parents of the future should not have some control over the kind of children they bring into the world. Ask any prospective parents for their preferences regarding their child, and most will agree that they want their child to be physically and psychologically "healthy," energetic, happy, outgoing, sociable, industrious, curious, creative, and intelligent. Of course, within that broad framework, different parents will disagree on the relative importance of, say, conformity versus creativity in their child.

Human Genetics

As the human genome is fully mapped and as human geneticists come to understand better the manner in which gene combinations are expressed in human phenotypes and behavior, the time will probably come when many genetic diseases (both physical and psychological) can be detected early in pregnancy (say, within six weeks of conception) and hence (at the parents' option) the embryo can either be repaired quickly by recombinant gene-splicing or be aborted if that is acceptable to the parents and society.

In this manner, society should be able to reduce the frequency of the genetically determined "psychological" maladies such as autism, severe attention-deficit disorders, severe mental retardation, familial dispositions toward Huntington's disease, epilepsy, schizophrenia, manic-depressive disorders, Alzheimer's disease, and other such afflictions. Although the diathesis–stress model of mental disorders is doubtless correct in emphasizing the interaction of both environmental and genetic factors in causing mental disorders, the fact remains that a person's genes determine his or her susceptibility to developing a mental disorder when confronted with the unavoidable stresses that arise in nearly all modern lives.

In principle, the human geneticists of the distant future, as did those in Aldous Huxley's classic *Brave New World,* will have the ability to manufacture and combine human eggs and spermatozoa that yield embryos having some specific combination or profile of physical and general psychological traits that the parents can select. The traits that could be genetically selected would be relatively general ones such as extroversion, industriousness, or sociability. Of course, the manner and content with which such broad traits are expressed in behavior would be determined by the child's social learning. That is, an industrious child might become a corporate magnate in Germany, a scientist in Bolivia, a rug merchant in Morrocco, or a drug smuggler in Miami: The trait means simply that whatever they do, they will work hard at achieving whatever ambitions their culture reinforces.

Several alternative methods are imaginable. By one method, the father and mother would supply the sperm and egg which would be taken to the genetics lab, examined and selected for absence of defective genes, then combined to produce an embryo. Early in gestation, the embryo's chromosomes would be checked and, if not developing properly, altered so as to produce an embryo closer to the desired genotype.

An alternative method would completely synthesize the chromosomes and genetic material for an embryo by following different biochemical prescriptions. This method is probably unrealistically complex for the near future.

Moral and Legal Complications of the Eugenics Program

The biochemical synthesis procedure briefly mentioned here has the feature that the fetus would have no biological parents, only someone who requested that it be created with certain properties. Because so much common law about children is premised on the idea that every child has parents, the synthetic method would call for radical revisions in laws of inheritance, parental responsibility for children, and other family-oriented customs.

Also, if children no longer were to be created by sexual reproduction, then sex between loving partners could become solely for pleasurable bonding rather than procreation, and that would raise concerns among certain religions which countenance sexual behavior only for procreative purposes.

The ability to select general traits, sex, and physical characteristics of one's children brings to the foreground the moral issues of deciding what kind of species *Homo sapiens* should become. By leaving the decision mainly in the hands of the parents, the species will be assured of at least some measure of genetic variability or biodiversity. The fear would be that successive generations would drift in the direction of some paragon image popularized, say, by Hollywood and the media, so that everyone would look like popular film stars, or similar ethnic beauties. A possible outcome of such genotypic sameness is that the species might perish either from sheer boredom with one another's appearance and personalities or from overwhelming new challenges.

One possible challenge is that new virulent bacteria or viruses could arise that could successfully attack the engineered genetic strains that might lack the relevant immune responses. One could argue that evolution, in its infinite wisdom derived from millennia of genetic experimentation, has created just the right range of genetic variability among humans so that the species can survive nearly any on-slaught from the myriad forms of bacteria and viruses that inhabit this planet. Perhaps, by selectively tinkering with that range of evolved genotypes, our human genetic engineers would be visiting upon us a host of unanticipated diseases against which our species would have no adequate defense.

Designing Our Own Milieu

Besides having the prospect of designing the genetic makeup of their children, the people of the late twenty-first century should be better able than us to encourage, moderate, and support their behavior by controlling their environment. New tools and inventions should provide people with powerful means for achieving their goals and avoiding the deleterious consequences of technology.

A simple example of how technology could reduce personal frustrations comes from the area of weight control. Medical science tells us that obesity is a serious health risk, especially when combined with high levels of serum cholesterol. Yet, despite struggling with unsatisfactory diets, many people in our society are over-weight. The problems of being overweight could be greatly ameliorated if food companies of the future had incentives (i.e., profits) to invent and use artificial fats and sweeteners that provided highly palatable substitutes for the high-calorie, high-fat foods we presently eat. At present, food companies use "popular demand" and the profit motive to justify feeding consumers the unhealthy junk foods that keep so many addicted to sugars and fats.

Another example of environmental manipulation in the future would be the self-conscious design of one's own work-space. Corporate executives, scholars, bureaucrats, scientists, and many others spend large portions of their work day at desks, reading reports and writing or dictating reports and correspondence. A ma-jor problem for such workers is getting access to relevant information in a timely fashion. The tools of information technology—computers networked into large document-sharing data bases; CD-ROMs containing hundreds of complete techni-cal encyclopedias; video disks with thousands of motion-picture or video illustra-tions—all will be expanded in power, made more user friendly, and permeate the work sphere of everyone. A small example familiar to psychologists is the *Psych-Lit* CD-ROM program of the American Psychological Association which lists ti-tles, authors, and abstracts of most papers published in a large number of profes-sional psychological journals and books.

A major challenge for psychologists of the future will be to design such information resources so they are optimally usable by everyone. People will have to be specially trained to scan large volumes of information quickly to extract the relevant bits for their immediate needs. Education of the future will be largely job-based and expertise-simulating rather than vast memorizing exercises: On-the-job trainers will be teaching students how to reason about problems in their specialty and how to search for answers to complex questions by perusing vast pools of technical literature. Cognitive psychologists will design various "thinking tools" for the computer to prompt the expert through a series of questions regarding some case or problem he or she is pondering. Automated abstracting services will be used increasingly to help knowledge-intensive professionals (such as scientists, engineers, physicians, lawyers, etc.) keep up with new information published in their fields. Very probably most of the technical literature in the distant future will be published only electronically, not in paper journals or books.

These environmental controls are external to our body—the typical perspective. But another entire area for exercising control is within our *internal environment*. The controls can operate either directly upon the brain or in the body and the endocrine system outside the brain. Let us consider several of these methods for regulating our internal milieu.

Monitoring and Controlling One's Internal Milieu

The neuropharmacology of mood disorders should be sufficiently understood in the future that scientists will know how to monitor moment-by-moment the levels of circulating endocrine secretions in a person's bloodstream just as an outdoor thermometer continuously measures the outside temperature. In this manner the levels of circulating cortisol will indicate a person's stress level, blood-glucose level will indicate hunger level, hormone levels will indicate sex drive, and so forth. Similar on-line, plasma-assay techniques should be able to display the blood level of alcohol for drinkers or the blood level of insulin for diabetics.

These biological signals could be used for several purposes. They could inform people of their internal states, so that immediate actions could remedy any unwanted state. For example, the diabetic could be warned to take an insulin injection, the drinker with high blood-alcohol warned to take a taxi rather than drive home, and the stressed person warned to take time out for relaxation.

If the signals were externalized for others to recognize, they could even serve as cues for social partners to behave in appropriate ways—for example, to signal to a spouse when the partner is exhausted, stressed out, frightened, angry, inebriated, sad, or sexually aroused, and to take appropriate actions to help the partner modify this disturbance of his or her internal milieu. In these cases the technology would be allowing us literally to "wear our emotions on our sleeves," so they could be easily read. Such a system could enable people to have a better understanding of and thus be more compassionate toward their friends and loved ones. Of course, enemies could use the signals to exacerbate the emotional disturbances in adverse directions.

Automated Homeostasis?

Some corrective actions of a biochemical nature, to rectify a hormonal upset, could perhaps be programmed to occur automatically through the use of a small computer-pack and an in-dwelling cannula with a "cafeteria" of synthetic endocrine agonists (or antagonists) that it could perfuse into the person's bloodstream. Each person's computer-pack might have stored a personally optimal "set point" for each circulating substance, and it would perfuse appropriate amounts of agonists or antagonists for that substance in order to maintain its monitored level near that set point.

Automated Medication Regimens

Such perfusion systems would also be very useful for reliably delivering medication to medical patients such as those afflicted with diabetes, heart disease, or thyroid deficiency. Something of this kind would be useful, too, for the delivery of psychoactive medications to chronic schizophrenics, depressives, and manic depressives. Current psychiatric practices with oral medications increase dose levels only very gradually over three to eight weeks, and are monitored weekly for unwanted side effects. As a result, psychiatric patients often become discouraged by the lack of immediate improvement in their functioning, so they stop complying with their prescribed medication schedule. Such noncompliance creates difficulties for the therapist who is trying to arrive at an optimal medication schedule for the patient.

A continuous monitoring system could overcome some of this problem by testing the level of drug (or drug metabolites) in the bloodstream and distributing the drug to reach a target level quickly. The target dosage would be adjusted by the physician who would be taking account of the patient's psychiatric symptoms along with the patient's judgment of well-being and negative side effects.

Monitoring Brain Neurotransmitters

More technically difficult would be a similar system designed to monitor the levels of effective neurotransmitters in the brain, such as dopamine, epinephrine, norepinephrine, serotonin, and other neuropeptides. The levels of these neurotransmitters might indicate or predict people's general mood—whether alert or sleepy, depressed, anxious, or relaxed—perhaps even before they are aware of their mood. The signals reflecting the level of different brain neurotransmitters could again be used with a computer-controlled, subdural system that feeds neurotransmitters into a carotid artery. The system could contain a negative feedback circuit to maintain specific target levels of brain neurotransmitters, by perfusing agonists or antagonists to raise or lower the imbalanced neurotransmitter. The administered drugs and chemicals would have to be altered so they could pass the blood-brain barrier—the body's means of blocking foreign chemicals from entering the brain.

People would be able to regulate their moods to some extent by programming into their perfusion pack different set points, to keep them alert, nonanxious, nonhostile, and nondepressed. In fact, people could experiment until they discovered that combination of neurotransmitters in particular brain regions that produced for them a panoply of feeling states, from alertness to sleepiness, from euphoria to calm relaxation. Such personal data could enable them to "dial up" any particular feeling state that they considered appropriate for the situation they were entering.

Some obvious governmental controls on the manufacture and distribution of relevant biochemicals would have to be designed into supplies for such systems to prevent their abuse. Conceivably, some people might try to "tune in and drop out" by maintaining an intense cocaine high most of their waking hours. Our society's present inability to control illicit drug trafficking and drug abuse does not augur well for the success of such drug-control programs. But a few methods have been successful, and they will be discussed now.

Treating Drug Addictions

It is generally believed that the most efficacious treatment currently available for severe heroin addictions is sustained methadone maintenance (Kreek, 1993). A significant level of methadone in the bloodstream accomplishes two ends: first, it eliminates or relieves the aversiveness of the usual withdrawal symptoms; second, it blocks the euphoric high that usually accompanies another heroin injection. Many methadone-maintained addicts falter and try a few more heroin injections in search of the euphoric high they experienced before; but with the methadone blocker, they get no high, and the conditioned link between an injection and euphoria weakens and eventually extinguishes.

A major stumbling block in our society is getting enough addicts into methadone treatment and keeping them on methadone indefinitely. (Evidence suggests very high relapse rates once an addict is withdrawn from methadone.) A technical solution would be to have physicians implant into the upper arm of each convicted addict some subcutaneous, slow-release methadone sticks (much as Norplant, a female contraceptive, is voluntarily implanted in the arms of women). The implants would slowly release methadone at the proper dosage in order to prevent withdrawal symptoms and block euphoric highs. Every few years the methadone would have to be replenished because evidence suggests that methadone treatment should continue indefinitely. A blood-monitoring system would be required to ensure that the addict does not remove the implants.

One can hope that similar therapies will be available to counteract the euphoria or high produced by other abused substances such as cocaine, amphetamine, LSD, alcohol, opium, morphine, and their derivatives. Perhaps the simplest treatment for these at present is to implant in the abuser an in-dwelling, slow-release chemical that causes nausea when combined with the illicit drug. For example, to counter the craving for alcohol (which is the most frequently abused drug), *antabuse* which causes nausea when combined with alcohol could be used. Like heroin addicts, alcoholics might be treated (with their consent) by having slow-release antabuse pellets implanted in their upper arms. In this manner, they would be made sick whenever they drank alcohol and would thereby learn to avoid alcohol. That, at least, would be a possible recommendation from science, for chronic abusers—say, drunk drivers with repeated offenses. Similar programs could be used to either prevent or cure addiction to cigarette smoking—a major cause of medical maladies. Of course, all of us can think of various practical, ethical, and political obstacles to such programs.

Treating Sleep Disorders

One hope is that the neuropharmacology of sleep will be understood sufficiently in the future so that psychologists will be able to alleviate certain sleep problems, especially insomnia: problems in falling asleep, depth and quality of sleep, or early-morning awakening. Perhaps by self-administering an appropriate sedative into the carotid artery, people could put themselves immediately into a restful sleep; and by setting a timer, select a sleep duration after which time an "awakening" antagonist would be perfused into the brain to bring on wakefulness.

Another desirable invention would be an artificial light box that travelers could enter briefly to accelerate their adjustment to the large day–night changes that can cause jet lag. At present, adjustment to jet lag due to long-distance travel is a slow, frustrating process; in a futuristic business environment requiring frequent long-distance trips, quickly resetting one's biological clock to track the local time would be a much desired goal. The method could use either internal electrical or biochemical stimulation of the suprachiasmatic nucleus, or external stimulation provided by a pulsed light box. By sitting for several minutes in the light box, travelers could have their biological light-dark cycles set to the local period. Such light boxes would be available for travelers at every airport, in airplanes, or in hotels catering to long-distance travelers. Such devices would be useful, too, for nightshift workers who often experience difficulty adjusting to working during darkness and sleeping during daylight hours.

A major obstacle to controlling beneficial sleep is that we do not presently understand much about what causes sleep or what biochemical functions it accomplishes. The cycle of "fatigue–sleep–revitalization" suggests that sleep is brought on by the accumulation of certain neurochemicals at particular brain sites, and that these are metabolized or cleared away during sleep. Clearly, however, the process is not totally "biochemical" because mental activity and anxiety can keep us awake and mental relaxation helps put us asleep. Nonetheless, as we come to understand more about the biochemical changes involved in the "refreshment process" of sleep, scientists of the future might be able to devise "instant refreshment" pills or injections that would have the effect of quickly providing the biochemical changes in the brain that currently can now be provided only by several hours of restful sleep. The refreshment injections would probably be combined with psychological procedures to relax and clear the mind. Such refreshment procedures would be especially helpful for doctors, paramedics, pilots, and combat soldiers who must stay alert long hours without a break for sleeping.

Sensory Augmenters

As our understanding of the physiology and psychology of sensory systems increases, so should psychologists and engineers become better able to design transducers that can either augment sensory receptors or shunt or replace defective ones. Today's augmenters are external amplifiers such as hearing aids or spectacles. Future augmenters might be implanted surgically, such as a new corrective lens for the eye or new tympanic-membrane amplifiers for the hearing-impaired. These would replace the external hearing aids and spectacles commonly used today, and would have primarily cosmetic and efficiency benefits.

The more difficult problem would be to restore vision to people who have had retinal degeneration or to restore hearing to people who have suffered degeneration or damage to parts of the middle or inner ear, or to the auditory pathways. In principle, a diaphragm could be mounted in the external ear to transduce sound-pressure signals similar to the transduction provided by the tympanic membrane; these signals could be relayed to an in-dwelling microchip that analyzes, then transforms, the sound pressures into a pattern of electrical impulses through a bundle of, say, 100 electrodes connected to different fibers of the auditory nerve. In this manner, the microchip would stimulate the auditory fibers to mimic the fiber firing pattern normally caused by vibrations of hair cells located along different regions of the basilar membrane. The job for auditory psychologists would be to help acoustic engineers select and test the significant acoustic parameters, say, from speech, that will provide maximal discrimination of the sensory information.

Perhaps something similar could be devised to replace a defective retina to help augment pattern vision, but the complexity of circuitry in the retinal ganglion layer suggests that the engineering task would be immense. Nonetheless, human factors psychologists might be able to design less than optimal, artificial retinas that would extract sufficient information from the visual array to help a visually impaired person move around to a significant degree.

Other obvious sensory augmenters would aim to create "supranormal" effects, such as allowing us to amplify weak visual or auditory signals. For example, human factors psychologists working in the auto industry could develop "night goggles" for auto drivers or appropriately treated windshields that would amplify contrast signals from visual-object patterns, thus enhancing their recognizability during night-time driving. Another sensor on the front of an auto could inform the driver of the distance to some roadway object ahead, the closing speed, and the estimated time before meeting. Such information could be used further by a microchip to calculate and signal drivers whether at current speed they have sufficient time to pass one road vehicle before reaching a second, oncoming vehicle.

Turning to a consideration of sensory pain, the goal of a sensory transducer would be to reduce or antagonize the pain sensations. One method for controlling somatosensory pains, say, that from an inoperable tumor pinching a nerve, would be to reduce the neurochemical substance in the dorsal spinal roots that carries pain sensations while encouraging at the same time the release of endorphins. A second method would be to use subdural electrodes to augment the firing of pain inhibition circuits in specific regions of the brain (periaqueductal gray area and raphé nuclei of the medulla; see Pinel, 1990). A third method would be to introduce into these areas opiate-like substances that block or antagonize pain signals. A fourth method would be to develop further psychological techniques for reducing pain, including cognitive restructuring, distraction, and sensate imagery.

Enriched Learning Environments

The schools of the future, if there are such institutions, will use more intelligent computer tutors with thousands of audioisual aids on CD-ROMs. The computer tutors would record the progress of each student in each subject matter, keep track of his or her skill level and learning strategies, and design individualized instructional materials appropriate for that student's profile. Students would progress through a collection of materials at their own rates and in a sequence determined partly by their interests along with inherent logical sequencing of the subject matter. Teachers and students' parents will largely play the role of cheerleaders, motivators, and guidance counselers rather than drill instructors for their students.

Schools of the future will expend far more effort to interest or motivate students to learn the material being taught. This will often be done by teaching concepts with entertaining visual illustrations and "real-life" contexts that connect the interests of the learners to the subject being taught. Real-life uses of the knowledge would be illustrated with video clips of people who use that knowledge or skill in their job or daily chores. Using what psychologists have learned about motivation and learning, the material to be learned would be presented in the context of a dramatic narrative that ties together items from diverse lessons such as math, physics, biology, and accounting. Such material would be integrated with the students' everyday life as far as possible.

Moreover, the presented material itself would be organized into tree structures or diagrams that brought out the logical dependencies among the concepts and principles, all with the intention of emphasizing the students' meaningful understanding of the material. In other words, the implementation of the educational curriculum would be based on principles gathered from basic research on learning and memory.

Memory Aids

Techniques that enhance the amount of information we can learn will be developed and disseminated more widely in the twenty-first century. Students in school will be taught not only the content or substance of the material, but also mnemonic techniques and devices—in other words, learning aids—that will enable them to absorb material more quickly and retain it longer. Textbook writers and newspaper reporters will present content in an organized fashion with many mnemonic aids to facilitate learning of the important points.

Similarly, the aging population of the twenty-first century will have the use of mnemonic techniques and devices that will help them avoid age-related declines in memory. Psychologists have already designed a collection of mental training exercises that could be put to greater use by the elderly. These exercises are designed to challenge and extend gradually the mental abilities of the elderly. A battery of exercises in concentration, visualization, relaxed alertness, reduction of test-anxiety, problem-solving, and so on, could be provided in graded doses to people of different ages as mental prophylactics against the usual ravages of an inactive, aging mind.

Smart Drugs

In addition, advances in the neurophysiology and neurochemistry of learning will undoubtedly help improve human memory. Several drugs have been found that improve simple learning, even when given shortly after the learning episode (McGaugh, 1989). These drugs appear to work by enhancing the extent and permanence of biochemical changes at the synapses of the brain circuits involved in representing the learning episode. To date, such facilitation has been found mainly for a few selected compounds given to enhance simple conditioned aversion in rats and mice. But the hope is that future psychological research will discover inexpensive drugs that will facilitate more extensive and complex learning in humans.

One impediment to school learning in young children is the syndrome of poor concentration and hyperactivity known as "attention-deficit disorder." Whether or not this is a coherent syndrome, the label nonetheless points to behavioral deficits in precursors of learning, so that a typical consequence is poor learning and below-grade academic achievement. Treatments for attention-deficit disorder include both the psychological and the pharmacological. Ritalin and other such stimulant drugs have the paradoxical effect of quelling the hyperactivity and apparently increasing the child's compliance with classroom routines. Future psychologists should be able to develop effective techniques for training such children to maintain attention or concentration on learning materials.

Language Learning

The future will bring an international diversity to science, business, and cultural affairs, and our descendants will have to deal with the problems created by attendant linguistic diversity. Techniques to enhance learning of language could be developed and applied more broadly in the twenty-first century. It is commonly believed (though disputed) that very young children learn a second language more easily than do adults who have been reared with only one language. The apparent advantage could be due to children's usually total immersion in the language culture they are learning and also the simplicity of children's language. Whatever the exact reason for the advantage, we might capitalize on the enhanced language-learning of children by providing immersion training in several languages throughout the first ten years of their lives.

An alternative way to deal with multilingual contacts is for people to wear a translator-computer in their shirt pocket hooked to an in-dwelling earphone. The listeners can dial up any one of a menu of speech translation programs for different languages, all being translated into the listener's native language. In that way, each participant in a conversation would be speaking and listening in his or her native language, with the pocket computers providing the speech-perception-with-translation interfaces. Perhaps once the language barrier between people is overcome, we shall be able to concentrate more on the importance of understanding the beliefs and psychological perspective of people from other cultures.

Electronic Communication

It is clear that telecommunications will be vastly improved in the future and will affect the way we interact. Each person would carry around a small cellular telephone with a unique phone number. Thus, dialing that number would always contact that portable phone, and the connection could be made over far larger distances than with current cellular phones. The person need not answer every call, but rather could select a mode whereby calls would be shunted to his or her message-recording number, and there prioritized according to the listener-provided information on the importance of the caller or category of caller.

Electronic mail systems will be greatly expanded into every home and office building and will most likely replace the slow mail system we have been accustomed to, except for mailing advertisements. The main innovation is that a speech-understanding system will be put in front of the mailer, so that senders need only speak their message into the decoder for it to be sent electronically either as a voice message or as a "printed" text to the receiver's computer screen.

Telephone and video conferencing will become cheaper and more popular as they increasingly replace physical meetings, especially those where participants travel long distances to a central meeting place. The social dynamics of teleconferencing will become a major topic in social psychology, and efforts will be made to supplement the verbal message with a variety of signals from nonverbal sources, such as the facial expressions and body language of speakers and listeners. Such signals are known to enhance or supplement the message carried by the words alone.

Final Comments

My discussion has touched on probable changes in people's lifestyle that technology might foster by the end of the twenty-first century, changes that psychologists will need to deal with. The so-called "universal laws" of behavior will not change much; that is, if psychologists were to test subjects of the late twenty-first century on standard experimental paradigms (say, memory scanning or short-term memory tasks), they would obtain roughly the same performance as our contemporaries in such tasks. The way in which people of the twenty-first century will differ enormously from us is in their standard technology, which will foster other changes in many of their personal capabilities and attitudes, which in turn may cause corresponding changes in their social beliefs and policies. Psychologists will need to be prepared to deal with the personal problems created by these revolutionary changes in life-style as well as the job stresses that will stem from these changes in personal capabilities and responsibilities.

User-friendly technologies could provide people with many ingenious tools to help them alter their external and internal milieus. In this manner, the technologies could empower people to attain their goals more easily and derive more satisfaction from their work and life pursuits. They would then live longer, happier, healthier, more productive and creative lives than people do today. After all, isn't that the Utopian goal of all social reformers, including psychologists?

Acknowledgments

The author's research is supported by a grant MH-47575 from the National Institute of Mental Health. However, the views expressed here are solely his own, and the grant from NIMH does not imply endorsement of these views by that agency. The author thanks Sharon Anthony Bower, who provided considerable motivation and input to the crafting of this paper.

References

Anderson, J. R. (1983). *The architecture of cognition*. Cambridge, Mass.: Harvard University Press.

Kreek, M. J. (1993). *Biological basis and pharmacotherapy for addictive disorders.* Speech given at Indo-U.S. Scientific Symposium: Mental Health and Neurosciences in the Decade of the Brain. Bangalore, India. February.

McGaugh, J. L. (1989). Involvement of hormonal and neuromodulatory systems in the regulation of memory storage. *Annual Review of Neuroscience, 12,* 255–287.

Newell, A. (1990). *Unified theories of cognition*. Cambridge, Mass.: Harvard University Press.

Pinel, J. P. J. (1990). *Biopsychology*. Boston: Allyn & Bacon.

3

The Impact and Promise of the Cognitive Revolution

ROGER W. SPERRY

Reflecting on a century past with an eye to the future, what I have to say is colored in no small part by a concern long shared with the late B. F. Skinner, namely, *"Can the American Psychological Association, or any other organization, count on another hundred years?"* Skinner's answer became increasingly less optimistic, especially in his last decade, concluding, *"The more we learn about human behavior, the less and less promising appear the prospects."* My own answer, reflecting a similar vein of increasing concern, sees a possible ray of hope in psychology's cognitive revolution and what it could mean in bringing new perspectives, beliefs, and values—in short, new mindsets and a new way of thinking—much needed if humanity is to survive the next century.

During its first hundred years, psychology is said to have gone through no less than three major revolutions. In addition to the recent shift to cognitivism, there were the two earlier revolts associated with J. B. Watson and Sigmund Freud. I will try to show that, of the three, the current so-called cognitive, mentalist, or "consciousness" revolution is far and away the most radical turnaround: the most revisionary and transformative.

A main theme to emerge goes in brief as follows: In the cognitive revolution, psychology is leading the way among the sciences to a new and improved—that is, a more comprehensive, adequate, and more valid—conceptual foundation for scientific (and for all) causal explanation and understanding. Any perceived irony here is indeed quite real. Psychology, after having been put down for decades by the so-called hard sciences as not being really a science, is now turning the tables—in effect, asserting that reductive physicalism or "microdeterminism," the traditional explanatory model of science (including behaviorism), has serious shortcomings and is no longer tenable.

Other disciplines, even physics, are beginning to agree and join in, discovering and adopting the new antireductive and emergent insights, including, for example, computer science, neuroscience, biology, anthropology, evolutionary and hierarchy theory, general systems theory and, of course, quantum theory, among others (e.g., Blakemore & Greenfield, 1987; Campbell, 1974; Gell-Mann, 1988; Gleick, 1987; Grene, 1987; D. R. Griffin, 1981; D. Griffin, 1988; Laszlo, 1972; Piaget, 1970; Stapp, 1982). Each of these, however, appears to have its own different, special version of how these innovations came about, each finding the origins within its own particular field.

I strongly believe that in the long run history will show that, among the sciences, psychology was actually the first to overthrow its traditional mainstream doctrine in favor of the emerging new paradigm. By the early 1970s, mainstream psychology already had adopted the new outlook (Dember, 1974; Matson, 1971; Palermo, 1971; Pylyshyn, 1973; Segal & Lachman, 1972); whereas the other fields have come to it only later on, especially during the 1980s and, in effect, have mostly just been following and developing varied forms and applications of what, in essence, is the same basic new core concept. At least that is the conclusion I come to and will try to support.

Overview

First, a quick review of some of the salient features of the much debated cognitive revolution as I see it: what the essential revolt was, what it means, and some of its consequences thus far. Most importantly, the cognitive revolution represents a diametric turnaround in the centuries-old treatment of mind and consciousness in science. The contents of conscious experience, with their subjective qualities, long banned as being mere acausal epiphenomena, or as just identical to brain activity, or otherwise in conflict with the laws of the conservation of energy, have now made a dramatic comeback. Reconceived in the new outlook, subjective mental states become functionally interactive and essential for a full explanation of conscious behavior. Traditional microdeterminist reasoning that brain function can be fully accounted for in neurocellular-physiochemical terms is refuted, as are former assumptions that traditional materialism provides—in principle, a complete coherent explanation of the natural world. The cognitive and consciousness revolution thus represents a revolt as well against the long-time worship of the atomistic in science. Reductive microdeterministic views of personhood and the physical world are replaced in favor of a more holistic, "top-down" view in which the higher, more evolved entities throughout nature, including the mental, vital, social, and other high-order forces, gain their due recognition along with physics and chemistry.

It is important to stress, however, that the cognitive changeover from behaviorism to the new mentalism does not carry us all the way from one previous extreme to the opposite—that is, to a mentalistic dualism. The shift, rather, is to a quite new heterodox position that integrates and blends aspects of prior opposed solutions into a novel unifying synthesis (Natsoulas, 1987). The new position is mentalistic in holding that behavior is mentally and subjectively driven. This view definitely, however, does *not* mean that the position is *dualistic*. In the new synthesis, mental states, as dynamic emergent properties of brain activity, become inseparably interfused with, and tied to, the brain activity of which they are an emergent property. Consciousness in this view cannot exist apart from the functioning brain.

A new reciprocal form of causal control is invoked that includes downward as well as upward determinism. This bidirectional model applies, not only in the brain to the control of emergent *mental* events over *neuronal* activity, but also to the emergent control by holistic properties in general throughout nature. Accordingly, it has been gaining ground in other sciences as well. What started as an intradisciplinary revolution within psychology is thus turning into a major revolution for all science. As a consequence, scientific descriptions, not only for behavior, cognition, the self, and so on, but for all physical reality are being vastly transformed—with wide humanistic, philosophical and epistemological as well as scientific implications. Like the Darwinian and Copernican revolutions, to which some authors now compare it, the cognitive revolution leads to a combined *ideological revolution* as defined by Karl Popper (1975). Alternative beliefs emerge about the ultimate nature of things, and a changed cosmology brings a new set of answers to some of humanity's deepest questions.

To many psychologists, such claims for the cognitive revolution will seem a lavish overstatement, even fanciful. I believe, however, that firm substantial backing can be found for each one of these assessments—plus many more, yet unmentioned extensions. Toward a preliminary understanding of why the impacts should be so profound and far-reaching, consider just the one fact: that the cognitive revolution, as here conceived, involves radical changes in, not just one, but in *two core concepts:* namely, *consciousness* and *causality,* both of which have extremely wide, almost ubiquitous application to everything we experience and try to understand. In view of this alone, it is obvious that the paradigmatic shift to cognitivism/mentalism, following centuries of rigorous materialism, is bound to have numerous major and far-reaching consequences—the list of which goes on and on.

Among further effects, this turnabout in the causal status of consciousness abolishes the traditional science–values dichotomy. That we are *in a new era* today in respect to values is well recognized (Edel, 1980). Thus the cognitive revolution, from an ethical standpoint, might equally well have been called a *"values"* revolution. The old value-free, strictly objective, mindless and quantitative, atomistic descriptions of materialist science are being replaced by accounts that recognize the rich, irreducible, varied, and valued emergent macro and holistic properties and qualities in both human and nonhuman nature. Subjective human values, no longer written off as ineffectual epiphenomena nor reduced to microphenomena, become the most critically powerful force shaping today's civilized world (Sperry, 1972, 1991a), the underlying answer to current global ills and the key to world change.

A different approach is also opened and a resolution offered for that age-old enigma, the freewill–determinism paradox. Blending previous opposites in a heterodox middle-way position, the new cognitivism retains both freewill and determinism, but each reconceived in modified form and integrated in a way that preserves moral responsibility (Deci, 1980; Libet, 1992; Sperry, 1964, 1970). Volition remains causally determined, but no longer entirely subject to the inexorable physiochemical laws of neurocellular activation. These lower-level laws become supervened by higher-level controls of the subjective conscious self in which they are embedded (just as it introspectively seems to be). The implications become critical for a scientific treatment of personal agency and social interaction (Bandura, 1989; Smith, 1983). Overall, we still inhabit a deterministic universe, but it is ruled by a large array of different types, qualities, and levels of determinism. In retrospect, we would not want it otherwise; especially, we would not want to live in an indeterminate, noncausal, and thus random and chaotic universe, totally unpredictable, with no reliability or any rational higher meaning.

In sum, the type of reality and worldview upheld by science is thoroughly transformed, being greatly enriched and more appealing as well as more credible. A fundamentally changed picture of ourselves and the world gives science an entirely new outlook on existence, a whole "new story" (Augros & Stanciu, 1984), plus a higher social role and enhanced public image. The vast gulf of mutual incompatibility that has long separated the world of science and that of the humanities (Jones, 1965; Snow, 1959) is abolished and replaced by a congenial continuum. Most important, perhaps, for those growing numbers among us who, like Skinner, see real concern about prospects for another hundred years, these renovations of the cognitive revolution provide a "new way of knowing" and understanding, a unifying new vision, in which some see a rational solution to our global predicament in the form of more realistic beliefs and values to live and govern by. For example, universally accepted global standards for such issues as world population control, conservation of world resources, and protection of our oceans and atmosphere are urgently needed.

Gaining Perspectives

Before going further, we need to clarify some frequent sources of misconception. First, at a time when it seems to be open season on personal theories of consciousness, it is important to recognize that what we deal with here is not just personal, obscure, or even minority theory or opinion, but rather, with the actual working conceptual framework and dominant doctrine since the 1970s, of the whole discipline of science that specializes in mind and behavior (Baars, 1986; Gardner, 1985), and thus best speaks for science as a whole on these matters. Moreover, my main focus here is not on the philosophical abstractions, such as whether mentalism or reductionism may ultimately prove correct, but on the recorded fact of a turning point in the history of science, and its cause.

Second, when I speak of behaviorism, I mean *behaviorism per se,* in the sense of an overriding paradigm, metatheory, or working conceptual framework for psychology in general. The reference is not to any of the various subordinate theories, practices, and approaches to behavior, learning, or brain function that incidentally may have become associated by coming into vogue during the half-century reign of behaviorism. It is the overriding conceptual paradigm itself that the cognitive revolution has overthrown, especially its renunciation (in common with the other natural sciences) of mental or subjective factors as valid constructs for causal explanation.

Third, our concern throughout is not with any esoteric, radical, or other recent fringe development, but with the central working premises of the solid scientific mainstream. Science viewed as a whole, its history, what it stands for, its principles, conceptual foundations, applications, and implications are what shape the present position and treatment. The remaining adamant "behaviorists" are taken to represent a respected minority challenging the basic new principles, but no longer representative of mainstream psychology.

Fourth, in view of salient misconceptions (e.g., Bunge, 1980; Chezik, 1990; Peterson, 1990; Pirolli & Goel, 1990; and others, see Natsoulas, 1991; Sperry, 1992), it is worth repeating that the type of mentalism upheld here is not dualistic in the classic philosophic sense of two different, independent realms of existence. In our new macromental or holomental synthesis, mental states as dynamic emergent properties of brain states, cause behavior but are not dualistic because they are inextricably interfused with their generating brain processes. Mental states in this form cannot exist apart from the active brain. At the same time, mental states are not the same as brain states. Perception, emotion, insight, judgment, and so forth, are mental states dependent on but different from the electrochemical and biophysical aspects of the brain. The two differ in the same way a dynamic emergent property differs from its component infrastructure. It is characteristic of emergent properties in that mental states are notably novel and often amazingly and inexplicably different from the components from which they are built. The recognized methodological difficulties posed by the use of introspection, however, are not remedied.

Furthermore, my reasons for bypassing quantum theory, the most frequently cited source of the new worldview, in favor of mind–brain theory needs at least brief mention (space does not allow full coverage). In the present view, quantum mechanics, as a conceptual framework, fails to give a complete coherent account of events at macro levels, nor does it subsume classical Newtonian laws as commonly inferred from the mathematical equations. Both quantum and Newtonian theory fail in our present view to cover adequately an important key principle, namely, that the collective spatiotemporal patterning of physical masses or of particles, energy sources, or other mass-energy entities exerts causal influence *in and of itself*. To explain and understand the macro world with its endlessly different entities and relations, one does not turn to this scheme with the expectation of finding specific answers in quantum mechanics or in any other superstring or "theory of everything." The subatomic features of a great cathedral and a sewage plant are the same. But these universal subatomic elements are supervened and superseded in two-way causation through the downward control exerted by higher-level components in which they are embedded. Again, what counts are the different spatiotemporal patternings of the components at all levels and between levels: their one- to four-dimensional Gestalts. This space/time causality, or pattern factor, prevents reduction, as a rule, from a macro level to a micro level. It also rules out the possibility that subatomic properties will move upward to the macro world. (A sheet of copper divided into three parts and each formed respectively into a sphere, a cube, and a tube still have the same atomic and subatomic properties as before. The macro properties, however, are different for each.) Thus, it is important to keep in mind that the new paradigm does not dispose of either quantum or Newtonian theory. It merely supplements these theories by adding the supervening, irreducible, but highly critical, space/time pattern factors.

Contested Historical Aspects

Some 20 years since the cognitive revolution marked a major turning point in the history of science, we still lack any satisfying consensus as to its exact nature and source, its driving rationale, or precisely what it means for the future. Within psychology itself, different interest groups continue to vie over these and related questions (e.g., Amsel, 1989; Baars, 1986; Bevan, 1991; Bolles, 1990; Chezik, 1990; Keil, 1991; Kendler, 1990; Lamal, 1990; Natsoulas, 1987; Simon, 1991; Sperry, 1980, 1991b; Wasow, 1989). If the overall impact and potential implications are anything like the sort inferred here, it becomes crucial that we try to understand better the true nature and essence of the cognitive revolution.

The story of this revolt, as I interpret it, was not one of finding new data to support the important role of cognition, plenty of which were already long evident. Instead, the story is one of discovering an alternative logic by which to refute the seemingly incontestable reasoning that heretofore had required science to ostracize mind and consciousness. How the discovery of this new logic came about is most easily explained in terms of the historical context out of which the new reasoning arose. Throughout the behaviorist/materialist era, extending well up into the 1960s, the age-old riddle of the mind–brain relationship involved a contradictory paradox: On the one hand, it seemed obvious from common experience that our behavior is *mentally* driven. Conversely, from the standpoint of neuroscience, it seemed equally obvious that a complete account of brain function, including the brain's entire input–output performance, could be provided in strictly objective neuronal–biophysical terms. In the explanatory system of neuroscience, researchers could find no place for the likes of conscious or mental forces, and the same was true of behaviorist psychologists. Behaviorism as "a philosophy of science" (Skinner, 1964) made the science of mind consistent with that of the neural and other natural sciences. On this basis, the antimentalist tenets of behaviorism seemed irrefutable all through its heyday. As humanist Andrew Bongiorno (personal communication, 1991), now in his nineties, recalls, "For half a century behaviorism reigned supreme in academe." To overthrow behaviorism would require an overthrow also of the conceptual foundations of neuroscience and of science in general.

What then led to the downfall of behaviorism? Or, put another way, what made cognitivism suddenly rise in its own right, no longer under the restrictive dictates of a reigning behaviorism, as in the earlier days of Edward Tolman? How did it become a new and independent paradigm predicating a worldview and tenets of its own that stood opposed to the long-dominant doctrine of the behaviorist/

materialist era? Whatever caused this turnabout, it came with a startling sudden-ness described in the early 1970s by Pylyshyn (1973, p. 1) as having *"recently exploded"* into fashion. It was as if the floodgates holding back the many pressures of consciousness and subjectivity were suddenly opened. What caused this abrupt turnabout has continued ever since to puzzle many leaders in the field (Boneau, 1992).

Mind-sets in 1964

As late as 1964, there was still no clear sense of the impending turnabout as evidenced in various conferences, books, and articles of and about the period (e.g., Bertalanffy, 1968; Feigenbaum & Feldman, 1963; Feigl, 1967; Nagel, 1971; Simon, 1962; Smythies, 1965). Within psychology, the debates between phenomenologists and behaviorists were ongoing as before, unable to shake the dominant reign of the behaviorist doctrine (Koch, 1963; Wann, 1964). In 1964, humanist Carl Rogers, who had searched over a long career for a scientific foundation for what he called "subjective knowing" was still referring to the concept of volition as "an irreconcilable contradiction" and "deep paradox" with which we just have to learn to live (Rogers, 1964). In September of the same year, the eminent neurophysiologist John Eccles reaffirmed at the Vatican Conference on Consciousness his reasoned conviction as a scientist, in line with physiological tradition, that consciousness is totally superfluous from the standpoint of neurosci-ence. But then, expressing what many of us nevertheless felt, he added, "I do not believe this story, of course, but I do not know the logical answer" (Eccles, 1966, p. 248). The finding of this logical answer was not far away and would be the key factor in making possible the cognitive revolution—as well as Eccles' own notable campaign embarked on shortly after, extolling what he called "psycho-physical interaction."

By 1971, it already was clear that many psychologists had come to recognize that their discipline was in the process of a major paradigm shift in which behav-iorism was being replaced by an opposing new mentalism or cognitivism (Matson, 1971; Palermo, 1971; Segal & Lachman, 1972). The revisionary concepts of the new paradigm—those concepts that finally broke the materialist logic in which science had been locked for over 200 years—were by then sufficiently clear and convincing to cause mainstream psychology to start swinging its support to the new mentalism. During this interim, therefore, between 1964 and 1971, some-thing must have happened to reveal the long-sought "logical answer" to the baf-fling impasse over consciousness and its role in science.

A Key Factor

What happened, I believe, was the discovery that the traditional logic by which consciousness had been excluded from scientific explanation was in fact basically flawed or incomplete, and that this inadequacy could be rectified through a different form of causal explanation. An alternative form of causal determinism was perceived that put mind and consciousness in a functionally interactive, nonreductive, and ineliminable causal role (Popper, 1965/1972; Sperry, 1964, 1965), thus breaking the long-standing impasse and "irreconcilable contradiction" of the mind–brain paradox.

The reason why this particular attempt to legitimize consciousness succeeded, where innumerable others had failed, lies in the use of a quite different approach. Previous efforts had stayed within the traditional reference frame, attempting to insert consciousness at points along the chain of causation that had already been well explained by the brain–behavior sciences—for example, at synaptic junctions between brain cells (Eccles, 1953). By contrast, the successful effort preserved this lower-level chain of causation and simply encompassed or embedded it within a higher-level (yet-to-be-described) cognitive system of cerebral processing. In this way, *subjectively experienced conscious qualities,* viewed as irreducible emergent properties of brain processing, could be looked at as objective interactive causal influences without contradicting the gains of earlier science. In other words, success was attained only by changing the rules of the game—that is, by inventing a whole different paradigm for scientific causal explanation.

Notably, this same seven-year period was also marked by a second extraordinary shift in the mainstream view regarding another age-old controversy—namely, the debate over wholism versus reductionism. After various ups and downs during the preceding century, reductionism had risen to a new high as we entered the mid-1960s, a period one philosopher called a "reductionist euphoria" (Nagel, 1971), bolstered especially by successes in molecular biology (Crick, 1966). But this wave of extreme reductionism soon gave way to a new flowering of holism and an acceptance of the concept of the irreducible whole (Checkland, 1981), which today still appears to be at an all-time high in the long history of this polemic.

In our present analysis, both of these shifts—that to mentalism and that to wholism—are directly linked, to the revised model for causal determinism. Both depend on the causal reality of irreducible emergent phenomena that interact as wholes. Subjective agency may thus be viewed as a special instance of top-down control, a special case of emergent causality. This emergent, top-down causality can be seen in such simple physical examples as the space-time trajectory of a molecule within a rolling wheel, a flowing eddy, wave action, a flying plane, among others. The existence and importance of top-down causation as an adequate description of the natural order appeared obvious (see Popper & Eccles, 1977, p. 209).

Psychology in the Lead?

The fact that the conceptual developments that legitimized consciousness also apply to emergent, "macro," and holistic properties in general is fast becoming recognized within other disciplines. Following the shift in psychology, which started in the 1960s and was established by the early 1970s, the new paradigm began to gain ground in other fields. Never before in the history of science have we seen such an outpouring of "new sciences," "new worldviews," "new visions" of reality, "new epistemologies," "new ontologies." The 1980s, especially, might well be called "the decade of emerging new paradigms." We saw the birth of the "systems view of the world" (Laszlo, 1972), the new "Worlds 2 & 3" of Popper (1965/1972), the "Tao of physics" (Capra, 1977), "the cognitive view of biology" and the new "science of qualities" (Goodwin, 1978), the "Aquarian conspiracy" (Ferguson, 1980), the "new view of animal awareness" (Griffin, 1981), "new dialogue with nature" (Prigogine & Stengers, 1984), "new story of science" (Augros & Stanciu, 1984), "the new philosophy of science" (Manicas & Secord, 1983), the "new evolutionary epistemology" (Greenberg & Tobach, 1988), the "reenchantment of science" in a "postmodern era" (e.g., Griffin, 1988; Toulmin, 1982)—and the list goes on.

All these developments share one major thrust—namely, the rejection of traditional reductionism. All these new visions, outlooks, sciences, philosophies, and so on, also depend on the presumed existence of some newly perceived flaw, incompleteness, or inadequacy in our time-honored traditional reasoning. And yet reductionist thinking has not been totally rejected; only the longtime assumption that it gives a complete and sufficient account. The day-to-day practice, methodology, and previous gains of science are little changed. Nothing is lost, but a whole new outlook on existence is opened up to us.

Toward a High-Quality Sustainable World

The second part of this chapter, "the promise," calls for a change of mind-set. Let us return to Skinner's concern about making it to another centennial as a thriving discipline. Most of the foregoing discussion is dwarfed in comparison to this question of survival, fast becoming the overriding imperative of our times—scientifically, politically, economically, and every other way—**a "cause of all causes which, should it fail, all others go with it."** Nothing in science today is of more basic importance than the effort to save science—and all the other great legacies of eons of evolution.

By now, it is widely agreed that what is needed to remedy our present self-destructive course is major changes in human thinking and behavior worldwide, in our life-styles, values, social and moral priorities, and the like. What group is in a better position or better qualified professionally than behavioral science to point out what has gone wrong and to suggest sound remedial actions? For the first time, the cognitive-mentalist paradigm makes possible a science-based approach to such global questions as, "What kind of world do we want, and what must we do to get there?" A new approach to moral issues can be phrased: "What ideals best guide existence on planet Earth?" and "What constitutes the highest measure for right and wrong and social justice?"

Though always debatable, directives at least give us a possible start, providing some targets at which to aim.

The bottom-line message runs something like this: *We can now look to science to save the world, not through new improved technology, green revolutions, and the like (which will only stave off and thereby magnify any eventual demise), but instead by providing more realistic and sustainable beliefs and values to live and govern by.* This message is not new, but it was given short shrift from both scientists and ethicists when voiced initially (Bixenstein, 1976; Edel, 1980; Sperry, 1972). The "value–belief" arguments still hold, and current attitudes seem more receptive.

Science, Values, and Survival

Today's mounting global ills will not be cured merely by applying more or better science and technology. Despite the marvels and apparent successes, the gains achieved are offset by the incessantly expanding demands of a growing human population. A context of rising population pressures makes it a simple truism that almost anything that enables more people to fare or thrive better—a new energy source, an aqueduct, another mass transit, or whatever, even environmental re-form—inevitably has the long-term result of a further escalation in our collective problems. Until population is stabilized, this "vicious spiral paradox" means that many seemingly desirable innovations, with obvious short-term benefits, just serve in the long run to put us deeper and deeper into a no-win proposition. Thus, slowly but surely, our civilization becomes ever more deeply enmeshed in a vicious spiral of mounting population, pollution, increased energy demands, environmental degradation, urban overcrowding and associated crime, homelessness, joblessness, and hopelessness. With one thing reinforcing another, we become more and more firmly entrapped each year.

What is needed to break this vicious spiral is a basic revision worldwide in human life-styles, aims, and attitudes, with a redirection of social values and policy toward more long-term priorities that will preserve an evolving quality of life for future generations. A major reconception of our human efforts is called for: a higher overarching perspective that includes ultimate goals and values, or as Einstein put it in reference to atomic power, "We need a new way of thinking if mankind is to survive."

Such a new way of thinking spawned by the cognitive revolution shows strong promise. Reversing previous doctrine in science, it affirms that the world we live in is driven not solely by mindless physical forces but also, and much more crucially, by subjective human values. Human values become the underlying key to world change—including our global predicament and its solution (Sperry, 1972; 1991a). The "battle to save the planet" becomes, in large measure, a battle over values.

The reason conventional values aren't working today—and have been driving us and our entire ecosystem toward collapse—is that some of our assumptions are wrong. Human values are not absolute, not immutable by natural law or divine ordination. Human values by nature are evolutionary, interrelated, dependent on the context in which they evolve (Pugh, 1977). To cling to unchanging values in a rapidly changing world can be fatal.

For centuries, it has been an assumption that because human life is special, even sacred, the more the better. "Go forth and multiply and take dominion . . ."

was morally good at the time the Scriptures were written. Two thousand years later, however, with the global situation reversed, and an exploding world population with its multiform side effects threatening to destroy everything we value, it follows today that because human life is precious, even sacred, *less is better*. Such an inescapable reversal of our assumptions overturns an entire complex of long-revered, centuries-old tradition. Today's world calls for a more far-sighted and modern vision of what it means to be humane.

Considering this massive world population growth, the ecological irreversabilities, and the attendant breakdown in the social fabric of society, a "point-of-no-return" is bound to occur well in advance of a final debacle. Indeed, there may be much less time than we think. Twenty-five years ago, we could still see a choice: either adopt new, more sustainable values by foresight, or have them thrust upon us by mounting intolerable living conditions (Sperry, 1972). Today, almost everywhere we turn, the signs of overcrowding and intolerability are already showing. Rising demands for subsistence in a direly depleted, degraded ecosphere are not the sole concern. In numerous subtle and unsubtle ways, excessive overpopulation desensitizes humanity and demeans the individual person into an increasingly expendable commodity. Our sense of the specialness of human life, its meaning, singular worth, dignity, and wonder undergoes an insidious, unobtrusive, but inexorable erosion to which our inherent human nature is particularly vulnerable. The process is so slow and the capacity of the human brain to adapt so great that the adverse trends, spread over decades or even generations, are adjusted to and taken for granted.

Instead of our longtime avoidance of sensitive population issues, we need the opposite: intensive study and open debate toward informed views of what optimal population levels might be, regionally and globally, and what **ideals might be worth striving for in an overall guiding plan for existence on planet Earth.** We urgently need some bright new Utopian goals toward which we can at least aspire.

Uniqueness, diversity, and contrast in our life and in our world lead to value and meaning. The wilderness and the urban settings each gain in contrast to the other, as do the many races and ethnic cultures of our world. A society overrun, dominated by, and designed to maximize, equalize, and homogenize "the human carrying capacity" will necessarily degrade and demean human life in all its diversity. The proven benefits of biodiversity we have seen in the wild applies to our human social order as well.

Overall, the immensity of the global rescue mission we now face, including the requisite changes in social and moral priorities worldwide, will require a unifying and higher allegiance that can transcend past loyalties, not to mention the international legislation needed to implement and secure the various reforms. Any one reform, taken by itself, seems challenge enough. Taken together, they are a formidable task. If we add the urgency of this mission, the collective hurdle seems almost insurmountable.

Already we are well past the point where we can leave to the next generations the type of ecosphere that we inherited and that they too deserve. Increasingly hard choices ahead will pit the exponentially growing needs of a human population against the rest of nature. Decisions not to have much-desired children, to forgo lucrative industrial profits, to abandon cherished livelihoods—all might be more readily embraced if they were reinforced by an informed public moral sense, one that has all the emotional power of a religious conviction. Indeed, to put an end to what thus far has seemed a losing battle, humankind will need to undergo a rapid conversion to accept a changed sense of the sacred, a changed sense of ultimate values, and the highest good. An overarching conviction to the highest good can readjust our hierarchy of social values and drive reforms at every social level.

The cognitive revolution in science can provide a new way of thinking that brings into focus more realistic insights about the kinds of forces that have shaped us, that move the universe, and that brought about the evolution of humankind. Environmentalism calls for a deep moral commitment that would preserve and enhance our world, and a recognition that the vast interwoven fabric of an evolving natural world, including humans, is inextricably intertwined. Evolution, driven by emergent and subjective pressures—cosmic, human, many little understood— becomes a purposeful and meaningful force in the governing of all living things. The highest good becomes the preservation of the quality of existence for future generations, not only our own. The sanctity of human life, and any higher meaning one wishes to attach to that life, must depend on the rights and welfare of coming generations. The United Nations, and other world courts and agencies, must build a system of world law and justice based on values that encompass not only the whole of nature but the future generations of humankind. Such bodies will also need to arouse a deep sense of outrage at what modern humanity is doing to itself and its future.

The promise of the cognitive revolution is multiform, but in the context of today's global ills and our imperiled future, its true success may rest on its ability to bring a higher level of meaning to science—one that recognizes and accepts as proper subjects of study the beliefs and value systems that may be our salvation for the twenty-first century.

Acknowledgments

This article is an abridgment of a Distinguished Centennial Address presented at the 99th Annual Convention of the American Psychological Association, San Francisco, California, August 1991. The address was read for Dr. Sperry by his former associate, Dr. Theodore J. Voneida, Professor and Chair, Department of Neurobiology, College of Medicine, Northeastern Ohio Universities, Rootstown, OH 44272.

The work was supported by funds donated to the California Institute of Technology for research on the mind–brain problem. I thank Theodore Voneida for his excellent reading and Mark Rosenzweig for the kind introduction. Constructive criticisms on an earlier draft were contributed by Joseph Bogen, Erika Erdmann, Polly Henninger, Jan Sperry, Ted Voneida, and anonymous referees. I also thank

Patricia Anderson, Norma Deupree, and Mary Jeffries for valued help in compiling the references and processing the manuscript.

References

Amsel, A. (1989). *Behaviorism, neobehaviorism, and cognitivism in learning theory: Historical and contemporary perspectives.* Hillsdale, NJ: Erlbaum.

Augros, R. M., & Stanciu, G. N. (1984). *The new story of science.* New York: Bantam.

Baars, R. J. (1986). *The cognitive revolution in psychology.* New York: Guilford.

Bandura, A. (1989). Human agency in social cognitive theory. *American Psychologist, 44,* 1175–1184.

Bertalanffy, L. von. (1968). *General systems theory.* New York: Braziller.

Bevan, W. (1991). A tour inside the onion. *American Psychologist, 46,* 475–483.

Bixenstine, E. (1976). The value–fact antithesis in behavioral science. *Journal of Humanistic Psychology, 16* (2), 35–57.

Blakemore, C., & Greenfield, S. (1987). *Mindwaves: Thoughts on intelligence, identity and consciousness.* Oxford: Basil Blackwell.

Bolles, R. C. (1990). Where did everybody go? *Psychological Science, 1,* 112–113.

Boneau, C. A. (1992). Observations on psychology's past and future. *American Psychologist 47*(12), 1586–1596.

Bunge, M. (1980). *The mind–body problem.* New York: Pergamon Press.

Campbell, D. T. (1974). Downward causation in hierarchically organized biological systems. In F. J. Ayala & T. Dobzhansky (Eds.), *Studies in the philosophy of biology* (pp. 139–161). Berkeley: University of California Press.

Capra, F. (1977). *The Tao of physics.* East Lansing, MI: Shambhala.

Checkland, P. (1981). *Systems thinking, systems practice.* New York: John Wiley.

Chezik, D. D. (1990). Sperry's emergent interactionism. *American Psychologist, 45:* 70.

Crick, F. (1966). *Of molecules and men.* Seattle: University of Washington Press.

Deci, E. L. (1980). *The psychology of self-determination.* Lexington, MA: D.C. Heath.

Dember, W. N. (1974). Motivation and the cognitive revolution. *American Psychologist, 29,* 161–168.

Dewan, W. N. (1976). Consciousness as an emergent causal agent in the context of control system theory. In G. G. Globus, G. Maxwell, & I. Savodnik (Eds.), *Consciousness and the brain* (pp. 179–198). New York: Plenum Press.

Eccles, J. C. (1953). *The neurophysiological basis of mind: The principles of neurophysiology.* Oxford: Clarendon Press.

Eccles, J. C. (Ed.) (1966). *Brain and conscious experience.* New York: Springer.

Edel, A. (1980). *Exploring fact and value* (Vol. 2). New Brunswick, NJ: Transaction Books.

Feigenbaum, E. A., & Feldman, J. (Eds.). (1963). *Computers and thought.* New York: McGraw-Hill.

Feigl, H. (1967). *The "mental" and the "physical."* (With "postscript after ten years"). Minneapolis: University of Minnesota Press.

Ferguson, E. S. (1980). *The Aquarian conspiracy.* Los Angeles: Tarcher.

Gardner, H. (1985). *The mind's new science: A history of the cognitive revolution.* New York: Basic Books.

Gell-Mann, M. (1988). Simplicity and complexity in the description of nature. *Engineering and Science, 51*(3), 2–9.

Gleick, J. (1987). *Chaos: Making a new science.* New York: Viking Press.

Goodwin, B. C. (1978). A cognitive view of biological process. *Journal of Social and Biological Structures, 1,* 117–125.

Greenberg, G., & Tobach, E. (1988). *Evolution of social behavior and integrative levels.* The T. C. Schneirla Conference Series (Vol. 3). Hillsdale, NJ: Lawrence Erlbaum.

Grene, M. (1987). Hierarchies in biology. *American Scientist, 75,* 504–510.

Griffin, Donald R. (1981). *The question of animal awareness.* New York: Rockefeller University Press.

Griffin, David (1988). *The reenchantment of science.* New York: SUNY.

Hook, S. (Ed.). (1960). *Dimensions of mind.* New York: Collier Books.

Jones, W. T. (1965). *The sciences and the humanities.* Berkeley: University of California Press.

Keil, F. C. (1991). On being more than the sum of the parts: The conceptual coherence of cognitive science. *Psychological Science, 2,* 283, 287–293.

Kendler, H. H. (1990). Looking backward to see ahead. *Psychological Science, 1,* 107–112.

Koch, S. (1963). *Psychology: A study of a science.* New York: McGraw-Hill.

Lamal, P. A. (1990). The continuing mischaracterization of radical behaviorism. *American Psychologist, 45,* 71.

Laszlo. E. (1972). *The systems view of the world; the natural philosophy of the new developments in the sciences.* New York: Braziller.

Libet, B. (1992). The neural time—factor in perception, volition and free will. *Revue de Metaphysique et de Morale, 2,* 255–272.

Manicas, Peter T., & Secord, Paul F. (1983). Implications for psychology of the new philosophy of science. *American Psychologist,* April, 399–413.

Matson, F. W. (1971). Humanistic theory: The third revolution in psychology. *The Humanist 31*(2), 7–11.

Nagel, T. (1971). Brain bisection and the unity of consciousness. *Synthese, 22,* 396–413.

Natsoulas, T. (1987). Roger Sperry's monist interactionism. *The Journal of Mind & Behavior, 8,* 1–21.

Natsoulas, T. (1991). Ontological subjectivity. *The Journal of Mind & Behavior 12,* 175–200.

Palermo, D. S. (1971). Is a scientific revolution taking place in psychology? *Science Studies, 1,* 135–155.

Peterson, R. F. (1990). On Sperry's model. *American Psychologist, 45,* 70–71.

Piaget, J. (1970). *Structuralism.* New York: Basic Books.

Pirolli, P. & Goel, V. (1990). You can't get there from here: Comments on R. W. Sperry's resolution of science and ethics. *American Psychologist, 45,* 71–73.

Popper, K. R. (1965/1972). Of clouds and clocks (Second Arthur Holly Compton Memorial Lecture, presented in April, 1965). In K. Popper (Ed.), *Objective knowledge* (pp. 206–255). Oxford: Clarendon Press.

Popper, K. R. (1975). The rationality of scientific revolutions. In R. Harre (Ed.), *Problems of scientific revolution* (pp. 72–101). Oxford: Clarendon Press.

Popper, K. R., & Eccles, J. C. (1977). *The self and its brain.* New York: Springer International.

Prigogine, I., & Stengers, I. (1984). *Order out of chaos: Man's new dialogue with nature.* New York: Bantam.

Pugh, G. E. (1977). *The biological origin of human values.* New York: Basic Books.

Pylyshyn, Z. W. (1973). What the mind's eye tells the mind's brain: A critique of mental imagery. *Psychological Bulletin, 80*, 1–24.

Ripley, C. (1984). Sperry's concept of consciousness. *Inquiry, 27*, 399–423.

Rogers, C. R. (1964). Freedom and commitment. *The Humanist, 29*(2), 37–40.

Rottschaefer, W. A. (1987). Roger Sperry's science of values. *The Journal of Mind & Behavior, 8*, 23–35.

Segal, E. M., & Lachman, R. (1972). Complex behavior or higher mental process? Is there a paradigm shift? *American Psychologist, 27*, 46–55.

Simon, H. A. (1962). The architecture of complexity. *Proceedings of the American Philosophical Society, 106*, 467–482.

Simon, H. A. (1991). What is an "explanation" of behavior? *APS Observer, 2*(1), 6.

Skinner, B. F. (1964). Behaviorism at 50. In T. Wann (Ed.), *Behaviorism and phenomenology* (pp. 79–108). Chicago: The University of Chicago Press.

Smith, M. Brewster. (1983). The shaping of American social psychology: A personal perspective from the periphery. *Personality and Social Psychology Bulletin, 9*, 165–180.

Smythies, J. R. (Ed.). (1965). *Brain and mind: Modern concepts of the nature of mind.* London: Routledge & Kegan Paul.

Snow, C. P. (1959). *The two cultures and the scientific revolution.* New York: Cambridge University Press.

Sperry, R. W. (1964). *Problems outstanding in the evolution of brain function.* James Arthur Lecture on the Evolution of the Human Brain. New York: American Museum of Natural History.

Sperry, R. W. (1965). Mind, brain and humanist values. In J. R. Platt (Ed.), *New views of the nature of man* (pp. 71–22). Chicago: University of Chicago Press. (Abridged in *Bulletin of the Atomic Scientists*, 1966, *22*(7), 2–6.)

Sperry, R. W. (1970). An objective approach to subjective experience: Further explanation of a hypothesis. *Psychological Review, 77*, 585–590.

Sperry, R. W. (1972). Science and the problem of values. *Perspectives in Biology & Medicine, 16*, 115–130.

Sperry, R. W. (1980). Mind-brain interaction: Mentalism, yes; dualism, no. *Neuroscience, 5*(2), 195–206.

Sperry, R. W. (1991a). Search for beliefs to live by consistent with science. *Zygon, Journal of Religion & Science, 26*, 237–258.

Sperry, R. W. (1991b). In defense of mentalism and emergent interaction. *Journal of Mind & Behavior, 12*, 221–245.

Sperry, R. W. (1992). Turnabout on consciousness: A mentalist view. *Journal of Mind and Behavior, 13*, 259–280.

Stapp, H. P. (1982). Mind, matter, and quantum mechanics. *Foundations of Physics, 12*, 363–399.

Toulmin, S. (1982). *The return to cosmology.* Berkeley: University of California Press.

Wann, T. W. (Ed.). (1964). *Behaviorism and phenomenology: Contrasting bases for modern psychology.* Chicago: University of Chicago Press.

Wasow, T. (1989). Grammatical theory. In M. I. Posner (Ed.), *Foundations of cognitive science* (pp. 161–202). Cambridge: MIT Press.

4

Mental Universals: Toward a Twenty-first Century Science of Mind

ROGER N. SHEPARD

In the 300 years since Newton propounded the universal law of gravitation, physicists have established this and many other laws and proclaimed them to hold universally. Thus, the inverse-square decrease of gravitational or electromagnetic force with the distance between material bodies is taken to hold not only in the local terrestrial environment (Aristotle's "sublunar realm") but to hold and to have held, unchanging in pristine splendor, throughout all space and time.

In contrast, the principles that have emerged from psychological laboratories, since psychological science split off from physical science some one hundred years ago, are generally assumed to apply, at most, to the particular species that happened to evolve on the one planet so far accessible to us—out of the billions upon billions of planets throughout the universe that may offer conditions similarly conducive to the origin of life. The branches of the evolutionary process that took place on Earth are presumed, moreover, to have been variously divided, redirected, or terminated through countless accidental occurrences of flood, fire, quake, volcanic eruption, cometary impact, climate shift, and continental drift, as well as through random genetic drift, the unpredictable runaway "arms races" between predators and prey, and runaway sexual selections between males and females. Such a history of accidental circumstances might seem to offer little basis for the emergence of universal psychological laws.

Mental Universals as Adaptations to Universals of the World

Not all aspects of the terrestrial environment have been chaotic or dependent on the particular accidental history of planet Earth, however. Many conditions are known to have prevailed everywhere on earth since the origin of terrestrial life, and some are believed to have held without change throughout the universe since the beginning of time. These include the already noted laws of physics and such associated facts as the following. On a planetary surface capable of supporting life, light and warmth will generally alternate with darkness and coolness with an invariant period (as a consequence of the universal law of conservation of angular momentum). On a biologically relevant scale of size, mass, and velocity, space is three-dimensional and Euclidean with a unique downward direction (conferred by the universal law of gravitation). Under the disequilibrium of energy essential to life, time is one-dimensional with a unique forward direction (conferred by the universal second law of thermodynamics). Holding even more certainly and under all possible conditions—including those inimical to life—are the abstract mathematical facts of logic, arithmetic, geometry, and probability. Far from being an arbitrary creation of the human mind, such mathematical facts have (in my view) universally held before the emergence of life, constraining what is possible in any world. Indeed, abstract mathematical constraints may have determined not only the form of the universe and its physical laws (as some theoretical physicist now suggest) but also the forms of evolutionarily stable strategies, of sustainable social practices, and of the laws of individual thought, whenever and wherever life emerged. Leibnitz's claim that this is the best of all possible worlds may have been correct only in that, at the level of abstract principles anyway, this is the only possible world.

Mental Universals Do Not Emerge from the Study of Brains

Researchers from many disciplines and laypersons alike often take it for granted that the only way to gain scientific knowledge about the mind is through a probing of the brain. They are mistaken. What little understanding we have so far gained about the workings of the brain has come only after we had already understood a problem in the world that the brain has evolved to solve. In view of the present state of development of psychological science, the proclamation that this was to be "the decade of the brain" expressed a wish more than an existing state of affairs or even a concrete plan.

True, powerful new technologies (including positron emission tomography, magnetic resonance imaging, genetic engineering, and neural net modeling) do offer hope that we may yet be heading into the "century of the brain." At least, we anticipate the emergence of practical methods for the detection, prevention, and treatment of significant neurological diseases, dysfunctions, and disabilities. But this does not mean that methods of probing the brain, however sophisticated and powerful they may become, will themselves lead to the formulation of general principles governing the mind.

As a very simple example, consider the question of why we have just three dimensions of color representation, when complete characterization of the spectral composition of light reaching the eye requires a potentially unlimited number of quantities (to specify the amount of energy at each wavelength in the continuum of visible light between roughly 400 and 700 nm). Undoubtedly, the discovery that there are just three classes of wavelength-selective photoreceptors in the human retina has significantly advanced us toward a detailed account of the earliest stages of visual processing and toward the identification and classification of different types of human color deficiency, the location of their relevant genes, and, perhaps eventually, the development of methods for their correction. Notice, however, that the existence of just three types of cones in the eye does not really answer our question; it simply replaces it with the further question of why we have just three classes of cones. Ultimately, a nonarbitrary answer to any "why" question about the human mind cannot be found in the brain but must be traced back to some nonarbitrary feature of the world in which the brain has evolved. The answer that I have tentatively proposed for the particular question of the dimensionality of color is that natural illumination has essentially three degrees of freedom of spectral variation. A correspondingly three-dimensional color system is needed therefore to compensate for these spectral variations in illumination, thereby to achieve constancy in the appearances of significant objects in the world (Shepard, 1990, 1992a).

The only constraints inherent in the brain itself that can provide ultimate answers to "why" questions about mental representations and principles are constraints that apply to the brain necessarily, simply because it is a physical system in the world and not because of anything peculiar to that one kind of matter that we call "gray matter." But if there are any universal constraints of this kind that determine universal principles of the mind (and I shall suggest two candidates later), we need not study the brain to discover such universal constraints. Such constraints, being universal, should be open to our investigation in any system, including those that are much simpler and more accessible than the brain.

Mental Universals Do Not Emerge
from a Study of Computers

There are also those who recommend that we use what we know about the computer as a guide to understanding the brain and hence, perhaps, the mind. Surely, the computer and the brain are alike in having the processing of information as their principal function. So, even if the probing of the brain alone cannot tell us about its function (and, hence, about the mind), to the extent that the brain is like a computer, a consideration of the computer may provide the needed insight about the brain because the computer is already well understood. After all, we built it.

What this argument overlooks is that whereas our brains evolved to solve the problems posed in the natural world, computers were designed by us to solve problems of a much more restricted and artificial type—initially and primarily problems of exact numerical computation based on relatively small sets of data. Although useful for certain purposes of science and commerce in modern technological society, such a computer would not enable a robot, however well that robot simulates the physical appearance of a human person, to survive on Wall Street, let alone to thrive in the jungle.

Again, we cannot hope to formulate the general principles governing a system without taking account of the world to which that system is adapted, whether by natural selection or by artificial design. The human brain has evolved an adaptation to a world that is very different from and less fully characterized than the world of numerical accounting. True, given the right program and sufficient time, a general-purpose computer (even of the extreme sequential type known as a Turing machine) can, in principle, carry out any well-defined information process. But our problem is precisely that we cannot define the process well until we know what problem must be solved. Moreover, as has often been remarked, if we should be lucky enough through an iterative, trial-and-error process of modifying a computer program until the computer did begin to behave adaptively in the natural world, we might end up knowing little more about general principles underlying the patchwork of ad hoc heuristics that arose through this artificial approximation to natural selection than we already know about general principles governing biological brains that arose through true natural selection.

The field of artificial intelligence may yet produce more intelligent, and (one hopes) more humane aids for the storage, retrieval, communication, and processing of information in science, business, entertainment, and the management of our daily lives in modern society. It has so far given us relatively little in the way of universal psychological laws.

Mental Universals Do Not Emerge from a Study of Cultures

Still others, particularly in the social and anthropological sciences and in the humanities, take umbrage at the very idea that human beings are subject to innate, let alone universal, principles. Such an idea seems inimical to two other valued, although seemingly already mutually antithetical, conceptions. The first is the conception of the human individual as a free agent, not subservient to any preexisting external constraints. The second is the conception of human culture, apparently assumed to have itself emerged independently of preexisting external constraints, acting as a powerful context within which each individual comes to play his or her appropriate role through individual learning.

There is no doubt that the cultural practices and the language of the group into which an individual is born constitute an extremely important part of the world to which that individual must accommodate if he or she is to survive and reproduce. There is also persuasive evidence that such accommodation is achieved largely through individual learning. A person who is suddenly transplanted to a very different culture may take on the ways of that new culture, but the conversion proceeds most quickly, completely, and irreversibly if the switch occurs sufficiently early in the person's life.

Two other possibilities also exist (even though the acknowledgment of their existence may be deemed less politically correct) for any two human populations that have remained geographically separated for sufficiently many generations. First, the differing demands (e.g., of climate, altitude, and set of prevalent pathogens) at the two locations will have produced some genetic divergence in physical attributes through natural selection (in addition to any that arise merely through genetic drift). Second, the differing social structures of each of the two societies are themselves likely to give rise to some additional genetic divergence, including divergences of cognitive and behavioral proclivities, through cultural selection. Differing demands of the reproduction roles of the two sexes can similarly give rise not only to physical differences but also to cognitive differences between the sexes. Moreover, sexual selection, having an inherently unstable positive feedback component, is potentially capable of leading to different cognitive divergences between the sexes in separated populations. If we are more cognizant of the physical than the psychological divergences, it may be only that they are more visible.

Genetic studies of families and of monozygotic twins reared apart are indicating with increasing specificity that genes determine not only such traits as eye color and blood group but also whether one has a particular type of color blindness, tone deafness, absolute pitch, spatial ability, or sexual orientation. Still, most differences of either a physical or psychological nature may be significant only to the extent that a particular culture deems them so. An individual adopted into a culture that has overcome its natural tendency to view differences with suspicion or animosity may become an accepted and successful member of its adoptive society despite a color of skin that is not optimally suited to the new climate or a turn of mind that is not specifically tuned to the new culture.

The important point, which is overlooked by those who would attribute all specific human cognitive and behavioral dispositions to cultural conditioning and who focus exclusively on the differences between cultures, is that the propensities that enable members of a species to establish and to maintain a social organization at all, like the capabilities that enable them to learn a language, must themselves have an innate, genetic basis. Other species, although quite similar in many ways, may simply be incapable of forming such a culture or learning such a language. Moreover, whatever an individual learns from the culture into which it is born depends on the principles that govern that individual's learning process. In the absence of preexisting principles of learning, such principles could not themselves be learned. Principles of learning must therefore have been shaped by natural selection to work in the kind of world in which the species has evolved. (For evolutionarily informed approaches to learning, see Cosmides & Tooby, 1987; Gallistel, 1990; Miller & Todd, 1990; Tooby & Cosmides, 1992.)

Ethnographically oriented investigators who look exclusively for the things that are unique to each culture will certainly find them. But they may fail to notice that at a more abstract level there are commonalities, which may have evolved as a reflection of abstract universals of the world that all cultures share. I give but one example: Ethnomusicologists have noted that the slendro and pelog scales underlying Indonesian music differ appreciably from the major and minor diatonic scales familiar to Western listeners. These ethnomusicologists have even noted that the gamelan in each Balinese village is tuned slightly differently from that in each other village. But these facts are in no way inconsistent with the equally demonstrable facts that the slendro, pelog, diatonic, and most other scales used in diverse cultures around the globe, share a number of abstract regularities. Despite their obvious differences, the musical scales in virtually all human cultures tend to have (1) just a few (usually five or seven) fixed focal tones per octave, (2) an asymmetric spacing (in log frequency) between these successive tones, (3) an exact replication of that same asymmetric structure in each successive octave, and

(4) an assignment of these focal tones to specific roles in a hierarchy of tonal functions, with certain tones (such as the Western tonic tone or the Indonesian gong tone) heard as more stable and played more frequently (see Kessler, Hansen, & Shepard, 1984).

The cross-cultural prevalence of such features suggests that they are not arbitrary. Psychoacousticians have long noted that some of these features may reflect physical universals of musical sounds, such as that tones separated by certain intervals (particularly the octave and the perfect fifth) produce less beating between harmonics and, so, sound more harmonious. Less widely recognized is that many of these features may have a more abstract group-theoretic basis independent of the physical, wavelike character of sounds. The asymmetric structures that are prevalent in musical scales turn out to be just those that permit each tone to be uniquely identified and unambiguously assigned a tonal function solely in terms of its relations to the other tones of the scale (Balzano, 1980). Only in this way are we afforded a fixed cognitive framework with respect to which music can have motion, tension, and resolution (Shepard, 1982).

More generally, the various forms of social structures and practices found around the world may not simply be totally unrelated conventions that arose arbitrarily in each culture, to be passed on from generation to generation purely by learning and imitation. They may also be constrained by abstract universals, such as those of game theory and evolutionary stability (Axelrod, 1984; Maynard-Smith, 1982), shareablity (Freyd, 1983), and parity (Liberman & Mattingly, 1989).

Three Possible Sources of Human Cognitive Universals

If there are mental principles that seem to be universal among humans (or even among all cognitively advanced animals), and if such principles are not ultimately explainable in terms of the brain, the computer, or the cultural context, where are we to look for their explanation? Only three possibilities occur to me and, of these, only two entail true universality.

1. Mental principles determined by the early breaking of symmetry

Any given principle might have arisen through a random symmetry breaking that occurred sufficiently far back in our evolutionary tree that the results are now manifested in all descendants from that common ancestral branch. Such a symmetry breaking would be analogous to the much more ancient one posited in chemistry and biology to account for the present complete domination of right-handed over left-handed DNA underlying terrestrial life, or to the still more ancient one posited in physics and cosmology to account for the apparent predominance of matter over antimatter throughout the universe. Some cognitive capabilities that appear to be universal among humans may also carry the inherited stamp of the random breaking of a symmetry that otherwise stood in the way of the realization of those capabilities.

I have suggested that the rules of syntax (as formulated, for example, by Chomsky, 1957) serve the principal function, which could itself be described as symmetry breaking, of specifying a regular way of mapping a multidimensional conceptual structure into a necessarily one-dimensional string of sounds or gestures, for purposes of communicating that structure to another individual (see Shepard, 1984, p. 431, footnote 6).[1] If the particular set of underlying syntactic rules common to all human languages is not more suited to serving this dimension-reducing function than some other, quite different sets of possible rules, the underlying form of human languages has not been dictated by any external constraint but has arisen arbitrarily from the necessity of breaking symmetry. If so, however, this human universal is likely to be found only in species that have descended from that same ancestral branch. It may not be shared by more remote species (such, possibly, as cetaceans?), even if they should prove to have evolved some form of language. Languages that originated independently, subsequent to the separation of their hosts' evolutionary lines, would be expected to have broken any symmetries, by chance, in different ways. Still more clearly, just as life that evolved entirely independently on a distant planet might be based on left- rather than right-handed molecules, that life, even if it also evolved a high level of intelligence, would not be expected to have broken cognitive symmetries in the way our own ancestors did in, say, the development of language on earth.

In short, if the development of a cognitive capability such as language requires an arbitrary breaking of some symmetry, the particular way in which that symmetry is broken cannot be a true universal; it is not likely to be common to all beings with that general type of cognitive capability, wherever such beings may have evolved. If there are any true mental universals underlying the capabilities that we share with all species of sufficiently advanced cognitive capabilities, those universals can pertain only to the original symmetry before it was broken, to a set of constraints on the possible ways it could be broken, and/or to the fact that it must be broken. Pinker and Bloom give another example of symmetry breaking in language: "There is no reason for you to call a dog *dog* rather than *cat* except for the fact that everyone else is doing it, but that is reason enough" (Pinker & Bloom, 1992, p. 470). The need for such symmetry breaking in language is an illustration not only of parity (Liberman & Mattingly, 1989) or sharability (Freyd, 1983) but also of the fact that even the seemingly arbitrary may be constrained by abstract, game-theoretic principles (see, e.g., Hurford, 1989).

2. Mental principles determined by the fact that the brain is itself a part of the world

The brain is necessarily subject to any constraints that apply to all physical systems in the world. We already know, for example, that any physical system in the world is necessarily confined to three-dimensional space, and that the rate of propagation of causal signals from one location to another in this space has some finite limit. Such universal physical constraints may explain the form of some mental laws. In particular, I have suggested (Shepard, 1981, 1984, 1989; Shepard

& Tenenbaum, 1991) that these spatiotemporal constraints of dimensionality and causal interaction may underlie Korte's third law of apparent motion and, possibly, a dimensional limitation on *morphophoric media* (Attneave & Olson, 1971), *indispensable attributes* (Kubovy, 1981), or *integral dimensions* (see Shepard, 1991).

3. Mental principles determined by evolutionary adaptation to the external world

As has undoubtedly become clear, I believe that the most general and important universal principles of the mind have arisen as evolutionary adaptations to universal regularities in the external world (Shepard, 1987a, 1991, 1992a). Naturally, such genetically internalized principles are expected to be physically embodied in the brain. But their embodiment there is a consequence of the external world acting through natural selection on the genes that control the development of the brain. Such embodiment is not, I believe, explainable solely in terms of the properties inherent in all physical systems (including not only brains but also computers, cars, atoms, and solar systems) simply by virtue of the fact that they are physical systems and, hence, directly and necessarily subject to the universal constraints of three-dimensional space, finite causal propagation, and thermodynamics.

I have also indicated that the universal external constraints that become internally represented through natural selection are probably not restricted to what we usually think of as the physical constraints governing the concrete material objects in the world. They are likely to include the even more general, abstract mathematical constraints of geometry, probability, group theory, and game theory. In addition to the example of the constraints on musical scales briefly mentioned here, I have previously developed the argument for the three particular cases of the representation of motions, colors, and kinds of objects (Shepard, 1987a, 1989, 1992a, 1994).

Motions. Laboratory studies indicate that the default mental representation of the motion of an object between two positions is determined not by the ways that a particular concrete object (whether a falling leaf, hopping rabbit, or spinning top) might be most likely to move between those positions, nor even by the laws of Newtonian mechanics that would govern such a motion in the physical world. To a greater extent, that representation is evidently determined by the still more abstract principles of kinematic geometry, which specify the geometrically simplest path of rigid transformation between any two positions in three-dimensional space (Shepard, 1984). This is true of (1) motions that are judged most simple or that are most accurately compared when an object actually moves (e.g., Carlton & Shepard, 1990a, 1990b; Shiffrar & Shepard, 1990); (2) motions that are subjectively experienced in apparent motion when two similar objects are alternately displayed in different positions in space (e.g., Farrell, 1983; Farrell & Shepard, 1981; Foster, 1975; McBeath & Shepard, 1989; Shepard, 1981; Shepard & Judd,

1976); and (3) motions that tend to be imagined when two differently positioned objects are to be mentally compared for identity or difference in intrinsic shape (e.g., Cooper, 1976; Shepard & Cooper, 1982; Shepard & Metzler, 1971).

Colors. The experienced color of an object does not correspond to the spectral composition of the light that the object scatters back to the eye, a composition that is determined as much by the variable spectral composition of the momentary illumination as by the intrinsic spectral reflectance distribution of the object's surface. Neither does the experienced color fully capture the spectral reflectance distribution of that surface, a distribution that has many more degrees of freedom than the three dimensions of human color space. Instead, the experienced color corresponds to a point in a representational space of surface colors whose three-dimensionality may be determined by the more abstract fact that natural illumination has three principal degrees of freedom and, hence, requires a three-dimensional representation in order to compensate for variations in illumination and thereby to achieve color constancy (Shepard, 1990, 1992a, 1992b, 1993).

Kinds. In the absence of prior knowledge about a particular object that an individual encounters and finds to have some significant consequence (e.g., of providing nourishment or inducing nausea and vomiting), the only basis that the individual has for generalizing to a new object that is more or less similar in appearance to the first is, again, a very abstract one. For all possible regions in its representational space that overlap the point corresponding to the first object and, hence, that might correspond to the set of objects of the kind having that consequence, the individual must, in effect, integrate over any prior weights associated with all those regions that also overlap the point corresponding to the second object. As a matter purely of probabilistic geometry, such integration yields a probability of generalization that, for a wide range of choices of prior weights, decreases with distance in representational space in close approximation to the simple exponential decay function that is empirically obtained when generalization data are submitted to multidimensional scaling. Indeed, the theoretically obtained function becomes exactly exponential if the prior weights are those prescribed for the condition of maximum entropy that is, minimum knowledge (Shepard, 1987b, 1991).

In each of these cases, psychological principles were found to take on a universal and invariant form only when they were formulated with respect to the proper representational space. To quote from the abstract of my most recent review of this approach (Shepard, 1994):

1. *Positions* and *motions* of objects conserve their shapes in the geometrically fullest and simplest way when represented as points and connecting geodesic paths in the six-dimensional manifold jointly determined by the Euclidean group of three-dimensional space and the symmetry group of each object.
2. *Colors* of objects attain constancy when represented as points in a three-dimensional vector space in which each variation in natural illumination is

canceled by application of its inverse from the three-dimensional linear group of terrestrial transformations of the invariant solar source.

3. *Kinds* of objects support optimal generalization and categorization when represented, in an evolutionarily shaped space of possible objects, as connected regions with associated weights determined by Bayesian revision of maximum-entropy prior probabilities.

These principles are also predicated on the assumption that Darwinian processes of natural selection provide the only basis for understanding how the human mind has come to be governed by universal, as well as domain-specific, principles. Psychologists have tended to resist this assumption, like social scientists and humanists in general, and many will undoubtedly continue to do so. The assumption runs counter to the cherished belief that a human being is a free agent not subject to preexisting, external constraints. Worse, from the perspective of the experimental psychologist, the assumption seems to let important determiners of human behavior recede from our grasp in the psychological laboratory, into a remote, unrecorded, unmanipulable, and perhaps largely unknowable prehistory.

In my attempts to overcome such resistance, I have advanced three counterarguments. First, like it or not, the truth is that the brain and hence the mind have been shaped by evolution; and within the limits of freedom possible to us, it is only the acceptance of the truth that can set us free. Second, learning is not an alternative to evolution but itself depends on evolution. There can be no learning in the absence of principles of learning; yet such principles, being themselves unlearned, must have been shaped by evolution. Third, the most general mental principles must have arisen as evolutionary adaptations to correspondingly general facts about the world; but these facts are not lost to us in the dim recesses of an unknown and inaccessible prehistory. By virtue of their very universality, these facts continue to dominate the world around us, undiminished and pristine, to this very day.

As psychology prepares to embark on the second century of its existence as an independent science, will it finally lay claim to the whole domain of mental principles? If, as I suggest, there are candidate mental principles that take unique advantage of the universal affordances of the world, the domain of their potential emergence through natural selection must vastly transcend the domains of terrestrial rats, pigeons, and humans. I, for one, am hopeful that psychological science will not be content to leave the discovery and formulation of universal principles of mind to some other perhaps bolder and more far-seeing science.

Acknowledgments

Preparation of this report was supported by the National Science Foundation (Grant No. DBS-9021648). I am indebted to my many collaborators in research, also to Leda Cosmides and John Tooby for helping me toward a better understanding of evolutionary theory, and to the editors for providing me with this opportunity to indulge in unfettered speculation.

Note

1. This suggestion was inspired by attempts I made back in 1957 to formalize such dimension-reducing rules for sentences sampled from several different languages. At the time, I was working with George Miller on a psycholinguistic evaluation of the prospects for mechanical translation and I was reading, in manuscript, Chomsky's *Syntactic Structures* (1957).

References

Axelrod, R. (1984). *The evolution of cooperation*. New York: Basic Books.

Attneave, F., & Olson, R. K. (1971). Pitch as a medium: A new approach to psychophysical scaling. *American Journal of Psychology, 84,* 147–166.

Balzano, G. J. (1980). The group-theoretic description of twelvefold and microtonal pitch systems. *Computer Music Journal, 4,* 66–84.

Carlton, E. H., & Shepard, R. N. (1990a). Psychologically simple motions as geodesic paths: I. Asymmetric objects. *Journal of Mathematical Psychology, 34,* 127–188.

Carlton, E. H., & Shepard, R. N. (1990b). Psychologically simple motions as geodesic paths: II. Symmetric objects. *Journal of Mathematical Psychology, 34,* 189–228

Chomsky, N. (1957). *Syntactic structures*. The Hague: Mouton.

Cooper, L. A. (1976). Demonstrations of a mental analog of an external rotation. *Perception & Psychophysics, 19,* 296–302.

Cosmides, L., & Tooby, J. (1987). From evolution to behavior: Evolutionary psychology as the missing link. In J. Dupré (Ed.), *The latest on the best: Essays on evolution and optimality* (pp. 277–306). Cambridge: MIT Press.

Farrell, J. E. (1983). Visual transformations underlying apparent movement. *Perception & Psychophysics, 33,* 85–92.

Farrell, J. E., & Shepard, R. N. (1981). Shape, orientation, and apparent rotational motion. *Journal of Experimental Psychology: Human Perception and Performance, 7,* 477–486.

Foster, D. H. (1975). Visual apparent motion of some preferred paths in the rotation group SO(3). *Biological Cybernetics, 18,* 81–89.

Freyd, J. (1983). Shareability: The social psychology of epistomology. *Cognitive Science, 7,* 191–210.

Gallistel, C. R. (1990). *The organization of learning*. Cambridge: MIT Press/Bradford Books.

Holland, J. H. (1975). *Adaptation in natural and artificial systems.* Ann Arbor: University of Michigan Press.

Hurford, J. R. (1989). Biological evolution of the Saussurian sign as a component of the language acquisition device. *Lingua, 77,* 187–222.

Kessler, E. S., Hansen, C., & Shepard, R. N. (1984). Tonal schemata in the perception of music in Bali and in the West. *Music Perception, 2,* 131–165.

Kubovy, M. (1981). Concurrent pitch-seggregation and the theory of indispensable attributes. In M. Kubovy & J. R. Pomerantz (Eds.), *Perceptual organization* (pp. 55–98). Hillsdale, N.J.: Erlbaum.

Liberman, A. M., & Mattingly, I. G. (1989). A specialization for speech perception. *Science, 243,* 489–496.

Maynard-Smith, J. (1982). *Evolution and the theory of games*. Cambridge: Cambridge University Press.

McBeath, M. K., & Shepard, R. N. (1989) Apparent motion between shapes differing in location and orientation: A window technique for estimating path curvature. *Perception and Psychophysics, 46*, 333–337.

Miller, G. F., & Todd, P. M. (1990). Exploring adaptive agency: I. Theory and methods for simulating the evolution of learning. In D. S. Touretzky, J. L. Elman, T. J. Sejnowski, & G. E. Hinton (Eds.), *Proceedings of the 1990 Connectionist Models Summer School* (pp. 65–80). San Mateo, Calif.: Morgan Kaufmann.

Pinker, S., & Bloom, P. (1992). Natural language and natural selection. In J. H. Barkow, L. Cosmides, & J. Tooby (Eds.), *The adapted mind: Evolutionary psychology and the generation of culture* (pp. 451–493). New York: Oxford University Press.

Shepard, R. N. (1981). Psychophysical complementarity. In M. Kubovy & J. Pomerantz (Eds.), *Perceptual organization* (pp. 279–341). Hillsdale, N.J.: Erlbaum .

Shepard, R. N. (1982). Geometrical approximations to the structure of musical pitch. *Psychological Review, 89*, 305–333.

Shepard, R. N. (1984). Ecological constraints on internal representation: Resonant kinematics of perceiving, imagining, thinking, and dreaming. *Psychological Review, 91*, 417–447.

Shepard, R. N. (1987a). Evolution of a mesh between principles of the mind and regularities of the world. In J. Dupré (Ed.), *The latest on the best: Essays on evolution and optimality* (pp. 251–275). Cambridge: MIT Press/Bradford Books.

Shepard, R. N. (1987b). Toward a universal law of generalization for psychological science. *Science, 237*, 1317–1323.

Shepard, R. N. (1989). Internal representation of universal regularities: A challenge for connectionism. In L. Nadel, L. A. Cooper, P. Culicover, & R. M. Harnish (Eds.), *Neural connections, mental computation* (pp. 104–134). Cambridge: MIT Press/ Bradford Books.

Shepard, R. N. (1990). A possible evolutionary basis for trichromacy. *Proceedings of the SPIE/SPSE symposium on electronic imaging: Science and technology*, Vol. 1250: Perceiving, measuring, and using color (pp. 301–309): Santa Clara, Calif.

Shepard, R. N. (1991). Integrality versus separability of stimulus dimensions: From an early convergence of evidence to a proposed theoretical basis. In G. R. Lockhead & J. R. Pomerantz (Eds.), *Perception of structure* (pp. 57–71). Washington, D.C.: American Psychological Association.

Shepard, R. N. (1992a). The perceptual organization of colors: An adaptation to the regularities of the terrestrial world? In J. Barkow, L. Cosmides, & J. Tooby (Eds.), *The adapted mind: Evolutionary psychology and the generation of culture* (pp. 495–532). New York: Oxford University Press.

Shepard, R. N. (1992b). What in the world determines the structure of color space? (Commentary on Thompson, Palacios, & Varela). *Behavioral and Brain Sciences, 15*, 50–51.

Shepard, R. N. (1993). On the physical basis, linguistic representation, and conscious experience of colors. In G. Harman (Ed.), *Conceptions of the mind* (pp. 217–245). Hillsdale, N.J.: Erlbaum.

Shepard, R. N. (1994). Perceptual–cognitive universals as reflections of the world. *Psychonomic Bulletin & Review, 1*, 2–28.

Shepard, R. N., & Cooper, L. A. (1982). *Mental images and their transformations*. Cambridge, Mass.: MIT Press / Bradford Books.

Shepard, R. N., & Judd, S. A. (1976). Perceptual illusion of rotation of three-dimensional objects. *Science 191*, 952–954.

Shepard, R. N., & Metzler, J. (1971). Mental rotation of three-dimensional objects. *Science 171*, 701–703.

Shepard, R. N., & Tenenbaum, J. (1991). *Connectionist modeling of multidimensional generalization*. Presented at the 32nd annual meeting of the Psychonomic Society, San Francisco (November 22–24).

Shiffrar, M., & Shepard, R. N. (1990). Comparison of cube rotations about axes inclined relative to the environment or to the cube. *Journal of Experimental Psychology: Human Perception and Performance 17*, 44–54.

Tooby, J., & Cosmides, L. (1992). The psychological foundations of culture. In J. H. Barkow, L. Cosmides & J. Tooby (Eds.), *The adapted mind: Evolutionary psychology and the generation of culture* (pp. 19–136). New York: Oxford University Press.

II

DEVELOPMENTAL THEORIES AND NEUROCOGNITION

Three distinctive chapters, by Howard Gardner, Jean Mandler, and Stephen Kosslyn, make up this part. The first chapter, by Gardner, deals with the question, Is there progress in the study of the mind?—especially as it relates to human intelligence. Mandler approaches the problem of the future of developmental psychology from the standpoint of one who has already experienced the future and is writing a retrospective account. Finally, Kosslyn, in Chapter 7, predicts a revitalization of Freudian ideas within the context of modern neuroscience.

5

Perennial Antinomies and Perpetual Redrawings: Is There Progress in the Study of Mind?

HOWARD GARDNER

I recently attended a conference filled with controversy. The purpose of the conference was to review studies of twins, with special reference to the insights about intelligence, personality, and psychopathology that can be gained from comparisons of identical (monoxygotic) and fraternal (dizygotic) twins reared together and reared apart (Bouchard, 1993). As a researcher who has questioned traditional views of intelligence and intelligence testing, I found myself caught in heated debate about whether intelligence is a single entity, one that is adequately measured by a standardized intelligence test; or whether the intellect is better viewed as a collection of separate faculties, which might be called distinctive factors of the mind, or intelligences. This controversy continued throughout the conference, adding spice if not clarity to the proceedings. When the conference had ended, one of the more senior persons in attendance remarked to a colleague, "I have not heard so much venom at a conference since the old days when we used to debate the effects of nature versus nurture. And it's equally unlikely that either side will be proved correct."

This innocent remark caught my attention because it captures my own view of scientific work in the human sphere—and because it anticipates some of the argument of this chapter. Although there are countless "little questions" in the area of the sciences of the mind, most persons are initially attracted to the disciplines because of curiosity about big questions: What is the mind? How does it develop? How does it relate to the body? Are we the products chiefly of heredity or chiefly of environmental factors? Are we one mind, one person, or are we more profitably viewed as a collection of mental faculties and of personality types? Moreover, even when our own research programs take us into more manageable questions— ones that have their own fascination, to be sure—most of us find ourselves drawn again to these old chestnuts; and especially so, when we are lecturing to new students, writing the introduction to a textbook, engaging in banter at a cocktail party, or, at the close our careers, trying to establish what, after all, has been learned from all that we've done.

Some questions may be answered decisively: Few scientists any more waste time trying to establish the truth of the biblical story of creation. Other questions will probably remain forever shrouded in mystery—even if the biblical story is not literally true, no scientific test can either prove or disapprove the existence of God. In this chapter I argue that the biggest questions in the sciences of the human mind fall somewhere in between these poles: certainly not beyond investigation yet unlikely to yield a complete answer. I begin the essay by presenting my own view of the changing terrain of the sciences of the mind. Then, using my own area of special interest—that of intelligence and creativity—I indicate the kind of progress that has been made and the kind of progress that is likely to be made in the future.

Of What Do the Sciences of the Mind Consist?

On my reading of the evidence, the questions that continue to fascinate the students of the mind were first posed by the Greek philosophers some twenty-five hundred years ago (Gardner, 1985, chapter 3). It was Socrates, Plato, Aristotle, and their peers, who first wondered out loud about the nature of the mind: its origins, its mode of operation, the functioning of memory, the status of imagery, the ways in which individuals learn and teach. This is not the only possible agenda for the study of the mind. For example, Eastern traditions have been oriented toward spiritual issues; Hindu and Buddhist spiritual leaders have spawned a different set of questions and, accordingly, a different approach toward answering them. But for better or worse, our own intellectual tradition has continued to ponder the aforementioned classical issues.

The major philosophical traditions within which current discussions are framed were first expounded in the seventeenth and eighteenth centuries. Thanks to the pathbreaking arguments put forth by Descartes, Locke, Berkeley, Hume, and Kant, a new and more rigorously defined set of issues came to the fore. It was as a result of these philosophical creations that all workers in the field routinely think in terms of issues like the nature of mental representations; the delineation of categories of thought; the extent to which knowledge is constructed by the individual himself, is inborn, or is read off of the surrounding environment; the relationship between language and other kinds of symbolic and cognitive faculties. Even those who have never read a word of classical philosophy, even those who spurn it as a useless preoccupation of benighted humanists, take the most fundamental questions from these writers, and from others inspired by them.

An equally decisive a step in the history of thought occurred in the latter part of the nineteenth century, when for the first time investigators began to examine these questions from an empirical perspective. When Helmholtz attempted to time a nerve impulse, when Donders sought to time a thought, when Fechner sought to measure sensation, when Ebbinghaus tried to unravel memory, these researchers were no longer seeking to resolve issues solely by argument; instead, they were looking for experimental evidence that could resolve—or, at the very least, increase our knowledge about—the longstanding philosophical questions from the Greek and the Enlightenment eras (Gardner, 1985, chapter 4).

Psychology and its allied fields were recognized as legitimate scientific disciplines about a century ago. And for many years it appeared as if psychology could provide empirical answers to the longstanding questions. Yet, a dispassionate history of the last hundred years scarcely reveals a field that is making steady progress. It is at least as convincing to argue that psychology has been a succession of, and a struggle among, a number of rival schools or paradigms: functionalism, structuralism, behaviorism, psychoanalysis, Gestalt psychology, and most recently, information-processing, connectionist, and sociobiological approaches (Fodor, 1968; Gardner, 1985, 1992a; Koch, 1981).

Some would contend that this struggle among schools is inevitable, the sign of a young and dynamic field, and would argue that there has been deep, underlying progress nonetheless. When it comes to certain areas—the study of visual perception, for example—this is a reasonable contention. For the most part, however, the schools have not succeeded so much as they have become exhausted: the names disappear but the struggles continue under new banners. Thus, for example, Chomsky's recent attacks against the behaviorists drew on Descartes' rationalistic view of mind, as well as on kinds of holist arguments that the Gestalt psychologists raised with respect to their atomistically oriented antagonists.

In the 1950s and 1960s, the study of the mind received a vital "shot in the arm," courtesy of the Cognitive Revolution. Inspired by the work of researchers like Miller, Chomsky, Simon, Newell, Bruner, and Piaget, researchers felt that they had discovered a new model of the mind—the serial digital computer—along with a set of methods by which its mechanisms could be laid bare (Gardner, 1985; Miller, 1979). And indeed for the next decade or so, cognitive science was promulgated as the royal road to the elucidation of the mind.

In my view, the cognitive scientific perspective has no ontological priority over other more, traditional views of cognition. Mind as computer, as information processing, has much to recommend itself. However, it is tenable to conceive of mind-as-cultural construction, in the manner of Vygotsky (1978), or as an evolved organ, as sketched by Geertz (1973). What cognitive science may have achieved, however, is a demonstration that the program of psychology could no longer proceed as it had in the past.

A New Topography of the Mind

Possibly dating back to the time of William James, there has been a faith among psychologists that the various subdisciplines of the field can work comfortably together and that they will eventually sum to a more integrated view of the human mind as a whole. This vision is still subscribed to by some writers of textbooks, members of the American Psychological Association, and others who call themselves psychologists (Gardner, 1992a).

However, the advent of cognitive science has convinced many of us that what perceptual psychologists are doing in their daily work is so different from what psycholinguists or social psychologists or clinical psychologists are doing that it no longer makes sense to think of us all as members of the same discipline. Even as we continue to carry out our ordinary disciplinary work, a new topography is being drawn up. No one can totally anticipate its lines of demarcation; but here is how I view the shape of what has been called psychology a decade or two from now.

Cognitive Psychology and Neurosciences

Those traditionally interested in questions about mentation—how we perceive, categorize, memorize, and the like—will join either an amalgamated field like cognitive science (in which computer modeling will play an important part), neuroscience (in which brain models and studies are dominant), or cognitive neuroscience (a recently coined hybrid that seeks to tie together the mind and the brain using both computational and neurophysiologically oriented approaches). Within these broad disciplinary camps, investigators will focus on problems (such as memory) and on domains (such as language, music, or spatial reasoning), bringing to bear the range of subdisciplines that now address those problems and contents. And so, for example, those interested in language will conduct psychological experiments, build computer models, carry out observational studies of language in different settings, seek evidence in clinical and brain studies, and the like. By the same token, those interested in the mechanisms of memory will approach their problem through the tools of computer modeling, brain experiments, and more traditional kinds of psychological experimentation. In the end, it is possible that the "story" told about spatial processing will resemble that told about linguistic processing, but this determination can be made only after more investigations of a comparative sort have been conducted within specific domains.

Cultural Studies

But what of the rest of what has traditionally been called psychology? I feel that part of psychology will become part of a new field that can be called "Cultural Studies." Much of what is now carried out in developmental or social psychology will be absorbed into a more general approach, carried out in conjunction with sociologists, anthropologists, and others who treat the culture-as-a-whole as their unit of analysis. I do not think that this work can aspire to science in the sense that we know it, because cultures change perennially and the very discoveries made in one generation can become deliberately refuted or struggled against in the succeeding one. Still, the kind of insights given by cultural studies can prove extremely valuable to those outside of the academy who are interested in classical psychological questions, ranging from the nature of prejudice to the nature of love, as well as to those who remain inside its walls.

Personality as Central

There will remain, I believe, a heartland of psychology: the study of the individual ego or personality, together with its pathology. For much of the lay public, and for some of our greatest psychologists, like Freud, this has always been the central area of psychology. In my own redrawn map, however, the study of personality will not remain the peculiar possession of psychologists. Instead, psychologists will share this terrain with writers, students of the arts, and others who take as their central *problematique* the human condition. Again, I do not believe that workers on personality will ever produce a science on their own; but the insights into personality that they will derive, as a result of their own work and their collaborations with those from the humanistic perspective, will be extremely valuable.

This, then, is my prospectus for mind studies as a whole. No longer a separate discipline called psychology, working on its own, but rather a blurring of the lines between disciplines as part of a cooperative effort to understand human functioning. Work will be problem-driven rather than discipline-driven. And investigators will study memory or language or music, rather than psychology or linguistics. If this vision seems utopian, I feel that it is not. When I wrote about Cognitive Science less than a decade ago, I predicted that there would soon be departments which called themselves Cognitive Science, and that psychology would not survive as a discipline. Since then the American Psychology Association itself has suffered a severe schism; there are dozens if not hundreds of cognitive science departments in the United States and abroad; cognitive neuroscience is well launched, with dedicated scholars and journals of quality; and, perhaps most significantly, serious bookstores have sections called Cognitive Science; and self-help books constitute the majority of entries in most Psychology sections.

A Case Study: The Intelligence Complex

One of the most important and enduring areas of research in the science of cognition has been work on intelligence. Indeed, the concept of intelligence, with its vaunted instrument the intelligence test, has often been considered the most impressive achievement of twentieth-century scientific psychology (Brand, 1993; Brown & Herrnstein, 1975). Yet, despite the attention paid to work on intelligence, it actually exemplifies an area where deep differences of opinion persist with respect to the most fundamental issues. As such, it provides a promising case study of the issues and topography that characterize contemporary studies of several cognitive processes and domains.

As is well known, work on intelligence and intelligence testing began around the turn of the century, when the French psychologist Alfred Binet was asked to determine which French school children would have difficulty in handling the requirements of school. In effect, Binet created the first intelligence tests, though the actual naming of the IQ was undertaken by Wilhelm Stern and the first standardization was due to the efforts of the American psychologist Lewis Terman. Following the successful administration of the Army Alpha to over one and a half million American recruits during World War I, intelligence tests—and the general concept of intelligence—became ensconced in the American scientific, educational, and popular imaginations.

In the following half-century, as the area of psychometrics coalesced, a finely tuned science of mental measurement emerged. American tests became admired throughout the educational world. Paradoxically, there were not parallel advances in the *theory* of intelligence, which remained much as it had been developed in the early years of the century by workers like Spearman, Terman, Cyril Burt, and Binet himself. For instance, there was little attention to the *processes* involved in the exercise of intelligence or to its neurophysiological underpinnings. However, sharp if inconclusive discussions erupted on a number of gritty issues: Is there single intelligence or a set of intellectual factors? If there are several factors, what relation obtains among them? How shall we best assess intelligence, through standard paper-and-pencil measures, or by some new techniques? Is intelligence largely an inherited capacity, or is it susceptible to environmental and cultural modeling and alteration? Are we most likely to learn about intelligence by probing the brain or by studying the details of human lives?

None of these questions is new, but none of them has yet been answered to any general satisfaction. Indeed, as my opening vignette suggests, they continue to be debated quite vociferously. I submit that the changes over the last decades, although not answering these traditional questions, allow us to address them in a much more sophisticated way.

The traditional view in intelligence—sometimes labeled the London School—holds firm to its classic position. As articulated by Spearman and echoed by Burt and Eysenck, the basic claims include the contentions that intelligence is primarily a general capacity to reason: that this factor is largely under genetic control; that it presumably reflects a certain general pattern of the brain and the nervous system; and that intelligence is best elucidated by studying the individual (or her brain) in isolation.

While it may seem that fidelity to this position entails clinging to the past, investigators have continued to accumulate strong evidence in support of this position. A general factor does indeed emerge from most psychometric measures as well as the so-called "positive manifold" (or positive correlations) among test scores. Behavioral genetics studies may confirm that some factor "g" (for general intelligence) is highly heritable, with nearly all authorities placing the heritability quotient at a minimum of 50 percent (Baker, 1993). New reaction-time measures and brain-wave studies may also document a certain behavioral and brain complex that seems to underlie this "g" factor. Accordingly, those who favor this position find little reason to look at social or environmental factors, though they readily recommend that those with lower IQs receive separate teaching approaches, which may be more appropriate for those who are intellectually less capable (Jensen, 1969, 1980).

Needless to say, this position is not popular among most educators and is anything but politically correct. Those who oppose this position on scientific and political grounds often put forth an entirely different set of propositions. These range from a denial that intelligence is important, to a claim that it is produced largely by social factors, to a denunciation of those who embrace the standard view as being racist, classist, or elitist.

Multiple Intelligences and Beyond

Impelled in part by a desire to move this discussion beyond the political realm, a number of investigators, including myself, have proposed a fundamentally different way of viewing the area of intelligence. Let me use my own "theory of multiple intelligences" as a test case (Gardner, 1983, 1993). I abjured the usual path of devising a new test of intelligence and looking for its component factors and correlations thereof. Instead, I began by examining the wide range of competences that are valued around the world and pondering what kind of a creature could evolve to carry out these several functions. Then, culling information from a wide range of sources, extending from the study of prodigies and *idiot savants* to the examination of neuropsychological case studies, I discerned at least seven separate mental faculties, which I dubbed the intelligences.

Whether these intelligences are truly independent of one another is an empirical question. It can be answered, however, only if one devises "intelligence-fair" ways of assessing human competences. I argue that, rather than assessing individuals by administering to them short-answer inquiries in a decontextualized setting, one is better advised to assess individuals in a rich context, where they can exhibit their own profile of cognitive strengths. Under ideal conditions, one would assess the intelligences of a young child by observing her at play (and at work) in a children's museum, rather than sitting the child down in a room and firing a set of short-answer questions or minute-long problems in her direction. When we have employed this procedure with young children, we have in fact been able to uncover a broader range of capacities, with most children exhibiting both characteristic strengths and weaknesses (Gardner & Hatch, 1989).

The move toward a plurality of intelligences, assessed by instruments far removed from standardized psychometric measures, represents one critique of the classical intelligence position. Since I put forth the theory of multiple intelligences, I have discerned two further shifts in the investigation of intelligences— shifts that are related to each other but that are best explained independently.

The shift toward *contextualization* argues that intelligence is always expressed, or not expressed, in a particular social and cultural setting. To observe intelligence in a decontextualist setting is either to distort it completely, or to look de facto at a very specialized kind of setting—the modern secular school room or office niche. In my view one can best observe intelligences at work by observing individuals in environments where their skills are customarily employed. And so one watches bettors at the race track, musicians learning a new piece of music, workers loading dairy cases unto a truck, merchants haggling in the bazaar, or tailors sitting at their workbenches. While one might be able to predict skill as a bureaucrat through the use of a standardized intelligence test, intelligence-in-action can be examined only by looking at the action itself (Ceci, 1990; Lave, 1988; Rogoff, 1990).

Whereas one new perspective requires taking into accounts the contexts in which mind is employed, the other removes intelligence from within the skin of the individual. The key concept here is the *distribution* of intelligence. On this account, intelligence inheres as much in the human and manmade artifacts that surround the individual as inside the head of the individual himself. Stripped of my notebooks, my pencil, my computer, and the persons with whom I customarily work, I lose much of my intelligence. My ability to perform intellectually is a function of how I am able to draw on these resources in order to help me solve problems or fashion products. Both the measuring and enhancement of intelligence need to begin by taking into account the ways in which we amplify our own perceptual and cognitive powers which, left unsupported, render us as virtually feral children. One promising approach would be to make available various kinds of artifacts to observe how individuals learn to make use of them in natural settings and then use them appropriately in more formal experimental settings (Salomon, 1992).

Stated at the extremes, there would seem to be little hope of reconciling the London position with the full-blown contextualized-distributed position. The first places all of intelligence in the head, in the brain, in the genes; the second recognizes the possibility of multiple intelligences in multiple contexts, the formative role played by education and other learning opportunies, the limits of a focus that fails to take into account the ways in which other individuals and artifacts can enhance or choke out intelligence.

And yet, as stated at the opening of this paper, I feel quite strongly that neither position is ever going to emerge as triumphant. Whether one veers toward the London pole or the contextualized pole is a function of the questions one is interested in, the measurements one wants to achieve, and the disciplinary matrix that makes sense to a researcher.

Take, as a first example, the contexts of interest. If one is interested primarily in performance in school, or in school-like contexts, one will veer in the direction of the London school. If, on the other hand, one is interested in a wide range of human talents, which can be expressed or suppressed across a gamut of cultural settings, then one will veer toward the contextualist view of intelligence. If one has been strongly influenced by a neurological perspective, one is inclined to look for brain correlates of intelligence. Note, however, that such a disciplinary proclivity does not commit a researcher to a hereditarian position; intelligence could be a result of congenital or of experiential factors that affect the growing brain, rather than a result of purely hereditary considerations. If one is influenced by an anthropological perspective, one will look to the role of different cultural milieus and forms of support in the emergence and expression of intelligence or to the dynamic interplay between ecological niches and biological systems over the millennia. And if one is affected by work in artificial intelligence or robotics, one may well be attracted to a distributed-network approach.

Some of us working in the area of intelligence have ourselves acknowledged the possibility of conciliation. In his important theoretical work on intelligence,

Sternberg (1985) allows for componential as well as contextual and experiential aspects of intelligence. Anderson (1992), sympathetic to a London position, highlights the importance of "g" in young children, while recognizing the greater utility of a multiple-intelligences position for later life. Perkins (1992) calls attention to a power dimension in intelligence, as well as one that is sensitive to strategic learning. And in my own writings, I have recognized the utility of standard psychometrics for understanding a certain kind of context, while calling for greater attention to the expression of other "intelligences" in different contexts (Gardner, 1992).

A Complex of Terms

There is another way in which the work on intelligence has been broadened. There is a heightened recognition that intelligence is part of a matrix of terms and concepts related to one another but emphasizing different fissures of the psychological terrain (Feldman, with Goldsmith, 1986; Sternberg, 1988, 1990; Sternberg & Davidson, 1986; Sternberg & Kolligian, 1990).

This complex of terms includes at least four different points: giftedness, expertise, creativity, and success. The gifted individual is one who, early in life, emerges as very strong in one or more areas of performance. The expert is the person who achieves a high level of performance in a culturally recognized domain. The creative individual is one who creates something novel in a domain that is ultimately accepted by individuals knowledgeable about that domain. And the successful person is one who is widely accepted and richly rewarded for a certain kind of contribution.

At an intuitive level, the distinctions among these individuals seem clear enough. Gifted musicians or chess players sometimes become adult experts like Yehudi Menuhin or Bobby Fischer, but sometimes they do not (Montour, 1984). Some people become experts in domains quite readily, whereas others take years to achieve an equivalent amount of expertise. Whether one is gifted is not a good predictor of whether one will be judged an expert; beyond normal levels of intelligence, creativeness seems to be an independent dimension, with high IQ neither necessary nor sufficient for creative expression; and the achievement of public success seems to be the most elusive property of all, even if, as Andy Warhol once quipped, we can all expect to become famous for fifteen minutes.

Giftedness

Among these hypothetical individuals, it is the gifted individual who is most likely to be accounted for by the traditional view of intelligence. This person often is blessed with a high "g" and will do well in school. If one expands the notion of giftedness to include areas like music or chess, then a different set of individuals will emerge. In each case, these individuals need the help of others in their community, but in the absence of considerable genetic endowment, the emergence of all individual as gifted is unlikely.

Expertise

Contrast this London-style gifted individual with the three other kinds of competences. To become an expert is not something that requires speed. The achievement of expertise is much more a function of the perseverence of the individual and the capacity of the larger society to provide timely instruction and support. If someone tells me about the educational provisions available in a society, and the motivation of the students, I can tell that person how much expertise will be achieved. In cases where a society values literacy, or musical competence, or spatial sensitivity, nearly all of its individuals—independent of genetic proclivities or IQ score—will achieve that level of expertise. The greater the distributed resources at one's disposal, the more likely one is to gain expertise.

Creativity

Creativity is something else again. Although a certain level of motivation and talent is required in the individual, these do not suffice to yield creative expression. In fact, one could know everything possible about an individual, and his or her brain, and yet have no idea about whether she is creative. This is because, as Csikszentmihaly (1988) has argued so persuasively, creativity is as much a function of judgments rendered by knowledgeable individuals in a field of endeavor as it is a reflection of specific kinds of psychological functioning in the brain. Accordingly, an understanding of the creative individual becomes inherently a sociological and an anthropological study, in which the individual's person and work are necessary but not sufficient contributors. To be sure, the role of judges can be discerned everywhere, but their role appears to be especially determinative when it comes to the designation of creativity.

Success

Finally, at the opposite end of the continuum from giftedness is the achievement of success. No doubt, as in the case of creativity, motivation and talent play some role. Yet, even more so than in the case of creativity, whether one achieves success is a function of the situation in which one finds oneself and the lucky events of one's life. Some individuals who will ultimately be judged creative never achieve success and die while still unknown. Conversely, many individuals who will ultimately be judged as neither gifted nor expert nor creative are nonetheless successful within a given society and at a given instance of time. The way to determine whether someone will be successful is not to study that person's brain or mind or personality but rather to probe the nature of the pressures and opportunities at work in the society in which he or she lives.

Part of what science does is to draw distinctions that have not been drawn before, it is hoped in ways that cut nature at its proper joints. If one takes the all-purpose term *intelligence,* and decomposes it into such loosely coupled concepts as giftedness, creativity, expertise, and success, not only does one prevent semantic confusion but, more importantly one obtains leverage with respect to the circumstances under which a London-School analysis can be helpful, as against those circumstances in which it proves more sensible to look at phenomena from pluralist, contextualist, or distributed perspectives.

I believe there may be a more general principle at work here. For many of the classic issues that have been posed in psychology and in cognate disciplines, it is unlikely that decisive answers can ever be given. Almost always, there will turn out to be some validity on each of the polemical sides of the discussion. Yet to the extent that one can disaggregate the concepts and their underlying assumptions, it should be possible to indicate which lines of evidence most strongly support one position, which lines of evidence most clearly bolster the opposite position, and, above all, how best to formulate the position that can give its due to the full range of argument. This is done, I should underscore, *not* in search of a simpleminded intermediate compromise; rather, this step is recommended because advances occur when one comes better to appreciate the circumstances that have led to the articulation of extreme positions, and when one points out the conditions under which either is right or wrong.

It is worth noting that this kind of analysis is by no means restricted to the area of intelligence and its related concepts. In the case of language, for example, there exists a longstanding tension between those of a Chomskian persuasion (Chomsky, 1957), who stress the innate properties of a linguistic device, and those of a sociolinguistic persuasion, who emphasize the extent to which linguistic moves must be taught and learned. At least some of this tension can be reduced once it has been acknowledged that adherents of the two positions direct their analytic attention to quite disparate aspects of language. When one's interest extends particularly to the phonological and syntactic structures of language, it is justifiable to look for underlying universal factors that may well be built into the human genome. If, on the other hand, one's attention is directed to the semantic and pragmatic aspects of language and communication, it makes sense to monitor carefully the strategies and emphases adopted by different cultures and subcultures.

A Glance Ahead

The ideas presented in this essay are themselves controversial; it will take time for them to be sifted through and, where deemed appropriate, absorbed into the evolving view of intelligence (and related concepts) within the cognitive disciplines. Still, in a volume that is explicitly devoted to prospective thinking, some speculations about the future of this work may be in order.

I expect that efforts to identify the core components of traditional intelligence will continue, and that such efforts may well succeed in identifying certain of the neurological and the genetic underpinnings of "g" (and, possibly, of other primary intellectual factors). Such work promises to shed light on the relative plausibility of singular and pluralistic accounts of intellect. So long as this work continues in isolation, however, its impact on cognitive studies in the larger sense will be limited.

To combat such isolation, concomitant efforts are needed in two other areas. First of all, it will be important to look at intelligence (and also to intelligence*s*) as this ensemble of constructs relates to other cognitive traits and processes, such as those involved in creativity, giftedness, expertise, and the like. Second, it will be equally important to consider each of these traits and processes as they unfold in different kinds of contexts, within and across cultures. If the preceding analysis introduced has validity, what counts in intelligence in one culture is not identical to intelligence in other cultures, nor is intelligence (or creativity) in school the same as intelligence (or creativity) at home, at the workplace, or in other institutions ranging from museums to church.

It may sound as if I am simply calling for more research on more topics, and that is true. However, to my mind, the real challenge is not to find out more about specific topics, but rather to figure out how these findings relate to one another and how they can be pieced together into a single composite that is scientifically coherent and compelling. A similar challenge confronts us as we look at topics that bear some resemblance to intelligence—such as language or music—as well as topics that are drawn from quite different domains of psychology—such as personality or will. To put it succinctly, either the sciences of human nature will be interdisciplinary and sensitive to cultural variation, or they will not be sciences at all.

Concluding Thoughts

Turning, in conclusion, to the issues raised in the opening pages of this chapter, it seems to me that the new topography of the sciences of the mind can be a valuable partner in unraveling the classical conundra of cognition. There will continue to be perennial antimonies, such as nature versus nurture, and singular versus pluralistic views of the intellect; but at the same time, our maps of these issues can be more finely drawn, with false distinctions eliminated, obscurities clarified, and new phenomena uncovered. None of the complex issues that philosophers and psychologists have grappled with for so long is likely to be resolved by work undertaken within a single disciplinary framework. Whether one is trying to understand language, or memory, or intelligence, the adoption of multiple-disciplinary perspectives is essential. Our understanding of these issues is most likely to be enhanced if we can—individually or severally—dissect these concepts from the perspectives of the range of disciplines and combinations thereof.

Perhaps equally important, over time, we may be able to discover which sorts of issues are most likely to be illuminated by the perspectives of one science, which issues are more likely to be illuminated by the perspectives of another. For example, with respect to the central issue examined in this chapter, questions having to do with native giftedness are more likely to be illuminated by brain sciences, while issues having to do with creativity and success will benefit reciprocally from a cultural and sociological focus. In the end, the study of man or woman will not advance by mimicking the other sciences; instead, neural, cognitive, cultural, and computational approaches will need to work together to bring order to those questions that have exercised its investigators since the issues were first posed in an era so remote from—and yet still so close to—our own.

Acknowledgments

I would like to thank Mindy Kornhaber for her helpful comments on an earlier draft of this manuscript.

References

Anderson, M. (1992). *Intelligence and development.* London: Blackwell.

Baker, L. (1993). Group report: Intelligence and its inheritance: A diversity of views. In T. Bouchard and P. Propping (Eds.), *Twins as a tool of behavioral genetics* (pp. 85–108). Chichester: Wiley.

Bouchard, T. J., and Propping, P. (Eds.). (1993). *Twins as a tool of behavioral genetics.* Chichester: Wiley.

Brand, C. (1993). Cognitive abilities: Current theoretical issues. In T. J. Bouchard and P. Propping (Eds.), *Twins as a tool of behavioral genetics* (pp. 17–32). Chichester; Wiley.

Brown, R., Herrnstein, R. (1975). *Psychology.* Boston: Little Brown.

Ceci, S. (1990). *On intelligence, more or less.* Englewood Cliffs, N.J.: Prentice-Hall.

Chomsky, N. (1957). *Syntactic structures.* Hague: Mouton.

Csikszentmihalyi, M. (1988). Society, culture, and person: A systems view of creativity. In R. Sternberg (Ed.) *The nature of creativity* (pp. 325–339). New York: Cambridge University Press.

Feldman, D. H., with Goldsmith, L. (1986). *Nature's gambit.* New York: Basic Books.

Fodor, J. (1968). *Psychological explanation.* New York: Random House.

Gardner, H. (1993). *Frames of mind: The history of multiple intelligences.* New York: Basic Books.

Gardner, H. (1985). *The mind's new science: A history of the cognitive revolution.* New York: Basic Books.

Gardner, H. (1992a). Scientific psychology: To bury it or to praise it? *New ideas in psychology,* 10(2), 179–190.

Gardner, H. (1993). *Multiple intelligences: The theory in practice.* New York: Basic Books.

Gardner, H., & Hatch, T. (1989). Multiple intelligences go to school. *Educational Researcher, 18,* 4–10.

Geertz, C. (1973). *The interpretation of cultures.* New York: Basic Books.

Jensen, A. (1969). How much can we boost IQ and scholastic achievement? *Harvard Educational Review, 39,* 1–123.

Jensen, A. (1980). *Bias in mental testing.* New York: Free Press.

Koch, S. (1981). The nature and limits of psychological analysis, *American Psychologist, 31,* 257–269.

Lave, J. (1988). *Cognition in practice: Mind, mathematics, and culture.* New York: Cambridge University Press.

Miller, G. (1979). A very personal history. Talk to Cognitive Science Workshop, Massachusetts Institute of Technology, Cambridge, Mass., June 1, 1979.

Montour, K. (1984). William James Sidis, the broken twig. *American Psychologist, 39,* 265–279.

Perkins, D. N. (1992). *Smart schools.* New York: Free Press.

Rogoff, B. (1990). *Apprenticeship in thinking.* New York: Oxford University Press.

Salomon, G. (Ed.). (1992). *Distributed cognitions.* New York: Cambridge University Press.

Sternberg, R. J. (1985). *Beyond IQ.* New York: Cambridge University Press.

Sternberg, R. J. (1988). *The nature of creativity.* New York: Cambridge University Press.

Sternberg, R. J. (1990). *Wisdom: Its nature, origins, and development.* New York: Cambridge University Press.

Sternberg, R. J., & Davidson, J. (1986). *Conceptions of giftedness.* New York: Cambridge University Press.

Sternberg, R. J., & Kolligian, J., Jr. (1990). *Competence considered.* New Haven: Yale University Press.

Vygotsky, L. (1978). *Mind in society.* Cambridge, Mass.: Harvard University Press.

6

The Death of Developmental Psychology[1]

JEAN M. MANDLER

When I was asked to review the history of psychology in the past century, it made me quite grumpy. They must think me past my prime. Although I am at retirement age, I am as busy in the laboratory as ever. I really don't have time to act the elder statesperson. Besides, the century isn't finished. There is still a decade to go, and if my current research is any indication, there will be a lot of action before 2100 rolls around. Anyway, it would be more fun to predict what will happen in the twenty-second century than merely to summarize the events of the twenty-first. Well, I suppose I can take a few hours off to imprint my memories onto the visual scratch-pad of my computer. The computer editor can turn it into language, because I can't be bothered to think so slowly.

It is true that I remember more than most. One hundred and five is not so old, but frankly, many of my contemporaries do tend to be somewhat forgetful. Some of them have already retired and are following the kinds of sybaritic pursuits that make them forget the historical implications of the early years of their careers. I actually remember my initiation into the study of development quite well. I even remember many of the professors teaching at my university in the first decade of this century. But things were really different then. Development was a separate field (yes, truly so; there was psychology, developmental psychology, social psychology, animal psychology—a whole list of psychologies; you've probably forgotten that, it was so long ago). I remember hesitating a long time before committing myself to a field that was considered by many to be a minor, if not actually trivial, subsection of the real thing. It was considered to be an appropriate playground for women psychologists (yes, there were psychologists and women psychologists in those days), where they could fool around with babies and do *that* sort of thing. When I was deciding on my major as an undergraduate in 2001, several professors counseled me to avoid the study of development, to go into connectionist modeling or neuropsychology instead, which were the then hot fields. They thought it was important to avoid the stigma of being in a soft "woman's" field.

But even then it was clear to me that development was the coming thing. A few connectionists and neuropsychologists of the time saw that as well, but on the whole, developmental issues were largely ignored. Many developmental psychologists kept abreast of current issues in the field at large and went to meetings on many topics, but my non-developmental colleagues were for the most part uninterested in developmental findings, and it was rare to find them at developmental conferences. (Yes, there were separate meetings in those days.) "Study anklebiters? We have enough trouble understanding adults," they said, or "It is the steady state we need to study." As if there were such a thing! I wasn't being farseeing, but it struck me as odd not to realize why the two giants that psychology had produced up to that time—Freud in the nineteenth century and Piaget in the twentieth—were thoroughgoing developmentalists. Right or wrong, both knew that to understand the mind one has to start at birth, watching mental structures being formed and developing into the rich, complex structures of adulthood. But this message was rarely understood by the psychological community at large, and so they were unprepared for the major change in the field that was to come.

Actually, I was sorry to see Piaget disappear from the scene. He was such a remarkable theorist. It would have been satisfying if he had lived to see the developmental approach vindicated. Yet 100 years after his death, the tenet that to understand psychology requires us to understand development is about the only thing that remains from his theory. (Of course, his belief that knowledge is constructed has also survived, but that view has been held by others and so does not seem uniquely his.) Even when I was an undergraduate at the turn of the century, it was clear that his theory had collapsed, and he was being relegated to the history books. I suppose in my temporary role as historian I should explain what happened, although many of you will already know it. But the demise of Piagetian theory was intimately linked with the understanding that development is the core of psychological study. Since many of you take that for granted, it may be of some use to describe how different the field used to be. I can't tell it all in a few pages, and besides there is much I don't know. But I will try to highlight what happened to developmental psychology (concentrating on cognitive development) and how it died from natural causes, to become reincarnated as psychology.

Piaget's theory had begun to crack during the last couple of decades of the previous century. It disintegrated from the end game backwards, so to speak. Piaget had posited that there is a stage of formal operational thought, reached for the first time in adolescence. This stage represented the final glory of the mind, in that by this age children could engage in abstract logical thought with the sophistication of the adult. This aspect of his theory had been under attack almost from the time that it was first formulated around the middle of the twentieth century, although the grounds may seem odd to you now. Although a few psychologists protested that even adults are not particularly logical in their thinking, the main complaint was that Piaget had used the wrong logic, not that he had glorified logic at the expense of other kinds of thinking. Only after many more decades did it became clear just what a small role logic plays in ordinary human thought.

Then his notion that there is a stage of concrete operations in middle childhood came under similar fire. During this period Piaget said that children were able to engage in certain kinds of deductive and inductive reasoning, but were limited in doing so to concrete, practical materials, and furthermore did not understand the complexities of higher-order logical reasoning. In this case one of the complaints was that the logic machine was already in place, once again missing a point that would be obvious today: Logical thought is only a small part of the ordinary workings of the mind. To be fair, there were some psychologists who realized that it was lack of familiarity with the physical variables that Piaget used in the problems he set, rather than a lack of logic, that caused the difficulties children experienced. But on the whole, I believe that most people did not realize that the main way children differ from adults is in the size and interrelatedness of their knowledge base. We know now, of course, that the ability to see patterns and relations among pieces of information in a problem is crucially dependent on how much you already know. Most of our most sophisticated and creative reasoning depends on that ability, rather than on the ability to form or follow chains of logical propositions.

About the same time it was also pointed out that Piaget's notion of a preoperational stage during the preschool years, in which thought was said to be haphazard and hazy, had never been fleshed out. His theory tended to treat this time of rich and varied learning merely as a holding period of semi-incompetence, with nothing much happening developmentally until logical reasoning began. Among other things, he overlooked the opening out of the child's social world, the cultural molding of thought, and learning the subtleties of pragmatic language use that constitute so much of the growth during this period. And given his preoccupation with logical thought, it is somewhat surprising that he missed the fact that the intuitive knowledge we use to understand logical argument is already well established by this time.

However, in spite of these criticisms of major parts of Piaget's theory, most psychologists thought his views on the sensorimotor foundations of development would survive. Indeed, it was largely accepted as fact in the textbooks of the day. Everyone knew that infants went through a prolonged stage of sensorimotor functioning before they began to think about the world—to form concepts, recall the past, solve problems mentally—in short, before they became human. There was actually quite a bit of resistance to the new evidence that began to trickle in during the 1980s and 1990s, indicating that infants possess a rich, conscious, conceptual life. We heard a lot about Occam's razor and the necessity of not attributing too much competence to infants. We were told that neural development was too immature to support anything much in the way of conceptual functioning or thought. We heard a lot about testability and accountability in science, and the dangers of regressing to mystical notions. Consciousness was often considered on a par with phlogiston in those days. The necessity of understanding consciousness has happened recently enough that most of you still bear some of the scars of the battles that were fought. Indeed, it has only been in the past twenty years or so that the term no longer elicits scorn from some antediluvian type.

But I digress. The point I wanted to make was that the demise of Piagetian theory as the essential framework for developmental work and the integration of development with the rest of psychology were related happenings. Although there were a number of factors at work, one that is sometimes overlooked was the roadblock that stage theory put in the path of this integration. As long as the human mind was thought to unfold in distinct, qualitatively different stages, bounded by potentially specifiable transitions, researchers who were concerned with adult thought did not need to worry too much about the earlier periods of development. This was especially true for the period of infancy. Clearly, a sensorimotor baby as described by Piagetian theory has little in common with the adult. If it has no concepts and no ability form images or think, it is so foreign to adult functioning that there is little reason to worry about what it is like. Such radical changes take place over time that explication of the infant mind cannot illuminate or guide the study of the adult mind. No road map here, just a different psychology to be mastered, and so easy to ignore, as animal psychology was ignored by most cognitivists in the second half of the last century.

So it was in part the discovery of the continuity between the infant and adult mind that made inevitable the resurgence of the developmental approach to psychology that Piaget promulgated. One might say that he lost all the battles but won the war. We have come to understand that the continuity from infancy to adulthood is one of the major assets in our research on the mind. Most of you take this for granted, but you should realize it is a fairly recent view. For most of psychology's history it was a canon of faith that one could study the adult mind sui generis. It was simply not realized that the sheer complexity of human psychological functioning literally makes it impossible to progress by observing only the operations of the steady *(sic)* state.

A related belief (also of ancient provenance) was the conviction that language provides the best entree to the workings of the mind. The result of this emphasis was just one more factor encouraging the separation of the study of adult functioning from its preverbal roots. It seemed obvious that preverbal thought could bear little relation to adult functioning, since rationality itself was thought to depend upon language. This view was almost a necessary by-product of a psychology that considered logical thought to be the heart of cognitive functioning. It may be difficult for some of you to believe what a centuries old tradition that was and how it permeated most scientific approaches to the mind. Consciousness was taboo, but it was accepted without question that what subjects (that's what they called people who performed in experiments) *said* provided the best evidence for the kinds of processing they did. (Sometimes, it was not just what they said, but the rate at which they produced words or how rapidly they pushed a button in response to linguistic materials.)

Some of the overwhelming emphasis on language and its use in recall, thinking, and problem solving was a philosophical hangover. Again, it may seem surprising to you how great a hold philosophers had over the psychological theories of the day. Psychology was the last remnant of science to remain part of philosophy's purview and its practitioners were understandably loath to give it up. As it became increasingly obvious that they had little to contribute to psychological knowledge, they clung to analysis of language. When I was at university, it was not uncommon for philosophers of the analytic persuasion to claim that they had been trained to reason more clearly and objectively than most psychologists and that their logical skills were needed to disambiguate the confused concepts most of us worked with. Furthermore, they believed that by analysis of language they could uncover the foundations of mind. Some of them hoped to prove that there is a "language of thought" (sic) that is propositional in character. To translate this view: They thought, and encouraged psychologists to think, that the predicate-argument structures of propositional logic were the basis of mind-stuff.

At this point you may well ask what led from the old view of the propositional basis of thought itself (as opposed to the propositional nature of language) to our present understanding that thought is nonverbal pattern-matching and pattern-creation, and that language is a (communicatively useful) gloss on, or translation of, largely nonverbal mental structures. As is usual with major paradigm shifts in science, there were many contributing factors. There isn't space here to cover them all, but I will briefly describe four in particular. They were (1) the growth of parallel distributed processing systems (connectionism) in cognitive science and the associated development of a new generation of powerful and sophisticated analog computers, (2) the restructuring of neuroscience, (3) the waning influence of Piaget in developmental psychology, and (4) the decline of Chomskian linguistics. What is more difficult to explain is how these various historical movements, which were at loggerheads much of the time, among them caused the revolution that put their separate disciplines out of business.

We might as well begin with the birth near the end of the last century of what was called at the time cognitive linguistics. Instead of assuming that linguistics was a discipline independent of psychology (I know that sounds weird, but then much of history does), this approach asserted that language was based on nonpropositional forms of representation, consisting of dynamic analog structures. It also claimed that these image-like patterns were not only involved in language understanding but were central to all human thought. This general view will of course seem commonplace to you, but you may not know how fiercely these ideas were resisted. (On the east coast of the United States, where Chomskian views of language predominated, they provoked much merriment.) But they were an opening wedge to a different view of thought.

At about the same time connectionism was born. It had a rocky start, because in its infancy it did not know how to handle the aspects of psychological functioning that, as I have described, were most valued by the rest of the field, namely, language-based symbolic thought and reasoning. But, helped along by the messianic fervor of many of its practitioners, it survived long enough as a movement to begin to have an impact on the field as a whole. Its successes were so impressive in the area of pattern learning and recognition that attention had to be paid to it. Even as it was being attacked, it drove another wedge into the hegemony of the dominant propositional models of thought. Merely by hinting at nonsymbolic ways in which reasoning and, yes, even language, might be implemented, it began to suggest new ways of doing psychology.

More important for this particular historical review, a number of people working on connectionist models of the mind began to realize that learning (development) was absolutely central. They were attempting to find out how parallel distributed systems discover regularities in the input they receive and organize themselves to respond on the basis of these regularities. This view suggested that they should pay more attention to developmental issues than their training as psychologists (or in some cases as engineers) had prepared them for. I remember my mentor at UCSD telling me how astonished she was to hear a plea at a general meeting of cognitive science in the 1990s for more information about how babies learn to form concepts. (She was happy to oblige).

This is where the simultaneously occurring shift in theories of infant development became relevant. There were several of these, but the one that I know the most about because of my own educational history, was the burgeoning of experimental results showing not only excellent pattern recognition and perceptual categorization in infancy, but also the beginnings of what used to be called the higher-order cognitive functions: concept formation, problem-solving, analogically-based thinking, and recall of the past. My mentor spent much of the latter part of her career showing that the foundations of conceptual thought were laid down in infancy, that they were nonverbal and nonpropositional in nature, that they formed the basis on which language is constructed, and that they created a central core of conceptual thought that lasts throughout life (Mandler, 1992; Mandler & McDonough, 1993). Sadly, she didn't live long enough to see the eventual acceptance of this point of view.

Then we come to neuroscience. What a troubled course that field has had! It is another field that has not survived in recognizable form from the last century. Essentially it split into two disciplines; one became (or perhaps I should say, continued to be) part of biology, the other became a subsidiary part of psychology. Vis-à-vis psychology, I have described how philosophy withered away from lack of work to do (or from lack of psychologists paying attention). Connectionism too began to play a subservient role because it couldn't (or didn't) provide psychological theory. Of course it thrived as a widely used modeling technique, but it did not fulfill its original promise as the golden road to psychological knowledge. Neuroscience couldn't provide psychological theory either, but it fared better because biology will always be with us as a separate level of analysis; neuropsychology did, as you know, however, cease to exist as a separate field.

When connectionist psychology was dominant in the early part of this century, it was assumed that it was correct because it was said to be modeling psychological processes in a neurally plausible way. There were many neuroscientists who scoffed at this idea. [You may have heard about that famous brawl in the twenties on the steps of NSF in Washington between a well-known connectionist and two (!) neuroscientists about whether the connectionist's model bore any relation to the real thing.] It is hard to say who was more deluded. Certainly, in spite of the increase in sophistication of the connectionist models from their earlier neurally naive forms, their claim to truth was wrong. But equally it became obvious that the neuroscientists were just as much at sea about what to look for next. I mention this famous dispute because to my mind it was the beginning of the end of the reductionist attempts to treat physical analyses of mind as more fundamental than mental analyses.

There was much dispute until quite recently as to who owns the study of mind. For the better part of a century many neuroscientists were convinced that the mind could not be understood without understanding the hardware underlying it. However, the way things stand near the end of the twenty-first century is that no one knows how to find their way through the vastness of the neural system without psychological data and theory as a guide. This dependence of neuroscience on psychology was long guessed at, but only became apparent with the advent of developmental neurocognitive studies about a century ago. Only then was it proven that the development of pathways most relevant to thought are crucially due to the particular learning experiences of the infant, that perceiving and behaving within a particular kind of physical and social world determine the way the brain organizes itself. Here was a clear case of having to understand the psychological events that babies are experiencing in order to understand how the brain develops.

Such a notion was disturbing to many of the neuroscientists of the time. They understood their task to be to find the physical mechanisms that would explain psychological events. However, now they were being asked to have a theory of the mental events they had wanted to explain, in order to understand the physical events that were supposed to explain the mental ones! Although they probably would have denied a view of the mind as epiphenomenal, many of them had a model of the brain as the sole "true" cause of mental events. In this model, to understand a brain event you must find its physical cause, and to understand a psychological event you must also find a physical cause. (This seems to us a somewhat greedy appropriation of causation to one's own field! Rather like a physicist claiming that the cause of liver functioning is the atomic structure of the organic molecules that compose it.) Nevertheless, the notion of psychological causes seemed to many to contradict the fact that minds require brains in order to think. (That minds require brains in order to function is obviously true for all animals, although now that we are beginning to build minds, the story will have to change somewhat.) In any case, the search for physical causes of mental events was slow to be replaced by the modern view that to understand psychological functioning one must seek psychological causes. The causal bridges that link one level of analysis of a phenomenon to another are not in themselves capable of doing the theoretical work of the higher level.

The modern view might have ended reductionist claims altogether, and it did in the sense that is now accepted that causal laws differ at each level of analysis of a phenomenon that is undertaken. On the other hand, a different kind of reductionism has arisen, albeit one that has turned the old attempt to reduce psychology to neuroscience on its head. Instead, we now see that neuroscience depends on the facts of psychology. The crucial knowledge that neuroscience requires is the psychological theory (sometimes called the computational theory) of what organisms think and do. It is not just that neuroscience requires behavioral measures to test its theories; more important is the fact that it is virtually impossible to understand that incredibly complex maze of continually developing neural connections without the theoretical computational level as a guide. If we don't understand what processing organisms are doing, we don't have a chance of understanding the algorithms required, and of course, without the algorithms we don't know what the neurons must do in order to implement them.

All of this meant that neither connectionist nor neural modeling could hold at the center of psychology. At the same time the crucial role of development began to become clear. We gradually realized that how organisms learn, and continually build on what they have already learned, is the secret to understanding the mind. So it was that development died as a separate field, and became instead the core of psychological theory, with infant development as the keystone. And, as you know, that is when psychology began to make new strides as a science and its paradigmatic disputes began to give way to a stable consensus.

These changes also explain why we have progressed further in understanding infant development than in understanding many aspects of adult functioning. It all turned out to be so much more complex than we had once thought. I suppose we should not be surprised that we are still working on the relatively simple cognitive structures of infancy and that many aspects of adult functioning are far beyond our ken. It is ironic that in the last century infant cognition was considered to be difficult to study because babies don't talk. Now that we know that most adult cognition is not language-based either, infant cognition seems relatively transparent, or at least more tractable.

To conclude this whirlwind tour of the twenty-first century, I suppose it behooves me to select among our many accomplishments a few that I consider to be the most seminal to the work that will come in the twenty-second. Not surprisingly, such a list will concentrate on the period of infant development because that has become so central to the field. Nevertheless, I approach this task with a good deal of trepidation. Obviously, only a fool would try to predict the future course of psychology (even though I did say that it would be more fun than summarizing the past). Bearing in mind the impossibility of the endeavor, my list goes as follows, roughly in the order of their accomplishment.

First, the final disappearance of the dispute over nature versus nurture was an important milestone, as was the disappearance of the ancient doctrine of innate ideas. We learned not only that there are no innate ideas, but why this centuries-old view is incoherent. We now understand that development does not require beliefs about the world to be built into the system, and why genetic structure cannot carry this kind of content information. It was not that nurture won, however; it too was put in its proper place. Recent research has begun to explicate in detail the innate processing mechanisms that account for the human ability to transform perceptual information into conceptual thought. This new line of work grew out of a school concerned with constraints on development that flourished near the end of the last century. Their theorizing however, tended to depend too much on the notion that one had to build in innate principles to guide development; otherwise it would be too open-ended and more variable than it is. It took some time before it began to be realized that the genetic basis of our sensory systems in conjunction with the physical world and the facts of cultural life provide most of the constraints that are needed. As research began to shift from principles to mechanisms, there turned out to be fewer mechanisms than originally suspected. Obviously, an important one of these is the mechanism that allows perceptual information to be redescribed into analog spatial representations of meanings. Another equally important mechanism is the one controlling the organization of these meanings into deeply interpenetrated, multi-leveled systems. As you know, the growth of these systems is under intense scrutiny today and is the area in which connectionist implementation has been the most useful. The complexity of this task, of course, is why we spend so much of our time studying the beginnings of these representational systems in infancy.

Next, we settled the dispute raging at the end of the last century over the issue of the relation between explicit and implicit memory. You may not remember much about it, since the issue was resolved fairly early in this century. Its resolution depended crucially on one of the most important accomplishments of our time, namely, making the inroads we have into understanding consciousness. The reason why the debate centered around contrasts such as implicit vs. explicit memory, procedural vs. declarative memory, and so forth, was because, as I mentioned earlier, the term consciousness was taboo. However, consciousness was a central clue to the organization of the mind and how it develops. Only when it became a respectable field of study (as it had been in the nineteenth century, albeit in the discredited form of introspectionism) could the memory issue be resolved. We have much still to do, and I predict that yet another century will pass before we understand consciousness thoroughly. However, we have obviously learned a great deal about the complex interplay of implicit and explicit processes, the constructive nature of consciousness, and its directing and channeling capacity.

The discovery of how conscious attention guides the intake and transformation of perceptual information beginning at birth, and the nature of the conceptual structures that are built up through this process (themselves not necessarily conscious, of course) was part of what led us to the modern view of language. The main function of language is to communicate. I suppose I am belaboring the obvious, but it is important to contrast the modern view with the older view of language as the primary medium of thought. We now understand that the role of language is to direct thought, not to create it, and especially to direct the thought of others. The communicative function is one reason why language is so redundant, imprecise, and full of overlapping meanings. It is extraordinarily difficult to create in another person's mind a mental model of what you wish to express. This is why so much of the educational curriculum is devoted to developing children's communicative skills.

At the same time, we should not overlook the role of language in constraining and steadying thought processes. This role is evident as soon as children begin to speak. The language community directs children's attention and begins to exert control over their previously less constrained analyses. Language helps keep thought within restricted bounds, to help it to stay orderly, so to speak. Unfortunately, this narrowing character of language often works to the detriment of creativity and is one of the chief problems we face with our schools today. This is not the place to discuss the turmoil in our educational system, but I cannot resist noting that the "back to language" movement's boycott of the current image-based computer systems in the schools is one of the major social problems we have to solve.

I do want to say a few more words in defense of language, however. It is true that we have learned that the nonverbal knowledge base set down in infancy is the core around which all later knowledge accrues. It is also true that we tend to operate nonverbally much of the time even as adults. Nevertheless, the current view of language as unimportant to psychological processing is undoubtedly exaggerated. It is not just that it gives a different shape to the knowledge base that has begun in the preverbal period. Its slow serial character is well suited to the slow serial character of consciousness. This is a fact we tend to forget in our new-found enthusiasm for the speed and depth with which so many other psychological processes (and the computer programs that simulate them) are carried out. Language is a necessary function, and we must strive in the next century to put it in proper perspective and not devalue it as so many do today. It constrains and oversimplifies our thought, to be sure, but it is invaluable as memory aid, as a check on veracity, as a repository of historical record, and most important, it remains our chief means of communicating with one another.

With that I will leave you to return to the laboratory, where I hope my work on infant-learning techniques to restore damaged brains will provide new hope for the twenty-second century. That is more important by far than these reminiscences of a twenty-first–century psychologist.

Note

1. This paper is a slightly condensed and cleaned-up version of a manuscript found in the lost luggage office of the San Diego Union Station when it was being pulled down. An anonymous person sent it to the University. I have no explanation for the time warp that seems to be involved, nor do I take responsibility for the views presented herein (although along with some oddities several ideas seem rather sensible). I publish it for those who will still be around to check out the future.

References

Mandler, J. M. (1992). How to build a baby II: Conceptual primitives. *Psychological Review, 99,* 587–604.

Mandler, J. M., & McDonough, L. (1993). Concept formation in infancy. *Cognitive Development, 8,* 291–318.

Suggested Readings with Annotations

Barsalou, L. (1993). Flexibility, structure, and linguistic vagary in concepts: Manifestations of a compositional system of perceptual symbols. In A. C. Collins, S. E. Gathercole, M. A. Conway, & P. E. M. Morris (Eds.), *Theories of memories.* Hillsdale, N.J.: Erlbaum. A discussion of nonpropositional representational systems.

Elman, J. L. (1993). Learning and development in neural networks: The importance of starting small. *Cognition, 48,* 71–99. The importance of development to connectionist modeling.

Fauconnier, G. (1985). *Mental spaces.* Cambridge, Mass.: MIT Press. Cognitive linguistic approaches to nonpropositional systems.

Fodor, J. (1975). *The language of thought.* New York: Crowell. A classic propositional account of the basis of thought.

Lakoff, G. (1987). *Women, fire, and dangerous things: What categories reveal about the mind.* Chicago: University of Chicago Press. Cognitive linguistic approaches to non-propositional systems.

Mandler, G. (1992). Toward a theory of consciousness. In H.-G. Geissler, S. W. Link, & J. T. Townsend (Eds.), *Cognition, information processing, and psychophysics: Basic issues.* Hillsdale, N.J.: Erlbaum. A discussion of consciousness.

Mandler, J. M. (1992). How to build a baby: II. Conceptual primitives. *Psychological Review, 99,* 587–604. An alternative view of infant development.

Mandler, J. M., & McDonough, L. (1993). Concept formation in infancy. *Cognitive Development, 8,* 291–318.

Mehler, J., Morton, J., & Jusczyk, P. W. (1984). On reducing language to biology. *Cognitive Neuropsychology, 1,* 83–116. A discussion of the relation between mental sciences and biology.

Piaget, J. (1952). *The origins of intelligence in children.* New York: International Universities Press. Piaget's theory of infancy.

Siegal, M. (1991). *Knowing children: Experiments in conversation and cognition.* Hove, U.K.: Erlbaum. An account of the importance of knowing the pragmatics of preschoolers' language understanding.

7

Freud Returns?

STEPHEN M. KOSSLYN

The twenty-first century may well see the return of many of Sigmund Freud's ideas to mainline academic psychology, which will be part of a grand synthesis of psychoanalysis, other forms of clinical psychology, behavioral psychology, cognitive psychology, and neuroscience. In his famous "Project for a scientific psychology," Freud (1895/1954) outlined goals that were simply beyond the reach of then-current research methods. Moreover, Freud lacked the scientific vocabulary to state his ideas clearly. The rise of cognitive neuroscience has ameliorated both deficiencies, and these developments may pave the way for many of Freud's deep insights and observations again to assume center stage in psychology.

This prediction may seem unlikely today because of a major, apparently unnoticed, paradigm shift since Freud's work. Freud was interested in the "why" of behavior; he wanted to know why people do what they do, and appealed to mental processes—including unconscious mental processes—as the source of a person's behavior. In large part because such processes are very difficult to observe, the behaviorists rejected a causal role for internal events in scientific psychology. Instead, they urged that we study only what is observable: stimuli and responses. However, they subscribed to the major goal of Freud's enterprise—namely that psychology should explain why one does what one does. Cognitive psychology was born in part as a reaction to the deficiencies of behaviorism, and in part in response to new conceptual tools and methods; it became clear that one must posit internal events in order to explain patterns of generalization and the like, and psychologists turned to the computer metaphor to theorize about such events (see Gardner, 1985). But something else happened at the time of the "cognitive revolution": Psychologists shifted their focus from questions of "why" to questions of "how." They began to ask about the details of how processing takes place to allow a person to store new information in memory, to recognize objects during perception, to use language, and so on. They neglected questions about why information is processed as it is in specific situations. Perhaps this is one reason why attempts to integrate Freud into cognitive psychology (e.g., Erdelyi, 1985) fell on deaf ears.

Cognitive psychology and its descendant cognitive science were not without their problems. In particular, it is not easy to use behavior to infer how internal processing takes place. The "imagery debate" is a case in point; Anderson (1978) proved that one can always have alternative theories of how information is represented, provided that one can adjust the theory of processing to compensate for differences in the theory of representation. Such concerns promoted the rise of cognitive neuroscience, in part because appeal to neuroanatomy and neurophysiology placed additional constraints on theories—limiting how footloose and fancy free one could be in positing representations and processing (see Kosslyn & Koenig, 1992; Kosslyn, 1994).

Cognitive neuroscience takes seriously the idea that the "mind is what the brain does," an idea that the young Freud embraced—and which colored his thoughts forever on. But the mind is more than a thinking machine; it is also a feeling machine. Researchers working within the cognitive neuroscience framework are just now discovering the neural bases of emotion (e.g., see LeDoux, 1987). This work has focused in large part on discovering anatomical pathways that are necessary for an animal to feel fear, but this clearly is only the beginning of a very important development: the use of the "how" of mechanism to facilitate a return to the "why" of thought and behavior. In many ways, "how" and "why" are intimately related; by analogy, given that one knows how a lens works, one can go far in discovering why people wear them in front of their eyes.

In this chapter I would like to outline one way I see psychology developing during the next twenty years or so. I would like to show how a cognitive neuroscience framework can lead one to make distinctions that not only illuminate Freudian concerns, but also generate empirically testable hypotheses. This chapter is unabashedly speculative, and many of the ideas are far-reaching. I want to show how, in principle, scientific psychology can once again make direct contact with the concerns of nonscientists who think about psychology and with the concerns of the society as a whole. I cannot say whether any of the specific ideas I sketch out here will survive, but I do believe that something like them will emerge during the early part of the next century.

Two Axioms and a Principle

One can root a neo-Freudian theory in two fundamental observations, which I treat as axioms (I shall assume that they are correct). These axioms, in combination with one empirically derived principle of brain activity, form the foundation for theorizing about the brain bases of many Freudian constructs. In particular, after developing the bare bones of a theoretical framework, I shall consider its utility for understanding one defense mechanism, repression.

The "explanation urge"

Human beings have an urge to explain events. They want to understand themselves and how they fit into their surroundings. This urge has been the subject of hundreds of studies in social psychology. For example, the urge to reduce "cognitive dissonance" (which arises when there is a contradiction between how one believes one would behave in a specific situation and how one actually does behave) relies on one's desire to explain; "dissonance" would not arise if one were not seeking explanations. Similarly, the "fundamental attribution error," of overemphasizing dispositional variables as causes of others' actions, is also a consequence of an urge to explain. This urge to explain is not a reflection of a more fundamental impulse to be curious or a desire to learn; cognitive dissonance reduction and its kin arise because we need to *explain,* not explore.

The explanation urge may well be one of the primary motivations for humans. It can override fundamental biological motivations such as reproduction and eating: Monks find it more comforting to accept a set of beliefs than to mate, and religious Jews or Muslims fast as part of their beliefs; in both cases, the beliefs provide comfort in part by offering explanations of many of life's mysteries.

The "survival axiom"

The explanation urge often has a focus, a purpose: One is trying to understand oneself and the environment in the service of survival. At a very early age, "survival" is primarily physical. But eventually it becomes not so much survival of the body, as survival of the "self." In this case, survival corresponds to protecting one's concept of the self and promulgating one's beliefs and goals as a way of perpetuating the self and increasing its power and security. From a cognitive neuroscience perspective, it is useful to distinguish between the "self concept" and "self characteristics." Self characteristics are the innate and learned behavioral tendencies, propensities, conceptions, and beliefs that govern one's behavior; a self concept is a theory of what those characteristics are—which need not be (and usually is not) entirely correct. The self concept corresponds to a "model" of one's self characteristics; this model is stored in memory in the same way that a model of the economy might be stored. (For further discussion of the "self concept," see Kosslyn, 1992.)

The survival axiom probably is a consequence of natural selection; it is difficult to imagine a complex social organism (such as a human being) without such a propensity.

Constraint satisfaction

Finally, the brain appears to operate according to the principle of constraint satisfaction (see Kosslyn & Koenig, 1992). Consider one example: One sees something and encodes a set of properties, each of which constrains what the object can be. Say that the object is red, which is consistent with its being a fire engine, an apple, someone's shirt, a tomato, a book, and so on. It cannot be a pear, a pea, a banana, and other objects that are not red. Now say that it is also round. That would rule out a fire engine, a book, a shirt, and other nonround things. Now say that it is about 4 inches in diameter. It could not be a cherry tomato or a beach ball. And say that it has a stem with leaves and has dimples on its bottom. Each additional piece of information constitutes an additional constraint, which narrows down the candidate objects; the more constraints, the more restricted is the range of viable possibilities.

Constraint satisfaction operates at multiple levels of scale in the nervous system, from the level of channels in the membranes of neurons to the level of small circuits to the level of large populations of interacting neurons (see Kosslyn & Koenig, 1992). This mechanism offers a natural way to implement the explanation urge: The explanation urge would be instantiated if the system is driven to find mutual consistency. When observations do not jibe, constraints are not being mutually satisfied and the system will be in a state of disequilibration. Such a state would cause an urge to "fit things together."

It is convenient to divide mental entities into two types, both of which are activated via a process of constraint satisfaction. On the one hand, *interpretations* are used to make sense of input. Interpretations exist at the level of individual objects, such as apples and oranges, and at the level of complex events, such as "deceit." Event-based interpretations rest on prior interpretations of individual objects or portions of events; for example, to interpret a person as trying to deceive you, you first would need to interpret the tone of voice, body language, facial expression, linguistic content, and so forth. Only after such individual interpretations are accomplished can one discover that they are not consistent with a single message—which is itself a pattern of activation that is consistent with the interpretation that the person is trying to deceive you.

In all cases, an interpretation consists of a packet of information that can be applied to a current object or event if the proper constraints are met. The constraints correspond to individual elements of the representation's "address" (such as a particular color, shape, size, and so on, for an apple).

On the other hand, *action plans* are used to generate a response (see chapter 7 of Kosslyn & Koenig, 1992). Typically, an activated interpretation itself serves as a constraint for action plans. If one interprets the input as an apple, and one is hungry, has money to buy the apple, and so forth, one may initiate a complex action plan that involves purchasing the fruit and eating it. If one interprets the input as a tomato, this action plan is less likely to be activated (at least in American culture, where tomatoes are rarely eaten as snacks). Kosslyn and Koenig (1992, chapter 7) summarize much of what is known about such processing.

Four Levels of Processing: Neural Systems

The rehabilitation of Freud's insights will rest on analyses of neural systems, and how emotion and cognition interact to produce behavior. In the next section, I show how this sort of approach can illuminate issues of interest to Freud. But before doing so, I must briefly sketch out an approach to conceptualizing neural systems. It is convenient to divide processing into four levels, each of which is operating at the same time and interacting with the other levels. These levels can be characterized in terms of differences in how constraints are processed. I first outline the salient features of each type of processing, and then consider how such processing can result in different types of repression.

Level 1: Constraint matching

When a stimulus is first encountered, a number of "bottom-up" processes occur; these processes extract salient stimulus attributes and match them to representations in unimodal perceptual memories (visual memory, if the object is seen; auditory memory if it is heard, etc.). For example, when viewing an apple, Level 1 processes extract the shape, color, texture, and size of the stimulus. There is evidence that many separate "channels" are used to extract information in vision; for example, color and shape appear to be extracted using separate neural mechanisms, which in turn are distinct from those used in extracting location (e.g., see DeYoe & Van Essen, 1988). These attributes are treated as constraints in a simple bottom-up constraint matching process, which leads to *stimulus recognition*. Stimulus recognition occurs when the input implicates a single representation in perceptual memory. When such a match occurs, one realizes that the object is familiar; one does not know its name, category, or any other information that is associated with the object in memory; this information is available only after *stimulus identification*, as is discussed in the next section.

After the input is recognized, information is sent to two separate systems. It is sent to a multimodal memory for stimulus identification, as will be discussed shortly. It is also sent to various subcortical structures, including the amygdala and neostriatum (e.g., see Amaral, Price, Pitkanen, & Carmichael, 1992; Le-

Figure 7.1. Brain areas that play key roles in the different types of processing. The striatum lies deep in the brain, beneath the cerebral cortex.

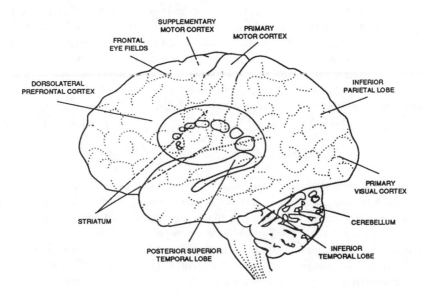

Doux, 1987; Mishkin & Appenzeller, 1987). If that object is an "unconditioned stimulus" (such as meat powder) or is a well-conditioned stimulus, it can "automatically" lead to behavior without identification. Mishkin and his colleagues (e.g., see Mishkin & Appenzeller, 1987; Mishkin, Malamut, & Bachevalier, 1984) document a "habit" system that relies on the striatum (also called the neostriatum); this area is illustrated in Figure 7.1 in relation to other brain areas discussed below. They have found that when a behavior can be performed based on simple stimulus–response associations, an animal can acquire that "habit" even when the hippocampus is removed; in contrast, if the task requires holding information in "working memory" while an animal is learning, removing the hippocampus devastates performance. The "habit" system as I construe it includes instinctual behavior [some of which probably relies on the ventral striatum (see Everitt, 1990) and the amygdala (see Kling & Brothers, 1992; see also Everitt & Robbins, 1992)], as well as behavior that has become "automatic" as a consequence of learning.

The critical characteristic of Level 1 processing is that it is entirely bottom-up; simply matching constraints to stored representations can lead to "automatic" behavior. This kind of behavior is like a cognitive reflex; one need not be aware of the reasons why those stimuli evoke those behaviors.

Level 2: Constraint interpretation

After the input has been recognized, it can be identified. Information flows from the unimodal perceptual structures into the frontal lobe (Goldman-Rakic, 1987) and to the temporal–parietal junction to be stored in a structure I call *associative memory* (see Chapter 8 of Kosslyn & Koenig, 1992). The process of recognition can be regarded as organizing the input into familiar categories. This input is then sent to associative memory, which includes associations between perceptual representations in different modalities, as well as between perceptual representations (the output from the recognition processes) and abstract information (such as names and categories; such associations are necessary if one is to name an object one sees). When an object has been identified, the associated information is activated—which in turn serve as constraints on action plans. One can apply all of the appropriate information in memory to the perceived object. For example, once one has identified a stimulus as an apple, one knows that it has seeds inside—even though they are not visible.

Level 2 processing relies on *explicit* memory, as opposed to Level 1 processing, which relies on *implicit* memory. Whereas one can voluntarily recall explicit memories and use them in a variety of contexts, implicit memories cannot be voluntarily recalled and typically are embedded in a specific type of processing (see Schacter, 1987, for explication of the distinction between the two kinds of memory representations). For example, one's telephone number is an explicit memory; one can recall it at will, tell it to someone else, divide it by the number 2, and so on. In contrast, motor skills are implicit memories; one cannot voluntarily recall how to swing a golf club properly unless one performs the action or imagines performing it, and such memories are limited to that particular action.

Associative memory contains interpretations and action plans, both of which are matched via constraint satisfaction. The input from the recognition system is but one constraint; one's internal states, previously activated representations of the context, and so forth, also serve as constraints. The goal of processing in associative memory is to identify the input and then to select the appropriate response. At any one time, the input will be identified only one way, and can be responded to in only one way (although several responses may alternate in rapid succession, only one can be performed at a time). Associative memory apparently operates via a so-called "winner-take-all" algorithm (see Feldman, 1985; Kosslyn & Koenig, 1992): Each representation is activated to the extent that the inputs serve as constraints that are consistent with it, and the more strongly each representation is activated, the more strongly it inhibits all of the other representations. If the "winner" only weakly suppresses the competing representations, however, the system may flip from one state to another—like a Necker Cube reversing before one's eyes (Feldman, 1985).

The winner-take-all process is governed not simply by how well the input satisfies the constraints associated with each representation. Some interpretations are more important than others: For example, if you are about to buy an apple when your child steps off the curb into the path of a car, you will interrupt the ongoing action plan and remain hungry to save the child. It is probably critical that the hippocampus receives massive inputs from the amygdala. The hippocampus plays a key role in storing new memories, and every memory may have an emotional association. Indeed, studies of emotion have consistently identified two major dimensions: valence and salience. Emotions are positive or negative to different degrees, and are stronger or weaker. This information presumably plays a critical role in the winner-take-all process: Representations that are associated with very salient emotions are more strongly activated than would be warranted by the input alone, and hence can inhibit other representations more effectively—allowing them to "win" even if they are slightly less appropriate for the extant constraints than other, less important, interpretations or action plans.

Sometimes more than one representation may be consistent with input, and the associated emotional salience may result in comparable amounts of inhibition. In this situation, there may be no immediate "winner." This is an unstable pattern of activation; the system is not in equilibrium. Computer simulations have shown that in such situations it is useful to lower thresholds to the point where some units "fire" spontaneously. This process is often thought of as throwing "noise" into the system (e.g., see Hinton & Sejnowski, 1986). Consider an analogy: Say that you had a bucket full of irregularly shaped objects (a sphere, a cube, a wedge, a rectangular solid, etc.), and you wanted to pack them into the bucket as tightly as possible. (This corresponds to fitting them into the most consistent overall pattern.) One way to do so would be to shake up the bucket, vigorously at first but then less vigorously as the objects began to settle down. Similarly, if thresholds are lowered so that noise is inserted into a network, and then noise is gradually eliminated, this will tip the balance so that one representation "wins."

The same mechanisms that underlie anxiety may also be used here. That is, in many situations networks can encode input more quickly if the firing thresholds of the units are lowered; this would produce a small amount of noise because some units would fire spontaneously. We can think of anxious anticipation as a kind of "priming" that greases the wheels, facilitating encoding. Such priming has a metabolic overhead, however, and thus would be less than salubrious if maintained over a long period of time.[1]

Level 3: Constraint seeking

On any given eye fixation, we encode only about two degrees of visual angle with high resolution. Thus, we may not encode enough information to recognize or identify an object immediately. In such circumstances, more than one interpretation is consistent with the input, and the winner-take-all process does not run to completion. Nevertheless, one representation may be most strongly activated (although not enough so to "win"). In such circumstances, one engages in Level 3 processing, and seeks additional information to allow the system to settle down.

For example, at first glance, an object might appear to be either an apple or a tomato. To decide, one needs only to look to see whether it has a stem, or a specific texture (for details of how such processing occurs, see Chapter 3 of Kosslyn & Koenig, 1992). When the new information is encoded, it serves as additional constraints, which are satisfied better by one competing interpretation— allowing it to inhibit the others. The differences between Level 3 processing and processing at other levels are schematized in Figure 7.2. The dorsolateral prefrontal lobes clearly play a critical role in the process of seeking additional information; patients with lesions to this area have disrupted eye movement patterns and information-seeking strategies (see Luria, 1980; see also chapter 9 of Kosslyn & Koenig, 1992).

Level 4: Constraint inventing

But what happens when additional information cannot be found, or does not resolve instability? The explanation urge leads one to keep trying to find an interpretation that is consistent with the constraints, but there is metabolic overhead in having several interpretations in competition for an extended period. In such circumstances, people seem to invent new constraints. These constraints are hypotheses or theories. Consider an analogy: Say that you are building a wall of irregularly shaped stones. The wall is not stable, in part because there are large gaps in it; you must hold onto the side, pushing stones in as the wall shifts. If only you could find a stone that would fit snug in a specific chink, the wall would be stable. But no such stone is handy. Thus, you use your free hand to pick up a stone and chip it down to the right size and shape, and then cram it in the hole. The stones are constraints, and the wall itself is an interpretation.

On my view, this process of "inventing" new constraints is at the heart of the human impulse towards philosophy, astrology, science, religion, and common gossip. The explanation urge leads us to abhor instability, when constraints do not fit together to implicate a single interpretation. Hence if need be, we invent new constraints. The right hemisphere apparently plays an essential role in this process,

Level I. CONSTRAINT MATCHING

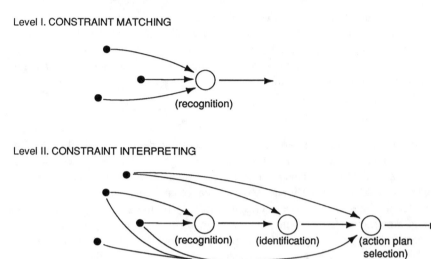

Level II. CONSTRAINT INTERPRETING

Level III. CONSTRAINT SEEKING

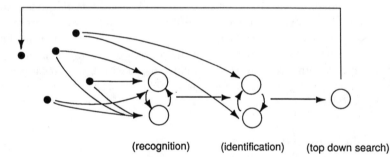

Level IV. CONSTRAINT CREATING

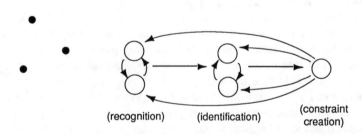

Figure 7.2. A schematic illustration of the four levels of processing. The theory posits that all levels are operating at the same time and are mutually interacting. The black dots at the left represent features of the input that serve as constraints; the open circles schematize processes that match or otherwise operate on constraints. Not illustrated, Levels III and IV also include a final phase in which an action plan is selected (after identification is achieved).

particularly the right frontal lobe. Patients with lesions in the right frontal lobe have difficulty "getting the point" of metaphors and jokes, even though their language abilities appear to be intact (e.g., see Brownell, Michelow, Powelson, & Gardner, 1983). Such patients may also have difficulty understanding the causal connections between separate events depicted in a complex scene. The four levels of processing and key brain areas are illustrated in Figures 7.1 and 7.2, respectively.

Freudian Theory and Levels of Neural Processing

The approach just outlined rests on fundamental assumptions about motivation and, hence, can allow us to address many "why" questions about behavior and thought. But what does all of this have to do with Freud? Freud's theory rested in part on the idea that unconscious drives bubble up from the id. The id obeys the pleasure principle; it wants gratification, and wants it now. The superego, on the other hand, incorporates the rules of society (primarily as transmitted by one's parents), and is just as rigid in its strictures as the id is in its desires. The ego is caught in the middle, and uses defense mechanisms to mitigate between the id and superego; these mechanisms block and rechannel drives, and do so unconsciously.

In my view, the "id" corresponds to Level 1 processing; it rests on innate drives, such as hunger and sex, as well as conditioned behaviors. These drives and behaviors run in the "habit" system; they are implicit representations, and hence are unconscious (Schacter, 1987). The "ego" corresponds to cortical activity in Levels 2, 3, and 4, which can inhibit the subcortical impulses (see LeDoux, 1992). The "ego" rests on processing of explicit representations, either as self characteristics or part of the self concept. The "superego" straddles the two other sorts of processing: It is embodied in Level 1, as additional "habits," and in Level 2, as "principles" (which are specific interpretation/action plan pairs). The entire system is modulated by temperament: The range of emotions and extremes of behavior are governed by a separate system, different from the one that sets the goals and works out strategies for achieving them.

The present perspective allows us not only to translate Freudian ideas into a cognitive neuroscience framework, but also to draw additional distinctions that eluded Freud. As an example, in the following section I consider his concept of repression—the unintentional "forgetting" of unpleasant memories and desires (which rests on forcing them into the unconscious, not actually discarding them). (Note that "suppression" is the intentional "forgetting" of unpleasant memories and desires—which does not seem as difficult to understand as repression.)

Five types of repression

Let us begin with two forms of repression that are closest to what Freud apparently had in mind. Both of these forms take place at Level 2, when constraints are interpreted. First, recall that, according to the present theory, when information arrives that does not fit any one interpretation particularly well, noise is added. In most situations, if a small amount of noise does not lead the ambiguity to be resolved, it is simply left hanging and one stores inconsistent information; people live with ambiguity all the time. However, in some cases it is very important to resolve the ambiguity. In such cases, the system continues to "shake the bucket" over an extended period of time. If enough noise is added for a long enough period, it will be impossible to modify the "weights" on connections in neural networks to store new information. This sort of process can produce a kind of "perceptual defense," preventing one from storing the new information.

Under what circumstances would this sort of repression occur? If one is looking at an apple or a tomato, such instability is quickly resolved by looking again and encoding additional information. But what if the interpretation of a fact is that "I am dishonest" but "I am honest" is an important part of one's self concept? The interpretation undermines one's self concept, and the survival axiom leads us to expect that the system will not take such revisions lightly. Interpreting the fact one way produces an output that is directly incompatible with another interpretation; this is a problem because both interpretations are likely to be activated by many of the same constraints (i.e., those pertaining to honesty), and so will be activated at the same time—which disequilibrates the system. Throwing in more noise will not solve the problem if the unpleasant interpretation is in fact a better fit to the data. Indeed, only the strong emotion associated with aspects of one's self concept allows such contradictory representations to hold their own, and not be swamped by the appropriate interpretation in the winner-take-all competition. This sort of process corresponds to the "callus" that Freud talked about, whereby the ego protects itself from unpleasant facts.

Second, another form of repression does not block information from being encoded, but rather blocks information that has been encoded from being recalled. Because the process of adding noise to settle a network takes time, in some situations information that would otherwise have been repressed during encoding is nevertheless stored. Specifically, if incoming information is important enough, it may be stored as a *flashbulb memory;* such memories apparently are encoded very quickly, in a form of one-shot learning (see Brown & Kulick, 1977). The degree of "importance" is presumably assigned during recognition itself, and a very high emotional salience results in the hippocampus's being "boosted" (via the amygdala) so that the interpretation of the input is stored very rapidly—so rapidly that the noise is added too late to disrupt the storage process.

As Freud conjectured, when the information is later activated, the same processes that typically protect one against threatening input during perception come to the fore, and now prevent one from remembering: In this case, noise is added if the interpretation is incompatible with an important feature of one's self-concept, and this noise prevents the information from being processed further.

Third, there is a far weaker kind of repression, which occurs at Level 3 (constraint seeking). At any one time, a person can seek only one specific type of constraint that will activate a specific type of interpretation. If an interpretation would activate an action plan that is likely to have unpleasant consequences, one may simply avoid seeking the information that activates that plan. Instead, one may seek information that will activate another action plan. For example, if one believes that returning a specific telephone call is apt to lead to an unpleasant conversation, one may be inclined to read the newspaper instead. One can put something out of one's mind by activating action plans that are incompatible with one that is likely to lead to unpleasant consequences.

Fourth, another kind of repression occurs when one engages in a behavior so much that it becomes "automatic," not requiring conscious monitoring (see chapter 7 of Kosslyn & Koenig, 1992). Once a behavior has become implemented in Level 1 processing, it is driven solely by stimulus input—and one may be entirely unaware of what one is doing. If one keeps engaging in an "annoying habit" (e.g., such as sucking one's lips) long enough, one can forget about it altogether. Changing habitual activity requires effort; the cortex must actively suppress "automatic" subcortical activity.

Finally, there is a type of repression that would occur if one engages in Level 4 processing—inventing new constraints. In this case, if the system is not in equilibrium because an interpretation is incompatible with important information in memory, one can rationalize or otherwise create new constraints that will bring stability. This is, of course, an example of "cognitive dissonance reduction." Much of psychotherapy may consist in unearthing the results of such processing, allowing one to disentangle information from the particular conceptual context (sets of interpretations) in which one has embedded it.

These conjectures seem consistent with many people's introspections and intuitions; but, more than that, they lead to testable predictions. I outline one such prediction in the final section of this chapter.

Further Directions and Implications

The present perspective has many implications for recasting Freud's theory in a cognitive neuroscience framework. I will touch on just a few of them briefly here.

Hydraulic processing?

Freud's theory rests on a hydraulic metaphor: Pressure builds up in the unconscious, which must be released one way or the other. This concept has permeated our language and is now part of our "common sense." But there is no evidence that it is correct, and it is at odds with the present view. Unlike Freud's theory, the present theory posits that one seeks constraints only when they are relevant. Although some interpretations may have low "thresholds" or have "loose constraints," and hence may be activated often, the unconscious is not dynamic; unresolved issues do not percolate, driving one to behave in specific ways. In my view, psychological "issues" center on interpretations that one hopes and wishes are not correct, on a conflict between the self concept and self characteristics. To the extent that input activates such conflicting information, the issue is "live;" to the extent that these representations are not activated, the issue would not affect one's thoughts or behavior. This is why people avoid certain situations.

Sex

Because of its biological importance, and importance to the preservation of aspects of one's self concept over time, issues about sex are very salient psychologically. Sex was of particular concern to people living in the Victorian age. In the Victorian age, interpreting one's behavior as sexual may have challenged core aspects of one's self concept. These days this happens less often; sex is only one of many possible issues people have. However, with the rise of AIDS, I would not be surprised if "morality" changes once again, and sex returns as a major issue for most people.

Catharsis

If the mind is not impelled by hydraulic pressure, then "getting it out" makes no sense. I distinguish between "getting it out" and "working it through." Catharsis is beneficial insofar as it helps one to invent new constraints, which resolve unstable patterns of activation.

Post-traumatic stress disorder

One of the most severe problems faced by Freud, with less than usual grace in his *Beyond the Pleasure Principle,* was what is now known as post-traumatic stress disorder (PTSD). When soldiers returned from World War I, they sometimes did not repress horrible things that happened to them but rather obsessed about them. According to the present theory, repression occurs only when events are interpreted in a way that is incompatible with a strongly held view, which typically is one that is intimately bound with one's self concept. The fact that an event is horrible is not enough to lead to repression; it must conflict with a stored interpretation that has high emotional salience, which prevents the interpretation of the input from inhibiting the stored interpretation. PTSD patients remember horrible events, which do not necessarily touch on their self concepts. These horrible events do not fit with one's beliefs and general conceptual framework, and hence when they are activated they lead to instability. Unlike conflicts with one's self concept, the information in memory is not strong enough to prevent the interpretation of events from "winning." Thus, it was not repressed in the first place, or when it is later recalled. And it is sufficiently strong emotionally that when any association begins to activate it, it overwhelms other representations and comes unbidden to consciousness (i.e., into short-term memory; see Kosslyn, 1992, for a discussion of the possible roots of the phenomenology of consciousness).

Unconscious wishes

The present approach leads me to suggest that there are two sorts of "unconscious wishes." First, "issues" are unfinished business, and when the relevant information is activated, one will seek additional constraints to stabilize processing; if this fails, one will invent such constraints. The behavior one engages in will be identical to that of "attempting to fulfill an unconscious wish"; but there is no wish, only incomplete constraint satisfaction when specific information is activated. Second, some repressed interpretations and action plans can be considered "unconscious wishes." Such representations govern behavior only if they are embedded in Level 1 ("automatic") processing. If repressed information is activated at Level 2, noise quickly obscures the information—rendering it uninterpretable and unable to govern behavior.

Regression

Regression occurs when one behaves in ways that were appropriate when one was younger, but are no longer appropriate. Such behavior can arise from two properties of the kind of system I describe. First, when noise is placed in computer simulations of neural networks, distinctions that are learned relatively late tend to become blurred. Thus, the network can use only highly overlearned, less fine-grained, input–output mapping functions. This observation leads us to expect that when an internal conflict arises, and noise is added, behavior will regress. Second, if the conflict is severe enough, behavior may be governed purely by Level 1 processing; these sorts of "automatic" responses are learned after much repetition and often may be learned earlier in life. Hence this sort of behavior will often appear to be a regression.

Moral behavior

In the *Ego and the Id* (page 17, Standard Edition), Freud quotes Groddeck as saying "We are lived." The ego is not in control, but is simply one part of a broader system, and other components may often be responsible for one's thoughts and behavior. From my perspective, most of one's behavior is a consequence of one's self characteristics, which determines how one interprets (via constraint-satisfaction processes) and responds to input (which depends on one's behavioral repertoire—i.e., set of action plans). The self concept is a special aspect of information in memory, which includes a model of "correct behavior." To the extent that one interposes one's self concept between an interpretation and an action plan, one can behave morally. That is, a dog does not deserve credit for "telling" us it is hot when its tongue is hanging out on a hot day; that's just part of being hot. Similarly, a child does not deserve credit for being "childlike"; that's part of being a child. In my view, one does not deserve credit for behaving morally if one is on automatic pilot (Level 1 processing) or if one is simply behaving along well-worn grooves (Level 2 and higher). To be moral, one must be deliberate; one must "take responsibility." This depends on interposing one's professed beliefs, in modulating behavior on the basis of what one thinks one *should* do—which is not necessarily what one wants to do based on constraint-satisfaction processes that are driven by the explanation urge and the survival axiom.

Conclusions

This project is undoubtedly premature. Most of the concepts that form the foundation of the present perspective will be foreign to clinicians and researchers interested in personality and psychopathology, and the use to which I am putting them will be uninteresting to most researchers who are familiar with neural network simulations and researchers in cognitive neuroscience. The present project may be doomed to fall into the cracks. But I have great confidence that this situation will change. As the conceptual and methodological tools alluded to in this brief sketch are further developed, they will surely intrude on all aspects of psychological theorizing.

One could justifiably ask whether it is worth pursuing this line of theorizing. Will we simply repeat the same mistakes made by Freud? I think not, for several reasons. First, I have begun to characterize a mechanism, and mechanisms leave observable "behavioral signatures." This version of the theory is testable. For example, consider the following prediction: Subjects take a bogus "personality test" and then see a set of statements that a computer purportedly generated to describe them; they are asked to decide whether each statement is correct. At the time they are making these decisions, skin conductance is measured, along with the time to make the decision. The subjects are later asked to remember as many of the statements as possible. According to the present view, items that required long times and that induced large skin conductance responses (SCRs) should be less likely to be remembered: These items were inconsistent with an important piece of information in memory (as evident by the long times and SCRs), and hence should be repressed. In contrast, items that required long times but did not evince SCRs should be remembered better; these items were subjected to "deeper" processing (see Craik & Lockhart, 1972), but were not in conflict with important stored information.

Second, each level of processing I have characterized is identified with specific neural systems. This opens a new way to study processing, using brain-scanning techniques such as positron emission tomography (PET). Such techniques will allow the theory to be testable in a way that Freud's theory is not.

Third, Freud modeled his science of "psycho-analysis" on the "hard" science of his day, and hence relied too much on the "coherence metric of truth." At that time, physicists had hundreds of years' worth of careful observations under their belts, and the goal was to formulate a theory that could fit all of the results together. Thus, physicists relied heavily on a coherence metric of truth. Freud apparently mimicked this approach: His goal was to formulate a theory that could fit together all of his clinical observations. But clinical observations are not hard data; they are colored by one's preconceptions and are not quantitatively precise. Moreover, there were relatively few such observations, which did not provide strong constraints on theorizing. Indeed, the plethora of spin-off theories (Jung's, Adler's, etc.) is a testament to how underconstraining the data were. The present approach relies on many different types of data, ranging from the neural, to the behavioral, to the clinical, and rests on hypothesis-driven empirical research. The goal is not simply to fit the facts, but to make predictions about new facts.

Fourth, Freud was imperialistic; he took all of psychology as fair game. The present goals are more modest. This approach may not help us to understand psychoses or disorders that arise because of neurotransmitter deficiencies. Rather, the present approach focuses on the functioning of the normal system.

In short, I predict that Freud will not remain in the shadows of academic psychology much longer; that he instead will be taken as grist for the mill of the next major development in cognitive neuroscience.

Acknowledgment

This chapter grew out of work conducted for the John D. and Catherine T. Mac-Arthur Foundation's "Mind/Body Network." I am grateful for their encouragement and support (in more ways than one) for high-risk interdisciplinary research.

Note

1. After writing this, I realized that a different kind of mechanism could produce the same results. This mechanism is involved in triggering a "fight or flight" response, one component of which is a neuromodulatory bath. This bath may lower thresholds in cortical systems to the point where noise is introduced. The details of this alternative story will be worked out elsewhere eventually.

References

Anderson, J. R. (1978). Arguments concerning representations for mental imagery. *Psychological Review, 85,* 249–277.

Amaral, D. G., Price, J. L., Pitkanen, A., & Carmichael, S. T. (1992). Anatomical organization of the primate amygdaloid complex. In J. P. Aggleton (Ed.), *The amygdala: Neurobiological aspects of emotion, memory, and mental dysfunction* (pp. 1–16). New York: Wiley-Liss.

Brown, R., & Kulick, J. (1977). Flashbulb memories. *Cognition, 5,* 73–99.

Brownell, H. H., Michelow, D., Powelson, J., & Gardner, H. (1983). Surprise but not coherence: Sensitivity to verbal humor in right hemisphere patients. *Brain and Language, 18,* 20–27.

Craik, F. I. M., & Lockhart, R. S. (1972). Levels of processing: A framework for memory research. *Journal of Verbal Learning and Verbal Behavior, 11,* 671–684.

DeYoe, E. A., & Van Essen, D. C. (1988). Concurrent processing streams in monkey visual cortex. *Trends in Neurosciences, 11,* 219–226.

Erdelyi, M. H. (1985). *Psychoanalysis: Freud's cognitive psychology.* New York: W. H. Freeman.

Everitt, B. J. (1990). Sexual motivation: A neural and behavioural analysis of the mechanisms underlying appetitive and copulatory responses of male rats. *Neuroscience Biobehavioral Review, 14,* 217–232.

Everitt, B. J., & Robbins, T. W. (1992). Amygdala–ventral striatal interactions and reward-related processes. In J. P. Aggleton (Ed.), *The amygdala: Neurobiological aspects of emotion, memory, and mental dysfunction* (pp. 401–429). New York: Wiley-Liss.

Feldman, J. A. (1985). Four frames suffice: A provisional model of vision and space. *Behavioral and Brain Sciences, 8,* 265–289.

Freud, S. (1895/1954). Project for a scientific psychology. In M. Bonaparte, A. Freud, & E. Kris (Eds.), *The origins of psycho-analysis: Letters to Wilhelm Fliess, drafts and notes: 1897–1902.* New York: Basic Books.

Gardner, H. (1985). *The mind's new science: A history of the cognitive revolution.* New York: Basic Books.

Goldman-Rakic, P. S. (1987). Circuitry of primate prefrontal cortex and regulation of behavior by representational knowledge. In F. Plum and V. B. Mountcastle (Eds.), *Handbook of physiology, Section 1: The nervous system; Volume 5: Higher functions of the brain* (pp. 373–417). Bethesda, Md.: American Physiological Society.

Goldman-Rakic, P. S. (1988). Topography of cognition: Parallel distributed networks in primate association cortex. *Annual Review of Neuroscience, 11,* 137–156.

Hinton, G. E., & Sejnowski, T. J. (1986). Learning and relearning in Boltzmann machines. In D. E. Rumelhart, & J. L. McClelland (Eds.), *Parallel distributed processing: Explorations in the microstructure of cognition. Volume 1: Foundations* (pp. 282–317). Cambridge, Mass.: MIT Press.

Kling, A. S., & Brothers, L. A. (1992). The amygdala and social behavior. In J. P. Aggleton (Ed.), *The amygdala: Neurobiological aspects of emotion, memory, and mental dysfunction* (pp. 353–378). New York: Wiley-Liss.

Kosslyn, S. M. (1992). Cognitive neuroscience and the human self. In A. Harrington (Ed.), *So human a brain* (pp. 37–56). Boston: Birkhauser.

Kosslyn, S. M. (1994). *Image and brain: The resolution of the imagery debate.* Cambridge, MA.: MIT Press.

Kosslyn, S. M., & Koenig, O. (1992). *Wet mind: The new cognitive neuroscience.* New York: Free Press.

LeDoux, L. E. (1987). Emotion. In F. Plum and V. B. Mountcastle (Eds.), *Handbook of physiology. Section 1: The nervous system; Volume 5: Higher functions of the brain* (pp. 419–460). Bethesda, Md.: American Physiological Society.

LeDoux, L. E. (1992). Emotion and the amygdala. In J. P. Aggleton, (Ed.), *The amygdala: Neurobiological aspects of emotion, memory, and mental dysfunction* (pp. 339–352). New York: Wiley-Liss.

Luria, A. R. (1980). *Higher cortical functions in man.* New York: Basic Books.

Mishkin, M., & Appenzeller, T. (1987). The anatomy of memory. *Scientific American, 256,* 80–89.

Mishkin, M., Malamut, B., & Bachevalier, J. (1984). Memories and habits: Two neural systems. In G. Lynch, J. L. McGaugh, & N. M. Weinberger (Eds.), *Neurobiology of learning and memory* (pp. 65–77). New York: Guilford Press.

Schacter, D. L. (1987). Implicit memory: History and current status. *Journal of Experimental Psychology: Learning, Memory, and Cognition, 13,* 501–518.

III

MEMORY, PERCEPTION, AND ECOLOGY

Chapters by Bennet Murdock, Robert Sternberg, Richard Gregory, and Michael Turvey and Robert Shaw are included in this part. Murdock restates the conventual wisdom in memory research and then makes extrapolations from that base to the future. Sternberg gives a fanciful impression of the "logical" continuation of original ideas by Miller and others, while Gregory's philosophic musings suggest a cosmic paradigm. The part closes with Turvey and Shaw's essay which calls for an ecological physics and a physical psychology.

8

Human Memory in the
Twenty-first Century

BENNET B. MURDOCK

Now that the nature of elementary particles and the basic framework of the genetic code have been worked out, the last, largely unexplored, scientific frontier is the nature of the human mind. Cognitive psychology is only one player in this game, but being a cognitive psychologist myself, I would like to think it takes a leading role. In general, cognitive psychologists are experimental psychologists whose domain of study is the higher mental processes—attention, perception, problem solving, thinking, and reasoning.

Memory, having a time-span ranging from seconds (or less) to decades, plays a central role in all of these processes. For example, how could we fixate our attention on something for any length of time unless we could remember what we were attending to? And, indeed, reasoning is the utilization of our store of knowledge, a knowledge that builds up over a lifetime and presupposes memory.

How does one study memory? Philosophers study memory by introspection and logic, psychoanalysts study memory by delving into the unconscious, and novelists write about memories using their own intuitions. Cognitive psychologists use scientific experimental methods. They do experiments, develop theories, and test models to explain their data. Let me dispose of three frequent objections to our approach. The first objection is this: How can you possibly hope to learn anything about human memory—it's so complex. That's what they said about the genetic code, but diligence and perspicacity paid off. Memory is certainly complex, and has many surprising aspects, but no one ever claimed that science is easy.

Second, there is so much variability from person to person, or within the same person from time to time, how can we hope to learn anything? The variability of memory doesn't preclude its understanding. If you toss ten coins and count the number of heads, all possible outcomes will occur if you make enough tosses. Probability theory provides a simple and complete description of the entire distribution of outcomes—a fact that has been known at least since the work of the Bernoulli's in the eighteenth century. Our understanding of memory may never be quite so precise, but probability theory plays an essential role in understanding the variability.

Third, how will you ever understand memory until you are able to open up the head and look inside? When we got our first laboratory computer (a PDP-12, well before PCs appeared on the market), I opened it up and looked inside. I knew at once that this was not the road to understanding. You could have inserted "electrodes" (probes) wherever you wanted and recorded its activity as long as you wanted, but I'm sure you never would have figured out how it worked. And the brain is surely orders of magnitude more complex.

To predict the future (which is the challenging goal of this collection of essays), we need to have some appreciation of the past. Let me, therefore, start with a very brief review of the first hundred years of memory research.

The First Hundred Years

How do we study memory? By using the standard scientific approach—collecting some reliable data, constructing a simple theory or model to explain it, collecting more data to test the model, revising the model in the event of unexpected findings, and so on, with the continuing interplay between theory and data. Unfortunately, in the memory area, theory development has lagged far behind data collection. We have more than enough experimental data, but still no generally accepted theoretical framework.

Let me give a simple example. One of the most robust findings in the study of human memory is the U-shaped serial position curve of serial recall. If you are given a short (e.g., 7 ± 2) list of items to recall, the curve that plots probability of correct serial recall as a function of serial position (ordinal list position of the item) will be an asymmetric U-shaped function showing considerable primacy (i.e., the beginning of the list is best recalled) and some recency (i.e., the end of the list is next best); the worst recall is for the item a bit past the middle.

These results were published by Nipher before the classic Ebbinghaus (1885/ 1964) monograph on memory (see Nipher, 1878, reprinted in Stigler, 1978). And we still have no completely satisfactory theory or model to explain these data. Nipher himself (who was a physicist) applied a simple binomial model for these data, the same type of probability model one would use for the coin tosses mentioned above. However, such a model is more descriptive than explanatory, and cognitive psychologists would like to know what mental processes underlie the "coin tosses."

Empirical research has been accumulating at an ever- increasing pace, and now, more than one hundred years later, we have a very sound and reliable data base for human memory. Although it may not be generally appreciated, we have accumulated a large number of empirical findings that should provide grist for a theoretical mill (e.g., see Crowder, 1976; or Murdock, 1974). In fact, a neurophysiologist once told me our data were much better than his.

To be more specific, we now have abundant evidence for different kinds of memory. We must distinguish at least three kinds of memory, and these depend on the types of information. There is item information, associative information, and serial- order information. Item information is occurrence information. Have we seen this person or heard this piece of music before? If so, we can say that he, she, or it is familiar. Associative information is the information necessary to associate or relate two "ideas"—anything from sense impressions to abstract concepts. Serial-order information is the information necessary to remember the order of occurrence of (three or more) items, objects, or events. Telephone numbers and the spelling of words are common examples.

The data on item, associative, and serial-order memory are quite different. Item information shows very slow and gradual forgetting over periods of at least a year (e.g., Nickerson, 1968), and there is no reason to think that it stops there. Much associative information is lost almost immediately ("What was the name of the person I just met?"). However, whatever survives a brief initial period tends to be quite stable, at least when memory is tested by associative recognition. Memory for serial- order information is quite different: Recall shows marked primacy (better performance on early list items) and little recency (better performance on late list items). Neither of these two effects is typical of item recognition or associative recall.

There is abundant experimental evidence on memory for these three different types of information (e.g., Murdock, 1974). In the last few years, two other topics have also become popular: priming and implicit memory. *Priming* of a written word refers to a facilitation of performance on some target item due to semantic relatedness *(semantic priming)* or visual relatedness *(episodic priming)* of a word presented earlier. If I show you the word "doctor" before I present the word "nurse," you will respond faster to the target item (nurse) than if it is preceded by some unrelated word; this is an example of semantic priming. On the other hand, if I show you "assassin" and later ask you to fill in the missing letters of the test item __s__a____n, you will do better on the task than if you had been presented with a neutral prime; this is episodic priming. (For a rather different example of priming, see McKoon & Ratcliff, 1980.)

Implicit memory (as opposed to explicit memory) takes place when priming occurs in a free-responding task. For instance, if I show you the word "Host" and later ask you to complete the fragment __ost with the first word that comes to mind, implicit memory ("remembrance without conscious recollection") would be illustrated if there were more "H" responses than other reasonable possibilities (e.g., "L," "M," "P"). It is sometimes even argued that experimental dissociations between explicit and implicit memory are evidence for different memory systems (e.g., Cooper & Schacter, 1992).

To understand the encoding, storage, and retrieval of item, associative, and serial-order information, as well as priming and implicit memory, we need theories or models that specify the underlying processes (or cognitive operations). As pointed out by McKoon, Ratcliff, and Dell (1986), the question is not how many memory systems there are, but how they work. This is why theories or models are so important. We now review briefly the theoretical developments that have occurred.

Theories and Models

Up until about 1960, the dominant theoretical position was interference theory, as formulated by McGeoch, Melton, Postman, and Underwood. In contrast to decay theory, interference theory claimed that the dominant cause of forgetting is interference, not disuse; "Iron rusts in time, but the cause is oxidation" (McGeoch, 1932). Similarity between the interfering and the to-be-remembered material was crucial, and interference could come from prior events ("proactive interference") and subsequent events ("retroactive interference"). It turned out that interference theory was not able to explain both proactive and retroactive interference with the same set of theoretical principles (Postman & Underwood, 1973), and with the advent of the information-processing approach (Broadbent, 1958), interference theory gradually fell into disuse.

The information-processing approach eschewed the stimulus–response emphasis of interference theory and concentrated instead on central processing mechanisms. Broadbent (1958) was perhaps the first to use flow charts to represent the dynamic processes of attention, perception, and memory. An example is shown in Figure 8.1. A decay theorist, he suggested that the limited memory-span capacity could be due to a combination of decay and a limited-capacity attentional mechanism. Performance in split-span task (simultaneous input on two distinct channels as in dichotic or dichoptic presentation) could reflect the switching of an attentional filter.

Information-processing notions were incorporated into the two-store models of Waugh and Norman (1965) and Atkinson and Shiffrin (1968). These models postulated two different memory stores: a transitory short-term (or "primary") memory and a more permanent long-term (or "secondary") memory. Data from free recall were used to illustrate the interplay between these two memories and to

Figure 8.1. Limited memory-span capacity due to a combination of decay and a limited-capacity attentional mechanism (from Broadbent, 1958).

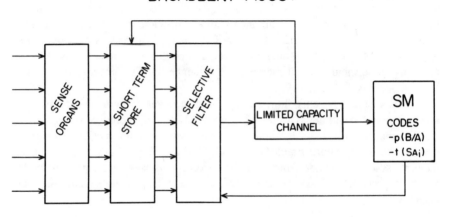

in support of these two-store models (e.g., Glanzer & Cunitz, 1966), but more powerful models are available today.

Two-store models focused on storage mechanisms and capacity limitations; the "levels of processing" approach (Craik & Lockhart, 1972) emphasized processing and showed how performance ("capacity") could be enhanced. Shallow processing, exemplified by rote rehearsal or attention to phonemic or orthographic properties of words, was contrasted with "deep" processing, where one attends to the meaning of words. Both recall and recognition are much better after deep processing than after shallow processing (Craik & Tulving, 1975).

Semantic-memory models (e.g., Anderson & Bower, 1973) were also popular in the 1970s. The semantic-memory models conceived of human memory as consisting of a large number of nodes where information (words, ideas, concepts) was stored with links or associations to connect them. An example is shown in Figure 8.2; such an approach can provide some insights into understanding the organization or structure of human memory. However, these models enjoyed only brief popularity; for one account of their rapid rise and fall, see Chang (1986).

Semantic-memory models postulate localized storage; each memory trace is stored in a different location. This "location" can be a small group of cells, a single neuron, or even lower- level events; this is unspecified. The problem is retrieval: How do you find information stored in memory? The search metaphor was accepted almost without question (Roediger, 1980), but a serial search through a memory store as vast as human memory seems a bit improbable.

The 1980s saw a dramatic change in the prevailing theoretical climate. Distributed-memory models appeared on the scene, and they provided a whole new perspective on human memory. Unlike node-and-link models, a specific item of information is not stored in a single location but dispersed over some large memory area. Furthermore, successive items of information are superimposed in this same area, so all information resides in a common memory store. A possible metaphor would be the wave action on the surface of a pond. You throw a number of different objects into the pond, and each object produces its own pattern of wave activity on the surface of the pond. These waves summate (superposition). The current wave action reflects the pattern resulting from all the objects to date. So, too, with human memory: The pattern of brain activity at any moment in time reflects, to varying degrees, all the events that have occurred in your lifetime.

This approach solves the retrieval problem. Where do you look to find something? You look at the waves on the surface of the pond; everything is mirrored there. But isn't it a hopeless babel of voices? How can you possibly preserve the identity of any one item or event when it is masked by countless others?

This is a matter of capacity. The capacity is not the size of the pond so much as the resolving power of our retrieval device. And, in general, there are three types of retrieval processes in human memory; the "three R's" are recognition, recall, and redintegration. *Recognition* involves a comparison process: Is the test item a member of a designated set (the objects in the pond, or the items in the list I have just shown you)? Or, in forced choice: Which of the several test items is a member of the designated set. *Recall* involves generation: You have to come up with the right answer. What was the third object thrown in, or what is the capital

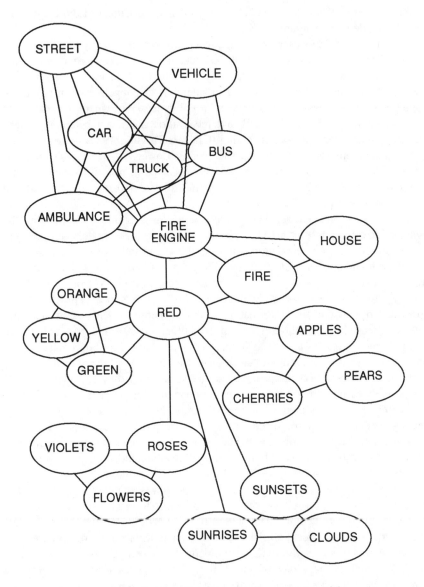

Figure 8.2. Example of a semantic-memory model.

of Australia? *Redintegration* also involves generation but with a partial cue. I show you a fragment of the object, and you tell me what it is. Or a note reminds you of a list of things to do.

How does capacity enter in? The greater the capacity of the system, the more we can recognize, recall, and redintegrate. To turn from the metaphor to an implementation of a distributed- memory system in a computer (which we can actually build or program, and test), assume we have a large array (or memory vector) which has N elements (or features). If each item or event is represented by an independent array or vector of N elements, then basically we can recognize with high accuracy N different items or events. As the number of items or events exceeds N, the system degrades (we start making mistakes), but the degradation (like human memory) is progressive or gradual, not sudden.

But, you protest, we have probably had millions of different experiences in our lifetime. Well, it is estimated that the brain has 10^{12} neurons and 10^{14} synapses, so this doesn't seem to be a problem. That is, the number of neurons or synapses could be N, so we have the capacity, the potential, to remember very many experiences. The system may be overloaded, but then our memory is not perfect.

Recognition is straightforward; we simply compare the probe item with the memory vector, assess its strength (familiarity), and make a decision. Of course, we need a comparison operation and a decision system (for detailed examples, see Murdock & Lamon, 1988, or Hockley & Murdock, 1987). What about recall and redintegration? Here we need an associative memory: *This* must be associated with *that* if *this* (i.e., the question or probe or cue) is to retrieve *that* (i.e., the answer or target). If we never learned that Canberra is the capital of Australia, the probe (what is the capital of Australia?) would not have much chance of making contact with the target.

There are various formalisms for an associative memory (e.g., Anderson, 1970; Murdock, 1979), but the capacity relation characterizes all of them. The greater the capacity of the memory, the more accurate the recall and redintegration. Recognition, recall, and redintegration can all go on in a distributed memory, but is the notion of a distributed memory really any more than a metaphor?

I would argue that it is. By now, there has been sufficient development of these ideas so that they qualify as bona fide scientific theories or models. They make quantitative predictions, are testable, and have been applied to a wide range of data (Murdock, 1993). As a very simple example, recognition accuracy should decrease as the length of the list increases, the presentation rate increases, or the lag (age) of the tested item increases. If one specifies the parameters of a recognition-memory model, it can predict what the magnitude of these effects should be.

A return to associationism is also worth noting. Associationism has been at the core of memory theorizing from philosophical works of the British associationists (Locke, Hume, Hartley, and the Mills; see Boring, 1929) through to interference theory. The role of associations in memory was downplayed with the popularity of information-processing models, organization, and levels. With distributed-memory models and connectionist (or neural network) models, associations return to center stage.

The Future

What will memory research be like in the future? Let me start with a very safe prediction: It will become more popular, and will attract the interest of specialists from many different disciplines. Why will it become more popular? As noted, the brain is probably the last scientific frontier, and scientific activity is driven by challenges. The data (at least some of the data) are rock solid, and this is an essential precondition for scientific investigation. And memory is important; it underlies all our cognitive processes.

Why will it attract the interest of many different types of specialists? Because they have special skills that could prove useful in understanding memory. Neurophysiologists have the necessary techniques and skills to investigate the biological basis of memory. Neuropsychologists have learned a lot about memory disorders, and the understanding of memory pathology may offer important clues to the understanding of normal memory. Physicists and mathematicians have quantitative skills and knowledge of physical systems that could (and some believe do) apply to biological systems. Last but not least, computer scientists (especially in artificial intelligence and computational modeling) have technical skills and simulation techniques that already are very important in developing and testing realistic models of human memory. (See Lewandowsky, 1993, for a readable account of computer simulation.)

Where does that leave experimental psychologists? Some people may think that leaves us out. Let me state emphatically that experimental psychologists studying memory are not playing in the sand box waiting for the "real" scientists (neurophysiologists?) to figure it all out. Neurophysiologists or neuroscientists can investigate in depth what is going on inside the skull, but as my PDP-12 computer example tried to show, they need some guidance as to what to look for. That's where we come in.

What we as experimental psychologists have to do is provide some guidelines, and that is why theorizing or modeling is so important. The first thing to do is figure out what the memory system is doing; then we can worry about how it does it. When we have theories or models that correctly predict the data, then we shall know we are on the right track. *How* the memory system does it is another matter, but the brain is probably clever enough to implement any operation or process our models require it to do. For example, in recognition–memory tests, the attention–likelihood theory of Glanzer (Glanzer, Adams, & Iverson, 1991) requires us to compute a likelihood ratio for two binomial distributions with different parameter values for the old and new-item distribution. Most of us probably couldn't do it with a pocket calculator and normal-curve tables, but if that explains the data (the regularities of recognition memory in particular), then it provides some useful clues as to how recognition memory might work.

Unfortunately, experimental psychologists are as divided on the big issues in memory as in other areas. As Julian Jaynes pointed out a number of years ago (Jaynes, 1966), physicists are all climbing the same mountain, and it is ever upward and onward. Psychologists, on the other hand, are like blind men staggering around in a dense jungle each crying, "Follow me."

Furthermore, experimental psychologists need a good press agent. To celebrate the decade of the brain, in September 1992 the *Scientific American* published a whole issue devoted to mind and brain. With one exception, experimental psychologists were conspicuous by their absence. When you see how completely the connectionists have taken the ball and run with it, it gives you pause for thought.

I'm afraid there is a real possibility experimental psychologists will be over-shadowed by other specialists and will play a subordinate role in memory research in the foreseeable future. Not only their divisiveness (as one critic put it, models are like toothbrushes—everyone should have one, but you would never dream of using someone else's; Watkins, 1990), but oftentimes we do Mickey-Mouse science. Recently, I was advised by one reviewer of a theoretical paper to leave out all the problematic issues for the model and deal only with what it could do. For a basic primer on the tenets of scientific research, I would strongly recommend the last chapter ("On Cargo-Cult Science") of Feynman (1986).

For the most part, however, we don't have the technical, mathematical, or computational skills of other specialists. Perhaps if we were in cognitive psychology departments, we wouldn't get so many students who flunked precalculus and want to help people. Our bread and butter is dealing with experimental data. We know how to design and conduct experiments, analyze results, spot confoundings and other problems, and (sometimes) how to interpret results. This is an essential part of the scientific enterprise, and in the area of memory, we can do it better than most.

One of the serious consequences of our data-driven approach is that the accumulation of data is so great that old data are forgotten and then are rediscovered and reported anew. My impression is that the current life-span of memory data is about ten years. If a study is not a classic, or if it does not get integrated into the current Zeitgeist, then in about ten years it will vanish from the scene only to be rediscovered in some young investigator's doctoral thesis. The wasted scientific effort is unfortunate.

The main reason this happens is that we do not have a generally accepted theoretical framework into which we can accommodate new findings. If we did, our tree of knowledge would grow and each little experimental finding that was theoretically relevant would end up in a terminal node somewhere. Archivists would continually update the documentations, and graduate students would be expected to master the data base before they embarked on original research. That way their "new" research would have a better chance of being original.

Actually, with the steady improvement of computer-based archives such as PSYCH-LIT, the situation may improve in the near future. The data base covered in these archives is continually expanding (though growing more in breadth than depth), and it is probably becoming more generally available. The problem, of course, is the retrieval cues. If you don't happen to put the right key words in your abstract, your article may not get the attention it deserves. Perhaps they will eventually put PSYCH-LIT on distributed-memory models or neural networks with context- sensitive retrieval.

The Turn of the Century

What will research in the memory area be like at the turn of the century? Probably very much the way it is today. We shall still have our current fads and fashions. Priming and implicit memory will be out, but something else will be in. As any chart of publication activity will show, topics come and go. The life-span of most topics is probably about ten years. The level of processing was in vogue from perhaps 1972 to 1982; semantic memory from perhaps 1975 to 1985; priming from perhaps 1985 to 1995, implicit memory from perhaps 1990 to 2000. I am not a historian of science, so these dates are very approximate.

Will the connectionist's bubble burst? A few years ago, a leading connectionist hazarded the guess that the enthusiasm would last another only year or two, unless there was a major breakthrough or technical development. There hasn't been one, at least to my knowledge, but I see no significant diminution of enthusiasm among the converts. My feeling is that the connectionist enterprise is much too strong and much too much a major scientific contribution to vanish overnight. They may not be the right models for human memory (McCloskey & Cohen, 1989; Ratcliff, 1990), but they are such an attractive approach for cognitive processes in general, they will certainly be alive and well at the start of the next century.

Will psychologists unite and use a common toothbrush? Not likely. Not only is it not hygienic, but I think experimental psychologists are of two types. One type (by far the larger) consists of the really out-and-out empiricists. They want to do experiments, and they don't care much about theories. Vulnerable to the criticism that their grant proposals and journal submissions are weak in theroetical relevance, they are forced at least to pay some attention to current theories and models. As the old adage (doesn't) say, you can lead experimental psychologists to the font of knowledge, but you can't make them drink (very much).

The other type consists of the committed theorists, who are very definitely the minority. They are interested in testing their theories with data, and collecting new data that are critical for the predictions of their theories. (For example, see Murdock & Kahana, 1993, for an analysis of the list-strength effect originally described in Ratcliff, Clark, & Shiffrin, 1990, and Shiffrin, Ratcliff, & Clark, 1990.) By and large, they are a contentious group not looking for compromise or synthesis. Again, it's the follow-me syndrome. Of course, theoretical psychologists are probably not unique in this regard. As a distinguished mathematician is reported to have said, "If I don't discover a major theorem, I'd rather it wasn't discovered" (Davis & Hersh, 1981).

Is the long-range solution to have both experimental psychologists and theoretical psychologists, just as we have experimental physicists and theoretical physicists? If so, this dichotomy is a long way off. And in both cases, I suspect this is more of a continuum or a matter of emphasis than a dichotomy. In both cases, experimentalists have to understand theory to do relevant experiments, and theorists have to know something about experiments to know what is testable.

The Far Future

What will the future look like well into the next century? Experimental psychology could merge with computer science, linguistics, neuropsychology, and perhaps even neurophysiology. When major departments change their name and call themselves "Department of Cognitive Science" or whatever, one suspects this might be a straw in the wind.

However, philosophy did not disappear when psychology took flight in the last century, and I doubt that experimental psychology will disappear when the cognitive scientists set up their own separate empires. Cognitive science in general is a burgeoning enterprise right now, and there is more than enough room for both. Consequently, I would not forecast the demise of experimental cognitive psychology, though what it will be called I would not venture to guess. Some fractionation will certainly occur. We have gone from one professional organization (American Psychological Association) to two (Psychonomics) to three (American Psychological Society) in a few decades, and I doubt that the trend will stop here.

For example, cognitive psychologists in Canada now seem to be marching under the banner of BBCS (the Canadian Society for Brain, Behavior, and Cognitive Science), and according to their recent newsletter, "BBCS . . . has become recognized as the main voice for experimental psychology and behavioral neuroscience in this country." Can't experimental psychologists speak for themselves? Physicists today can proudly look back on their history and identify themselves with Galileo, Newton, Faraday, Einstein, Schroedinger, and Heisenberg. Can anyone imagine physicists calling themselves SNIPs (Spin Nuclear Investigators of Particles)?

Apart from our identity crisis, what else might characterize our activities then? I think that the main change is that we will be much more sophisticated both experimentally and theoretically. Not only will our experimental techniques become more powerful, but our theories and models will grow and develop too. And perhaps it is not too optimistic to hope that theory and data will be more tightly related. Experiments will be closely tied to theory, and, in one way or another, discrepant findings will be assimilated and explained by the extant theories.

Perhaps by then cognitive psychologists will realize that 2×2 contingency tables and mean reaction times are not going to tell us very much about how the mind works. Experimental dissociations, the bread and butter of our current field, are theoretically vacuous even now as single-system models can explain them as well as multi-system models (Murdock, 1989). Mean reaction times, too, can be quite uninformative. This has been known for a long time (Woodworth, 1938; Ratcliff & Murdock, 1976), but progress along these lines has been slow (though see Mewhort, Braun, & Heathcote, 1992). Maybe the pace will accelerate in the next century.

By the next century, distributed-memory models of one sort or another (formal mathematical models, computer-simulation models, or connectionist models) will have succeeded where interference theory failed: to "achieve an unquestioned superiority as the only significant analysis of forgetting" (Postman, 1961). They have too much face validity to think otherwise. They are large- capacity systems, they allow superposition, they are direct- access systems so there is no search process, and they are biologically realizable in slow-acting neural networks. Some of them (e.g., the linear associator model of Anderson, 1970, or the convolution–correlation model of Murdock, 1979) are even mathematically tractable since they are simple linear models. There are problems with the current models, but there are already significant accomplishments (Raaijmakers & Shiffrin, 1992). Given the progress that has been made in the past 10 to 15 years, it is reasonable to assume that eventually the major problems will be solved and we shall be into a cleaning-up phase. Perhaps gradually in the next century, the last scientific frontier will disappear, and we shall be able to settle down to a period where we consolidate our gains.

Acknowledgments

Preparation of this paper was supported by NSERC Grant APA146 from the Natural Sciences and Engineering Research Council of Canada. I would like to thank Michael Kahana for many useful comments.

References

Anderson, J. A. (1970). Two models for memory organization using intracting traces. *Mathematical Biosciences, 8,* 137–160.

Anderson, J. R., and Bower, G. H. (1973). *Human Associative Memory.* Washington, D.C.: Winston.

Atkinson, R. C., & Shiffrin, R. M. (1968). Human memory: A proposed system and its control processes. In K.W. Spence and J. T. Spence (Eds.), *The psychology of learning and motivation: Advances in research and theory* (Vol. 2, pp. 89–195). New York: Academic Press.

Boring, E. G. (1929/1950). *A history of experimental psychology.* New York: Appleton-Century-Crofts.

Broadbent, D. E. (1958). *Perception and communication.* New York: Pergamon Press.

Chang, T. M. (1986). Semantic memory: Facts and models. *Psychological Bulletin, 99,* 199–220.

Cooper, L. A., & Schacter, D. L. (1992). Dissociations between structural and episodic representations of visual objects. *Current Direction in Psychological Science, 1,* 141–146.

Craik, F. I. M., & Lockhart, R. S. (1972). Levels of processing: A framework for memory research. *Journal of Verbal Learning and Verbal Behavior, 11,* 671–684.

Craik, F. I. M., & Tulving, E. (1975). Depth of processing and the retention of words in episodic memory. *Journal of Experimental Psychology: General, 104,* 268–294.

Crowder, R. G. (1976). *Principles of learning and memory.* Hillsdale, NJ: Lawrence Erlbaum Associates.

Davis, P. J., & Hersh, R. (1981). *The mathematical experience.* Boston: Houghton Mifflin.

Ebbinghaus, H. (1885). *Über das Gedächtnis* (H. A. Ruger & C. E. Bussenius, Eds., and trans.). New York: Dover, 1964.

Feynman, R. P. (1986). *Surely you're joking, Mr. Feynman!* New York: Bantam Books.

Glanzer, M., Adams, J. K., & Iverson, G. (1991). Forgetting and the mirror effect in recognition memory: Concentering of underlying distributions. *Journal of Experimental Psychology: Learning, Memory, and Cognition, 17,* 81–93.

Glanzer, M., & Cunitz, A. R. (1966). Two storage mechanisms in free recall. *Journal of Verbal Learning and Verbal Behavior, 5,* 351–360.

Hockley, W. E., & Murdock, B. B. (1987). A decision model for accuracy and response latency in recognition memory. *Psychological Review, 94,* 341–358.

Jaynes, J. (1966). The routes of science. *American Scientist, 54,* 94–102.

Lewandowsky, S. (1993). The rewards and hazards of computer simulation. *Psychological Science, 4,* 236–243.

McCloskey, M., & Cohen, N. J. (1989). Catastrophic interference in connectionist networks: The sequential learning problem. In G.H. Bower (Ed.), *The psychology of learning and motivation: Advances in research and theory* (Vol. 24, pp. 109–165). New York: Academic Press.

McGeoch, J. A. (1932). Forgetting and the law of disuse. *Psychological Review, 39,* 352–370.

McKoon, G., Ratcliff, R. (1980). Priming in item recognition: The organization of propositions in memory for text. *Journal of Verbal Learning and Verbal Behavior, 19,* 369–386.

McKoon, G., Ratcliff, R., & Dell, G. S. (1986). A critical evaluation of the semantic–episodic distinction. *Journal of Experimental Psychology: Learning, Memory, and Cognition, 12,* 295–306.

Mewhort, D. J. K., Braun, J. G., & Heathcote, Andrew. (1992). Response time distributions and the Stroop task: A test of the Cohen, Dunbar, and McClelland (1990) model. *Journal of Experimental Psychology: Human Perception and Performance, 18,* 872–882.

Murdock, B. B. (1974). *Human memory: Theory and data.* Potomac, MD: Erlbaum.

Murdock, B. B. (1979). Convolution and correlation in perception and memory. In L. G. Nilsson (Ed.), *Perspectives in memory research: Essays in honor of Uppsala University's 500th Anniversary* (pp. 105–119). Hillsdale, N.J.: Erlbaum.

Murdock, B. B. (1989). The past, the present, and the future: Comments on Section 1. In H. L. Roediger & F. I. M. Craik (Eds.), *Varieties of memory and consciousness; Essays in honor of Endel Tulving* (pp. 93–98). Hillsdale, N.J.: Erlbaum.

Murdock, B. B. (1993). TODAM2: A model for the storage and retrieval of item, associative, and serial-order information. *Psychological Review, 100,* 183–203.

Murdock, B. B., & Kahana, M. J. (1993). An analysis of the list–strength effect. *Journal of Experimental Psychology: Learning, Memory, and Cognition.*

Murdock, B. B., & Lamon, M. (1988). The replacement effect: Repeating some items while replacing others. *Memory and Cognition, 16,* 91–101.

Nickerson, R. S. (1968). A note on long-term recognition memory for pictorial material. *Psychonomic Science, 11,* 58.

Nipher, F. E. (1878). On the distribution of errors in numbers written from memory. *Transactions of the Academy of Science of St. Louis, 3,* ccx–ccxi.

Postman, L. (1961). The present status of interference theory. In C. N. Cofer (Ed.), Verbal learning and verbal behavior (pp. 152–179). New York: McGraw-Hill.

Postman, L., & Underwood, B. J. (1973). Critical issues in interference theory. *Memory & Cognition, 1,* 19–40.

Raaijmakers, J. G. W., & Shiffrin, R. M. (1992). Models for recall and recognition. *Annual Review of Psychology, 43,* 205–234.

Ratcliff, R. (1990). Connectionist models of recognition memory: Constraints imposed by learning and retention functions. *Psychological Review, 97,* 285–308.

Ratcliff, R., Clark, S. E., & Shiffrin, R. M. (1990). The list-strength effect: I. Data and discussion. *Journal of Experimental Psychology: Learning, Memory, and Cognition, 16,* 163–178.

Ratcliff, R., & Murdock, B. B. (1976). Retrieval processes in recognition memory. *Psychological Review, 83,* 190–214.

Roediger, H. L., III. (1980). Memory metaphors in cognitive psychology. *Memory & Cognition, 8,* 231–246.

Shiffrin, R. M., Ratcliff, R., & Clark, S. (1990). The list–strength effect: II. Theoretical mechanisms. *Journal of Experimental Psychology: Learning, Memory, and Cognition, 16,* 179–195.

Stigler, S. M. (1978). Some forgotten work on memory. *Journal of Experimental Psychology: Human Learning and Memory, 4,* 1–4.

Watkins, M. J. (1990). Mediationism and the obfuscation of memory. *American Psychologist, 45,* 328–335.

Waugh, N. C., & Norman, D. A. (1965). Primary memory. Psychological Review, 89–104.

Woodworth, R. S. (1938). *Experimental Psychology.* New York: Holt.

9

The Miller's Tale: A Speculative Glimpse into the Cognitive Psychology of the Future

ROBERT J. STERNBERG

Gordon H. Miller wiped the sweat from his forehead, but to no avail; it reappeared instantly. He cursed himself for having proposed this trip. He hadn't anticipated three-hour waits in sweltering airports. If only the air conditioning worked! If only the world could get the ozone layer back! There were a lot of "if onlys" these days in the 2040s. But Miller knew what an honor it was, or supposedly was, to be the first scientist in the Disunited States granted money and approval to cross regional borders in decades.

The breakup of the USSR in the 1990s—leading to the Soviet Disunion—had been by almost any standard too successful. After the initial economic struggle, the new countries had thrived, showing that they didn't need a massive federal government with its hungry tax collectors and bloated bureaucracies.

The former Soviet republics also provided inspiration to politicians worldwide. Smelling blood, everyone wanted to jump onto the disunion bandwagon, and Americans were no exception. Perennial losers smelled victory at last. No one had expected Massachusetts to be the first to secede from the United States, but the Dukakis–Tsongas team had convinced them. No longer would they be the only state to have voted for McGovern, or the state with the worst bond rating in the country. As of the year 2000, they became their own country, the only independent nation-state in the world with Greek as its official language—outside Greece, of course. New Hampshire, always ready to "live free or die," quickly followed in 2003 with Harold Stassen III at the helm—his first victory since the civil lawsuit against a pet-owner who failed to use a pooper-scooper when his dog had soiled Stassen's pristine lawn. In the next ten years, more and more states left the union, some banding together to form new conglomerates. Texas, which had always thought it was a country unto itself in any case, seceded just two weeks after the governing Manifest Destiny Party annexed Oklahoma. By 2015, Californregon, Nor-Sou Dakota, Micheconsin—almost the whole bunch—had followed suit. Only New Mexico blazed its own trail, hooking up instead with Mexico, which most people had always thought it belonged to anyway. Once the American Disunion had occurred, nearly all forms of communication between the former states, now nations of sorts, broke down almost completely.

Now Gordon Miller, funded by the National Institutes of Mental Wealth (there was still a token disfederal government in Washing Town, staffed by the descendants of the old House and Senate members), was taking an expedition. He wanted to find out what psychologists across the Disunion had done in the three decades since they had last had any communication. Miller was a professor of cognitive psychology at Princeford University, whose motto was "We Treat Each Student Like a Prince." (Actually, all psychologists at Princeford had the name "Gordon H. Miller," for obscure historical reasons.) Despite the heat, he really was excited to start his exploration of the state of cognitive psychology, and he eagerly awaited his departure for Carnal Watermelon University in Pittstop.

Pittstop

Miller was met at the Pittstop airport by a Carnal Watermelon delegation, which greeted him with the customary shower of watermelon pits. The welcome was less than warm, though the seeds had been preheated. No, there was something almost mechanical about the greeting. Then Miller realized that he had been welcomed by robots, mechanical creatures! He felt oddly as though he were a pawn in a chess game. The robots escorted him in a robocar to the university, where they were met by robocops who ushered them to the robodepartment. By now Miller had an idea of what to expect, and he was not disappointed.

"We have computerized robots here who are programmed to perform any function cognitive psychologists have ever wanted to understand," said Complex Simon, chair of the department. He was also a human being. "Our robots can think, remember, perceive, even spit out watermelon pits."

"What's the theory of thinking that drives their thought processes?" asked Miller, impressed in spite of himself.

"That's easy," answered Simon. "I've a printout of the program right here." Simon handed Miller 150 pages of program code.

"So what's the theory?" repeated Miller.

"The program is the theory," replied Simon.

"But what's the view of thinking underlying the program?" asked Miller.

"A detailed view," replied Simon, "a very detailed view. We're not like those psychologists who can't specify their claims operationally. Every theory here is sufficient to generate a running program. Our theories work—literally."

"How do you know which elements of the theory are really claims about humans and which simply make the program run?"

"Who cares?" Simon said. "What's important is that the programs simulate human performance."

"How do you know they do things the way humans do?"

"Is this some kind of an ACT or what? We have extensive data from college students doing the Tower of Ho Ho Ho Chi Minh City."

"Don't get SOAR. I just don't see how the types of simulations you do tell us whether humans really use the same processes."

Simon was obviously annoyed. "You seem to be missing the point. Our programs can do anything anyone can do. Our programs can even rediscover what has been discovered by the most creative scientists in history."

"Can they discover anything new?"

"Not so far. But have *you* discovered anything new lately?"

"Don't get personal," Miller said. "I was just asking. I was concerned that you might be begging the question of creativity by essentially inserting the creative part into the input. You seem to view creativity as ordinary problem solving, but maybe that's because the programs just do ordinary problem solving."

"I take it back," said Simon. "You have created something recently—hard feelings. I'm very busy. Good day."

Miller moved on to the next Carnal Watermelon lab, where he was met by three psychologists. "Welcome to the connectionist lab," all three said in unison.

Miller knew about connectionism. It had once been the wave of the future, but it had begun to go out of favor when respected scientists were discovered to be spending all their time trying too hard to make connections. Desperate to make their computer programs work, they had tampered with so many parameters that the programs could simulate anything, which ultimately became the problem. The programs were so powerful that no one could show any of them to be wrong.

"You're dealing with massively parallel systems, I suppose," began Miller.

"Yes," the three psychologists said together.

"I used to read about these systems in graduate school. My impression was that they modeled basic cognitive processes quite well, but didn't do as well with the higher processes."

"That *was* true," they said, in unison.

"Ah, I see. How did you solve it?" asked Miller.

"We view all processes as perceptual processes here," they replied.

"How did that solve the problem?" asked Miller.

"What problem?" they responded, altogether confused.

"The problem of modeling higher cognitive processes."

"Higher than what? All processes reduce to perceptual ones, and our models can handle these well, well." (The latter "well" was from one of the three psychologists, who missed a beat and didn't reply as well as the others did.)

Miller was feeling discouraged, but gave it one more try. "I'm really impressed by this software," he began, and then realized he was almost shrieking in frustration. Calming himself, he added, "Do you ever test human subjects anymore?"

"There's n-no longer any n-need t-to-oo-ooo," was the somewhat garbled response.

The three were definitely out of sync now, and it was showing. Miller decided it was time to depart. "This has been an unparalleled opportunity to observe first-hand what you're doing here. Thank you!"

"Y-our-ur'e w-welc-come," they called asychronously as Miller rushed out.

Miller spent the rest of the day climbing up several of the seven hills of Pitts-top, and then hopped on a commuter plane to his next destination, Philacream-cheese.

Philacreamcheese

Philacreamcheese was the home of a department that had been quite highly es-teemed in the days before the Disunion. Miller was eager to meet the faculty, who had been considered a thoughtful group of academics.

"Hello, and congratulations on the opportunity to visit our distinguished de-partment," said a man in academic garb, waiting for him in the airline terminal. Obviously, people here had a sense of humor. Miller squinted to read the name tag on his flowing robe. It said, "Philosopher King." Yes, people here definitely had a sense of humor.

"Thank you," Miller replied, shaking hands. "I'm Gordon Miller, of Prince-ford University."

"Cup of coffee?"

"I think not."

"Then you are not," replied the Philosopher King.

"I beg your pardon," stammered a startled Miller.

"Oh, a Cartesian allusion," said the Philosopher King loftily. "I wouldn't have expected you to pick it up. Just a little inside joke."

"Uh . . . yeah. Well, I'm interested in learning about the kinds of research being done at your university," said Miller, as they walked to the baggage claim.

"Kinds of what?" asked the Philosopher King.

"Research."

"Really, if you mean bringing people into a lab and asking them questions—no one here has done that for years. We're thinkers here," chuckled the Philoso-pher King. He led Miller out into the airport parking lot.

"Oh, I see. How do you learn about human behavior without actually observ-ing it?"

"We use rational deductive analysis—one learns much more through deep, penetrating logical analysis than through mindless empirical studies. Indeed, no one's done a worthwhile empirical study in decades."

"How do you know that," asked Miller, "when there's been essentially no communication among psychologists for decades?"

"We reasoned it out. It's just a matter of rational analysis. There are no empir-ical studies worth doing. Here's my car. Would you like to put your bag in the trunk?"

"Wait a minute. How can you figure by rational analysis whether there are empirical studies worth doing?" Miller held on firmly to his briefcase and travel bag.

"Can't you?" asked the Philosopher King.

"Not really," said Miller.

"We have some openings in our graduate and postgraduate programs if you'd care to apply for one."

"Uh, I think not."

"Which brings us back to where we started. You don't really exist. *Non cogitas, ergo non est.* Q. E. D." The Philosopher King chuckled self-satisfiedly to himself.

Miller decided that this conversation wasn't much to his liking. In fact, there was no point even in getting in the car with this man to see the university. Checking his watch, he made a run for it; at the ticket desk he changed his booking to get on the next flight to Taxachusetts.

Taxachusetts

The flight to Taxachusetts was brief, and the airport was not far from the university, where Miller was met by a welcoming committee. They looked very much like any other psychologists, except for their noticeably large heads.

"Welcome, welcome," one of them said. "We think you'll be quite impressed with what you see when you visit our university, the Haardvark Institute of Technology." (Once there had been two separate universities, but they had combined when they discovered that they could save on regional taxes, the highest in the Disunion.)

"At the HIT, our approach is purely biological," continued another psychologist. "We long ago realized that all mental phenomena are reducible to biological phenomena. The old cognitive models were really a cloak for our ignorance."

"That's very impressive," said Miller, who himself was sympathetic to this approach.

"Yes, it is," said the HIT psychologist, her forehead bulging slightly. "For example, we can tell you quite precisely where each cognitive function occurs in the brain."

"Suppose, then, I want to understand how children acquire language. Can you tell me that?"

"Absolutely. We can show you every neural pathway, every language center of the brain."

"Pardon me, but I was referring to *how* they acquire language," Miller attempted to clarify.

"I just told you, we can show you . . ."

"I see. Well, suppose I want to know the role of the mother in language acquisition."

"We can show you exactly what parts of the brain are activated when the mother talks to the young child."

"And suppose I want to know why people often make and then follow through on decisions based on faulty information?" Like coming here, Miller thought to himself.

"We have identified exactly the areas of the brain where both good and bad decision-making occur."

Miller wasn't getting answers that addressed the issues he was interested in. But he wasn't stupid; he was beginning to get the idea.

"And if I want to know why I'm in a bad mood right now?"

"We can show you where that's happening too," replied the psychologist. Miller wasn't really listening any more, though. He could have sworn that the bulges in her head were actually shifting around as she answered each of his questions. He became fascinated with the undulating movement . . . but then he realized he was staring.

"Uh . . . sorry. I suppose you have some kind of biological test of intelligence."

"Yes," she said, unperturbed, "that we have too. We know exactly which evoked potentials to measure."

"Can people improve their intelligence?"

"Sure, we're not determinists. And when people improve their intellectual skills, the improvement shows up as a change in the pattern of evoked potentials."

"You're saying the EPs change as a result of the increase in mental skills?" Miller asked incredulously.

"Right."

"But, then, what's the cause and what's the effect?"

"Biology is always the cause, and behavior is the effect. That is our motto here at HIT."

"But you said . . ."

"Yes, I understand. But the improvements themselves are biological. They have to be."

Was it cat and mouse? Or chicken and egg? Miller didn't care anymore. He excused himself from the group, pleading a splitting headache.

"We can show you exactly where in the head. . . ."

But it was too late. Miller had escaped to find his hotel. Once in his room, he took two aspirin and fell sleep. He dreamed he was an explorer, trying to find his headache so he could annihilate it. When he reached his headache, it was waiting for him, holding a sword. The headache challenged him to a duel. Miller started to accept the challenge, but then remembered that he didn't have a sword, so instead he took out a gun and shot the headache right between the eyes.

When he woke up, the headache was gone. So was his wallet. Someone had subsidized his tax payment at Miller's expense. He needed a new credit card, fast. He called Ex-American Ex-express.

"If you would like to obtain a credit card, have brown eyes, and weigh over 173 pounds, press '1' now," a voice chimed. "If you have lost your credit card, have green hair, and love the Red Sox, press '2' now. If . . . ." The recording was giving him another headache, and he hung up. Obviously, Ex-American Ex-express had not hired any human-factors types. And then he had a thought. Maybe they had. They had known exactly how to get him off the phone quickly and effectively. Hmm. . . .

Checking to make sure his head wasn't bulging, he packed so he'd be ready to leave for Georgeous in the morning. Then he went back to sleep for the rest of the night.

Georgeous

Early the next day, Miller departed for the long lost city of Atlantis, Georgeous, where a group of once well-reputed psychologists lived. They had long had an abrasive habit of calling themselves the "Emery Board," for reasons that were not entirely clear. Still, well-informed sources said that you couldn't meet a Neisser group of people.

"Greetings!" Miller exclaimed to the pleasant group of psychologists who awaited him at the Emery Board offices. The walls of the offices were huge glass windows looking out on the surroundings. The noonday sun was streaming in. "I'm glad to be here, and I hope I'll have a chance to visit your psychology labs."

"Labs? Did you say labs? Why would we want labs? What can you learn in labs? When we do research, we do it naturally, in the real world!" One woman spoke for the others, while they pointed out the windows to emphasize her point.

"Ah, very interesting," Miller said. "Is it very hard to control variables?"

"Is the Pope Catholic? Of course it is, but we want to understand the role of context," she said.

"And what do you see that role as?" Miller asked.

"How you think and behave depend largely upon the context you're in."

"Are you saying that you can't make any generalizations across contexts?" queried Miller.

"Of course you can," the psychologist replied. "Context affects what you do without regard to which context you're talking about."

"And which context *are* we talking about?" Miller demanded.

"All contexts."

"So behavior is dependent on context—that I understand. But, then, how do you go beyond that?"

"Beyond what?" the Emery Board psychologist asked.

"The statement that context matters."

"You say how it matters in each instance."

"Which is?"

"Depends on the instance," she gently reminded him.

"So what general principles have emerged from this work?" Miller kept at it.

"That behavior is always dependent upon the context in which it takes place, for one."

"And for another?" Miller asked.

"That each context is capable of affecting behavior in its own way."

"Well, thank you. Perhaps now I could talk to one of your colleagues?"

"Sure," said the psychologist, opening a door into another office. "Here's Professor Dom Spec."

"I'm Gordon Miller. How do you do? And you study . . . ?" asked Miller.

"Domain specificity," replied Dom Spec.

"Let me guess. You've found that human behavior is completely domain-specific."

"That's right. How did you guess?"

"And you can't generalize across domains because each domain has its own set of behaviors," Miller continued.

"Exactly."

"So the domain is like what I just heard about context."

"Well, it depends on the domain. . . ."

"And there are no general principles?"

"Not true at all," said Dom Spec. "It's generally true that behavior depends upon the domain."

Perhaps the Atlantis midday sun had been too much for Miller. He felt oddly hot under the collar. He feared he wasn't communicating successfully with his Disunion colleagues so far on this trip, and he said as much.

Sympathetically, Dom Spec advised, "I suspect that it will depend on which nation-state you visit. Each is its own domain, and . . ."

Miller excused himself and left. After checking into his hotel, he changed his clothes for a swim in the pool. His goal was to forget the morning's conversation, which was easy, because now he was in a new context.

Maybe this trip wasn't worth the hassle. Psychology had always swung in pendulum shifts from one extreme to another without finding the middle ground. In the years of Union, the corrective for this problem had been communication. When departments had been in contact with one another, they had been forced to resolve their differences, clarify their positions, and answer tough questions. But without interdepartmental communication, Disunion academic departments had been free to pursue their own courses; in many cases, apparently, to the point of absurdity. Years of isolation had made them blind to their extremism, not to mention their shortcomings.

Miller sighed. He'd try a few more of the departments scheduled for the trip, but if things didn't improve, he'd call it quits. The next scheduled stop was Bandway. His plane left the next morning.

Bandway

The folks from Bandway picked him up at the airport. They arrived in a ridiculous-looking vehicle that must have been two hundred years old. It looked like something out of a history book.

"Greetings," said the driver. "I'm Professor Tagalong."

"Hello," said Miller. "That's a strange vehicle you've got there. What's it called?"

"Oh, this," Tagalong replied. "This is a bandwagon. It's a bit old, huh? In fact, it's as old as psychology itself. It's our symbol here in Bandway. Go ahead and take one of these postcards. It has a picture of a bandwagon on it."

Miller shoved it in his pocket and jumped on the bandwagon for a ride to the university. Bandway University was impressive, as were the facilities in the psychology department. Obviously, one could do just about any experiment here. Miller thought it odd, however, that no one was using any of the labs, despite the fact that it was midday on a Wednesday. And as he looked more closely, he noticed a thick layer of dust over the equipment, suggesting either that it was never cleaned, or, worse, that it was never used. He asked Tagalong about this as delicately as he could.

"I notice that your cleaning staff doesn't keep your equipment clean. What gives?"

"I wish that were it," Tagalong said. "To be honest, most of this equipment has never been used."

"Might I ask why not?"

"It's very simple, really," he said. "Since the Disunion we haven't really known what other people are doing."

"So?" Miller asked.

"It's hard to jump on a bandwagon if you don't know where it is. The only bandwagon we've been able to locate is the one you took to come here, and it's old, old, old. We're looking for something a bit fresher, which is why we're so glad you're here. What do *you* study? Can you use some help?"

"Why not just study what *you* want to study?"

"Really, that wouldn't do much good. Who would then jump on *our* bandwagon?"

This stop also seemed to be leading nowhere. Miller thanked his hosts and dejectedly prepared himself for the West Coast leg of his voyage, a visit to Californregon.

Californregon

The flight to the West Coast was a long one, especially because the plane had to land in many of the former states to clear customs and win approval to use their air space. Finally, however, they landed in Californregon.

At the airport, Miller was met by a husky young scientist who held up a sign with Miller's name on it. Once Miller identified himself, the young scientist bowed and introduced himself in a take-charge manner as Gorgan Flower from Stanyota University. History books said that the university had once had a different name, but then Toyota Motor Company bought it at a distress sale caused by the former federal government's lowering of grant overhead costs to 3 percent. At that point, Toyota didn't want even a hint of association with the old name, not to mention the Ford Motor Company.

They rode in a shuttle jeep to the university. It was a bouncy, noisy trip that precluded conversation. Nonetheless, there was lots to look at. Routes 101 and 280 had both been closed as a result of earthquake damage, and now people just fended for themselves on the bumpy terrain. The one thing every vehicle seemed to have was four-wheel drive. People got around; that much was obvious. But where Miller was going he could not decipher, given that all the signs were in Japanese.

When they arrived, they were escorted into Jordan Hall. A portrait of one of the kings of Jordan hung on the wall. It didn't much matter which—they were all named Hussein, and all looked alike to Gordon Miller.

At that point, the scientist who had accompanied Miller to the university turned to him and boomed, "Welcome to Stanyota, Professor Miller."

"Thank you. I'm very interested in what you're doing at Stanyota," replied Miller, "especially given your history of being the best psychology department in the old United States."

"Right you are, young man." This was a strange comment, since Gordon Miller was the oldest man present. "We continue to be at the forefront—at the cutting edge of the field."

"What are the main research programs here?" asked Miller.

"Yes, yes. To be honest, we're constantly researching how to keep ahead of the competition. You don't stay Number One by sitting on your butt."

"But what, exactly, are you studying?" persisted Miller.

"If we told you that, you could do what we're doing, and then we wouldn't be at the front of the pack, would we? Does Macy's tell Gimbel's?" laughed the professor heartily.

"But those are ancient department stores, and both went bankrupt ages ago."

"Exactly my point. They went bankrupt because everyone knew what they were doing and then figured out how to do it better."

Miller was frustrated. He'd traveled awfully far to be told that the research here was a trade secret.

The Stanyota professor took pity on him. "All right, I'll give you a hint. Plastics."

"What do plastics have to do with anything?"

"If I told you that . . ."

"Okay, forget it. Thanks a lot for your time."

And with that, Miller sauntered off to his nearby hotel, The Quake Walk, to make some notes. That afternoon, Flower called to invite him to a university sporting event called "The Citation Classic." Miller attended, fascinated by the unfamiliar game. Ten Stanyota faculty members sat at a long table. Each professor was given a large volume of published research, and the player who found the most citations to his or her own work in 30 minutes won. It was brutal.

The next day, from Palo Bajo, home of the university (it had been renamed after sinking 30 feet deeper into a financial hole after the last quake), he took a helicopter to Don Diego, home of a branch of another great university, the University of Californregon. The city was apparently named after the alter ego of Zorro, a famous patriot who had slashed his signature "Z" into the clothing of many an antagonist. But as soon as they arrived at the university, it was obvious that there was trouble—big trouble.

Two swordsmen were dueling. Was it a match between Zorro and his nemesis Sergeant Garcia? No, it was a match between representatives of two departments, psychology and cognitive science, both of which wanted officially to represent behavioral studies at their university.

Miller was perplexed. "Why are you fighting?"

One of the masked swordsmen turned his way. He scowled. "This pretender to the throne claims to represent psychology when in fact he deserted psychology years ago. He has no right to be here."

"On the contrary, psychology at UC Don Diego isn't psychology. Cognitive science is the true psychology, the true study of the mind," claimed his opponent. "It's been that way ever since the Norman Conquest."

Miller missed the reference, but was puzzled. "I'd be glad to meet with you both." But he realized that he had entered a turf battle, much like the one fought between two ancient countries, both of which had claimed to be the true "China." Miller also noticed that the two swordsmen were tired.

"How long have you been fighting like this?" he asked.

"At least fifty years," one of them replied, not letting down his guard for an instant.

"You mean that in all this time, there hasn't been a conclusive finish to the battle?"

"I've won," they both said simultaneously.

"How can you get anything done if you're always fighting?" Miller asked. But they were no longer listening; they were too busy parrying blows.

Miller thought to ask them to point the ways to their respective departments, but then, gazing beyond the duelers, he thought better of it. In the distance, he could see two seemingly endless lines of people. They were fencing.

The trip to Californregon had been yet another disaster. He hadn't learned a thing, or at least not anything he had wanted to learn. So he decided to write off yet another destination and try one last university stop, Centralia.

Centralia

Centralia was, as its name implied, in the center of the Disunion. In older times, it had been known for its hard-boiled experimental approach to psychological problems—the opposite, for example, of the Philacreamcheese approach. The plane took off bumpily, signaling the beginning of a hard trip—not nearly as hard as the data he was likely to be hearing about in Centralia, however.

When he landed, he was greeted by a team of psychologists who immediately asked whether he would be willing to be a paid subject in an experiment. Miller politely declined.

"Well, then, why did you say you were here?" asked one of the psychologists, who introduced himself as Biff.

"To learn about what you're doing," Miller said.

"No better way to learn about our research than to be part of it."

Miller could see his point, but he still wasn't interested. "What are you studying right now?" he asked.

"I'm comparing recall of three-syllable words to recall of four-syllable words."

"And why are you doing that?"

"To see which is better recalled. Actually, I would have thought you'd see that."

"What do you expect to find?" Miller asked.

"A difference," Biff said.

"Why?"

"Because I found a difference for two- versus three-syllable words."

"Congratulations. But is there some theory of learning or memory behind the research?" Miller asked.

"You bet," Biff replied. "My theory is that recall varies with the number of syllables in the word to be recalled."

"Uh, how long have been studying this issue?"

"Only three years," Biff said. "Before that, I was comparing recall of nouns versus recall of verbs."

"Let me guess," Miller said. "Your theory was that there would be a difference."

"Exactly," Biff proudly proclaimed.

Miller had had enough. He was out of there. This research trip was over. What a waste of a week this had been.

Washing Town

Just one more stop—Washing Town, where he had been given his grant money for the trip in the first place. As he had been asked to do, he stopped in at the National Institutes of Mental Wealth, the funder of the research.

"Thanks for dropping by," said Casper Cash, the grants coordinator. He was fairly undistinguished, except for his suit and cape. Emblazoned on the suit was a "$." Cash lit a fat cigar with a five-dollar bill, and noticed Miller's resulting look of astonishment.

"I can see why you'd be surprised. I used to light these with ten-dollar bills, but times are tough. Even the cigar wrappers these days are cheap."

Miller noticed that the wrapper was a one-dollar bill.

"And what did you learn on your trip, Professor Miller?"

The question was embarrassing. Miller couldn't think of even one thing he'd learned that was worth knowing. "Oh, I learned one or two things," he said, trying an understated diplomatic approach.

"Good, good," said Cash. "Exactly what we were hoping for."

"I'm sorry that I didn't . . . *What?*" Miller tried not to sound flabbergasted.

"We hoped that you'd learn one or two things."

"You didn't expect me to learn more?" Miller asked.

"Oh, no. When we give a grant, our expectation is that our grantee will learn one or two things—no more, no less."

"Are you saying that you don't want grantees to learn more?"

"I'm saying that a good solid grant teaches us one or two new things, and let's be honest, usually they aren't really very new. And besides, no one really cares a whole damn lot anyway, 'cept the person who wrote the grant—maybe. Actually, usually he's happy just to get the grant. Damn waste of effort that he actually has to do the research, but that's the game."

Miller couldn't believe his ears. "Are you telling me that you don't expect people to learn very much?"

"Course not, just between you, me, and the lamppost."

There actually was a lamppost in the office, and Miller was seated directly between it and Cash.

"What do you do when you get a proposal that might teach us more than one or two things, or that might really be interesting?" Miller wondered.

"We turn it down, of course. The research probably isn't very tight, and if it is, that's even worse. Doubtless it will threaten some reviewer, and that'll be the end of that. And rightfully so. In fact, we turn threats over to the Disfederal Bureau of Investigation. Every game's got its rules, and we don't like people who can't play by ours. Just last week I got a proposal with margins that were too small. I threw the sucker right into the circular file. The guy thought he could buy himself extra room by extending the margins by 1/16 of an inch on each side. We fixed his wagon. There's only one wagon we ride around here."

"Let me guess," Miller said, "the bandwagon."

"How'd you know?" asked Cash.

"Just a hunch."

"Well, I guess you sure did learn a thing or two on this trip. Yeah, well, be careful about flashing around your knowledge like that. We didn't really expect you to learn anything very revolutionary. If we had, we'd never have funded you."

Miller dutifully thanked Cash and left. What a depressing end for a depressing trip.

Return to Princeford

Miller returned home to Princeford, utterly discouraged. He lay down on his bed to try to forget, and then he woke up in a cold sweat. The whole thing had been just a nightmare! It never happened! He'd been so tired, he'd fallen asleep in his clothes! Relieved, he ripped them off, not noticing the postcard that slipped from his pocket. In another room, someone chuckled.

Miller showered and went back to bed, falling asleep instantly. Almost silently, a door opened and closed. The house remained quiet.

In the morning, Miller woke up refreshed, got dressed, and ate breakfast. Putting on his jacket to go to work, he noticed the postcard lying on the floor. Stunned by a half-formed memory, he stopped short and stooped to pick it up. No, it didn't look familiar. What was that rickety wheeled wooden thing in the picture? And what were these words written on the back? "Those who do not learn from the future are doomed to live it." What the heck? What kind of nonsensical joke was this? He tossed the card into the wastebasket and left the house whistling.

But as he got closer and closer to the bus stop, his whistling ceased and his mood darkened. "This is going to be a rotten day," he remembered. "Boy, do I have a lot of phone calls to make. What a time sink. And there's that departmental lunch . . . and the faculty meeting . . . and oh God! I haven't even started to work on my presentation for the national conference on the future of cognitive psychology next week. Good grief . . . why can't I just sit peacefully in my own office, doing my own work in my own way, without all these outside demands? What purpose—"

Then, for the second time that morning, Miller stopped short, this time in mid-complaint. Dashing back to the house, he snatched the postcard from the trash. He stared at the picture and the words again, pondering and remembering. A smile spread over his face slowly as he straightened up. Carefully he folded the postcard into his wallet, and again left the house. This time, however, he whistled all the way to work.

When Miller arrived at his office, he immediately began preparing for the national conference on the future of cognitive psychology. He realized he had learned a great deal on his trip. He had met a variety of investigators, each working in a different milieu. Each thought about problems in a different way, and they even thought about different kinds of problems altogether. What the investigators thought about, and *how* they thought about it, was a joint and interactive function of their cognitive abilities, personal traits, styles, interests, and the environments in which they were working. One could not possibly understand their thinking in isolation—outside this broader context. And if their thinking about thinking could be understood only in this way, then clearly that was the way thinking needed to be thought about. Therein lay a future of cognitive psychology, although certainly not the only one. Cognitive psychology needed to be integrated not only with fields outside psychology (as in cognitive and neuroscience), but with fields within psychology itself. Fields within psychology should not have been dividing as they became more specialized; instead, they should have been coming together. The best specialist would always be the best generalist.

Yes, Miller realized, there were things that could be done now, before it was too late. He took the postcard from his wallet, drew a large "X" across the picture of the bandwagon, and prepared to tell his tale, "The Miller's Tale."

Acknowledgments

This work was supported under the Javits Act Program (Grant No. R206R000001) as administered by the Office of Educational Research and Improvement, U. S. Department of Education. The findings and opinions expressed in this report do not reflect the position or policies of the Office of Educational Research and Improvement of the U. S. Department of Education. Thanks to Susan Papa for editorial assistance in preparation of this article.

10

The Future of Psychology

RICHARD L. GREGORY

There is only one way to predict the future—reflect on the past. What we see from looking back is very much dictated by our personal interests and philosophies; but as these can be made explicit, we can compare and share expectations, and fears and hopes, for predicting and planning futures. Value judgments enter right at the start!

Observations and experiments must always be interpreted, from assumptions that may or not be useful. Thomas Kuhn expressed this very clearly with his "Paradigms" of science, such as Darwin's nineteenth-century natural selection for the origin of species, and the nineteenth century's ether for carrying light. Kuhn tends to think of paradigms as large scale and very grand; but we may equally consider small or even microparadigms as essential for science—and quite often as disastrously misleading. The future of science depends on whether what we see as useful paradigms turn out to be guides to truth or prisons of the intellect.

Let me give three actual clear examples of micro-paradigms misleading intelligent people. The first example is a professor of psychology who wanted to record eye movements with a camcorder, using infrared light. How? He said: "I will use infrared sensitive tape." The second example is a microscope salesman, who explained the reduced brightness of a more magnified image as due to the greater thickness of the short focus lens. Lastly, giving a lecture recently, the slide projector gave too large an image for the screen. As I moved it *forward,* the organizer thought I was mad. The point here is, of course, things normally look smaller as one moves back—but not for slide projectors! It is all a matter of switching on to an appropriate paradigm. To my mind, the future depends on paradigms. Occult notions held up psychology for centuries. Will computer-paradigms illuminate, to create conceptual and technical advances? Or will they, too, turn out to be misleading paradigm traps?

Let us look back, to reflect on the future. Since the beginning of recorded thought, there has been a drastic though gradual change—from explanations of the physical world in terms of psychology to explanations of psychology from physical analogies. To express this somewhat differently: Through the last several millennia what originally appeared as physical, and what now appears as psychological, has changed over. For example, magic dominated how the stars and earthly events were seen; but now magic is generally explained from physical principles. There remains, however, a hinterland, neither quite mind nor matter, with phenomena such as psychosomatic illnesses, effects of placebos, and the experimental subject of psychophysics. All these lie somewhat uneasily between mind and matter.

Computers live in this mind–matter hinterland. Although their hardware lies firmly in physics (though a bit spooky, as quantum effects are important), their rules, or working algorithms, are not quite physical—though like our minds they are powerless without hardware implementation. The key concept here is *cognition*—intelligent use of knowledge. Over the last few years, the status of studies of cognition has risen in the scientific community, so that, from being tainted by an aura of magic it is now the very center of information technologies and of the brain sciences. It is a reasonable bet that the philosophy and science of cognition will continue to grow in importance, over the next century and beyond.

Looking back, we see a plethora of paradigms for describing the universe and mind. Mind has not always been limited to brains. Take the planets, the "wanderers" of the sky. Right up to Johannes Kepler early in the seventeenth century, the planets were seen as intelligent beings, cavorting gods and goddesses. Then, with Kepler's laws and the Newtonian system of universal gravity, they were seen very differently—as insignificant parts of a machine that runs forever, without machine-minders, as it has momentum with no friction. Like the cycles and continuing dates of an everlasting calendar clock, the future was seen as contained in its present and past. So there was no room for intelligence in the physical universe.

From the seventeenth century, the behavior of the heavenly bodies has been attributed not to properties of matter, but rather to characteristics of surrounding space, which was conceived to be far more than nothing. Earthly matter was a different matter—to be seen with very different paradigms before the science of chemistry. Alchemy (though abandoned late in life by Bacon and Boyle in the seventeenth century) had high significance for Newton, who wrote (though he never published), over four million words on the philosophy and practice of alchemy. He may have been attracted to gold (he became Master of the Mint) but what attracted him most was the *power of symbols*. Newton saw their power in his mathematics (which he related to the mind of God, physical laws being ideas in God's mind) and in the symbols and rituals of alchemy, as keys to understanding. So Newton saw cognition, intelligence, in matter.

How was intelligence recognized? With the newly invented telescope, Kepler saw circular craters on the moon as designed "Artificial" creations of intelligent moon-living beings, used as protection from the heat of the sun. The far more random lunar mountains he regarded as "Natural" and not a product of intelligence. It is curious that although Kepler was a professional astrologer, employed by Princes to predict their futures, the planets lost their intelligence when they were seen to obey Kepler's laws and to move in nearly circular elliptical section orbits, even though circular ripples in ponds were not seen as a sign of intelligence. Straight lines are better evidence of intelligence than circles; yet one has only to look at modern architecture to see how we are ruled by rulers! Does this suggest that architects are intelligent? Any more intelligent than igloo builders? Not really. Straight lines suggest artificial rather than human intelligence, and not everything artificial demonstrates intelligence. Indeed, there can be artificial stupidity: So artificial intelligence is not altogether a tautology.

With the developments of physics and engineering over the last half millennium, theories of mind have been inspired and enriched by human inventions. Mind has been likened to electricity and magnetism; to hydraulic pumps and pipes; to telephone exchanges (more or less automatic); to predictive gun-ranging devices; to interactive analogue nets; to digital computers (human or self-programed). More specifically, error correction in skills has been likened to servo-mechanisms found originally in windmills; some properties of memory have been explained in terms of holograms. Concepts for measuring the cost of transmitting information in telegraphs or telephones have been applied to the nervous system, and there are many more paradigms for mind derived from technologies.

At present, the key concept from technology is *information*. But so far we have met a wall to understanding the meaning of "meaning." When Claude Shannon and Warren Weaver devised their measure of information for costing telegraph messages and telephone calls, they had to accept such a very restricted use of the word "information" it precluded meaning. Their definition was based on probabilities; but since it left out what messages signify, it abandoned the accepted and most important significance of the word and concept "information."

An important task for the future is to define "information" to include meaning. But there would seem to be many kinds of meanings—so we might need several *kinds* of concepts, with various scales for measurements. Psychology has often erred by trying to measure very different things, along the same scale. This has been socially as well as conceptually disastrous for measuring intelligence along the single dimension of the IQ scale.

By assuming that the intelligence of a carpenter, a cook, a clerk, a concert pianist, a comic, a chemist, a call girl, a college professor, a capitalist, and a crook are of the same *kind* of intelligence is a rank impertinence, denying each their rightful degrees of freedom to be different in kind. To rank them on a single scale is indeed so silly that we should seek some psychological explanation for this most famous error of psychologists.

An explanation may be that, as simple scales claim the respectability of the physical sciences, they might enhance the reputation of psychology. For it was indeed a major move to see that all forms of energy are ultimately one, and that *temperatures* of anything can be measured on a single scale. The very powerful concepts and units for measuring energy, mass, force, velocity, and so on, in physics and engineering are intimately related to conceptual models of physics and engineering—including very general and very deep paradigms for thinking and seeing. As we have learned that conceptual models are vitally important in physical science, we may well see that the troubles of psychology are due to inadequate, often inappropriate, mental models of mind. In Kuhn's terms: We lack good *"Paradigms"* in psychology, so psychology is not a "normal" science.

So far, paradigms for thinking about mind have come from physics-based technologies. But now that we begin to have technologies of mindful machines, the ancient antithesis of matter and mind is closing. Cartesian dualism looks more and more suspect with the increasing powers of AI and the respectability of cognitive concepts.

Cognition is not simply physical or mental, and it has a kind of dualism. A computer needs hardware, and it needs software. There can't be software programs without hardware implementation. We can now see Descartes' dualism of different *entities* (bizarrely linked by the pineal gland) as a mistake. The dualism of cognition is not different entities (body and soul, or brain and mind) but rather different *aspects* of the same thing. They are different as functions of a machine are different and yet entirely dependent on the "anatomy" and "physiology" of the machine. All machines have this aspect dualism of form and function.

Computers seem extremely different from other machines because they accept questions and produce answers. The (non-Cartesian) dualism, here, shows up because descriptions of hardware and descriptions of software need entirely different languages, and it is not possible to translate either one into the other as the concepts hardly overlap.

Let us look at this more generally with a noncomputer example. The parts of a steam engine can be described in terms of the channeling of physical principles as a function of the shapes of its parts. The parts can also be described in terms of contributions toward an end result—speed, power, or whatever. The cylinder, piston, connecting rod, valve gear, boiler, etc., all obey physical principles; but to appreciate them we need to know how they restrain and direct physical forces to achieve an end. Without specifying the end, or purpose, it is impossible to consider appropriateness or efficiency. This applies to making sausages, printing words, or whatever. The machine must be described with an end in view. If its use changes, descriptions of it change too.

Here there is danger. The danger is confusing the *description* with what *is being described*. The temptation is especially great when computing, or information handling, is involved. For the steam engine there is no danger of a mathematical description, of the changing forces and so on in engine, being used to *replace* the engine. For it is obvious that equations will not turn the wheels or pull the carriages. The equations are descriptions: They are not themselves physically effective. But in accounts of computers and brain function, it is surprisingly easy to think of descriptions as substitutable for what is being described. There are mathematical algorithms for describing supposed visual processes; but it does not follow that the brain in fact carries out such algorithms, in order to see. A filter may be described with an equation: It does not follow that the filter has to *solve* the equation.

This is important and rather obvious when we compare an analogue with a digital processor. A simple circuit may be made with a capacitor and a resistor, and used, let us say, for integrating. It may be described with equations of integrations, but it does not follow—indeed it is entirely false to suppose—that the capacitor and resistor solve integration problems by following mathematical algorithms. This is what a mathematician would do, but this circuit is not a mathematician. What is confusing is that a digital computer might solve it like a mathematician. And they might come up with the same or very similar answers—though by entirely different means. The danger is that, just as the early astronomers put God into the working of the universe, we put digital computers into brains. Judging from myself and most of my friends, our brains are very poor at computing in this way, yet we are good at many things mathematicians find very hard or impossible to solve.

One would not be tempted to make this mistake of putting the description into what is being described for, say, a steam engine. This is because the engine doesn't provide answers, so it doesn't look brainy. Yet it *could* be used to produce all sorts of answers. Values might be read off it, for various conditions, so though bizarre it might be used as analog computer. So might any repeatable physical system: Pendulums, falling weights, eddy currents (as in a speedometer) can and are used to compute, or at least to provide, quantitative answers. If one uses the machine differently, the same components are directed to very different ends. They may need to be differently described, and differently judged. What looked appropriate and efficient may now look bizarrely inappropriate and absurdly inefficient, or vice versa.

Analog computing is so essentially different from following the steps of algorithms digitally that a different word seems in order. It might save confusion to call analog processing *"commuting"*—moving and changing data. Thus, reading values from a graph would be commuting. Commuting is very useful, though it has its limitations, as it saves the tedium and time of digital computing. An essential question to ask of brain mechanisms is: Which are analog (commuters); which are digital (computers)? At present, we are returning to essentially Hebbian (named for Canadian psychologist Donald Hebb) concepts of analog nets. These may be *described* with algorithms, though they don't necessarily *carry out* algorithms. They may be simulated on a digital computer, but then much of their special powers are lost.

To see the brain as a digital computer or as an analog commuter is to accept extremely different paradigms. Paradigms for thinking can be guides or prisons. They can throw light for understanding; but they can trap us into deadends. Then, they are like cosmological black holes. But fortunately (as for black holes trapping light) photons do occasionally escape. Illuminating discoveries do sometimes emerge from even the most sterile paradigms. Scientific progress would hardly be possible if this were not so. Perhaps the historical paradigms of mind—hydraulic pumps and pipes; telephone exchanges; predictive gun-ranging devices; mills that seek the wind—have suggested useful observations and experiments, and have provided some important insights, even though they are essentially misleading.

For the future, I see digital computers and analog commuters as ever more powerful tools for amplifying the power of our brains (or minds), and also as the bases of paradigms for describing how brains (or minds) function.

As we are bad at performing algorithmic processes, and we lack precise memory, it seems absurd to preclude computers from examinations. We might as well ban pencils and pens (and indeed it was verbal memory that seemed most important in the Middle Ages, so writing was banned in examinations) as to expect people to be efficient without machine-aids.

Since even the smallest, simplest, pocket calculator is so much better than us at arithmetic, the Turing test is hardly the point. It is impossible to confuse us with computers—because in many ways even the simplest computers are far too smart! Their intelligence is different from ours; but this is so also for the cook, the call girl, the car salesman, and the calculating genius. They are all different, so this should not prevent us from calling machines "intelligent." The supreme intelligence known to us are the processes of natural selection that have created the plants with their wonders of photosynthesis, animals with eyes, and our brains. This beats anything we can think up or explain. That evolution is itself blind and purposeless should not rule it out as being intelligent, though we can see and we have intentions. Natural selection, acting by trial and error, is the supreme, though in many ways different kind of intelligence from ours. We cannot ask it to predict the future.

It is a safe bet that computers of various kinds will become more and more powerful, to take over, even more completely, the tedium of number crunching and much of thinking. We are left with deciding on such matters, as what matters. Do we need violence for TV to wake us up? Should we adopt voluntary euthanasia? Computers are not a lot of help for such decisions.

Given that commuting and computing are relegated to machines, what will there be for us to do? One answer is seeking good paradigms. For as we are always trapped in paradigms, it is as important now to find good paradigms, as it was to get out of the dark dank caves of our beginnings. My prediction is that *we will become philosophers*. More specifically, philosophy will become the most important university subject. From their emphasis on finding good paradigms, William James and Hermann von Helmholtz will be seen as the greatest founding psychologists. Freud might just slip in.

The only safe prediction is that technologies will continue to dominate how we think. Radically new technologies could change psychology out of recognition. It is safe to say that new technologies will change understanding—both by suggesting new paradigms and by providing the means for investigating and testing paradigm-related ideas. As technologies became more cognitively mindlike, our minds will increasingly become embedded in technologies—quite soon, hardly to be distinguished. Then we shall have to exercise our consciences on what do about machine consciousness—and hope they will do the same for us.

A fundamental clash of psychological paradigms is passive *direct* versus active *constructional* accounts of perception and memory. The difference is as dramatic as saying that perceptions are *samples of reality*, or that they are *descriptions*. Even more dramatic: Are perceptions virtual realities?

If one thinks of perceptions as descriptions, like predictive hypotheses of science, as I do, then direct theories seem deeply misleading: a black hole imprisoning thought, precluding truth. It inhibits thinking about perceptual prediction, gap filling, pictures, creative processes, phenomena of illusions. It may be so that a direct theory is a black hole; yet it has to be admitted that the generals and camp followers of this paradigm do make important discoveries. It is fortunate that philosophically sound paradigms are not always necessary for discovery—but they help!

I find the notion—the paradigm—that perceptions are predictive hypotheses as illuminating and helpful. I believe it to be true. And we might think that the most important result of science is inventing paradigms for illusion-free, creative conceptual seeing. For me the future lies in developing this Hypothesis notion, which leads to looking for procedures, rather like methods of science, for brain processes of perception. This may, however, appear paradoxical in the light of the warning above against confounding descriptions with what is being described: Such as saying that the brain *works with* algorithms when algorithms are useful for *describing* functions. The perceptions-are-hypotheses paradigm might look paradoxical because hypotheses are descriptions! According to this account, visual perceptions are no closer to reality than are theories of hypotheses of science. Yet according to this view, these virtual realities of perception and science are the closest we can ever get to truth.

What, then, of the new computer technology of virtual reality that allows us to interact with computer-generated worlds? Although at present this is frankly disappointing, it does offer immense promise for investigating cognitive processes of perception and learning. For the experimenter can invent any world, even with logical incompatibilities, to discover what can or cannot be seen and learned and understood. The inputs will be pure and precisely defined; not contaminated with extra (leading or misleading) cues. Indeed, one suspects that in maze-learning experiments, sometimes the maze learns more, from scent trails, than the animals learn.

Computer-processed brain imaging is now showing us physiological aspects of cognitive processes. Computer-generated virtual reality may reveal hidden aspects of the brain's virtual reality, that is our perception.

11

Toward an Ecological Physics and a Physical Psychology

M. T. TURVEY AND ROBERT E. SHAW

It is reasonably fair to say that the major achievement of the nineteenth century was a formal and rigorous understanding of the previously intuitive idea of "energy" and that the major achievement of the twentieth century has been a similar grasp of the previously intuitive idea of "information," at least as that idea bears on systems of communication. As we peer into the twenty-first century, we can see science shaping up to address the intuitive idea of "knowledge," more precisely of "knowing about" as a property that some material systems can possess with respect to themselves and to other material systems. One suspects that a major scientific goal of the next century, perhaps *the* major goal, will be a formal and rigorous understanding of "knowing about."

In some quarters there may be an argument given that we have already made good progress on this topic, to the point of understanding that the topic is closely related to the exact idea of computation developed in this century as an integral component of science's formal grasp of information. "Knowing about" is a species of computation over discrete symbol strings—that is, representations. From other quarters will come the claim that we are only now beginning to make good progress on this topic, given the newly appreciated formalization of a neural network as a parallel communication of continuously graded signals among very many, computationally simple, processing elements. From the neural network perspective, "knowing about" is a species of dynamics—specifically, of the time evolution of neural-like states.

Seen from these two departure points, the challenge of "knowing about" reduces to that of developing and understanding particular mechanisms with the ability to mimic the cognitive phenomena (e.g., memory, language, perception, learning) that characterize organisms, especially humans, and of collecting these achievements into a single unified "knower." For reasons that will become apparent, we suspect that the foregoing attitude-cum-strategy will prove unsatisfactory, and will be (or ought to be) discarded long before the twenty-first century reaches a close. Contrary to the current hopes and aspirations, it seems to us most unlikely that "knowing about" can be equated with, and understood by, the embodying of cognitive capabilities by an arbitrarily chosen material system using processes whose reality is guaranteed only by their implementation (Pollack, 1993). Similarly, it seems to us that the goal of a unified computational account (symbolic or subsymbolic) of cognition is a case of misplaced emphasis.

To be blunt and to the point, "knowing about" as a natural phenomenon will demand a radical extension of physics and, quite possibly, an inverting of the classical understanding that the functional order defining living things (e.g., learning, patterns of mating behavior, directed locomotion in cluttered surroundings) is too special an aspect of nature to sustain universal generalizations of the kind that typify physics (cf. Rosen, 1991). When turned on its head, the classical understanding becomes: *Material systems that express "knowing about" are more general in respect to the principles that underlie them than the material systems that physics currently addresses.* Rather than a reduction of "knowing about" to the contents of any current physics, an amplification of physics by the rigorous study of "knowing about" is envisaged. Again, to be similarly blunt and to the point, it is not the unification of different hypothesized mechanisms of cognitive phenomena that should be sought but rather the *unification of cognition and nature* (see also Pollack, 1993). This sought-after unification is between the laws and principles formative of nature and the defining qualities of material, epistemic systems. Importantly, the assertion above, inverting the ordinary treatment of cognition as special and contemporary physics as general, forewarns that achieving unification will be pursuant to a conceptual revolution in physics that discloses the basis of "knowing about" as generic. It is precisely for such reasons that "knowing about" is so challenging now and will be so challenging for the men and women of the next century: It demands a dramatic, and far from obvious, overhaul of our fundamental orientations, physically and philosophically, toward living things, their surroundings, and the relations that hold between them.

Psychology on the Cusps Between the Past, Present, and Next Centuries

Around the beginning of the twentieth century, the structuralist and functionalist controversy was in full swing—each claiming to pave the royal road to a scientific psychology. For the structuralists the central question was "What is mind?" and the preferred experimental method was introspection. The method defined psychology as an anthropocentric science. Only humans have language and the ability, thereby, to communicate mental content as immediately experienced. For the structuralists, their view of mind went hand in hand with an acceptance of the burgeoning field of physiology as a way of modeling the brain, the seat of consciousness, and of explaining the connection of the elements of mind to the bodily sensations residing in the brain. Structuralism boasted that psychology was distinguished as a science by its methods for getting to the foundational aspects of mental content and to "mental chemistry" (how elemental experiences combined). Not surprisingly, structuralists championed mind and body as separate and interactive and the belief that volitional thoughts were to psychology what mechanical forces were to physics ("Doesn't the mere thought of moving the body motivate its limbs?").

Functionalism grew out of a positive reaction to the pragmatism of evolutionary biology and a negative reaction to the narrow focus of structuralism's questions and methodology. Rather than being a coherent school comprising singleminded adherents to strict doctrine, as structuralists were, functionalists were eclectic on method and pragmatic about theory. For them the central question was not "What is mind?" but "What is mind good for?" Their quest was not simply to know about mind but to know how mind works in accomplishing adaptive ends for the whole organism whatever its species. Hence, the questions posed by the functionalists tended to be practical, biological, and molar, whereas those posed by the structuralists tended to be disinterested, physiological, and molecular. For the functionalist, the issue was not so much what experiences constitute the mind but what adaptive purposes justify the existence of mind. The functionalist philosophy might best be described as a kind of double aspectism, a neutral monism or perspectival realism, with the mind being viewed as "the brain looked at from the inside" and the brain as "the mind looked at from the outside." Both consciousness and behavior were processes whose streaming through time defied analysis into the fundamental elements sought by structuralists.

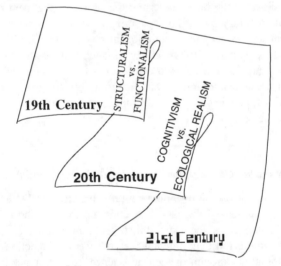

The twentieth century has borne witness to many changes in psychology and the branches of natural science to which it is closely allied. Not surprisingly, the opposing perspectives of structuralism and functionalism prominent at the cusp of the nineteenth and twentieth centuries have gone. They were displaced early in the present century by new psychologies such as behaviorism and Gestaltism. As the twentieth century unfolded, however, structuralism and functionalism began to reemerge in new and more compelling forms. A kind of structuralism is the currently dominant perspective in psychological research and theory. Cognitivism interprets mental states as the computational states of a Turing machine or as the time-evolving states of a connectionist (neural network) machine. Cognitivism's lineage is largely structuralism. The inheritance includes a bias toward human intellectual prowess, an emphasis on the physiological underpinnings, and Cartesian dualism (strengthened by the appreciation that mentalism and materialism can coexist comfortably within a computational perspective on mind). The coherence of cognitivism or cognitive science, such as it exists, is induced by a rejection of logical and methodological behaviorism and an embracing of mind as the topic of study. Mind is imbued, however, with functionalistic goals as well as traditional structuralist properties. Where the structuralists at the cusp of the nineteenth and twentieth centuries were strict doctrinaires, the structuralists at the cusp of the twentieth and twenty-first centuries are eclectic, encouraged by the explosion of computer and medical technology to borrow concepts and principles from a multitude of disciplines.

The functionalism to be found at the present cusp between centuries is in the form of "ecological realism," a perspective that emerged in the latter third of the century largely inspired by the American psychologist James J. Gibson. To greater or lesser degree, this perspective is heir to themes developed under pragmatic functionalism (especially as envisioned by the Americans C. S. Peirce, William James, and John Dewey), act psychology (a mental functionalism), and Gestalt psychology (especially its holism). Like the functionalism of old, the concerns of ecological psychology are more molar than molecular, and its goals focus on the individual adaptability in evolutionarily functional contexts of all organisms, both within and across phyla. The streams of behavior and consciousness that figured prominently in the first round of functionalism are replaced with active organisms qua perceivers engaged in dynamical transactions with their functionally defined environments. This second round of functionalism, Ecological Psychology, shapes the vision of the future science of mind expressed in the present article.

Organism–Environment Mutuality and Reciprocity

The disposition to know is a natural property of a certain class of material systems called organisms. Historically, all attempts to understand this property have been shaped by the metaphysical stance of dualism. Psychologists and philosophers have long referred to the dualism of mind and body, identifying the need for two distinct languages (mentalese and physicalese) to describe what appear to be two radically contrasting aspects of nature. Close relatives of the dualism of mind and body are symbol–matter dualism, subjective–objective dualism, and perception–action dualism. To adopt dualism in any of the preceding forms is to cleave to a particular methodology in which the two things referred to are defined independently of each other, studied independently of each other, and interpreted through independent scientific accounts. Thus, for example, the experimental study of perception and theories of perception have generally proceeded independently of the experimental study of action and theories of action with the upshot that efforts to understand how perception controls action and action enhances perception are forced to introduce arbitrary and special mediators (e.g., schemas, set points, inferential processes). Dualism, therefore, has unwelcome scientific consequences: By sanctifying the logical independence of mind and body, symbol and matter, perception and action, subjective and objective points of view, dualism as a doctrine encourages conceptual divisions in science that give rise to mysteries (vs. potentially tractable scientific problems) that become apparent as soon as questions are raised about how the states or processes in question are connected.

The dualisms mentioned are, in our view, subordinate to organism–environment dualism; it is the keystone that holds them in place, as depicted in Figure 11.1. In a theory of "knowing about," the two principal players are the organism and the environment. Organism–environment dualism establishes the grounds for this theory as the logical independence of the two terms, meaning that a theory of the organism (the "knower") can be built independently of a theory of the environment ("the known"), and vice versa. The presumed logical independence has sponsored theories of "knowing about" in which organisms are continually in the business of figuring out the world in which they act, much like detectives facing the scene of a crime with only vague clues as to the perpetrator. More profoundly,

Figure 11.1. The classical dualisms formative of psychological theory in the present and past centuries are subsidiary to and locked together by organism–enviroment dualism.

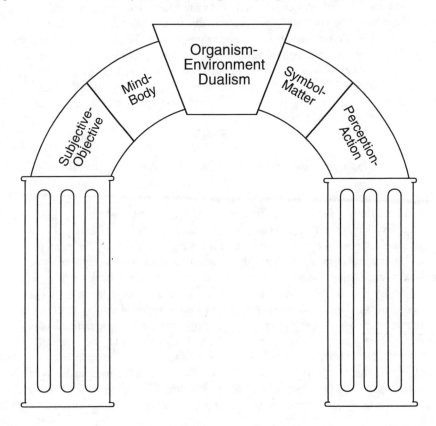

the overarching dualism of organism and environment sanctifies the interpretation of living things as the products of a process—that is to say, evolution, which lies beyond the laws and principles governing inanimate nature, is essentially unpredictable, and contingent (rather than necessary or entailed). Under this conceptual umbrella, the origin of systems exhibiting "knowing about" was a frozen accident, lacking lineage with, and necessary relation to, the generic principles formative of nature. *In our view, the most important conceptual step to be taken in the twenty-first century, with respect to the foundations of a scientific attack on "knowing about," is the rejection of organism–environment dualism and the acceptance of organism–environment mutuality and reciprocity.*

In 1913, Lawrence Henderson published a small volume entitled *The Fitness of the Environment* in which he sought to balance Darwin's evolutionary thesis of the fitness of living things for their environments with an account of the fitness of our planet for life. For example, he addressed the importance of the heat capacity of liquid water in maintaining a relative constant temperature of the earth's surface, a feature essential to the survival of organisms which can function only within a restricted temperature range. Henderson's work was given a mixed reception. Some found it stimulating, others thought it was platitudinous (Blum, 1951). The investigation of the evolution of the earth as a system, conducted largely since Henderson's time, has affirmed Henderson's hypothesis of the reciprocal fit between living things and their terrestrial surroundings (see Swenson, 1989, and Swenson & Turvey, 1991, for reviews). *A key observation is the increase over geological time of entropy production in the biosphere with the growth and differentiation of organisms.* Figure 11.2A shows a progressive departure of the Earth, as a global single system, away from equilibrium as indexed by the increase in atmospheric oxygen. The transformation of the redox state of the planetary system—from a reducing state when life first appeared some 3.8 billion years ago, to a mildly oxidative state some 2 billion years ago, to its presently highly oxidative state—can be taken as a measure of a progressive ordering or internal entropy reduction of the planetary system as a whole. This progressive increase of order in the small, at the scale of the earth, is also a measure—by the balancing requirements of the second law of thermodynamics—of an increasing rate of entropy production in the large, on the scale of the universe.

The atmosphere at the outset of life was mildly reducing, meaning that the earliest life forms were anaerobic, acquiring their energy resources through fermentation. About 3.5 billion years ago, proto-cyanobacteria (ancestors of "blue-green algae") achieved a linkage between the limitless supply of photons from the sun and the essentially limitless supply of electrons in water to bring about the release of oxygen into the atmosphere. As a consequence, life proliferated at an accelerated rate, atmospheric oxygen accumulated (beginning about 2 billion years ago once the oxygen sinks, such as iron formations, were filled), and the planetary redox potential shifted from reducing to oxidative. Atmospheric oxygen functioned as an internal resource or potential that operated over evolutionary time to drive the planetary system even further from equilibrium.

Figure 11.2B elaborates the preceding theme by showing that not only did terrestrial entropy production increase with increase in the quantity of order or

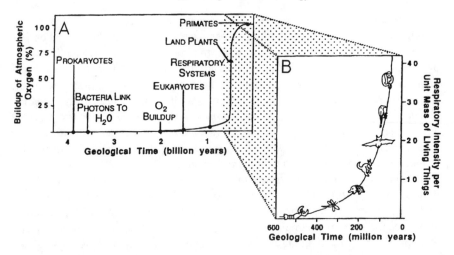

Figure 11.2. Over geological time, measured in billions of years, atmospheric oxygen accumulated gradually at first and then at a (comparatively) rapid pace with increasing numbers and varieties of life forms until it reached its current level of 21% of the atmospheric gases (100% on the vertical axis of A). The accumulation began about 2 billion years ago when the earth's oxygen-binding chemicals became saturated and the oxygen released by bacteria during photosynthesis was free to enter the atmosphere. The oxygen buildup is a measure of a progressive ordering or internal entropy production of the planetary system as a whole. Within the last billion years (B), the rate at which the planet's chemical energy was "burned up" through the use of oxygen increased as the rate at which the respiration per unit mass of living things increased with the numbers and levels of living things progressively amplified (pictured in B). An important reading of A and B is that living things and the planet constitute a unitary system abiding by a principle of maximizing the rate of entropy production.

living matter over geological time, but so did the intensity of entropy production. Specifically, Figure 11.2B depicts the respiration intensity per unit mass of living things over the past 600 million years. Aerobic respiration (oxidative phosphorylation) is the process by which living things employ oxygen to release the energy potential from their food. In aerobic respiration, one molecule of oxygen is used for the conversion of each atom of organic carbon. The mass specific respiration intensity is the rate at which chemical resources are dissipated or burned by oxygen into waste or heat products per unit mass of body weight. It is, therefore, a measure of the specific, or per-unit-mass, rate of entropy production. In combination, Figures 11.2A and 11.2B reveal the global nature of evolutionary ordering: Higher-ordered states require higher rates of dissipation to maintain their spatial and temporal extents; the increase in atmospheric oxygen over evolutionary time, due to the activity of living things, provided the potential required for progressively higher-ordered states. As can be seen, the sharp increase in the respiration intensity function in Figure 11.2B corresponds to the sharp increase in the buildup of atmospheric oxygen in Figure 11.2A; the higher-order states acted as sinks that dissipated the oxygen potential.

Schrödinger's (1945) "Life feeds on negentropy" highlights that living things are not equilibrium states but rather steady states maintained away from equilibrium by a continuous flow of energy and matter. A living thing must continually convert energy into organization, and thus the order defining a living thing adds ceaselessly to the universal entropy. Figures 11.2A and 11.2B underscore that, with the production of more order, with more numerous and more richly organized living things, and with the progressive production of higher states of order, the additions to the universal entropy are made at a greater rate. To Schrödinger's "Life feeds on negentropy" should be added "Life enhances the rate of entropy production in the large."

In sum, the significance of the phenomena captured in Figures 11.2A and 2B is the following: *Living things and their surrounds are not logically independent of each other. Together, they constitute a unitary planetary system abiding by a single and directed evolutionary strategy that opportunistically produces—in progressively more varied and intense ways—the means for the global unit to generate entropy* (Swenson & Turvey, 1991). Organism–environment dualism, a metaphysical hypothesis, is replaced by organism–environment mutuality and reciprocity, a scientific fact that Henderson (1913), most surely, would have acknowledged gleefully. Presumably, this fact of the global relation of Life and Earth is foundational to inquiry into the local relations of organisms and their niches that constitute the subject matter of a science of cognition. It suggests, for example, that there must be reciprocal expressions of organism as knower and environment as known.

Toward a Functional Semantics

Different organisms can occupy the same space or habitat but not the same niche. The term *habitat* refers to where an organism lives, the term *niche* refers to how it lives. The point is that two or more species can live in the same location but to do so they must go about their lives in very different ways. A principle of competitive exclusion is often advanced as the reason for defining a niche abstractly, as that thing in which two sympatric species (those with the same or overlapping areas of geographical distribution) do *not* live. One principal goal of evolutionary ecology is descriptions of the surfaces and substances surrounding an organism that capture uniquely the fit of that organism to its surroundings and clarify the partitioning of any given habitat into distinct niches. In the latter third of the present century, Gibson (1966, 1979/1986; Reed & Jones, 1982) coined the term *affordance* to provide a description of the environment that was directly relevant to the conducting of behavior. An affordance of layout is an invariant combination of properties of substance and surface taken with reference to an organism and specific to an action performable by the organism. An affordance of a change in layout (an event) is an invariant combination of changes in the aforementioned properties, again in reference to an organism and its action potential (Shaw, Flascher, & Mace, 1993). For example, one invariant combination of properties affords grasping by a person, another affords support for climbing by a person, another affords catching by a person, and so on. Affordances are opportunities for action, and the perception of them is the basis by which an organism can control its behavior in a forward-looking manner—that is, prospectively. To assume this essential role, however, the term affordance cannot refer to states of affairs that depend on perception or conception for their existence but must refer to real opportunities. From our perspective, this relatively innocuous identification of a niche as a space of real opportunities for action promises to revolutionize the study of cognition.

As an organism moves with respect to its surroundings, there are opportunities for action that persist, opportunities for action that newly arise, and opportunities for action that dissolve, even though the surroundings analyzed as objects and the relations among them remain the same. In the efforts to model cognition in the present century, the knowledge base presumed to be needed by organisms or agents has been identified as denumerable static objects and relations. The affordance interpretation contradicts this presumption. A change of pace or a change of location can mean that a brink in the ground now affords leaping over, whereas at an earlier pace or location it did not. Further, subtle changes of action can give rise to multiple and marked variations in the opportunities for subsequent actions. The environment-for-the-organism is dynamic and action oriented, whereas the environment-in-itself—that which has been the target of most modeling in the latter decades of the present century—is fixed and neutral with respect to the organism and its actions (Kirsch, 1991). *The new century will witness a thoroughgoing attempt to build a functional semantics if for no other reason than the need to build robots that work with respect to environments that are real* (Effken & Shaw, 1992).

Can we catch a glimpse of the building blocks of this function-oriented semantics? In conventional physical analyses, the property of a thing that is potential, or latent, or possible—that is, not occurrent—is referred to as a *disposition*. The primary characteristics of a dispositional property are three in number, and they are basic to developing the notion of affordance. First, the disposition to do something is prior to doing that something. For example, a crystal will actually refract light provided that it is refractive to begin with; if it was refractive to begin with, then it was so whether or not it was exposed to light. Second, dispositionals (or causal propensities) come in pairs. For example, (all) light rays are refracted if and only if (some) pieces of matter are refractive. In respect to the organism–environment mutuality and reciprocity thesis, it is noteworthy that reciprocity occurs in the very definition of a dispositional property. Third, dispositionals never fail to be actualized when conjoined with suitable circumstances. The character of an affordance can now be more clearly expressed; it is a real possibility, it is a dispositional property, and it is reciprocated or complemented by another dispositional property: an effectivity. An *effectivity* is the causal propensity for an organism to effect or bring about a particular action. Whereas an affordance is a disposition of the surrounding environment, an effectivity is the complementing disposition of the surrounded organism (Shaw, Turvey, & Mace, 1982; Turvey & Shaw, 1979). Thus, an affordance is a particular kind of physical disposition, one whose complement is a property of an organism (Turvey, 1992). The upshot is that, from the perspective of investigating "knowing about," an organism and its niche constitute two structures that relate in a special way such that understanding of one is, simultaneously, an understanding of the other. If the form of this special relation could be made precise, then an important step would be taken toward understanding the class of material systems that exhibit "knowing about."

Mutuality implies a sameness—a commensurate dimension—over which organisms and their environments might transact business. But the relationship between organism and environment must reflect their different functions in the ecosystem—a bipolar dimension over which they act and react in reciprocal but distinct ways that nevertheless fulfill one another. Consider the analogy to numbers which add up to one: They are mutual in that they may be added to one another (symmetry) but reciprocal in that they may have different values (asymmetry). The symmetry property can be reconciled with the asymmetry property by moving to a higher level of analysis, namely, to the notion of the numbers being complementary in the sense that they complete one other. Likewise, taken together, the organism and environment may be mutual and reciprocal—symmetric and asymmetric—but at a higher level they are complementary duals; they combine to make a whole—an ecosystem. It is apparent, therefore, that the asymmetry of *dualism* (where organisms and environments are merely incommensurate kinds) must give way to the symmetry notion of *duality* (where the two are commensurate kinds); otherwise there can be no synergy, without which there could be no ecosystems. Under this synergy, biology and physics come together with psychology to define a science at a new scale—the ecological scale—at which physical law might conceivably become more unitary. The alternative treats the relationship between knower and known as a metaphysical dualism, with the organism as knower and the environment as the known, coming under different laws, or worse, viewing the environment as being lawfully independent of its function for supporting the organism, and the organism, as a perceiver-actor, whose functions lie outside the scope of any law.

In sum, the special relation in question between organism and environment seems to be the particular kind of isomorphism captured by the mathematical notion of duality. Duality is an abstract rather than a concrete idea; it refers to a relational property, a correspondence, holding between a pair of mathematical objects. The duality holds, even if two objects are of unlike kind, so long as some property of the first object plays the same role among its total property set as that played by a property of the second object among that object's total property set. For example, with respect to a series of perceptions and a series of actions, as might be exhibited over time in fulfilling a goal, a duality would be an operation that establishes a correspondence between the properties of the two series even though the two are quite different (Shaw & Alley, 1985).

The discussion of duality that was initiated by the implications of Figure 11.2 and encouraged by the issue of a functional semantics has, in the immediately preceding comment, focused upon the fit between perception and action under an intention to do so and so. Most of what follows is concerned with the steps needed to understand that fit.

Controlled Locomotion as the Paradigmatic Form of "Knowing About"

For most scholars grappling with cognition in this final decade of the twentieth century, the dominant tendency is to equate knowledge with concepts and to inquire about their form and about the inferential processes (explicit when cognition is defined as symbol manipulation and implicit when it is defined as connected subsymbols) that operate upon them. The grounding of the concepts—that is, how they can refer to the environment of the knower—and the origins of the constraints on the inference mechanisms—that is, the reasons that these mechanisms should function in just that way that renders their consequences sensible (meaning that one could, in principle, act upon them)—are not of paramount concern. (For criticisms of this attitude from our perspective, see Carello, Turvey, Kugler, & Shaw, 1984; Turvey & Shaw, 1979; Turvey, Shaw, Reed, & Mace, 1981; for similar criticisms from within conventional cognitive science, see Harnad, 1990; Johnson-Laird, Herrman & Chaffin, 1984.) In sum, cognition tends to be investigated as a disembodied, rational process: Concepts and inference mechanisms can be lifted away from the organism–environment systems, and perception–action subsystems that express them, and modeled in their own terms. Accentuating the already troublesome features of this modeling strategy is the fact that it requires a designer who must determine what constitutes the objects, events, and relations to be conceptually represented on the basis of his or her own experience, creating a frozen (static) ontology peculiar to the designer's whims (Carello et al., 1984; Clancy, 1992; Turvey et al., 1981). A major promise of the neural network perspective is that the preceding difficulty is circumvented because concepts in that perspective are not prescribed but emergent, arising from the interactions among very many subsymbolic processing units. Unfortunately, a critical examination of NETtalk (Sejnowski & Rosenberg, 1987), often offered as the primary example of successful emergence, reveals that the conceptual distinctions eventually exhibited by the network are already implicitly coded by the designers into the patterns fed to the network (Verschure, 1992).

The disembodying of cognition is consonant with organism–environment dualism and reinforced by the choice of what counts as a paradigmatic cognitive phenomenon. Popular choices are the human capabilities of syntax, problem solving, remembering, expert knowledge, and the like. These phenomena seem to be so focused *at* or *in* the individual, and so trivially dependent on the current environment and ongoing behavior, that they invite analysis in purely formal, abstract terms and the modeling of the environment and behavior (conceived as inputs and outputs, respectively) in the same abstract terms. In consequence, broaching the problems of how the symbols, inference mechanisms, and task ontologies are grounded rarely occurs in the context of the preceding choices of paradigmatic cognition. And even if an attempt were made, it is not clear that these research domains can provide a sound basis for addressing the grounding issues. We have two reasons for this pessimism: First, grammar, problem solving, remembering, expert knowledge, and the like, are too far beyond the pale of the current stock of scientific tools by which nature's phenomena are understood in general law-based terms, reducing thereby their potential as a basis for substantial progress;

second, and perhaps more important, they cannot be considered as fundamental forms of "knowing about" nor can they be considered as having posed major challenges in the evolution of material systems with the property of "knowing about." Returning to Figure 11.2, most of the past 3.5 billion years seem to have been consumed by the establishment of the ability to move in a controlled and directed manner—to tumble, crawl, walk, run, jump, fly, swim, slide, burrow, and so on, among the environment's persistent and variable clutter, perceiving the actions the material layout allows with sufficient efficacy to discover energy resources and to implement the circumstances for procreation. We suspect that grammar, problem solving, remembering, expert knowledge, and the like, are capabilities that arose straightforwardly once controlled locomotion, at each and every length scale occupied by living things, was firmly in place (see also Brooks, 1991). On these considerations, scientific inquiry into "knowing about" begins with *controlled locomotion.* What will become extremely apparent as we examine what is involved in controlling locomotion is that *understanding "knowing about" will demand both a broadening and an enrichment of the current understanding of "energy" and "information," an appreciation of the confluence among all three intuitive ideas, and a physically grounded understanding of an even more inexact idea, namely, "intention."*

Figure 11.3 depicts a dragonfly weaving its way about in a thicket of the kind

Figure 11.3. Controlled locomotion by a dragonfly is a very cognitive matter.

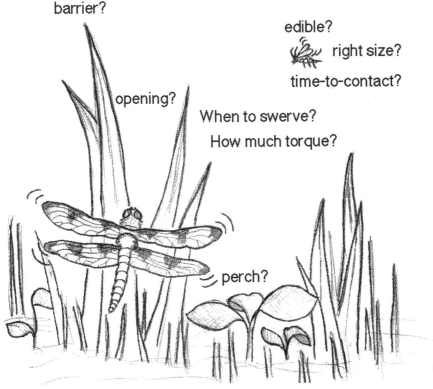

typifying New England in the summertime. A dragonfly feeds on small insects, such as mosquitoes. In seeking its prey, the dragonfly must perceive paths through the thicket. To do so, it must perceive obstacles to its forward locomotion and openings that permit it passage, given its size. Given the many objects within the thicket—insects, birds, leaves, berries, flowers, and so on—the dragonfly must perceive selectively those objects that are edible for it, commonly insects within a certain length scale and degree of softness. It must also perceive places that it can alight upon, places to rest between searches. In traveling through the thicket and in direct pursuit of a prey, the dragonfly must perceive when an upcoming twig or an upcoming prey will be contacted if current conditions (wing torques, forward velocity) continue, so that suitable adjustments can be made both with respect to the body as a unit and with respect to the most forward limbs that are used to effect a catch or a landing; it must perceive the amount of required rotation, elevation, and yaw in three-dimensional space when it and a prey are not aligned; it must perceive the distances of prey, when more than one is within range; and it must perceive when to decelerate, and whether it is decelerating appropriately when the catch is close to occurring and similarly when it is descending onto a perch.

The dragonfly–thicket system expresses why it is that controlled locomotion is such a fundamental form of "knowing about." To satisfy its intent in the thicket, the dragonfly must know where it is, where it can go, when it can go, and how it can get there. Let us see what kinds of things students of cognition in the twenty-first century may have to grapple with in order to account for how the lowly dragonfly locomotes successfully.

Direct Perception

The dominant view of perception on the cusp between the twentieth and twenty-first centuries is that it is very much a matter of inference, very much a process that involves reasoning-like steps, albeit "unconscious and irresistible." To a significant degree, this view is shaped by the widely held understanding that the light distributions available to the eye, the sound distributions available to the ear, and so on, fail to specify the properties of organism–environment systems. The energy patterns ambient to an organism are traditionally thought of, at best, as containing cues or clues to the world. Consequently, in the standard view of the twentieth century, "perception" becomes a roundabout or indirect way of getting acquainted with, and maintaining contact with, one's surroundings. Perception is interpreted scientifically as a kind of justification, via inference, of an organism's perceptual beliefs. This interpretation, which casts perception in the mold of proposition-making activity with either true or false consequences, renders perception a potentially questionable basis for an organism knowing about its surroundings.

The ecological approach places tight constraints on the use of the term "perception." By promoting a conception of law that allows meaningful relations between organism and environment to hold, it constrains the use of the term "perception" to relations governed by such laws. Further, it reserves the term "perception" for designating only really possible and actual states of the organism–environment system. These constraints on its usage vindicate perception as *the* incorrigible basis for an organism knowing about its surroundings (Turvey et al., 1981).

Consider the statement *"O perceives E,"* where *O* stands for organism and *E* stands for an environmental property. Under the ecological analysis, this statement presupposes a law, *L:* A property *P* of an ambient energy distribution (e.g., light) is lawfully related to *E* in that it is unique and specific to *E* in *O*'s niche. Now, given *L,* *"O perceives E"* designates a factual state of affairs if (1) *E* is present, (2) the *P* resulting from (1) and *L* is available to *O,* and (3) *O* detects the *P* defined in (2). *The incorrigible basis for an organism "knowing about its environment lies in the satisfaction of L and the three conditions.* The statement '*O* perceives *E*' picks out a property of the organism–environment system emergent when *L* and the three conditions are fulfilled. The importance of calling it a "property" is that a property (as opposed to an attribute or a concept) is present or absent, existent or nonexistent, but not true or false.

Given the satisfaction of *L* and the three conditions, an organism (in principle) is directly aware of *E.* In the formulation dominating the twentieth century, an organism is directly aware of something else—such as the states of its nervous system or of an internal representation—and only indirectly aware of states of the world. The notion of perception as indirect goes with organism–environment dualism; the notion of perception as direct goes with organism–environment mutuality and reciprocity.

Physicalizing and Intentionalizing Information

Consider the possibility already identified, that the emergence and extension of material systems exhibiting "knowing about" accords with a physical selection principle, namely: Those things, processes, etc., are selected that increase entropy production at the fastest rate. This consideration provides a glimpse of how it could be possible that cognition is intimately connected to principles of the most generic kind and not merely a contingent feature of nature at the terrestrial scale: Material systems with the property of "knowing about" can interact in more diverse ways with their surroundings than material systems restricted to force-based interactions, extending, thereby, the opportunities for the global system to degrade energy.

Colloquially, one would say that the interactions between organism and surround typifying "knowing about" are information-based. Consider, for example, the dragonfly vis-à-vis thicket in Figure 11.3. In speaking this way, however, one seems to be using the term information in a very different sense from the mathematical formulation of information as the minimum equivalent number of binary steps by which a given representation may be selected from an ensemble of possible representations. This mathematical theory of information was developed to address the formally defined states of affairs of communication and representation and not the physical states of affairs by which informed interactions might occur between an organism and its surround. It is a theory suited, at best, to the organismic capability of discriminating. Within the theory, information processes are viewed as selection processes that must be made from among a specific set of alternatives; and if the selections are to convey information, the set of choices must be known in advance. But discrimination among members of a set presupposes that the members are perceptible, meaning that the capacity to discriminate is derivative and, by itself, a poor basis for "knowing about." Furthermore, foreknowledge of the environmental entities to be encountered is incompatible with the intuitive understanding that information detection should be the basis for adjusting behavior to novel circumstances. Organism–environment interactions require information in the sense of information *about* something, information specific *to* something; that is, information of a kind that permits the perception *of* something rather than the discriminating among things (Gibson, 1966, 1979/ 1986). Even more poignantly, the actions by which "knowing about" is expressed require that information about environmental facts be referential to the energy for behaving with respect to those facts. For the dragonfly of Figure 11.3 aiming itself at a prey, to see the distance-to-contact is to see the work required, to see the time-to contact is to see the (schedule of) impulse forces required, to see the direction-to-contact is to see the torques required (Shaw & Kinsella-Shaw, 1988).

In sum, the response in the twenty-first century to the challenge of "knowing about," a challenge expressed quite substantially by our dragonfly, will require a theory of information that takes information to be physical—that is, a law-based property of real states of affairs as opposed to simply a logical or mathematical attribution. Pursuit of the theory will consist, in significant part, in the empirical determination of properties of ambient energy distributions that are specific to behaviorally relevant properties of organism–environment systems. A lot of mathematics and physics will be needed in this enterprise, and much of it will have to be developed. Importantly, in keeping with the argument that systems expressing "knowing about" are more general in respect to the principles that underlie them than the systems accommodated by contemporary physics, it will have to assume that the intuitive idea of information *in its most fundamental form* can only be captured in organism–environment systems. The development of the requisite understanding will be founded on answers to questions such as: What kinds of energy magnitudes and energy forms are involved? What kinds of structures carry or contain information? What are the physical conditions for generating information? What is the (thermodynamic) cost of detecting it? How is information connected to dynamics? How is information perspectival, that is, scaled to the systems that use it? Let us see what directions the answers to some of these questions are likely to take.

1. What Kinds of Energy Magnitudes and Energy Forms Are Involved?

Oddly enough, this question is closely linked to the question of what makes a system complex. There are a number of ways of addressing this complexity question in present-day science, but the most basic, and at the same time the most relevant for our present purposes, focuses on the degree to which the flows of energy from the interior to the exterior of a system can be time-delayed (Iberall & Soodak, 1987; Yates, 1986). The ability to delay external-to-internal-to-external-to . . . energy flows affects dramatically a system's mode of interaction with its surroundings; the system's enslavement to the external force field is weakened. The time-delaying of energy flows provides a local, internally based, source of forces that can compete actively with the external forces. Our dragonfly can fly against gravity and into a breeze. As system complexity magnifies—that is, as the internal forces increase with respect to the external forces—system–surround interactions will become increasingly less dominated by force (dimensionally, MLT^{-2}), momentum (MLT^{-1}), and kinetic energy (ML^2T^{-2}). That is, the basis for the interactions will become increasingly less dependent on observables defined through the mass *(M)* dimension (Kugler & Turvey, 1987, 1988) and increasingly more dependent on observables defined solely through the dimensions of length *(L)* and time *(T)*. These observables are geometric (fashioned from *L*), spectral (fashioned from *T*), and kinematic (fashioned from both, for example, LT^{-1}, LT^{-2}).

Consider that living things are immersed in energy distributions; our dragonfly, for example, is immersed in light. The forces impressed upon them by these enveloping distributions are low relative to the forces that can well up from the interior of organisms—for example, the forces of enveloping optical distributions or enveloping distributions of volatile materials with respect to the forces generated by a flying insect or a running mammal. It is these low energy distributions that connect the dragonfly to the thicket's behavioral opportunities or affordances. They are the basis for force-free epistemic contact to be contrasted with the forceful non-epistemic contact characteristic of the systems-and-surrounds studied in classical mechanics.

2. What Kinds of Structures Carry or Contain Information?

The descriptions in the optical case, for example, are of the spatiotemporal structure—that is, the adjacent and successive order—that is imposed on the ambient optical distributions by the layout of environmental surfaces (attached and detached objects, places, one's body, movements of one's body, surface displacements, deformations, collisions, etc.). An ecological conception of information is founded on the assertion that invariant relations exist between layout properties of general significance to the governing of activity (affordances) and macroscopic, noninertial properties of structured ambient (optical, mechanical, chemical) energy distributions (Gibson,1966; 1979/1986). The latter, therefore, can specify the former. In the case of the dragonfly of Figure 11.3, the structured light available during flight consists of transformations of different intensities, spectral contrasts, and specular highlights in different directions. The mathematics and physics of fields are needed to reveal, for example, the optical properties lawfully generated by gaps that are pass-throughable and by edible objects that are interceptible.

The distinction between information about something and the something in question deserves emphasis, as highlighted by the following analysis of Gibson's (1966): Fields of diffusing volatile materials fill the air and are ambient to each and every animal. The sources of these odors are other animals and their products, plants and their products, and a few types of inorganic things. (For the most part, the minerals of the earth, the air, and the water, are odorless.) The information carried by a diffusion field specifies its source but is not chemically identical with its source. Thus, the body odor of an individual animal is specific to its body but does not have the same chemical composition. Behind the explication of the information carried by fields of diffusing volatile materials is an ecological chemistry. This chemistry expresses the fact that some vapors (and, in the case of tasting, some solutions) are informative about their sources without being chemically identical with them. Analogous tasks confront ecological optics (Gibson, 1961; Reed & Jones, 1982), ecological acoustics (Gibson, 1966; Lee, 1990; B. Shaw, McGowan, & Turvey, 1991), ecological mechanics (Gibson, 1966; Solomon, Turvey, & Burton, 1989), and so on.

Also deserving of emphasis is the distinction between available information and detected information. Energy distributions ambient to a point of observation are structured in ways specific to the surface layout surrounding the point of observation and to the point of observation's position relative to those surroundings. They provide, therefore, opportunities for "being informed," more essentially, for planning and controlling goal-directed behavior. These opportunities exist because of the invariant relations between the properties of the surround and observation point and the properties of structured ambient energy distributions. These opportunities are not dependent on living things; they are simply available as a consequence of the lawful regularities at the ecological scale. It is, however, to be understood that the laws of information, like the laws of mechanics, electromagnetism, and thermodynamics, are necessarily involved in the make-up of living things. The meters (perceptual systems) and actuators (muscle synergies) of organisms can no more lie outside these information laws than the metabolic, respiratory, circulatory, hormonal, etc, processes can lie outside the mechanical, electromagnetic, and thermodynamic laws.

3. How Is the Information-That-Is-Detected Related to the Energy-That-Is-Controlled?

Given an onboard source of energy (e.g., chemical energy carried in the muscles), what are the constraints on its deployment to bring about directed movements? Perception by the dragonfly of the direction-to-contact with a mosquito is rendered as the application of a specific torque to bring about the coincidence of axes—of dragonfly and prey—in three-dimensional space. Patently, to generate this specific torque, the dragonfly must allocate a specific amount of its energy resources. At first blush, information about direction-to-contact and the energy for torque-to-contact seem to be two very different and unrelated things. If they are indeed so very different, then it is difficult to comprehend how the dragonfly, or any other creatures such as ourselves, can routinely interconvert them. The daily challenge of directed actions would be analogous to attempting to convert one currency into another (e.g., deutsche marks for dollars), routinely and reliably, in the absence of an exchange rate. If information and energy are independent and without a common basis, then the conversion must be arbitrary and the fitting of actions to the surroundings a matter of happenstance. In our view, the strong version of organism–environment mutuality implies that information and energy are logically dependent and relate in the double dual manner expressed above (Shaw & Kinsella-Shaw, 1988). This is a profoundly important hypothesis about the two focal topics of the past and present centuries: *When properly understood, information and energy are reciprocal aspects of nature. This reciprocity is neither required nor revealed by a physics that considers natural systems that exhibit the quality of "knowing about" as special systems. The reciprocity is brought to the forefront only when systems exhibiting "knowing about" are understood as more general in respect to the principles that underlie them than the material systems currently addressed by physics.*

That there may be a common and intrinsically defined energy-dissipation principle underpinning animal activity is suggested by the following remarkable fact: Locomoting animals exhibit an independence of energy cost and speed such that the amount of energy used to run a given distance (say, 10 m) is nearly the same whether it is run at top speed or at a leisurely pace. When mass-specific rates of energy consumption are plotted, as in Figure 11.4A, for a given animal as a function of locomotory speed, a straight line is obtained from an intersect with the vertical axis at zero (e.g., Full, 1989). This linear dependency of mass-specific rate of energy consumption on speed holds for bipeds, quadrupeds, and polypeds, for arthropods and vertebrates, for limbed and limbless animals. It is a dependency of great generality, suggesting a fundamental principle governing locomotion that is independent of morphology, physiology, size, and taxa. Spelling out the types of quantities involved in the linear dependency we see that

$$\text{Net cost of locomotion} = \frac{\text{Energy per unit mass/Time}}{\text{Distance/Time}}$$

$$= \frac{\text{Energy per unit mass}}{\text{Distance}}$$

That is, the net cost of locomotion indicates the amount of energy required to move a unit mass of animal a given distance. The slope of mass-specific rate of energy consumption versus speed varies inversely with mass, as shown in Figure 11.4B. On the basis of the empirically determined slopes, it can be concluded that to move a unit of mass 1 meter, a cockroach of 3 gram dissipates twice as much energy as a crab or mouse of 30 g and nine times as much energy as a dog of 3 kilogram; small animals on a per gram basis require more energy per time and per distance. Conversely, if an arthropod, a reptile, a bird, and a mammal have similar mass, then the energy to be dissipated by each to move 1 meter will be nearly identical.

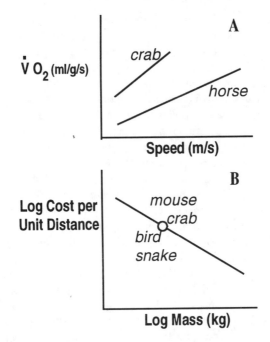

Figure 11.4. (A) As a crab and a horse run faster, the energy they expend increases in direct proportion to their speed—more so for the lighter crab, however, than the heavier horse. For both crab and horse, the constant slopes mean that the cost of traveling a given distance is a fixed amount, regardless of speed. (B) This constant cost depends on the mass of an animal. Animals different in form and locomotory style but of the same mass require the same amount of energy to move the same given distance.

We might hypothesize, therefore, that the dragonfly of Figure 11.3 is relieved of the burdensome task of determining how much energy to use for this or that path through the thicket at this or that speed by a fundamental principle that is at once thermodynamical and informational. The form of this principle escapes current science, but its relevance to everyday locomotion has been duly, if implicitly, appreciated by dragonflies for well nigh 350 million years.

Intentional Behavior as a Symmetry of the Ecological Scale

The dragonfly's perceiving and acting are conjoint in that they serve a mutual aim (catching small insects and maintaining, in consequence, onboard energy resources). At the same time, they are disjoint in that they serve that aim in reciprocal ways, by the detection of information that constrains action and by the performance of actions that constrain perception. In a circularly causal manner, the dragonfly's perceiving alters its actions, thereby engendering new opportunities for perceiving, and thereby entailing further modifications of its actions. Intuitively, understanding the conjointness and disjointness of perception and action is a cornerstone of the theory of "knowing about."

The dragonfly's pursuit of prey is an example of intentional behavior. Such purposive movements (Tolman, 1932) or goal-directed actions are a hallmark of living things and are as commonplace terrestrially as the motions addressed by physical theory. Cybernetical efforts to capture intentional behavior, conducted for most of the latter half of the present century, sought to render intentional behavior as a combination of initial conditions (a set point) and control laws. Rather than providing understanding, this move regressed the general problem of intentional behavior to the highly particular problems of how and for what purpose given systems were designed (Kugler, Shaw, Vincente, & Kinsella-Shaw, 1990; Weir, 1985).

The thesis that systems expressing "knowing about" are the most general in respect to the principles that underlie them, suggests that intentional behavior is likely to demand a physical account of the most profound kind, with extremely broad implications. In contrast to the material systems that have come under the scrutiny of past and present physics—systems that must be aimed by extrinsically imposed initial conditions (classical mechanics) or pulled by a preexistent attractor (deterministic chaos)—a material system such as the dragonfly literally aims itself toward targets. Stated more completely, the dragonfly as an intentional material system exhibits both a significant insensitivity to extrinsically imposed initial conditions (the thicket is cluttered in variable ways at all length scales, a fact which the dragonfly does not seem to find overly bothersome) and an uncommon sensitive dependence on final conditions (a mosquito is usually caught, regardless of the number and variety of impediments) (Shaw & Kinsella-Shaw, 1988). It is as if the transformations of perception and action leave invariant the dragonfly's state of "wanting that it catch that particular mosquito" (philosophers sometimes refer to verbs that are followed naturally by "that" as *intentional idioms*). Relatedly, it is as if the dragonfly's intending, or "wanting that it catch that particular mosquito," binds the variables of information detection, energy control, and goal state, in a special way so as to effect a geodesic (a least distance, least time trajectory) and to conserve some particular (but as yet unknown) quantity.

These observations suggest that a useful approach to the natural phenomenon of intentional behavior can be provided by the mathematical theory of groups, a tool to which physics has turned repeatedly this century with great success whenever and wherever issues of invariance and conservation arise. A *group* is a set *G* of transformations or symmetry operations equipped with three rules: Any two operations can be combined to give a third (and this product is associative), there is one that does nothing at all (the identity), and every operation has an inverse (the combination of the two being the identity). A group is closed. No elements outside *G* are attainable by combining elements contained within *G*. In its applications in physics, a group is a measurement device that reveals certain, ideally essential properties, while ignoring others. Can a group be defined that captures the minimal essential structure, the basic symmetry, of intentional behavior? And if so, what hidden structure is it likely to disclose?

Our suspicion is that overseeing any efforts to identify the symmetry group for intentional behavior should be the thesis of organism–environment mutuality and reciprocity, strongly interpreted (Shaw, Kugler, & Kinsella-Shaw, 1990). This thesis dictates a number of reciprocities. Some aspects of intentional behavior refer to an interior frame of reference, the biology of the dragonfly. Other aspects refer to an exterior frame of reference, the thicket surrounding the dragonfly. By the strong mutuality thesis, the processes referred to these two frames should be reciprocal. Similarly, some aspects of intentional behavior are *hereditary,* in that what is happening now is entailed by what occurred previously, and other aspects are *anticipatory,* in that what is happening now is entailed by what will happen next. By the strong mutuality thesis, these past-referring and future-referring processes should be reciprocal. Also by the strong mutuality thesis, a reciprocity should exist between the informational and energetic aspects of intentional behavior, a reciprocity that has already been underscored in remarks above.

It is roughly apparent that fulfilled intentional behavior, such as the dragonfly maneuvering through the thicket to nab a gnat, consists of four operations: detecting information, intending a particular goal, controlling energy, and successively realizing the goal. In order to lay hold of the symmetry of intentional behavior, we shall need to represent these operations in a manageable form. We need to assign numbers to them. Two of these operations act on states in the exterior frame of reference—detecting information about the environment and one's self, and controlling energy to bring about specific movements of one's self with respect to the environment. The other two operations—intending a goal and realizing it—act on states in the interior frame. Capturing the contrast between the exterior and interior pairs can be achieved by using the real numbers $+1$ and -1 to represent the exterior pair as real operators and by using the imaginary numbers $+i$ and $-i$ to represent the interior pairs as imaginary operators. Since information about an environmental fact is a basis for anticipatory control, its detecting can be treated as the operator -1, to convey its acausal, time-backward nature; in contrast, the energy controlled to move in a particular manner, as the basis of hereditary control, can be treated as the operator $+1$, to convey its causal, time-forward nature. In a similar vein, since intending a goal is anticipatory and realizing a goal is hereditary, these can be treated as the operators $-i$ and $+i$, respectively.

Figure 11.5 depicts the preceding mathematical structure for the dragonfly of Figure 11.3. It defines a group (operations are associative, each has an inverse, and there is an identity). The question posed was how the variables of information detection, energy control, and goal state are bound together under the mosquito-catching intent. That they might do so by virtue of a group structure provides an answer that points to symmetries at nature's ecological scale shaping the functional order characteristic of that scale. We underscore the significance of symmetry in our final remarks.

Direct Perception: Symmetry Again

It is fairly obvious that perception is *the* means by which organisms know about their surroundings. The dragonfly picks its way through the thicket and aims itself at suitable prey by means of perception. If perception is not merely contingent

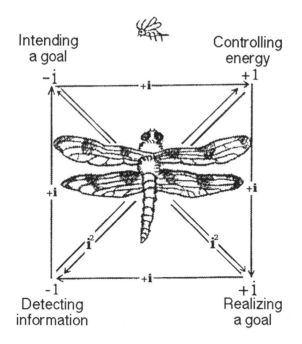

Intending
a goal

Controlling
energy

$-i$ $+i$ $+1$

$+i$ $+i$

i^2 i^2

-1 $+i$ $+1$

Detecting
information

Realizing
a goal

Figure 11.5. The persistence of an intention ("catch that mosquito") over variations in information detection, energy dissipation, and proximity to the "catch," together with the coherent fitting together of these variations, invites a group structure analysis. The depicted group is a cyclic group with its four operations linked by the flow operator i.

but entailed, following necessarily from maximizing the global rate of entropy production, then perception is a phenomenon to be understood in terms of lawful regularities and symmetry principles defined at the ecological scale of organisms and environments, rather than in terms of mental states, and formal languages of representation and computation. This leads to what may well prove to be, in the next century, the most important handle for taking hold of "knowing about" in a rigorously scientific manner—namely, *the understanding that perception must be "direct"* (i.e., achieves direct apprehension without intermediaries such as inference or matching to mental schemas). This handle, fashioned for us in its contemporary form by Gibson (1966, 1979/1986), provides a means for appreciating organisms as knowers and the environment as known in mutually compatible terms. *Direct perception is consonant with organism-environment mutuality and reciprocity:* Where the interpretations of perception that have dominated the past and present centuries have portrayed the dragonfly and its surroundings in disharmony, perception as direct renders the dragonfly and the functional description of its surroundings harmonious. Very importantly, direct perception does not create the epistemological paradoxes that have befallen all other theories of perception, paradoxes that would be expressed by phrases such as "the dragonfly's visual system invents its surroundings," "the thicket and prey are illusions of the dragonfly's brain," "tne dragonfly has foreknowledge of space," "the dragonfly has foreknowledge of the basic concepts needed to interpret the signals from its sensory organs," and so on. For Gibson, perception is specific to the environment and to self-movements because (1) information is specific to the environment and to self-movements, and (2) perception is specific to information.

Specificity is an intuitive idea of considerable power, as highlighted in our expectations for a biologically relevant information theory. It should become evident in the next century that the top priority of a science of cognition is a *general theory of specificity,* of how one thing can specify another and how specificity can be preserved over different and time-varying components of an organism–environment system (e.g., the components of the dragonfly–thicket system and the perception-action cycles that it manifests). This contrasts with the pursuit, by many scholars in the latter part of the present century, of a *general theory of representation* (e.g., Fodor, 1975). What is gained from the specificity of perception to the environment and self-motion? Nothing less than the grounding of "knowing about." Patently, for those who would seek a general theory of representation, any viable theory of what concepts an organism may be said to have and how they might be said to refer, presupposes and requires a theory of specification (Shaw et al., 1982).

The directness of perception follows, presumably, from nature being constrained in particular ways. Consequently, science in the twenty-first century can expect to advance significantly by pursuing, in as rigorous and as thoroughgoing a manner as possible, the implications of the postulate of direct perceiving. The reason why direct perceiving can be used in the way suggested is that direct perceiving, like organism–environment mutuality and reciprocity, and the persistence of intention over perception–action cycles discussed above, implies a symmetry. The importance of this implication is that, if it happens to be the right symmetry, then the conceptual route to understanding "knowing about" will have been identified. As we have learned so well this century, symmetry dictates design. The idea of constraining experimentation and theory building by symmetries is the ultimate intellectual legacy bequeathed to contemporary and future scientists by Einstein.

Perceiving is a "polyphasic" phenomenon, and the notion that perceiving is direct implies that the various phases of matter involved (mechanical, plasmic, biological, and psychological) must obey certain fundamental compatibility relations (Shaw & McIntyre, 1974). For the required compatibility, not only must laws be invariant within a phase but also they must exhibit conjoint invariance across phase boundaries. Direct perceiving implies a symmetry in the structure of the interactions among the laws of matter's different phases. To come to terms with perceiving as a natural state of affairs, therefore, is to understand lawful relations that are invariant over a change in phase. We have no illusions about the difficulty of pinning down the nature of the symmetry principle that fixes the directness of perceiving. It seems to us that neither the data nor the theoretical expertise available at the tail end of the twentieth century are at the level of sophistication required to formulate the intrinsic symmetry of the governing physical laws. To an important degree, contemporary data and theory are not up to the task because of a widespread and historical tendency to treat perception and action as if they were phenomena (1) outside the purview of universal physical principles and well-tried physical strategies, and (2) to be explained by accounts far less abstract, and considerably less general, than those that address motion and change in non-living material (Kugler & Turvey, 1987; Turvey, 1990a, 1990b). Only by reversing this tendency can the science of the twenty-first century hope to reveal the symmetry that underwrites the perceptual abilities of organisms and the action capabilities that they support. Such will be the charge for the new century's students of cognition who would wish to understand the "knowing about" that is exhibited every summer by the likes of dragonflies in the thickets of New England and by the human observers, like ourselves, who choose to watch and wonder about them.

Acknowledgments

Preparation of this manuscript was supported in part by National Science Foundation Grants BNS 90-11013 and BNS 91-09880 to Michael Turvey and National Institute of Child Health and Human Development HD-01994 to Haskins Laboratories. The contributions of Claudia Carello to the conceptual content of this paper and to its artwork is gratefully acknowledged.

References

Blum, H. F. (1951). *Time's arrow and evolution*. Princeton, NJ: Princeton University Press.

Brooks, R. (1991). Intelligence without representation. *Artificial Intelligence, 47,* 139–159.

Carello, C., Turvey, M. T., Kugler, P. N., & Shaw, R. E. (1984). Inadequacies of the computer metaphor. In M. Gazzaniga (Ed.), *Handbook of cognitive neuroscience* (pp. 229–248). New York: Plenum.

Clancy, (1992). The frame of reference problem in the design of intelligent machines. In K. V. Lehn (Ed.), *Architectures for intelligence (Proceedings of 22nd Carnegie Symposium on Cognition)* (pp. 357–423). Hillsdale, NJ: Erlbaum.

Effken, J. A., & Shaw, R. E. (1992). Ecological perspectives on the new artificial intelligence. *Ecological Psychology, 4,* 247–270.

Fodor, J. (1975). *Language of thought*. New York: Cromwell.

Full, R. J. (1989). Mechanics and energetics of terrestrial locomotion: Bipeds to polipeds. In W. Weiser & E. Gnaiger (Eds.), *Energy transformations in cells and organisms* (pp. 175–182). New York: Thieme Verlag

Gibson, J. J. (1961). Ecological optics. *Vision Research, 1,* 253–262.

Gibson, J.J. (1966). *The senses considered as perceptual systems*. Boston: Houghton Mifflin.

Gibson, J.J. (1979/1986). *The ecological approach to visual perception*. Hillsdale, NJ: Erlbaum.

Harnad, S. (1990). The symbol grounding problem. *Physica [D], 42,* 335–346.

Henderson, L. J. (1913). *The fitness of the environment*. New York: Macmillan.

Iberall, A., & Soodak, H. (1987). A physics for complex systems. In F. E. Yates (Ed.), *Self-organizing systems: The emergence of order* (pp. 499–520). New York: Plenum.

Johnson-Laird, P. N., Herrman, D. J., & Chaffin, R. (1984). Only connections: A critique of semantic networks. *Psychological Bulletin, 96,* 292–315.

Kirsch, D. (1991). Foundations of AI: The big issues. *Artificial Intelligence, 47,* 3–30.

Kugler, P. N., Shaw, R. E., Vincente, K. J., & Kinsella-Shaw, J. (1990). Inquiry into intentional systems 1: Issues in ecological physics. *Psychological Research, 52,* 98–121.

Kugler, P. N., & Turvey, M. T. (1987). *Information, natural law, and the self-assembly of rhythmic movement.* Hillsdale, NJ: Erlbaum.

Kugler, P. N., & Turvey, M. T. (1988). Self organization, flow fields, and information. *Human Movement Science, 7,* 97–129.

Lee, D. (1990). Getting around with light or sound. In R. Warren & A. Wertheim (Eds.), *Perception and control of self-motion* (pp. 487–506). Hillsdale, NJ: Erlbaum.

Pollack, J. (1993). On wings of knowledge: A review of Allen Newell's *Unified Theories of Cognition. Artificial Intelligence, 59,* 355–369.

Reed, E., & Jones, R. (1982). *Reasons for realism: Selected essays of James J. Gibson.* Hillsdale, NJ: Erlbaum.

Rosen, R. (1991). *Life itself.* New York: Columbia University Press.

Schrödinger, E. (1945). *What is life?* New York: Macmillan.

Sejnowski, T., & Rosenberg, C. (1987). Parallel networks that learn to pronounce English text. *Complex Systems, 1,* 145–168.

Shaw, B., McGowan, R., & Turvey, M. T. (1991). An acoustic variable specifying time-to-contact. *Ecological Psychology, 3,* 253–261.

Shaw, R. E., & Alley, T. (1985). How to draw learning curves: Their use and justification. In T. D. Johnston & A. T. Pietrewicz (Eds.), *Issues in the ecological study of learning* (pp. 275–304). Hillsdale, NJ: Erlbaum.

Shaw, R. E., Flascher, O., & Mace, W. M. (1994). Dimensionen der Ereigniswahrnehmung. In W. Prinz & B. Bridgeman (Eds.), *Enzyklopädie der Psychologie, Wahrnehmung, Konition,* Vol. 1 (pp. 457–528). Göttingen: Hogrefe, Verlag für Psychologie.

Shaw, R. E., & Kinsella-Shaw, J. (1988). Ecological mechanics: A physical geometry for intentional constraints. *Human Movement Science, 7,* 155–200.

Shaw, R. E., Kugler, P. N., & Kinsella-Shaw, J. (1990). Reciprocities of intentional systems. In R. Warren & A. Wertheim (Eds.), *Perception and control of self-motion* (pp. 579–620). Hillsdale, NJ: Erlbaum.

Shaw, R. E., & McIntyre, M. (1974). Algoristic foundations to cognitive psychology. In W. B. Weimer & D. S. Palermo (Eds.), *Cognition and the symbolic processes* (pp. 305–362). Hillsdale, NJ: Erlbaum.

Shaw, R.E. & Turvey, M.T. (1981). Coalitions as models for ecosystems: A realist perspective on perceptual organization. In M. Kubovy and J. Pomerantz (Eds.), *Perceptual organization* (pp. 343–416). Hillsdale, NJ: Erlbaum.

Shaw, R. E., Turvey, M. T., & Mace, W. (1982). Ecological psychology: The consequence of a commitment to realism. In W. Weimer & D. Palermo (Eds.), *Cognition and the symbolic processes* (pp. 159–226). Hillsdale, NJ: Erlbaum.

Solomon, H. Y., Turvey, M. T., & Burton, G. (1989). Gravitational and muscular variables in perceiving extent by wielding. *Ecological Psychology, 1,* 265–300.

Swenson, R. (1989). Emergent attractors and the law of maximum energy production: Foundations to a theory of general evolution. *Systems Research, 6,* 187–197.

Swenson, R., & Turvey, M. T. (1991). Thermodynamic reasons for perception–action cycles. *Ecological Psychology, 3,* 317–348.

Tolman, E. C. (1932). *Purposive behavior in animals and men.* New York: Century.

Turvey, M. T. (1990a). The challenge of a physical account of action: A personal view. In H. T. A. Whiting, O. G. Meijer, & P. C. W. van Wieringen (Eds.), *The natural-physical approach to movement control* (pp. 57–93). Amsterdam: VU University Press.

Turvey, M. T. (1990b). Coordination. *American Psychologist, 45,* 938–953.

Turvey, M. T. (1992). Affordances and prospective control: An outline of the ontology. *Ecological Psychology, 4,* 173–187.

Turvey, M. T., & Shaw, R. E. (1979). The primacy of perceiving: An ecological reformulation of perception for understanding memory. In L-G. Nilsson (Ed.), *Perspectives on memory research.* Hillsdale, NJ: Erlbaum.

Turvey, M. T., Shaw, R. E., Reed, E., & Mace, W. (1981). Ecological laws of perceiving and acting: In reply to Fodor and Pylyshyn (1981). *Cognition, 9,* 237–304.

Verschure, P. F. M. J. (1992). Taking connectionism seriously: The vague promise of subsymbolism and an alternative. *Proceedings of the 14th annual conference of the Cognitive Science Society.* Hillsdale, NJ: Erlbaum.

Weir, M. (1985). *Goal-directed behavior.* New York: Gordon & Beach.

Yates, F. E. (1986). Outline of a physical theory of physiological systems. *Canadian Journal of Physiology and Pharmacology, 60,* 217–248.

IV

LANGUAGE AND CATEGORIZATION

This part, containing chapters by James Jenkins, Willem Levelt, Dominic Massaro, and George Lakoff, generally deals with language processing and theories of categorization. Jenkins traces the sometimes contentious history of mental structures in this century with a broad based view of the future; Levelt's whimsical conversation with Professor Wundt is an effective introduction to the issue of the universal products of the mind, including linguistics, logic, law, anthropology, and economics; Massaro advances time by a century and gives a prophetic analysis of the properties of signal and percept; Lakoff's chapter ranges widely, from language to personality to mind–body issues, and is a stimulating tour de force of ideas and Western philosophy.

12

Unintended Consequences and the Future of Psychology[1]

JAMES J. JENKINS

Historians are always interested in the notion of *unintended consequences*. Some person, organization, or government performs an action aimed at a specific goal, a goal for which the action may in fact be successful, but in some other domain the action has surprising consequences that no one intended when they set out to achieve the first goal.

The classic example of unintended consequences is the "noble experiment" of prohibition in the United States in the 1920s. Obviously the well-meaning people who argued for a constitutional amendment to make alcohol illegal hadn't the slightest idea that one of the by-products of that amendment would be the formation of smuggling mobs and the reign of terror that accompanied the large scale organization of crime. (The populace apparently learned little from that episode either, as witnessed by the late-twentieth-century repeat of the prohibition regarding drug use, which seems to have had much the same consequence.) A different kind of example in the 1990s followed the end of the long "cold war" that the western democracies waged against the dictatorship of the Soviet Union. Everyone rejoiced in the "victory" in that war, but no one foresaw the awful ethnic and religious wars that followed the collapse of the USSR.

My present occupation comes about from a minor unintended consequence of one of humankind's great achievements. When the United Governments of the Northern Hemisphere decided to set up a permanent base on Mars, they planned for everything—or so they thought. Obviously, you don't succeed in a venture like that by just hoping that things are going to turn out all right. The experts pretested everything from the oxygen regeneration system and waste recycling to the minimal strength and weight of materials that could be tolerated in the weak Martian gravity.

They knew from the start that the psychological problems were going to be critical. The social psychologists understood that they couldn't set up a closed society of nine people in intimate contact with one another for ten years without coping with the fact that they would want to kill each other before the first long lap of the voyage was over. Even in the psychologically primitive 1930s, when Admiral Byrd set up the Furthest South Station close to the south pole, he elected to man it himself *alone* because he believed that even the two best-adjusted members of his party could not get along with each other through the long antarctic night—and that was only six months, not ten years.

So, of course, the planners picked one of the best young psychologists around, John Carter, with Ph.D.s in Physics *and* Experimental Psychology *and* a postdoctoral residency in Clinical Psychology. They knew that he could be helpful on the day-to-day "hard science" side, good on the problems in ergonomics and human engineering, and, perhaps most importantly, capable of doing the more subtle matters of personality monitoring and compatibility control. By now everyone knows how he finally came to take control of the mission and how he kept the crew sane with the invention of the Reality Game after the return ship malfunctioned. When they finally did get back, he was an international hero, of course, with wealth and fame thrust upon him.

What was the unintended consequence? Carter decided after his world tour that he really wanted to go back into psychology; that was the catch. Not even the most far-thinking planner had thought about the fact that a professional who has spent five years in mission training and then been completely out of touch with his field for ten more years would be hopelessly out of date in his professional field. [All of us should have known of course. One of my best graduate students had a good academic job and was ready for tenure when he took five years out "to find himself." (That was a common endeavor in the 20th century.) After he discovered that he had been there all along, he tried to get back into the field, but it was too late. He didn't even know what the problems were, much less the current techniques and models.]

Well, in the case of Carter, the upshot of it all was that a grateful government decided to try to make it up to him with special tutoring. They hired me to "retread his head"; all on the QT of course. I was supposed to fill him in on the important events in the field during the fifteen-year period and on its current status so he could "be a psychologist" again. I decided to retire from my Distinguished Professorship in Experimental Cognitive Neuroscience and spend a year or so full-time trying to bring him up to date, or as much up to date as possible. (Just trying to stay up with the field is like trying to catch up with an avalanche; the field keeps thundering along in 500 different journals while you're chasing it.)

To make sense of my story and to understand what I was trying to do, you have to know a little bit about the nature of American psychology back in the twentieth century. All the interesting developments revolved around the concept of mental structure. The notion that the mind was structured was really an idea that had to be rediscovered during the second half of that century. Of course, in Europe there was a lot of sympathy for the idea of mental structure even from the turn of the century, but after Part II of the Great World War, psychology was pretty much an American monopoly. Behaviorism was in charge in the United States. You couldn't talk about "mental faculties" or "memory" or "levels of analysis" or "mental structure," because those ideas were regarded as fundamentally unscientific. In the great midwestern universities where the psychologists bragged about being "dustbowl empiricists," you couldn't even talk about "making up your mind" without having your colleagues look at you strangely.

The only interesting thing you *could* talk about was learning. And to keep subjective elements out of that study, psychologists devoted their energies to the study of animal learning. As a result, the "Golden Age of Learning Theory" ensued. People who persisted in being interested in *human* learning had to follow in Ebbinghaus's path. They studied "verbal learning." In this case, to stay respectable and to avoid the contaminating effects of previous learning, the investigators studied the learning of items for which the learners essentially had no history— that is, nonsense syllables, and nonsense designs, or random dot patterns. Of course, all of this had the result of hiding the effects of mental structure, whatever they might be.

In the second half of the century, however, a few adventurous souls began to follow the lead of the psychologists Hebb and Bousfield. (Most people know something about Hebb who was pushing the idea that learning changed assemblies of brain structures, but very few people seem to know about Bousfield.) Although only a few people paid any attention to Bousfield's work (and he couldn't get it published in the standard journals), he persisted in the study of *mental organization*. These organizations showed up readily when people tried to recall words. He found that the recall even of messy categories like "all the pleasant words you know" was quite orderly as was the recall of "all the unpleasant words you know." During the 1950s and 1960s, Bousfield and many of the young psychologists who listened to him excitedly explored the effects of structure in free recall. If subjects were given lists of words in random order but the words were drawn from meaningful categories, the lists tended to be recalled pretty much category by category. Even if the words were not obviously related, it was discovered that the subjects tended to impose some structure on them when they tried to recall them. Further, it shortly became clear that the more structure there was in the list and the more the subjects did things that made the structure clear (by sorting or categorizing, or evaluating the words), the better they recalled the lists—*even when they were not trying to learn them*. That is, there were automatic effects of stirring up those mental structures.

That was an important finding, of course. People could remember words better by attending to how they related to mental structures than by trying to remember them. About that time psychologists realized that they didn't have the faintest idea what people did when they were told to "learn"; that instruction simply covered the fact that the learners did anything they thought would help—which frequently was no help at all. For example, most naive learners believe that the best way to remember something is to repeat it over and over, but when that technique was explicitly tested, it turned out that it was pretty poor. The best way to remember something was to relate it to some *mental structure,* either unique to the domain or area of the topic being learned or to some all-purpose structure developed just to help people recall material. (These special "remembering structures" were called mnemonics and their use goes back to the ancient Greeks, but psychologists didn't study them seriously until studies of structure in memory became acceptable in the second half of the century.)

Well, once studies of mental structure became legitimate, psychologists began to study all kinds of structures. In the 1960s and 1970s Garner showed (to everyone's surprise) that perception of patterns and designs was a function not of the individual items that were shown to subjects but, rather, of the total set from which they were drawn. Other psychologists began looking at story structures (What makes stories easy to remember?), the structure of oral history and folk tales (How do they hold their form over generations of telling and retelling?), the structure of dialogue, the layout of problem spaces, and everything imaginable in the laboratory.

Finally it occurred to psychologists and educators to study the structure of academic subject matters—that is, the things that we try to teach students in our schools. Presumably these are structures that really matter—unlike stories and folk tales.

As a result of all of this work, it became clear that perception, memory, and knowledge are all structured. Some structures are simple linear strings like lists; some structures are circular like the properties of colors; some structures are hierarchies like classifications of plants or animals (lots of psychologists liked that), and some are tree structures, like sentences. The most interesting areas of knowledge turned out to be complex multidimensional collections of many kinds of structures, blending procedural skills, declarative knowledge, and organizational properties of rules, forms, and structures.

Finally, when the structures of some of the subject matters were becoming clear, psychologists tackled the question of how to teach structures. Obviously, it just doesn't do to say, "Learn this hierarchy of relations and you will understand all you need to know about this subject matter." It doesn't work that way. The structure of a subject matter is an end product of a lot of different experiences and complexes of interrelationships; it is not in itself a causal entity. At first we didn't know how to arrange experiences that would have the different kinds of structures as outcomes.

Studies in lots of different fields showed that experts knew thousands and thousands of facts, not all of which appeared to be well organized. And the experts seemed to employ hundreds (sometimes thousands) of rules in complex networks of relationships, many of which they couldn't tell you about because they were expressions of tacit knowledge acquired through years of experience. The experts themselves had rarely tried to coax the knowledge to the surface to look at it in explicit, verbal form.

Finally in the last decade of the century, investigators began to realize that orderly structures could be looked at as specialized mathematical groups. That insight (which had been suggested by the mathematician Poincaré and the philosopher Cassirer early in the century) led to a fundamental idea that revolutionized learning, namely, that you didn't need to teach the students everything that you wanted them to know. What you had to do was to discover the "root," so to speak, of the mathematical structures that represented the knowledge. If you could isolate a "generator set" (the right basic set of rules and elements), you could teach that set very thoroughly. After the students had learned that, they would be capable of *generating* all the aspects of the whole group when they were needed.

It is a little hard to explain this to outsiders but think of a really simple system, like adjective–noun descriptions. Suppose you had a bunch of forms, like circles, squares, triangles, half moons, pentagons, and the like, and suppose they came in a lot of different colors. You could learn ten form names, ten color names and one rule *(put the color name in front of the form name)* and all of a sudden you would be able to name 100 colored forms correctly. That's just a simple combinatorial group, but look how efficient it is; you learn 21 things and you get 100 different labels for free. Or think about multiplying; you learn the "times table," just 100 products, and some rules about how to write numbers down and how to "carry" numbers, and—Voilà! You can multiply any number by any other number. Look at that power; you learn a few things and then you can do an *infinite* number of different multiplications. Do you begin to see the power? This led a lot of psychologists to get really serious about finding the mathematical structures that underlie perception and memory and the different fields of knowledge.

Well, while one group got hot on this business of finding the underlying structures, another group of psychologists continued studying experts to see how they operated. To their surprise they found (as Herb Simon had suggested a long time ago) that for lots of problems the experts didn't problem-solve, they just *recognized the problem* as one of a given kind out of their vast store of experiences, and applied the appropriate remedy. So they were super-fast in getting to solutions but in a sense they were "unconscious" about the way they solved problems!

Well, that was the state of the field when Carter got busy preparing for Mars. While he went off to train to be a hero, we moved on to the next stage of development in psychology. The one new technique that had not yet been thoroughly exploited by scientific psychology was *virtual reality*. Of course, John was involved with virtual reality in the elaborate trainers that were devised for the Mars mission, with simulations of landings, space craft emergencies, working in low gravity, and all that kind of thing. But that kind of training had been going on since they first built flight simulators after the Great Wars. No one realized what would happen when the scientists and educators got hold of the tools. There's another unintended consequence.

Somebody put two and two together and decided that there was a solution to the problem of professional training. If the quick solutions of experts are "recognitions" based on experience, rather than brute force problem solving, why not arrange to give students *massive amounts of experience* via virtual reality? This ought to be the way to attain real results! It should be more efficient and more satisfactory than any amount of traditional classroom lecturing about facts, rules, and principles. And, besides, it might be a lot of fun!

To be honest, I have to confess that no educator invented this idea; it happened spontaneously, and then we all saw how good it was and formalized it. If my historical research is correct, the movement started innocently enough with a project in Minnesota that was designed to build an expert system in pediatric cardiology. As the psychologists on that project tried to figure out what the experts knew and how they functioned, they began to simulate cases on the computers. This let them study what the experts were doing and thinking as each item of information was discovered or revealed. They added the virtual reality aspects to the cases to make them more lively and realistic than just having a screen full of data. If you were in the study, you could "see" a kid brought into the hospital, "hear" his mother report his symptoms, "listen" to his heart and lungs, "palpate" the body, and "feel" his reflexes, "send him off" for tests, or whatever. While the expert was going through all this, the psychologists made the experts do divided attention tasks so they could see when the cardiologists were really immersed in the case and know when an important item of information came in that captured the cardiologist's attentional capacity. That was all well and good, and the investigators of expert knowledge progressed nicely in teasing out the structural, algorithmic base of the experts' knowledge.

But another unintended consequence occurred. The medical students began fooling around with the cases; playing with them as if they were video games. I suppose it went something like this:

Student 1: Hey, here's the case of the kid from Frostbite Falls. Let's see, he comes to the hospital at 5:30 P.M. He's got a lot of heart symptoms. [Listening to the heart.] Man, that sounds lousy; he's in trouble all right. And his mother says he's been squatting a lot; that's supposed to be a bad symptom, isn't it? What do we do now? The choices I've got here are: *Order lab tests* (specify tests).
                                                                  Provide maintenance.
                                                                  Go eat dinner and hurry back.
Student 2: I know that case, you can't get lab tests at that time of night—for hours and hours anyway, and if you go eat dinner, the kid dies. Bingo, you killed him! Then you not only feel bad, the machine locks up and you have to start the case all over. The first thing you have to do is watch over the kid's maintenance. Oh, and watch out for jaundice too. If this case has jaundice, the diagnosis will be coarctation of the aorta. I don't know why, but it will be.

"*I don't know why but it will be.*" That's the tipoff of course. The students were getting to be "recognition experts" through vicarious experience. Their professors seized on this; after all, that's what internships were for, weren't they? You do internships to build up "practice." Now, with virtual reality, students didn't need to be in a clinic waiting for experience to cumulate; they could cram weeks of "hands on" vicarious experience into every day! It didn't take a rocket scientist to realize that schools could bombard medical students with cases of all sorts, rare cases, common cases, typical cases, deceptive cases, you name it. The ordinary limits of internships no longer applied. Most physicians who had been trained in university hospitals never got to see common things like chicken pox, or croup, or even indigestion because the most common disorders never get to a teaching hospital. But now, the fledgling doctors could be given anything you thought might be useful.

It went this way: The subject matter experts would work on a problem or set of problems until they understood its structure down to the finest detail. Then they would create the algorithmic procedures that would let the teachers generate any of the infinite varieties of the problem that they wanted. And, because the systems were rule-based, the machines could deal appropriately and realistically with the consequences of anything that the students did. It was a tremendous task, of course, but it was made easier by the fact that the developers could draw on the massive data bases that had been built up in special content areas and tie them into the particular cases without having to do all the work again. For example, if the student prescribed medications that would result in harmful combinations, the virtual reality could predict the consequence from its pharmaceutical data base and make it happen. In advanced systems the machine could even explain *why* it happened, but most students were not much interested in that; they hurried on to find proper combinations and got on to the next case. In short, when any disorder was thoroughly understood, it could be instantiated in virtual reality and the practical treatment of the disorder could be taught through experience with hundreds of exemplars.

We shouldn't really have been surprised that this was possible. All of us acquire the complex structure of our native language by exposure. And the people from whom we learn not only don't know the underlying structure of the language, they don't even know that they are teaching! Just the same, all of us develop enormous expertise in the use of that language. Now, in the language case you can argue that we get a lot of assistance from special brain structures that have evolved to do language, but, of course, the same thing must be true for all sorts of aspects of living in this world. For social animals like us, there are certainly genetic predispositions for relating to other members of the species both alone and in groups.

The advantages of the new teaching techniques were tremendous in all the professions. The best thing in medicine was that the students didn't hurt anybody in the course of their training. If they screwed up, they just replayed the case until they got it right! (In the old days that was the way they trained weather men about tornadoes. There was no comprehensive theory about tornadoes. So, they had the students draw and analyze one historic tornado map after another. After a couple of weeks of doing that, the student could just glance at a map and say, "That's a tornado map"—and he'd be right.) Practice and corrective feedback over hundreds of instances lead to good intuitions! So who cares about formal knowledge? Let engineers design; let architects build; let the psychologists diagnose, and then let them live with their products on an accelerated time scale while the virtual machines, virtual buildings, and virtual patients suffer the wear and tear and the stresses and strains that are calibrated into their virtual lives.

Well, like everything else, there were some unintended consequences of that development as well. A strange anomaly arose. The scientists who were probing for the deepest structures of knowledge were able to design devices that enabled practitioners to be trained who could do their jobs by intuition! As you might have predicted, psychology departments (like a lot of other disciplines) simply split apart. The scientists trying to determine the algorithmic bases of subject matters found they had more in common with mathematicians and the designers of robots than they did with their former colleagues who were trying to solve practical organizational and social problems or doing diagnosis and therapy. The old twentieth-century split in psychology between the clinicians and the academics was mild compared to the chasm that opened between the RATS (as the rationalist, algorithm-building psychologists were called) and the INTS (the intuitive psychologists who did the applied work of the field).

The RATS were jealous of their fluent, speedy colleagues. The RATS could solve problems, of course, but it took a long time because they had to generate every step that they needed. Each case was the equivalent of developing a whole system from the ground up. The INTS on the other hand could whip through problems, recommending action steps, diagnosing, prescribing, and treating, without having any means to explain what it was that underlay the decisions they were making—just pure clinical judgment. So we had slow, ponderous thinking machines on the one hand who knew everything there was to know about deduction, hypothesis testing, and principles of explanation and, on the other hand, the whiz kids who could solve problems, but couldn't explain or justify what they recommended. The upshot was that the INTS, who were in some sense the product of the RATS, walked away with all the money and glory. (You can see that this is a kind of Frankenstein story.)

The irony, of course, was that without the RATS the INTS wouldn't have had their virtual realities in which they honed and sharpened their intuitions by dealing with myriads of virtual patients. On the other side, without old-fashioned skilled practitioners, the RATS wouldn't know what the problems were and wouldn't have any experts from which to tease out the dimensions of expertise. (And they wouldn't have received any financial support for their studies of the algorithmic base of the disorders and social structures. It was certain that the government wasn't going to support those kinds of mind games if there hadn't been some real payoff in the society.)

So despite the fact that their destinies were linked, the RATS and the INTS went their separate ways; they simply could not tolerate each other in the same departments. Things continued that way for a while in all of the fields. The RATS and their computer brethren did their studies of experts and developed the systems that trained the professionals that did the work of the world. The INTS diagnosed, designed, healed, and what-have-you and took refresher courses when the algorithm for a new, deeper, insight was worked out.

> "Learn to treat the new future-shock neurosis!
> Twenty cases in one evening.
> Three hundred cases in a week.
> Expertise guaranteed! Sign up now!"

But, as you should expect by now, there were a few unintended consequences that ruined the entire scheme. The first thing that happened was that the professional certification procedures broke down. The RATS didn't need to be certified, of course, because they were academics, so no one cared whether they were competent or not. The INTS on the other hand, were important to society, but no one knew how to test them because their knowledge was mostly nonverbal. The only thing you could do was give them the textbook cases and see if they gave the proper school solution. Given the uncertainty of psychological practice and the need for long time periods to evaluate results, it might be years before you could decide whether someone was qualified. So, certification was largely a shambles; authorities usually asked how many hours of virtual training the candidates claimed and certified on that basis.

When the RATS reached the point where the experts in the field were those who had been trained by the virtual reality technique, the field went into crisis and the work came to a shuddering halt. Even though the RATS used their most sophisticated techniques, the only coherent and consistent things they could find were their own algorithms! What was worse, the algorithms were increasingly buried under a set of "superstitious beliefs" (in the old sense of Skinner's analysis of superstitious behavior). The INTS were bright people of course, and like all bright people they had tried to "figure out" what was going on. Quite naturally, they began to invent theories of behavior to account for what they saw in their clients and what they saw themselves doing. Well, the outcome was bizarre! Because they had never been trained in the history of the field and lacked any foundation in cognitive psychology, learning theory, social psychology, or personality theory, they were devising anew almost all the schemes that anyone had thought of in the entire span of western thought. A group in New York, for example, had decided that there must be four kinds of fundamental personalities: optimistic-active, pessimistic-inactive, aggressive-active, and calm-inactive, a typology that goes back to the ancient Greeks. A group in Florida (where people don't wear many clothes) had converged on body types and supposed that personalities were the result of the three dimensions of obesity, muscularity or boniness. (Shades of Sheldon!) A group in Alaska developed a theory that personality was a product of climate and held that mood was closely related to the amount of sunlight one was exposed to. Still another group believed that everything was a product of how one talked to oneself and advocated that every morning patients should recite "Every day in every way I am getting better and better" in front of a mirror. And so it went. Every scheme, good or bad, that anyone had devised was reinvented. What was worse, as the practicing INTS developed theories, their beliefs changed, and they began challenging their intuitions and altering the carefully calibrated responses they had learned in their virtual reality training.

You can see that the situation in both branches of psychology was intolerable. The RATS had no more original expertise to study, and the INTS were throwing off their training in an effort to *understand* what they found themselves doing. The quality of practice declined, and some patients seemed trapped forever in shifting paradigms of superstitious personality theory.

But one light seemed to be shining in the psychological darkness. Stories of remarkably successful application of psychology were coming out of Minnesota. Responsible leaders of RATS and INTS went to the Twin Cities to examine the stories. What they found was in a way almost a joke—or at least a pun. The heart of the success was a pair of twins! You may remember that in the last century there was lot of publicity given to the twin studies at the University of Minnesota. The investigators developed a twin registry and studied hundreds of twin pairs. Most of the publicity went to the dramatic studies of twins reared apart, but, of course, those can be interpreted only in terms of twins raised together.

Well, in the course of all those studies of twin pairs a sizable number of twins decided to become psychologists of one sort or another. The case of interest was a pair of identical twins (Bill and Hank James) who went down the two separate tracks; one trained as a RAT and the other as an INT! And then, miracle of miracles, they rejoined and worked together. Can you see the picture? One set of genes trained in both ways! No matter what problem was presented, the client got the best of both worlds: a quick appraisal and classification of the problem if it was one for which the "canned programs" had prepared Bill, and the deep, searching examination of the problem and the generation of the phenotype from the basic generative principles of personality, or social, or organizational psychology if the problem was unique. The pair was awesome in efficiency and power!

The effect on the field was something akin to the application of antibiotics in the field of medicine. Before antibiotics, there were a lot of "schools" of medicine; you could pretty much believe whatever you liked. But after antibiotics, the field changed. One school of thought had something that REALLY worked. In the face of such strong evidence, the debates died away and medicine moved into a new era. The work of the James twins had somewhat the same effect on psychology. The combination of approaches did something enormously more than either approach alone.

Well, eventually there was a "psychology summit." The leaders of all of the associations of the RATS and the INTS convened in Geneva and thrashed about for two furious months in hammering out a new agreement about how the various parts of the field of psychology were going to relate to each other. They decided that both groups could survive whole only if they merged their knowledge and skills and tried to combine their specialties in the head of each trainee. The new trainees were to be known as RAINS, not just a combinations of the old names but a recognition of the training needed to bring the whole field to fruition.

Oh, . . .
"Hello, John!"
"Good to see you Jim. Can we begin?"

Note

1. Inserting scientific references into this "story" seemed inappropriate. Instead, I have limited myself to listing some suggested reading. The reader will have little trouble discovering which of these is related to the various segments of the story.

Suggested Reading

Baars, B. (Ed.). (1986). *The cognitive revolution in psychology*. New York: Guilford Press.
Bousfield, W. A. (1953). The occurrence of clustering in the recall of randomly arranged associates. *Journal of General Psychology, 49*, 229–240.

Brown, R. (1973). *A first language: The early stages.* Cambridge, Mass.: Harvard University Press.

Burroughs, E. R. (1939). *John Carter of Mars.* New York: Ballentine Books.

Byrd, R. E. (1938). *Alone.* New York: G. P. Putnam.

Cassirer, E. (1944). The concept of group and the theory of perception. *Philosophy and Phenomenological Research, V,* 1–35.

Feltovich, P. J., Johnson, P. E., Moller, J. H., & Swanson, D. B. (1980). The role and development of medical knowledge in diagnostic expertise. Paper presented at the meeting of the American Educational Research Association, April 1980.

Foss, D. J. (1968). Learning and discovery in the acquisition of structured material: Effects of number of items and their sequence. *Journal of Experimental Psychology, 77,* 341–344.

Franks, J. J., & Bransford, J. D. (1971). Abstraction of visual patterns. *Journal of Experimental Psychology, 90,* 65–74.

Garner, W. R. (1974). *The processing of information and structure.* Potomac, Md.: Erlbaum.

Garner, W. R. (1991). Afterword: A final commentary. In G. R. Lockhead & J. R. Pomerantz, (Eds.), *The perception of structure* (327–332). Washington, D.C.: American Psychological Association.

Hyde, T. S., & Jenkins, J. J. (1969). Differential effects of incidental tasks on the organization of recall of a list of highly associated words. *Journal of Experimental Psychology, 82,* 472–481.

Jenkins, J. J., Wald, J., & Pittenger, J. B. (1978). Apprehending pictorial events: An instance of psychological cohesion. In C. W. Savage (Ed.), *Cognition and perception: Issues in the philosophy of psychology, Vol. 9: Minnesota studies in the philosophy of science* (pp. 129–163). Minneapolis: University of Minnesota Press.

Poincaré, H. (1952/1913). *Mathematics and science; last essays.* New York: Dover Publications.

Shaw, R. E., Wilson, B. E., & Wellman, H. (1986). Abstract conceptual knowledge: How we know what we know. In V. McCabe & G. J. Balzano (Eds.), *Event Cognition: An ecological perspective* (pp. 59–78). Hillsdale, N.J.: Erlbaum.

Simon, H. A. (1992). Alternative representations for cognition: Search and reasoning. In H. L. Pick, Jr., P. Van den Broek, & D. C. Knill (Eds.), *Cognition: Conceptual and methodological issues* (pp. 121–141). Washington, D.C.: American Psychological Association.

13

Chapters of Psychology

WILLEM J. M. LEVELT

An Interview with Wilhelm Wundt (1832–1920)

Sehr geehrter Herr Professor Wundt, what is your opinion about the place of psychology among the sciences of mind?[1]

As the science of the universal forms of direct experience, it is the foundation of the sciences of mind. Psychology is at the same time the most general science of mind and the foundation of all others, such as philology, history, economics, law, etc.[a]

Are these special sciences of the mind, then, "chapters of human psychology," just like, for instance, developmental psychology or general psychology?

The psychological analysis of the most general products of mind, such as language, mythical representations, moral norms, is psychology's due, in part as a necessary expansion of its territory over the phenomena of shared mental life, in part as an aid in grasping complex psychological phenomena at all.[b]

But is it realistic to expect that anthropologists (whom you call "Völkerpsychologen"), linguists, or historians who study these products of mental life will ever consider themselves psychologists?

It could appear that psychology, too, would be best served if the one who ventures to address the anthropological issues combines the qualifications of the historian and the philologist with those of the psychologist. But for two reasons I believe that there is little prospect, at least for the time being, that this wish will be fulfilled. First, given the current partitioning of scientific research, one can hardly expect the philologist or historian to approach the issues in a way that would satisfy the present standards of scientific psychology. Second, maybe one should not even blame him for this, because his task and the perspectives with which he necessarily approaches the issues are essentially different.[c] However, anthropology as such will remain part of psychology.[d]

You are called the father of experimental psychology. Will these other "parts" of psychology be experimental in nature?

Just like the natural sciences, psychology has two exact methods at its disposal: The first one, the experimental method, serves the analysis of the simpler

Figure 13.1. The author (left) interviewing Wundt (right).

psychological processes; the second one, the observation of the universal products of mind, serves the study of higher psychological processes and developments.[e] *Where, then, do you see the boundaries of the experimental method?*

Its limits are reached only where specific mental phenomena and products arise from living in a human society; these are inaccessible to experimentation, such as is the case for language, mythology, and morals.[f] These mental products are the objects of observation.[g]

Finally, what is your conception of the mind–body relationship?

Such a relationship can be nothing else than two mutually connected causal chains, which, however, cannot affect eacsh other because of the incomparability of their parts. I have already called this the principle of psychophysical parallelism.[h] So, for instance, the elements that figure in a spatial or temporal mental image will also entertain a regular relation of coexistence or succession in their physiological substrates.[i]

Thank you, Professor Wundt, for these helpful comments.

From Wundt to Marr

Where are we now, almost a century later? In this section I will argue that, in spite of substantial progress in the study of mind, Wundt's double distinction is by and large still valid. The first one concerns (simple) process versus (complex) product, the second one experiment versus observation; these distinctions are still ruling the relations between psychology and the other sciences of mind.

Process versus product: Marr's three levels of explanation

According to David Marr (1982), the "top level" of understanding any information-processing device is its abstract *computational theory*. This is a formal characterization of the input-to-output mapping of the device. Or, in Wundt's terms, it is a (formal) description of the system's *product*. One example of such a theory is a visual grammar, a formal characterization of three-dimensional interpretations for some domain of two-dimensional scenes. Another example is a generative grammar, a formal characterization of the well-formed sentences of a language. As we saw, language is Wundt's pet example of a complex psychological product. The goal of linguistics is to provide a computational theory of this product of mind. In Wundt's terms we are at this level dealing with anthropology, which is a proper part of psychology.

Marr's second level is the *algorithmic theory*. It deals with how the computation is done, how an input representation is transformed into an output representation.[2] There are myriad ways of generating a language's well-formed sentences, and myriad ways of parsing two-dimensional stereo patterns into three-dimensional configurations of objects. The psychological aim here is, of course, to come up with an algorithm that faithfully models how we, human beings, generate sentences or parse stereoscopic scenes. The algorithmic theory is a *process* theory. This is the traditional domain of psychology, dating back to Wundt and earlier. Time and again, Wundt stresses that the primary psychological phenomena are events, processes *("Vorgänge")*, not objects.

Marr's third level deals with the *physical implementation* of these processes. How is a mental process realized in the nervous system? Wundt was still largely in the dark about these implementational issues (though his ruminations about the substrate of spatial and temporal images are certainly consonant with the later discoveries of retinotopic mapping in the visual cortex and the recent work by Georgopoulos et al., 1989 on the time course of mental rotation in the motor cortex).

How does the product/process distinction relate to psychology's place among the sciences of mind? My thesis is that, by and large, general psychology in the twentieth century has kept to its traditional role of studying processes, of seeking explanations at the algorithmic level. And it has been very good at that. But the corollary is that it has tended to ignore the universal products of mind; it has largely left computational theorizing to what I shall call the special sciences of mind, linguistics, logic, law, sociology, anthropology, and, as I shall argue below, economics.

Psychology has not been in the forefront asking questions such as: What is a *possible* human language? What are *possible* systems of human spatial orientation? What are *possible* kinship systems? What are *possible* musical systems? What are *possible* conceptions of other people's intentional states?" And so on. In short, psychologists have tended to ignore the issue of universals of human cognition, our genetic cognitive endowment.[3]

Instead, and in the best of cases, psychologists have accepted one or another existing cognitive system as a given and studied how it functions. And here, they have been quite successful. We now have sophisticated process theories of visual scene analysis, of word and sentence parsing, of the perception of rhythm and tonality, of inference making, and so forth.

In the worst of cases, though, psychologists have continued to stay away from the naturally given systems. In the tradition of Ebbinghaus (who was the first to study verbal memory experimentally, but by means of nonsense syllables), they have so much "purified" their experimental materials that the ecologically given system (of memory, of object recognition, of spatial attention, or what have you) is immunized. The resulting theories of processing are often mathematically sophisticated, but of questionable generalizability (i.e., ecological validity). To conclude this point, psychologists have been more than happy to accept Wilhelm Wundt's experimental psychology, but they have been far less inspired by him as the father of *Völkerpsychologie*. Although products of mind are often the object of study in developmental psychology (e.g., What is the structure of children's number system, their lexicon, or their conception of time?), they seldom are in Wundt's core area, general psychology. By and large, general psychology (i.e., the study of general principles of mental life) has taken the complex products of mind for granted, leaving their analysis to the special sciences of mind, such as linguistics, anthropology, law, logic, sociology, musicology, and what have you. And there has never been much prospect indeed for Wundt's wish in this respect to be fulfilled—that students of these products of mind are themselves sophisticated in psychology. In other words, psychology has left some of its most precious gems to the care of other disciplines.

Experiment Versus Observation

Wundt's position here was straightforward. Simple psychological processes should be studied by the experimental method. Complex mental processes, however, are inaccessible to experimentation and should, therefore, be approached indirectly—namely, by analyzing their products or outcomes. It is society that stabilizes such products (a language, a system of norms, etc.). They are inaccessible to experimental study; observation is the only appropriate method here.

At this point, one should say that what Wundt established as the father of experimental psychology flourished substantially—better than he could have foreseen. Already in Wundt's own time, there were remarkable efforts to study experimentally higher-order processes such as reading, thinking, sentence comprehension; this in spite of Wundt's castigations (Wundt, 1907, 1908). But it is especially since the so-called cognitive revolution of the 1950s and 1960s that the experimental method became successfully applied to complex mental processes as well. One of the main forces here has been psycholinguistics. The experimental work by George Miller and his associates on syntactic processing in language comprehension still stands as a landmark of experimental innovation and creativity. Now, thirty years later, we have at our disposal a wide gamut of experimental methods that trace processes of lexical access, syntactic parsing, and discourse interpretation "on line." A very similar development is currently under way in the study of our skill of speaking (Levelt, 1989, 1993). For Wundt, the creation of sentences—one of the key issues in his psychology of language—was entirely in the domain of *Völkerpsychologie*—that is, inaccessible to experimentation.

Not only has the experimental method conquered the domain of complex mental processing, it also came to be used in the study of outcomes or products of complex processing. We now ask our subjects to judge the well-formedness of sentences; we ask them which bet they prefer, or which of two visual patterns they find more pleasing.

Although these developments have shown Wundt's assignment of methods to be untenable, it still governs the relations between psychology and its neighboring sciences of mind. Psychology is the only science of mind where the dominant methodology is experimental. One does see an occasional experiment in anthropology and a few more in economics, but that is about it. The major method for the other sciences is systematic observation: questionnaires, statistics, participant observation, introspection, diary studies, or whatever the local art may be. After almost a century, Wundt's assignment of research methodologies to disciplines (whether or not "parts of psychology") is still in force. Although there can be good reasons to opt for one methodology over another (for instance, it would be plainly impossible to approach historical issues by means of experiment), these methodological predilections often lack intrinsic motivation. It is, in fact, remarkable to what extent psychology and experimental psychology have become associated in twentieth-century psychology—often to the degree of near synonymy. It is somewhat like defining history as the science of archive searching.

Linguistics and Microeconomics: Two Computational Chapters of Psychology

In this section I elaborate on the sketched relationship between psychology and the other sciences of mind in light of two examples—linguistics and microeconomics. I argue that, in spite of their huge differences in subject matter, they entertain the same formal relationship to psychology. And that relationship is probably quite similar for other sciences of the mind.

Linguistics

Generative theories of grammar, Marr (1982) argued, are computational theories. They delineate the well-formed linguistic representations (syntactic, phonological, etc.) that the mind is capable of computing. Psycholinguistic theories, on the other hand, are algorithmic in nature. They deal with the mental processes that generate or parse the structural representations postulated in the computational theory.

Marr gave the advice to proceed from top to bottom in cognitive science. First produce a formal account of what the device is intended to compute, then start bothering about how it does the computing. The physical implementation will rarely, if ever, be a major constraint on the algorithmic theory, according to Marr (1982). Chomsky's position has been similar:

> There seems to be little reason to question the traditional view that investigation of performance will proceed only so far as understanding of underlying competence permits. (Chomsky. 1965, p. 10)

In other words, it makes little sense to create theories of human language parsing (theories of performance, algorithmic theories) without a solid understanding of the mental grammar in the language user (a theory of competence, a computational theory).

This is a rather ascetic position. Linguists are, not surprisingly, not too pressed to complete their chapter of psychology. And psycholinguists, I fear, don't have the patience to wait for that glorious moment. Are they, then, meanwhile messing about in gloom? Not in my experience. Instead, the two enterprises are not entirely independent. In fact, one of the attractions of Marr's distinction between computational and algorithmic levels of explanation is that one has to bother about the correct *assignment* of an explanatory factor. Is it computational or algorithmic? Chomsky and Halle pointed out this problem a quarter of a century ago, in a less ascetic, more balanced mood:

> It must, incidentally, be borne in mind that the specific competence–performance delimitation provided by a grammar represents a hypothesis that might prove to be in error when other factors that play a role in performance and the interrelation of these various factors come under investigation. . . . When a theory of performance ultimately emerges, we may find that some of the facts we are attempting to explain do not really belong to grammar but instead fall under the theory of performance, and that certain facts that we neglect, believing them to be features of performance, should really have been incorporated in the system of grammatical rules. (Chomsky & Halle, 1968, p. 111)

This implies the possibility that algorithmic research may affect the computational theory. Hence, the two enterprises should go hand-in-hand, as has been Professor Wundt's good advice all along.

Any computational theory involves an idealization, an abstraction from process and implementation. Chomsky's rigorous idealization for linguistics goes like this:

> Linguistic theory is concerned primarily with an ideal speaker-listener, in a completely homogeneous speech-community, who knows its language perfectly and is unaffected by such grammatically irrelevant conditions as memory limitations, distractions, shifts of attention and interest, and errors (random or characteristic) in applying his knowledge of the language in actual performance. (Chomsky, 1965, p. 3)

During the almost three decades following this demarcation, we have learned to ask two questions. The first one is: Are the computational assumptions correct,— that is, are they psychologically valid? And the second one is: Are we making the psychologically correct assignments to the computational and the algorithmic levels of explanation?

Storms have raged over these issues. We have seen dramatic changes and diversification in grammatical theorizing. Some, such as Gazdar et al. (1985), continued Chomsky's generative program—that is, to write grammars (of minimal generative capacity) that generate all and only the sentences of a natural language. These theorists maintain the psychological assumption that the generative rule-based grammar is a correct representation of the language user's linguistic knowledge.

Others, including Chomsky himself, came to entirely dismiss the notion that a language can be formally generated: *"Further formalization is pointless"* (Chomsky, 1986, p. 91). The user's linguistic knowledge is not a system of generative rules: *"There are no rules at all, hence no necessity to learn rules"* (Chomsky, 1987, p. 68). Instead, according to Chomsky, our innate language capacity (or "universal grammar") is a network of modules, each of which is based on principles that are invariant among languages. For instance, there are only a finite number of possible phrase structures within the syntactic module. They differ in terms of only a few parameters. Learning a language is setting those parameters. (Why this should make further formalization pointless is, however, less than obvious.)

The psychological validity of these, and many other computational proposals, is the subject of empirical research. Are Gazdar's rules reflected in the way we parse sentences when we listen or read (Fodor, 1989)? Are young children really "setting parameters" when they acquire their native language (Weissenborn, Goodluck, & Roeper, 1992)? And so on. Each computational theory carries its own research agenda.

And with respect to the second question, what to assign to the computational and what to the algorithmic level (to "competence" or to "performance" in the linguistic jargon), the fights have been fierce as well. Initially (during the early 1960s), the relation was considered to be quite transparent: Each (computational) rule of grammar would correspond to an (algorithmic) operation in perception or production. As a consequence, the more complex a sentence's syntax, the harder it would be to process. But counterexamples soon emerged. A sentence like *The horse raced past the barn fell,* for instance, is much harder to parse than its simple syntax justifies. And this, Fodor et al. (1974) argued, is the result of our perceptual strategies or heuristics. When a sentence begins with a noun phrase followed by a verb, our first guess is that the noun phrase and verb relate as actor and action, and that is usually correct. But the heuristic doesn't work for the example sentence (the horse *was* raced past the barn before it fell). This heuristics approach solved a range of enigmas in sentence processing. It also limited the role of the computational theory. The latter was merely there to characterize the well-formed output of parsing—that is, the ideal structural target of processing. But whether or how the target was reached became a problem *sui generis*. As a consequence, the algorithmic theory became much less dependent on the theory of syntax than it used to be. In fact, modern processing theories of language are compatible with almost any sophisticated grammar. The primacy of the computational theory over the algorithmic theory, as proclaimed by Chomsky and by Marr, has disappeared; the two enterprises are developing concurrently with surprisingly little interaction. Too little, to my taste. But the abandonment of primacy claims, one way or another, is a major step ahead.

Let us now move to an entirely different discipline, microeconomics, and notice that it entertains the same formal relationship to psychology.

Microeconomics

Microeconomics deals, in part, with human decision-making—in particular, with the consumer's choice behavior. That part of microeconomics is a theory of choosing between means that are in short supply. And since most commodities in life (such as food, jobs, spouses, education, or fresh air) are in short supply, this part of microeconomics is *ipso facto* a quite general theory of human choice behavior. It should be noticed that other, and highly successful, parts of microeconomics don't have individual choice behavior as their object. Operations research, for instance, deals with the efficiency of production or transportation processes, not with consumers' choices. The following discussion, however, concerns only the aspect of microeconomics interested in consumer choices.

For Adam Smith (economics' eighteenth-century founding father), economic theory should take the *individual* consumer's behavior as its starting point. According to Smith, the behavior of aggregates derives in regular ways from individual choice behavior, variable as this may be. What would Wilhelm Wundt's view be on this matter?

Professor Wundt, I forgot to ask you this: How does an economical system emerge? Is economics also a chapter of psychology?

Every attempt to understand economical history in causal terms leads to a psychological analysis. What else are supply-demand relationships, the spur of competition, and the other leverages of labor and trade than psychological motives?[j]

Thank you, professor. I won't intrude again.

This nicely parallels Wundt's view on language. Language, according to Wundt, is in the final analysis a process in the individual speaker. But in an aggregate, a language becomes a more or less stabilized product.

As a theory of the individual consumer's choice behavior, microeconomics is another chapter of human psychology. But it is a computational chapter. Modern microeconomic theories are typically axiomatic-deductive formal systems that generate sets of well-formed or "rational" choices. A rational choice is one that, given a limited set of resources, allocates these in such a way that the decision-maker's own satisfaction is maximized. Although economic theories differ in important details with respect to their definition of rational choice, the rational choice *paradigm* is at the basis of almost all present-day consumer theory.

The parallels to generative linguistics are ubiquitous. Both are deductive theories, involving similar idealizations. In economics one is dealing with an ideal decision-maker, just as generative linguistics postulates an ideal speaker-listener. An ideal decision maker is one who is fully informed about his or her own needs and preferences, and possesses all relevant information about the choice alternatives and their utilities—just as the ideal speaker-listener "knows his language perfectly." Moreover, the ideal decision maker is not subject to limitations of attention or memory; all relevant information is always available. This is, again, precisely the same idealization as was made in generative grammar. Finally, the market community is homogeneous; all consumers are alike in terms of informational state and subjective utility functions. This parallels the "completely homogeneous speech-community" of linguistics.

As a computational theory, microeconomics is a theory of rational outcomes or choices—of *products* of behavior. The rational choice parallels the well-formed sentence in linguistics. In neither case are we dealing with *actual* products of behavior, but with *virtual* or *possible* products. In that sense both kinds of theory are normative (see Massaro, 1991); they tell you what product is all right and what product is not.

And neither of the theories are *process* theories. The rational choice paradigm is as much ignorant of how a choice comes about, as is the generative grammar paradigm about how a sentence is produced.

Above we discussed two questions that were raised with respect to the demarcation between computational and algorithmic theories in linguistics. Exactly the same issues have been hotly debated in economics.

The first one was, Are the computational assumptions correct; are they psychologically valid? In other words, are consumers rational agents? In economics, there has grown a kind of monstrous alliance to deny the validity of the assumptions. Arrow (1986), for instance, argues that the assumptions are incoherent. If all individuals are alike in utility function and information state (the homogeneity assumption), and rational decision implicates complete exploitation of information, then there would be no trading at all. Trading results from economic agents being *different* in their state of knowledge or utility function.[4]

Others argue that the paradigm is well-nigh vacuous. Hogarth and Reder (1986) write:

> However, to apply the rational choice paradigm, few—if any—psychological assumptions are needed. The economic implications of the paradigm are compatible with virtually any account of the decision-making process so long as this generates appropriately sloped supply and demand curves.

And essentially the same is argued by Simon (1986), when he remarks that *"neoclassical economics becomes, as has been observed more than once, essentially tautological and irrefutable."*

Tversky and Kahneman (1979, 1986), psychological intruders in the economic playground, take another tack. They turn to the axioms of expected utility theory—that is, to the foundations of the rationality paradigm—and test their psychological validity *by means of experiments*. The results are shocking; there is substantial and systematic violation of all axiomatic assumptions. This is like the systematic and substantial violations of linguists' grammaticality predictions that Levelt (1972) found in an experiment where (other) trained linguists judged the well-formedness of sentences.

The second question was, Are we making the psychologically correct assignments to the computational and the algorithmic levels of explanation? This issue has been actively pursued in economics with equal force. For decades, Herbert Simon has been in the forefront here. He is the preeminent *algorithmic* economist. According to him, the only thing of real interest is *how* people make their decisions. Decisions are made in a context of limited information about cost and supply functions, a particular framing of the choice situation, under severely limited attentional conditions, guided by particular beliefs and expectations. Within these limitations, the consumer will still have good reasons for each step in the process. In other words, economic agents have "procedural rationality." But there is not the slightest hope that procedural rationality will have "substantive rationality" (i.e., computational rationality) as an emergent property. Says Simon (1986, p. 39):

> I would recommend that we stop debating whether a theory of substantive rationality and the assumptions of utility maximization provide a sufficient base for explaining and predicting economic behavior. The evidence is overwhelming that they do not.

Arrow (1986, p. 201) is as rabid in undermining the computational underpinnings of the rational choice paradigm. The rationality assumptions

> certainly imply an ability at information processing and calculation that is far beyond the feasible and that cannot well be justified as the result of learning and adaptation.

This agrees with Simon's position. The obvious untenability of the computational assumptions on which subjective utility theory is based led to various adaptations that can be interpreted as "assignment shifts." The computational theory started "importing" factors that had been previously assigned to the algorithmic level.

One example is the move to drop the assumption that the economic agent is fully informed. Information is among the scarcities that a decision maker has to cope with. In Search Theory (Stigler, 1961) the state of information is a variable, whose cost is a factor at the level of the computational theory. Smith (1985) similarly attaches a price tag to computational effort—that is, agent's costs of thinking.

Another example of shifting boundaries between computational and algorithmic theory is provided by the Rational Expectations model (Lucas, 1981) in which agents behave fully rationally, given their state of information. But process factors may create systematic distortions in that informational state. For instance, managers systematically err in ascribing price movements to general versus industry-specific changes. In other words, agents are subject to illusions—which is an assignment to the algorithmic level. Tversky and Kahneman were among the first to stress the irrational force of such illusions.[5]

Whereas the latter two examples are still adaptations of the rational choice paradigm—essentially preserving the computational theory—Kahneman's and Tversky's Prospect Theory (1979) shifts most of the explanatory work to the algorithmic level. Making a choice is a two-phase process. During the first phase the decision problem is "framed" in terms of potential acts, contingencies, and outcomes. This framing process is subject to norms, habits, expectancies, and so on. During the second phase the prospects resulting from the first phase are evaluated, and the best one is selected.

It is an empirical issue how framing and evaluation are achieved by the subject. According to the authors, the decision maker uses a set of powerful heuristics to arrive at a representation of the problem. These heuristics do not derive from the axioms of rational choice, but they are "procedurally rational" (Simon's term) given the limited information on which the consumer has to act.

What is left, then, for a computational theory? Or in Marr's terms: What is the agent trying to achieve? According to Prospect Theory it is, first, to avert losses and, second, something like living by the adage "a bird in the hand is worth two in the bush." Consumers are certainly not maximizing expected utility. These aims are formally specified by means of an evaluation function, which is the computational part of Prospect Theory.

These developments in microeconomics are highly similar to those in linguistics. The algorithmic theory has become largely independent of the computational theory. Heuristic procedures that are still reasonably effective under conditions of limited information and limited temporal resources replace foolproof rational procedures that require omniscience and unlimited computational resources. The computational theory has become more realistic; at the same time, it has ceased to dictate the structure of the algorithmic theory.

The present section exemplified psychology's formal relationship to computational sciences of the mind by considering linguistics and economics in some more detail. In both cases, the situation evolved from one in which the computational theory dictated the structure of the algorithmic theory to one in which the algorithmic theory became independently motivated. Is there reason to expect that this more balanced relation will also extend to the implementational theory? I shall return to that question after a few remarks on the cultural relations among the sciences of mind.

Science Culture

The sciences of mind developed from a common core; many of them emancipated from philosophy no more than a few hundred years ago. The easy way of interpreting the resulting partitioning is that it naturally follows the "joints of nature." Linguistics deals with one faculty of mind, economics with another one, and so on. But this is obviously false. Which faculty of mind is the subject of anthropology? Certainly, it must include the abilities to talk, to trade, to exercise moral judgment, etc. And how is anthropology different from sociology? In that it studies "non-Western" people? Are there "Western" versus "non-Western" faculties of mind?

Clearly, the present partitioning of the sciences is a rather arbitrary result of our cultural history. Capitalism grew economics, colonialism grew anthropology, and so on. And each science of mind cultivated its own local culture, its own pet topics, its own cherished methods.

But in spite of their ever growing divergence, the "computational" sciences of mind have still kept commonalities in scientific culture. These, however, are just as arbitrary as are their differences. I have already mentioned the tendency, canonized by Wundt, for these sciences to evade experimentation as a method. Economists do study "experimental markets" (see Smith, 1962, for a pioneering study), but this methodology is as marginal as the systematic experimental elicitation of sentences by linguists or the controlled field experiment in anthropology.

Another cultural commonality among the computational sciences of mind is to capitalize on intuitive judgment. The linguist's or native speaker's intuition that "this is a grammatical sentence" still counts as critical evidence in the evaluation of a theory of grammar. This in spite of obvious problems of measurement and interpretation (Levelt, 1974, Vol. 3). Similarly, the economist's intuition that "this choice is rational" is still an important guide in constructing theories of choice, or at least in selling them: *"To add credibility to the story, appeal is often made to everyday intuition concerning individual behavior"* (Hogarth & Reder, 1986, p. 3).

Such examples can easily be multiplied. But the point can already be made: Neither the partitioning of the sciences of mind nor their differences and commonalities of method are deeply principled in nature. Instead, we are all subject to an arbitrary legacy of history. But in the next section I argue that there is hope for the next century. The new generation of scientists of mind is increasingly dressed in blue jeans wearing the label "cognitive science." That term is as ill-defined as the traditional ones, but it is at least nondivisive and nondogmatic.

Marr's Three Levels According to Escher, Exemplified by the Theory of Speaking

Wilhelm Wundt was right: Psychology is the foundation of the sciences of mind. Its task is to disentangle how the mind and all of its faculties function. And Marr was right too: To study the mind's operations, one must consider what it tries to achieve, what computational problem it tries to solve. Ever since Wundt's time, the latter kind of question has been largely left to the "special" sciences of mind. And they have considerably grown apart, both among them and away from psychology.

This has been to the detriment of both psychology and of the special sciences. The most remarkable effect on psychology has been the morbid growth of *processitis,* the tendency to study processes irrespective of their functions and of the representations that are relevant to those functions. Behaviorism, built on the ultimate stimulus–response process, was killed by this disease (and its heir connectionism is a vulnerable next candidate). But processitis has been a lingering condition of psychology since the cognitive revolution. For instance, many psychologists still consider it to be an art to clean away from their experimental materials everything that could be of any ecological validity to the subject (the Ebbinghaus syndrome). The special sciences of mind likewise suffered by naively relying on outdated psychology (such as rational choice theory, behaviorism, or psychoanalytic theory).

But there can be well-founded hope that these seemingly irrevocable developments are coming to an end. As I have already indicated, the twentieth century is

Figure 13.2. Marr's three levels according to Escher. Copyright © 1953 by M.C. Escher/
Cordon Art—Baarn—Holland.

closing its books with an ill-defined item called "cognitive science." It is not a
coherent science in terms of object, methodology, or education, but it certainly is
a gigantic melting pot where disciplinary boundaries no longer hold. This is the
right climate for growing irreverent offspring, for whom Marr's three levels are
like Escher's litho *Relativity,* where climbing is decending and descending is
climbing, without any preestablished priority or hierarchy among levels.

Let me exemplify this new state of affairs by referring to our most complex
and species-specific skill, the ability to talk. Returning to his ascetic position,
Chomsky (1988) argued that the scientific study of how we express our thoughts,
the ordinary use of language in everyday life, is beyond reach, if not principally
then at least factually for the time being. Why? Because there is no prospect of
solving "Descartes' problem"—namely, how it is possible that we can act in a
free and undetermined way. Talking is free, undetermined action in that sense.
Hence, there is no hope for a theory of speaking.

This is both logically and factually false. Logically, because even if we don't
know where thoughts to be expressed come from, we can study how, given such

a thought, it becomes expressed in language (and why wouldn't we be able to investigate where thoughts come from?). It is factually false, because since the 1960s there has been substantial theoretical and empirical progress in the study of how we speak (for a review, see Levelt, 1989). This progress concerns both the issue of how speakers generate thoughts to be expressed, and the machinery of giving these thoughts syntactic, phonological, and articulatory shape. We have a clear case here where the (or, rather, one) computational perspective has been deeply misleading with respect to the feasibility of an algorithmic theory (let alone its physical implementation).

As a matter of fact, if anywhere, it has been in the study of language and speech production that Escher's democratic relation between levels became a living reality. Let us first consider the computational and algorithmic levels.

The speech-producing mechanism appears to have a highly modular organization. Among the various component modules, there is one that controls grammatical encoding—that is, the selection of appropriate words from the mental lexicon and the incremental production of syntactic structure. Another module controls phonological encoding—that is, it computes the phonological shape of the utterance. For each module, its scientific analysis consisted of determining its characteristic input and output representations (semantic, syntactic, phonological) and the operations that mediate between them.

For instance, the grammatical encoding module takes conceptual or semantic structures as input and generates syntactic surface structures as output. The phonological encoding component takes surface structures as input and generates phonological plans (both segmental and suprasegmental) as output. There is no way in which the computed representations are logically "prior to" the operations. There are quite restrictive operational requirements on the theory. For example, one central property of any psychologically sophisticated model of speech production is that production is "incremental"; both syntax and phonology are generated "from left to right" without much look-ahead. This, in turn, restricts the character of the input and output representations (semantic, syntactic, phonological) that can figure in such a theory. There is no primacy either for the computational theory (the theory of representations), or for the algorithmic theory (the process must run on relevant representations).

And what about Marr's implementational level? Historically, the theory of speaking has been the neurologists' playground since Broca discovered the speech–motor center in the left brain. The smarting shortage of interested psychologists gave the neurologists a free hand. And we should be grateful for what they accomplished. The careful delineation of aphasic syndromes, initially as a means to accomplish in vivo anatomical localization of cerebral disorders, led to the first *functional* models of language production. And these models were mostly modular in nature. Each module subserved a particular function in the process of speaking (such as activating word meanings or activating the articulatory shapes of words) and could ideally be localized on one of the lobes of the left hemisphere. This paradigm of negotiating between functional and cerebral modeling has fruitfully continued to the present day.

And equally active is the direct negotiation between cerebral modeling and representational or computational theory. A substantial part of present-day cognitive neuropsychology is concerned with the types of representations that are accessible or computable under different kinds of brain damage. Grodzinsky (1990, p. 17) argues that these breakdown patterns are as criterial for a theory of grammar— that is, the computational theory—as is its compatibility with an algorithmic or functional theory:

> The internal structure of the theoretical account of a domain, then, effectively dictates which patterns of impairments are possible, and which are impossible. An examination of deficit descriptions can be used to evaluate the theory. If the predictions it makes are correct, and if it is found to be compatible with breakdown patterns, we can conclude that it meets the neuropsychological constraint of breakdown-compatibility. This will be added to two other proposed constraints on the theory of grammer: those of *learnability* and *parsability*.

And the search for the brain's modular specialization for different types of linguistic representation continues at increased speed. The aphasiological evidence is being complemented by two further sources.

There is, first, the evidence stemming from single-cell recordings during open brain surgery. Creutzfeldt, Ojemann, and Lettich (1989), for instance, found neurons in the left superior temporal gyrus that specifically responded to compound words such as *horseshoe* (as opposed to monomorphemic words, such as *spaghetti*). Cellular and cell assembly models of linguistic units (such as phonological features, syllables, phrases, and clauses) are beginning to be developed (Braitenberg & Pulvermüller, 1992). Critical here is the realistic modeling of cortical circuits, such as is the case for the "canonical microcircuits" that Douglas and Martin (1990) proposed on the basis of their extensive anatomical and physiological studies of brain tissue. The so-called "neural" networks of connectionism have very little to do with these real cortical circuits. Rather, the make-believe "neural" network modeling of connectionism is the latest excuse for behavioral scientists to stay away from issues of implementation, continuing the tradition of behaviorism.

There is, second, the explosive development of noninvasive (or almost noninvasive) brain imaging technology. The brain's metabolic activity during the execution of linguistic tasks can now to some extent (and in different ways) be traced by positron emission tomography (PET) and through functional nuclear magnetic resonance imaging (MRI). The first PET studies of speech production have recently appeared (Peterson et al., 1988; Wise et al., 1991). They show that different aspects of word retrieval (semantic, phonological/phonetic) in speech production involve different areas of the brain, and thus are beginning to reveal the relations between representation and implementation at the brain's macro scale.[6] Functional MRI is the greatest promise here. There is the expectation that its superb spatial resolution will soon be matched by a temporal resolution of one second or even less. The new imaging technologies will be material in redressing the still existing imbalance between computational and algorithmic theory, on the one hand, and implementational theory, on the other.

The successful dissection of our faculty of speech sets an example for the study of mind beyond the year 2000. Major leaps are to be expected if representa-

tion, process, and implementation are studied in close interdisciplinary cooperation. Any claims to priority among these three will be counterproductive. And
don't believe that Escher's picture is an impossible one.

Notes

1. Wundt's responses are free but faithful translations of the following German texts:

[a] *Als Wissenschaft von den allgemeingültigen Formen unmittelbarer Erfahrung . . .
ist sie die Grundlage der Geisteswissenschaften . . . Psychologie . . . ist* [sie] *selbst
die allgemeinste Geisteswissenschaft und zugleich die Grundlage aller einzelnen, wie
der Philologie, Geschichte, Nationalökonomie, Rechtswissenschaft usw* (Wundt, 1914,
p. 18).

[b] *daß . . . die psychologische Analyse der allgemeinsten geistigen Erzeugnisse, wie
der Sprache, der mythologischen Vorstellungen, der Normen der Sitte, der Psychologie
teils als eine notwendige Ausdehnung ihres Gebiets auf die Vorgänge des gemeinsamen
seelischen Lebens, teils als ein Hilfsmittel für das Verständnis der verwickelteren psychischen Vorgänge überhaupt zufällt.* (Wundt, 1914, p. 10).

[c] *Nun könnte es scheinen, als wenn auch der Psychologie dann am besten gedient
wäre, wenn derjenige, der sich an die völkerpsychologischen Probleme heranwagt, die
Eigenschaften des Philologen und des Historikers mit denen des Psychologen verbände.
Aus zwei Gründen glaube ich jedoch, daß dieser Wunsch, vorläufig wenigstens, kaum Aus-
sicht hat, verwirklicht zu werden. Erstens wird man bei der gegenwärtigen Teilung der
wissenschaftlichen Arbeit schwerlich erwarten dürfen, daß der Philologe oder Historiker
die Sache in einer den heutigen Forderungen der psychologischen Wissenschaft genügen-
den Weise in Angriff nehmen werde; und vielleicht wird man ihm dies nicht einmal verden-
ken können, da die Aufgaben und, was damit unvermeidlich verbunden ist, die Gesichts-
punkte, mit denen er an die Probleme herantritt, wesentlich abweichend sind* (Wundt 1904,
p. v).

[d] *Gleichwohl wird die Völkerpsychologie als solche ein Teil der Psychologie bleiben*
(Wundt, 1904, p.vi).

[e] *Demnach verfügt die Psychologie, ähnlich der Naturwissenschaft, über zwei exakte
Methoden: die erste, die experimentelle Methode, dient der Analyse der einfacheren psychischen Vorgänge; die zweite, die Beobachtung der allgemeingültigen Geisteserzeugnisse,
dient der Untersuchung der höheren psychischen Vorgänge und Entwicklungen* (Wundt,
1914, p. 30).

[f] *Grenzen sind ihr erst da gesetzt, wo durch das Zusammenleben der Menschen geistige
Vorgänge und Erzeugnisse eigener Art entstehen, die, wie die Sprache, die mythologischen
Vorstellungen, die Sitten, der experimentellen Einwirkung unzugänglich sind* (Wundt 1919,
p. 11).

[g] *. . . daß in diesem Fall geistige Erzeugnisse die Objekte der Beobachtung sind
(Wundt, 1914, p. 29).*

[h] *Eine solche Beziehung kann nicht anders denn als ein* Parallelgehen *zweier mitein-
ander verbundener, aber vermöge der Unvergleichbarkeit ihrer Glieder niemals direkt
ineinander eingreifender Kausalreihen angesehen werden. Ich habe dieses Prinzip . . .
bereits als das des* psychophysischen Parallelismus *bezeichnet.* (Wundt, 1919, p. 550).

[i] *So werden z.B. die Elemente, die eine räumliche oder zeitliche Vorstellung konstitu-
ieren, auch in ihren physiologischen Substraten in einem regelmäßigen Verhältnis der
Koexistenz oder Sukzession stehen* (Wundt, 1914, p. 396).

[j] . . . *daß jeder Versuch, die Erscheinungen der Wirtschaftsgeschichte ursächlich zu begreifen, auf eine psychologische Analyse hinausführt. Was sind in der Tat die Verhältnisse von Angebot und Nachfrage, der Sporn der Konkurrenz und die anderen Hebel des Arbeits—und Handelsverkehr anderes als psychologische Motive . . . ?* (Wundt, 1908b, p. 397).

2. There is a potential source of confusion here. On the one hand, Marr calls the computational theory a representation. A grammar, for instance, is a representation of the language. On the other hand, he also calls the input and output of an algorithm a representation. I use "representation" only in this latter sense. However, this does not affect my use of Marr's tripartition. The theory of representations—that is, their ultimate explanation—is the computational theory. The algorithmic theory takes representations for granted; it is explanatory only for the ways in which they are created or transformed.

3. Remarkable exceptions in the history of psychology are, among others, to be found in the Gestalt school of psychology, Heider's social psychology, Piaget's genetic psychology, Michotte's "Kantian" psychology, Gibson's ecological psychology, and Rosch's prototype theory. All deal, in different ways, with outlining well-formed or "possible" products of mind.

4. The corresponding argument has never been made within the other chapter of psychology, linguistics. If the linguistic community is completely homogeneous, all language users knowing their language perfectly and being without limitations in terms of their interests or states of attention, would there be any talking? At any rate, there will be no language *learning*, because learning presupposes the existence of an incompletely informed state, for which there is no place in the idealization. There can be only a magical switch from the intitial state to the fully informed state.

5. Tversky and Kahneman's theory of cognitive illusions, and more specifically their experimental approach to testing the rationality axioms, has not survived without criticism. See, for instance, Gigerenzer (1993).

6. We shall also have to live with dramatic overinterpretations. The beautifully colored, symmetrical PET-scan images are becoming the Rorschach pictures of popular brain science: Every interpretation is accepted. The recent "Mind and Brain" issue of *Scientific American,* for instance, depicts verbs as being located in the prefrontal lobe and nouns in the temporal lobe of the left hemisphere, momentarily ignoring the speaker's quite productive ability to use denominal verbs and deverbal nouns.

Acknowledgement

The following persons have disagreements with this chapter: Colin Brown, Peter Hagoort, Dom Massaro, Antje Meyer, and Jan Pen. But all of them helped me substantially on an earlier draft.

References

Arrow, K. J. (1986). Rationality of self and others in an economic system. In R. M. Hogarth & M. W. Reder (Eds.), *Rational choice: The contrast between economics and psychology* (pp. 201–215). Chicago: The University of Chicago Press.

Braitenberg, V., & Pulvermüller, F. (1992). Entwurf einer neurologischen Theorie der Sprache. *Naturwissenschaften, 79,* 103–117.

Chomsky, N. (1965). *Aspects of the theory of syntax.* Cambridge, Mass.: MIT Press.

Chomsky, N. (1986). *Barriers.* Cambridge, Mass.: MIT Press.

Chomsky, N. (1987). Language in a psychological setting. *Sophia Linguistica Working Papers in Linguistics,* p. 22. Tokyo: Sophia University Graduate School of Languages and Linguistics.

Chomsky, N. (1988). *Language and problems of knowledge. The Managua lectures.* Cambridge, Mass.: MIT Press.

Chomsky, N., & Halle, M. (1968). *The sound pattern of English.* New York, N.Y.: Harper and Row.

Creutzfeldt, O., Ojemann, G., & Lettich, E. (1989). Neuronal activity in the human temporal lobe. I. Responses to speech. *Experimental Brain Research, 77,* 451–475.

Douglas, R.J., & Martin, K. A. C. (1990). Neocortex. In G. M. Shepherd (Ed.), *The synaptic organization of the brain* (3rd edition, pp. 389–438). New York: Oxford University Press.

Fodor, J. D. (1989). Empty categories in sentence processing. *Language and Cognitive Processes, 4,* SI 155–209.

Fodor, J. A., Bever, T. G. & Garrett, M. F. (1974). *The psychology of language.* New York: McGraw-Hill, 1974.

Gazdar, G., Klein, E., Pullum, G. & Sag, I. (1985). *Generalized phrase structure grammar.* Oxford: Blackwell.

Georgopoulos, A. P., Lurito, J. T., Petrides, M., Schwarts, A. B., & Massey, J. T. (1989). Mental rotation of the neuronal population vector. *Science, 243,* 234–236.

Gigerenzer, G. (1993). Cognitive illusions illusory? Rethinking judgment under uncertainty. In K. I. Manktelow & D. E. Over (Eds.), *Rationality.* London: Routledge.

Grodzinsky, Y. (1990). *Theoretical perspectives on language deficits.* Cambridge, Mass.: MIT Press.

Hogarth, R. M. & Reder, M. W. (1986). Introduction: Perspectives from economics and psychology. In R. M. Hogarth & M. W. Reder (Eds.), *Rational choice: The contrast between economics and psychology* (pp. 1–23). Chicago: The University of Chicago Press.

Kahneman, D., & Tversky, A. (1979). Prospect theory: An analysis of decision under risk. *Econometrica, 47,* 263–291.

Levelt, W. J. M. (1972). Some psychological aspects of linguistic data. *Linguistische Berichte, 17,* 18–30.

Levelt, W. J. M. (1974). *Formal grammars in linguistics and psycholinguistics* (3 vols). The Hague: Mouton.

Levelt, W. J. M. (1989) *Speaking: From intention to articulation.* Cambridge, Mass.: MIT Press.

Levelt, W. J. M. (Ed.). (1993). *Lexical access speech production.* Cambridge, Mass.: Blackwell.

Lucas, R. E. (1981). *Studies in business cycle theory.* Cambridge, Mass.: MIT Press.

Marr, D. (1982). *Vision.* New York: Freeman.

Massaro, D. (1991). Psychology as a cognitive science. *Psychological Science, 2,* 302–307.

Peterson, S. E., Fox, P. T., Posner, M. I., Mintun, M., & Raichle, M. E. (1988). Positron emission tomographic studies of the cortical anatomy of single-word processing. *Nature, 331,* 585–589.

Simon, H. (1986). Rationality in psychology and economics. In R. M. Hogarth & M. W. Reder (Eds.), *Rational choice: The contrast between economics and psychology* (pp. 25–40). Chicago: The University of Chicago Press.

Smith, V. (1962). An experimental study of competitive market behavior. *Journal of Political Economy, 70,* 111–137.

Smith, V. (1985). Experimental economics: Reply. *American Economic Review, 75,* 265–272.

Stigler, G. J. (1961). The economics of information. *Journal of Political Economy, 69,* 213–225.

Tversky, A., & Kahneman, D. (1986). Rational choice and the framing of decisions. In R. M. Hogarth & M. W. Reder (Eds.), *Rational choice: The contrast between economics and psychology* (pp. 67–94). Chicago: The University of Chicago Press.

Weissenborn, J., Goodluck, H., & Roeper, T. (Eds.). (1992). *Theoretical issues in language acquisition.* Hillsdale, N.J.: Erlbaum.

Wise, R., Chollet, F., Hader, U., Friston, K., Hoffner, E., & Frackowiak, R. (1991). Distribution of cortical neural networks involved in word comprehension and word retrieval. *Brain, 114,* 1803–1817.

Wundt, W. (1904). *Völkerpsychologie, Vols. I & II: Die Sprache.* Leipzig: Engelmann.

Wundt, W. (1907). Über Ausfrageexperimente und über Methoden zur Psychologie des Denkens. *Psychologische Studien, 3,* 301–390.

Wundt, W. (1908a). Kritische Nachlese zur Ausfragemethode. *Archiv für die gesamte Psychologie, 11,* 445–459.

Wundt, W. (1908b). *Allgemeine Logik und Erkenntnistheorie,* Bd. 3. Stuttgart: Fischer.

Wundt, W. (1914). *Grundriss der Psychologie.* Leipzig: Kröner.

Wundt, W. (1919). *Menschen- und Tierseele.* Leipzig: Voss.

14

From Speech-Is-Special to Talking Heads: The Past to the Present

DOMINIC W. MASSARO

The Setting

Scene: Telecom Channel 46, January 7, 2101

Good audience, why partake in this antiquated pastime of scientific inquiry? Existence opened in mystery and will close in mystery. Our telecom channels have been designated to please, not puzzle. For those into delectation, the other telecom channels offer instantaneous desserts. Virtual Reality 3 presents Marilyn Monroe's rendezvous with Madonna III. If this tryst is too boring, the multistimulation of Bach's Brandenburg concerti is guaranteed to bombard all sensory stations—sensory overload at its finest. Julia Child's gastronomic channel is serving up Stegosaurus, as reconstructed from simulations of the fossil record.

If you haven't already dissolved my talking head *con* accompanying hand gestures, let me entice you not only to read my lips, but also to engage in the highest mode of thought of our ancestors. We do not have to dispute the consensus reached during the last century that *Homo sapiens* are not capable of knowing everything. Uncertainty in the outcome of our inquiry, however, should not preclude your participation. It's factual that thinking, problem solving, and inquiry are no longer taught in school or viewed as essential to success and happiness. Why do we need to penetrate the mysteries of the universe when we are nurtured and protected by intelligent machines of every kind? Who needs cogitation when we have every escapist philosophy imaginable, ranging from neurolinguistic programming to sleep learning to subliminal perception? Who can deny the exultation we find in walking on hot coals without pain, the ease of becoming an expert on some esoteric topic while asleep, and the ego boost we achieve in overcoming yet another frailty of our being by using the latest subliminal self-help disk? A recent discovery has revealed that the scientific puzzles deliberated during the twentieth century may still be worth pondering.

Supporting the rubble of the great quake of 1999, finally unearthed a century

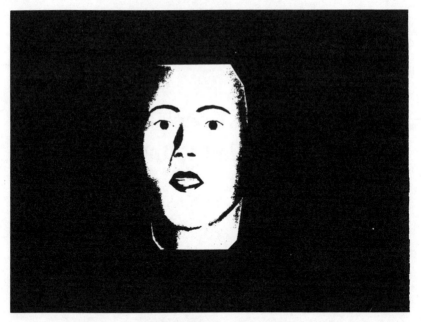

Figure 14.1. Talking head of a communication channel.

later, were books (bound pages of written language) of unprecedented importance. Although human readers of twentieth-century English were no longer available at the time of the discovery, the Smithsonian's computers and speech synthesizers were still functional and capable of translating this primitive written language reasonably well into the spoken language of that time. Although twentieth-century speech sounds odd, it can be understood fairly easily. Why is our current spoken language no longer identical to this earlier form? There was an increased rate of sound change when we eliminated the written form of language. Remember that the major revision of written English early in the twenty-first century was aimed at establishing a regular correspondence between spelling and sound. Hypermediasts succeeded where Ben Franklin, Mark Twain, and George Bernard Shaw had failed. Now written language mirrored its spoken form. No longer could *fish* be spelled *ghoti* (*gh* as in "rough," *o* as in "women," and *ti* as in "nation"). Even with spelling-to-sound regularity, however, universal literacy was still beyond the reach of formal schooling. Notwithstanding the pledged intentions of youthful politicians, because of the huge budget deficit remaining from the twentieth century the excessive cost and time required to teach literacy exceeded society's resources. Education and quality failed under Clintonomics in the same manner as under Reaganomics.

Given the dominance of the English language, all written language became extinct soon after the disappearance of written English. The scientists at the time consummated their research with the belief that reading was an unnatural act in contrast to the understanding of spoken language from which written language was derived. (As will be noted on the disk *Speech Perception and Cognitive Skills,* however, written language could also be acquired naturally without formal schooling.) Given simulated environments of talking beings that more closely engaged our natural processing, children no longer were required to struggle with written language. They could plug into (or be plugged into) any spoken lesson at any time and at any age. Contrary to the predictions of many of our intelligentsia of the time, the extinction of literacy was not accompanied by the fall of civilization. Written language was no more necessary for sagacious mentality than was color vision.

Within these ancient writings existed a review of speech perception research. Believe it or not, this topic evidently plagued the old sciences of the mind—dubbed cognitive science at the end of the twentieth century. With this discovery, we learn that some twentieth-century scientists anticipated the current view of perceptual, cognitive, and linguistic functioning. Today, we realize that evolution did not specifically give us the special skills required for our cognitive and technological world. Our sophisticated world is well beyond the comprehension of any one of us, but together we are an intelligent society. Multiple Pleistocene heads are better than one. Understanding spoken language is only one of many domains of pattern recognition in which we impose meaning on an event by using multiple sources of information. We explore this domain because (1) the availability of the ancient writings on the topic offer new insights, (2) spoken language is typical of many of our worldly interactions, (3) it is essential to appreciating the richness of communicating via talking heads, (4) spoken language consumes many of our waking hours, and (5) it is at least as important as fishing, even virtual fishing. We begin our inquiry by gaining an appreciation of the skill involved in speech perception.

Speech Perception: An Amazing Skill

Let us begin our study with the state of the art in speech science at the end of the twentieth century. Calling up the video archives from that time, we can experience the virtual reality of the following scenes. In a psychology laboratory, a six-week old infant in a baby chair has a pacifier in his mouth. As he sucks on the pacifier, the experimenter presents the sound /ba/ (as in *banana*) contingent on the infant's sucking. Given this feedback, the baby increases his sucking rate but soon becomes bored and sucks less. Now, however, the /ba/ sound is changed to /da/ and the infant increases his sucking rate again. The infant must have noticed the sound change from /ba/ to /da/. This initial research led to the development of the ingenious management devices available to today's caregivers. Bored infants are a thing of the past.

A petite three-year-old girl sits at a table of toy figures. She is told a short story and she must describe the story with the toy figures. To the child, she is playing a game, but to the psychologist and psycholinguist, she is displaying a remarkable ability to perceive and understand language. As an example, the child is told, "The fence the horse kicks." The child takes the horse and has it kick the fence. This interpretation illustrates that the child has learned a constituent of the syntactic structure of English. The child's experience with subject–verb propositions is responsible for her understanding that the horse kicks the fence.

A small shipping company invests several thousand dollars to install an automatic speech recognition system. The operator reads the address on the package and simply calls out its destination for the machine to recognize. Contrary to the assurances of the manufacturer, the machine makes a variety of catastrophic errors. The system is most likely to fail when a talker speaks at a faster or slower rate than normal, when the talker forgets that he is talking to a machine and speaks with a lazy tongue, or when the talker has a cold. Why couldn't they design a machine to recognize speech as well as a three-year-old child?

The mysteries of understanding speech engaged speech scientists during the last four decades of the twentieth century. At the end of the twentieth century, scientists wondered how many more decades would be necessary to achieve enough understanding of spoken language understanding to build a machine to simulate this perhaps last specialization of *Homo sapiens*. As expressed by George Miller (an ancestor of our hero in the Miller's Tale; see Chapter 9), "It enabled this big-brained, loudmouthed, featherless biped to overrun the earth. . . ." (Miller, 1981, p. 1). Humans might not be able to claim language as uniquely theirs, but there can be no argument about speech. Chimpanzees and apes can learn to sign but they aren't so constructed to speak. (It wasn't much later, however, that chimps at Yerkes laboratory and elsewhere were successfully learning how to *understand* spoken language; Savage-Rumbaugh et al., 1993.)

Perhaps because of the special nature of speech, the dominant belief at the end of the twentieth century was that *speech perception is special*. It had been reasoned, for example, that a speech "organ" (in the brain) had evolved to carry out this unique function. A speech organ is necessary because speech is a highly specialized domain that necessarily requires a specialized processing system. The minority alternative view was that understanding speech is just one domain of many that requires discrimination, categorization, and understanding. We also discriminate, categorize, and interact with everyday objects and events. Why should speech be any different? Although the controversy was not resolved, the specialization of speech perception became scientific dogma while the minority view was eventually forgotten. Spoken language became the dominant form of communication, and we are now communicating via talking heads and accompanying hand gestures rather than by the written word. (Speed readers had to learn to search and skim spoken language with the same speed and prowess that they used on written language.) We shall see that our current form of communication is consistent with this minority view. Your puzzle now is to undertake a retrospective examination of these two hypotheses of speech perception. Adopt the mental software of a twentieth-century citizen confronted with this dilemma, and your disciplined inquiry will bear rewards that only a peek inside Father Nature's Trousers (or under Mother Nature's Skirt) can supply. To experience this twentieth century inquiry, we shall enter its timeline to ponder how spoken language is understood. Put on your thinking caps because this inquiry from the twentieth century challenges inhabitants of the twenty-second.

Is Speech Perception Specialized?

A central issue in speech perception and psycholinguistics is the so-called modularity of speech and language. Noam Chomsky (1980) envisioned language ability as dependent on an independent language organ (or module), analogous to other organs such as our digestive system. This organ follows an independent course of development in the first years of life and allows the child to achieve a language competence that cannot be elucidated in terms of traditional learning theory. This mental organ, responsible for the human language faculty and our language competence, matures and develops with experience, but the mature system does not simply mirror this experience. The language user inherits rule systems of highly specific structure. This innate knowledge allows us to acquire the rules of the language, which cannot be induced from normal language experience because (advocates argue) of the paucity of the language input. The data of language experience are so limited that no process of induction, abstraction, generalization, analogy, or association could account for our observed language competence. Somehow, the universal grammar given by our biological endowment allows the child to learn to use language appropriately without learning many of the formal intricacies of the language. At the same time, however, other linguists are documenting that the child's language input is not as sparse as the nativists had argued (Sampson, 1989).

Although speech does not have an advocate as charismatic and influential as Chomsky, a similar description is given for speech perception. In addition, advocates of the special nature of speech are encouraged by Fodor's influential proposal of the modularity of mind. Our magnificent capabilities result from a set of innate and independent systems, such as vision, hearing, and language (Fodor, 1983). Speech-is-special theorists now assume that a speech module is responsible for speech perception (Liberman & Mattingly, 1989; Mattingly & Studdert-Kennedy, 1991). Given the environmental information, the speech module analyzes this information in terms of possible articulatory sequences of speech segments. The perceiver of speech uses his or her own speech–motor system to achieve speech recognition.

The justification for a speech module is analogous to the one for language more generally. Performance is not easily accounted for in terms of the language input. In speech, it is asserted that the acoustic signal is deficient and that typical pattern recognition schemes could not work. Put another way, it is reasoned that speech exceeds our auditory information-processing capabilities. In terms of the modularity view, our speech perception system is linked with our speech production system—and our speech perception is somehow mediated by our speech production. For theorists in the speech-is-special camp, the objects of speech perception are articulatory events or gestures. These gestures are the primitives that the mechanisms of speech production translate into actual articulatory movements and are also the primitives that the specialized mechanisms of speech perception recover from the signal. Before evaluating experimental evidence and other relevant findings concerning the special nature of speech perception, we begin with a historical sketch of the psychological study of speech perception.

A Historical Glimpse of the Twentieth Century

Speech perception wasn't always considered specialized. The turn of the nineteenth century was a heady time for psychologists. Fechner, Donders, Wundt, and their converts had paved the way for an experimental study of mental life. With tools such as a tachistoscope to present visual displays for short measurable intervals, and named as such to tongue-tie undergraduates before computer monitors made them obsolete (the T-scopes, not the undergraduates), experimenters could gain control over stimuli and derive stimulus–response relationships. Some of the best known work involved reading written words (which also captivated many "cognitive" psychologists during much of the twentieth century). One of the main findings to surface from this research was the important influence of context on reading. As documented in Edmund B. Huey's (1908) seminal text, our knowledge about spelling, syntax, and meaning facilitates the recognition of the letters on a page of text.

In contrast to the plethora of studies carried out on the written word, apparently only one was done on the spoken word. William Chandler Bagley's dissertation under Edward Titchener showed influences in speech perception that were analogous to those found in written language. Members of Cornell's psychology department were asked to recognize mutilated words with missing segments. This manipulation is reminiscent of Pillsbury's (1897) studies of the recognition of written words with missing letters. As can be seen in the examples, readers easily recognized the words even though they were spelled without all of their letters.

Table 1. Examples of the letters exposed and the word read by a subject in Pillsbury's (1897) study

Letters Exposed	Words Read
kommonly	commonly
fashxon	fashion
foyever	forever
disal	deal
uvermore	evermore
danxe	danger

In Bagley's (1900) experiment, the naturally spoken words were recorded and played back on Edison phonograph cylinders. The results demonstrated that the context of the sentence improved recognition (and even perception) of the mutilated words. Word recognition was improved if the word was placed in the middle of a sentence, for example. This intuitive result was published in the leading psychological journal of the time, but was quickly forgotten, and speech more or less fell outside the domain of experimental psychology. Bagley's seminal study was not cited in Woodworth's *Experimental Psychology* (1938) and a twentieth-century survey of psychology in America omitted any reference to speech perception (Hillgard, 1987). It also remained somewhat foreign during the "cognitive revolution," at the end of twentieth century, and only the technical goal of speech recognition by machine delegated speech perception its fair share of attention from experimental psychologists and other explorers of the mind.

At the beginning of the twentieth century, the psychological study of speech perception came, not from within psychology, but from an applied problem: a reading machine for blinded veterans returning from World War II. The goal was to design a machine that would read typewritten English and convert the letters into distinct sounds. The nonsighted listener would learn to recognize these sounds and read by ear. The scientists quickly found that the words spoken by machine were very difficult to understand and were not easily learned. This led Alvin Liberman and his colleagues to question why humans recognize natural speech so easily. Their inspiration was that we perceive speech via the same mechanisms used to produce speech: Speech was special. The nonsense sounds emanating from the speaking machine had little to do with how speech was spoken and, therefore, were gibberish to the listener. The next three decades of research from Haskins Laboratory was centered on the theme of the specialized nature of speech perception.

Evolutionary History of Speech

If speech perception is a highly unique and modular function, we would expect it to have a relatively long evolutionary history. Our speech is critically dependent on the characteristics of our respiratory system and vocal tract. Thus, it is of interest to determine the evolutionary history of the biological system used for speech. That is, a unique process would be expected to have a unique evolutionary history. Speech as we know it, however, appears to be relatively recent in our evolutionary history. Before the artificial speech of the last few decades, speech could be produced only by biological entities.

Using fossil records, Lieberman (1991) argued that speech as we know it was not possible just over 100,000 years ago. As can be seen in Figure 2, Neanderthal had a larynx positioned high, close to the entrance to the nasal cavity. The tongue was also positioned almost entirely in the mouth as opposed to being half in the pharynx, as it is in our mouths. Computer modeling showed that the Neanderthal vocal tract could not make many of our everyday speech sounds and would speak in a highly nasalized fashion. These characteristics would make speech a less than optimal communication system, primarily because the primitive segments of speech would be highly similar to one another. If Lieberman is correct, it wasn't until *Homo sapiens* evolved around 100,000 years ago that speech could have taken the form we know today. Although Lieberman's analysis is still being debated (Bradshaw & Rogers, 1993), it seems certain that speech is relatively novel by evolutionary standards.

Because speech (as we know it) is so recent in our evolutionary history, it seems unlikely that a unique skill evolved to perceive speech and understand language. It appears that the astonishing brain growth of our ancestors occurred sometime before the development of speech and language as we know them. Given that the fundamental stuff of thought and language were probably already

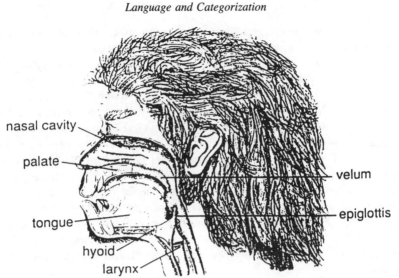

Figure 14.2. The reconstructed airway of the La Chapelle-aux-Saints Neanderthal fossil. (After Lieberman, 1991.)

present, it is unlikely that specific brain structures had to evolve to empower speech production and speech perception. Our gift of language, thought, and culture must be due to exploiting the plasticity of the brain for communication. Although spoken language eventually emerged as the higher-level programming language of human computer systems, there doesn't appear to be anything in our evolutionary history that forces the conclusion that speech is special.

The Mystery of the Missing Phoneme

Linguists had invented the phoneme as the building block of speech. Phonemes are the minimal units in speech that can change the meaning of a word. The word *ten* has three phonemes: We can change the /t/ to /d/ to make *den,* the /e/ to /ae/ to make *tan,* and the /n/ to /l/ to make *tell.* Psychologists believed that recognizing speech must, therefore, necessarily involve recognizing phonemes. However, it did not seem to be possible to find the phoneme in the speech signal. Consider the syllable /da/: It has two phonemes /d/ and /a/. If we play this syllable in isolation, we hear /da/. Now if we repeatedly shorten this syllable by removing short segments from the end, we should eventually hear just /d/. Not true. Our percept changes from /da/ to nonsense, not from /da/ to /d/. Therefore, some magic must be involved in hearing both /d/ and /a/ given the syllable /da/.

The magic didn't stop here. We would expect to find some constant characteristic in the speech signal for a given phoneme. However, this was not the case. Figure 14.3 gives a visual representation of the sounds /di/ and /du/. Given that /d/ is first phoneme of both sounds, we should see the same signal at the beginning. We don't: The higher band of energy increases in /di/ and falls in /du/. One of the original arguments for the specialized nature of speech perception implicated this uncertain relationship between properties of the speech signal and a given phonemic category. It was emphasized that, in contrast to other domains of pattern recognition, one could not delineate a set of acoustic properties that uniquely defined a phoneme.

This argument holds very little force under close scrutiny. First, the psychological reality of phonemes can be questioned. Preliterate children and illiterates have trouble accessing the phonemes in spoken language. We modern illiterates, for example, have difficulty perceiving eight different speech segments in the word *strategy*. Most of us would say that it has just three segments. Similarly, a subjective experience of *ma* can occur without individual percepts of /m/ and /a/. It follows that phonemes might not be perceived at all, and much of the mystery can be overcome if the perceptual units of speech are larger than phonemes. In addition, some variability between the actual signal and the perceived pattern is not unusual in human pattern recognition. Therefore, the relationship between signal and percept in speech does not require us to accept that speech perception is specialized.

If phonemes were functional in speech perception, we would expect them to be ordered sequentially one after the other. However, they appear to be squashed together. This smudging of phonemes and their contextual variation is due to coarticulation—the articulation of one segment being influenced by the articulation of preceding and following segments. As visualized by Hockett (1955), phonemes are like a conveyer belt of eggs run through a wringer so that it is difficult to discern at what point one egg ends and the next begins. This overlapping of phoneme segments in speech has also been enlisted in service of the argument that speech is special. However, the absence of a strict sequence of phonemic units

Figure 14.3. Spectrograms of the synthesized speech syllables /di/ and /du/.

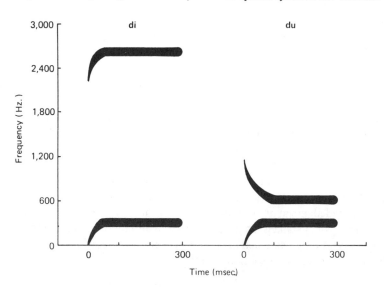

does not necessarily require a specialized speech perception process. Perhaps, the most comparable situation is handwriting in which the visible characteristics of a letter are influenced by its adjacent neighbors. (***Narrator's overlay:*** This example is lost on us because we do not read, but a similar situation holds for movements in dance.)

Rate of Speech Processing

One traditional argument for a special processor for speech is that the transmission rate of the speech signal appears to exceed our perceptual capacity. Phonetic segments—the minimum linguistic units of speech that are approximated by the letters of the alphabet—occur at a rate of between 10 and 20 per second. Supposedly, humans cannot identify nonspeech signals at even half this rate. There are several counterarguments to the rate argument, however. First, speech has a fast rate only when phonetic segments are taken as the psychologically real unit of analysis. Although many linguistics promote the linguistic reality of these phonetic segments, there is no evidence that these segments are psychologically functional in speech perception. If larger units (such as syllables) are assumed to be the functional perceptual units in speech perception, then the rate of presentation of these signals is well within the range of our information-processing capability.

Second, a word could be recognized without necessarily recognizing the phonemes that make it up. If a sequence of arbitrarily selected sounds is presented, listeners have trouble identifying the order of the elements that make up the sequence unless each sound is presented for a quarter of a second or so. On the other hand, these same listeners can *discriminate* one of the sequences from another when the sounds are much shorter—in the range of 5 to 100 milliseconds (Warren, 1982). A sequence of short speech segments produces a unique percept that is necessarily informative for a communication system. Two different sequences of identical components are discriminated from each other because one arrangement is heard as different from the other. One might sound "bubbly" and the other like a "shrill," and people can even learn to label and identify these sequences.

A final problem with the argument that the rate of speech processing is greater than other forms of auditory information processing is the positive contribution of context. Our ability to process speech at a fast rate holds only for familiar speech. Even linguists have great difficulty transcribing a language that they do not know. Knowing a language allows us to perceive and understand speech given a deficient signal or very little processing time. For example, we can hear the first /s/ in the word *legislatures,* even when the relevant segment has been replaced by a tone (Warren, 1970). Similarly, we can perceive the speech of a language we know when it is speeded up at two or three times its normal rate (Foulke & Sticht, 1969). Finally, when spoken language is represented in written form, literates can read as quickly as they can listen. The impressively fast rate of processing spoken language does not require a specialized processor.

Categorical Perception

Categorical perception serves as the cornerstone for the view that speech is special. We can usually discriminate among more instances than there are categories of the instances. For example, we can discriminate among thousands of different colors, but have only a few dozen or so labels for them. Speech is believed to be different. The dogma is that perceivers are limited in their ability to discriminate differences among different speech sounds belonging to the same phoneme category. According to this view, the speech sounds within a category are identified only absolutely, and discrimination is possible for only those sounds that can be identified as belonging to different categories.

Psychology and the speech sciences seem imprisoned by the notion of categorical perception perhaps, in part, because of phenomenal experience. One's phenomenal experience in speech perception is usually that of perceiving categories. If perception simply refers to our reported linguistic experience, then we cannot deny categorical perception because we naturally attend to the different categories of language. We cannot be swayed by linguistic experience because we have learned that it does not necessarily mirror the underlying processing. If perception refers to the psychological processing, however, then it is clear that the processing system is not limited to categorical information. Many empirical investigations have now demonstrated that perceivers are capable of perceiving differences within a speech category. For example, the ambiguity of tokens of a given syllable can be made synthetically and presented as test items. People can reliably indicate the degree to which these different tokens represent the speech category. In addition, the ambiguous tokens require more time for categorization than do clear tokens. These results indicate that people can discriminate differences within a speech category and are not limited to just categorical information. The richness of the representation of a speech token is not obscured during speech perception, but retains its graded composite of information. Most likely because of the discrete structure of human communication via spoken language, however, decision processes simply map the rich continuous information into one of the discrete categories used in our language. The toddler must choose between perhaps a ball and a doll when his caregiver asks him to put away his doll, but may mutter something that is roughly a good match for either of these two words. Given that speech is not perceived categorically, the case for the modularity of specialization of speech is weakened considerably.

Development of Speech Perception

Modularity of speech necessarily has a large innate component. It is still common to attribute categorical perception to infants as well as adults (Eimas, 1985; Gleitman & Wanner, 1982). Although early studies appeared to find that infants noticed differences only between sounds from different speech categories and not between sounds from within the same speech category, follow-up studies quickly demonstrated that infants discriminate differences within, as well as between, categories. More generally, research with infants reveals that they discriminate the multiple dimensions of the auditory speech signal. However, the meaning of these differences in the language must be learned and infants are not prewired to categorize the signals into innate phonetic categories. The infant is analogous to the adult learning to label and identify sequences of meaningless sounds. It is as false to attribute categorical perception to the infant and child as it is to claim that fully developed adults are categorical perceivers (Massaro, 1987).

It was also experimentally demonstrated that infants and young children do not discriminate and categorize speech signals as well as adults. Their caregivers seem to be aware of this limitation because there is also a substantial amount of "parentese" during the first years of life. "Parentese" is spoken when the caregiver speaks clearly and slowly to the child. As with most skills, the child manifests a slow acquisition of the fundamental distinctions of our spoken language. Children have difficulty discriminating speech categories and their ability to discriminate increases gradually throughout childhood.

Narrator's overlay. These discoveries of the slow and gradual development of speech are relevant to reading written language. When both were present in society, it was easy to conclude that reading was an unnatural act relative to speech. Speech seemed to be acquired naturally, whereas reading required some formal instruction. With hindsight, however, we now understand that the advantage speech may have enjoyed was primarily its persistent presence from the womb onward. On the other hand, the infant and toddler did not interact intensively with the written word, and most children are shielded from it until some formal schooling. You are probably unaware of the scandalous infant-read experiment that was undertaken at about the time that literacy was becoming extinct. Infants, from the time of birth, were equipped with specialized goggles that presented the written transcription of all spoken language in her environment. (The experiment originally used females because of their assumed superior language skills, but follow-up studies with males showed the same result.) The state of the art in speech recognition by machine had improved sufficiently to translate the spoken language of the infants' caregivers into a written form as it was being spoken. These infants procured literacy with no formal schooling and hand-in-hand with its spoken form. These results were suppressed by government agencies that had just renovated all the libraries (building containing books) so they could be sold as high-income housing. The shredded books made excellent insulation, and this innovative housing easily satisfied the current stringent energy requirements.

Retrospectively, we can comprehend that the research attempting to prove that speech is special was verificationist in approach, rather than adhering to the sacred scientific tenets of falsification and strong inference. Speech researchers weren't alone: The most striking example from the end of the twentieth century involved the putative language of bees (Wenner & Wells, 1990). Experiments had convinced most scientists that bees communicate the direction and distance of food to their cohorts by an elaborate dance upon reentry to the hive. These experiments and the language hypothesis even earned a Nobel Prize. It was only many years later that a few investigators seriously considered alternative hypotheses. It was then possible to design experiments without a confirmation bias. When these experiments were carried out, the bee language hypothesis failed. Similarly, advances in the understanding of speech perception came about when falsification and strong inference guided the research. *End of Narrator's overlay*

The Nonspecialized Nature of Speech Perception

Not only is the documentation for the special nature of speech perception weak, there is also corroboration to support the idea that speech perception is simply one of many domains of pattern recognition. No specialization is required for speech any more than for recognizing objects, melodies, and written language. We review a few of these sources of evidence here.

Contextual Effects in Speech Perception

A strong source of evidence against the modularity of speech perception involves the strong contribution of linguistic and situational context to speech perception. We perceive language more easily when we have some expectation of what the talker is going to say. Many of our conversations involve situations in which we find ourselves predicting exactly what the talker will say next. One hundred years after Bagley's first demonstration, experiments are still demonstrating that sentential context can facilitate word recognition. Situational context can also improve word recognition (Pollack & Pickett, 1963).

Speech Perception by Nonhumans

There is another source of evidence against the hypothesis that speech perception is carried out by a specialized module unique to humans. If speech perception is special and mediated in any way by speech production, then discrimination and recognition of fundamental speech categories should be impossible for nonhumans. However, some nonhuman animals can discriminate fundamental speech segments. Chinchillas (a small rodent with auditory capabilities close to humans) can discriminate fine distinctions in our spoken language. Even quail can learn to discriminate a set of syllables beginning with the stop consonant /d/ from a set of syllables beginning with the stops /b/ and /g/ (Kluender, Diehl, & Killeen, 1987). If there is information in the auditory speech signal that can be processed using normal perceptual mechanisms, we would expect that speech perception would not be limited to humans. More recently, chimps at Yerkes appear to be learning how to understand spoken language when regularly paired with other meaningful symbols. (Savage-Rumbaugh et al., 1993)

Reading Speech Spectrograms

As shown in Figure 14.4, speech spectrograms are visible representations of the acoustic characteristics of speech. When a device that translated speech into spec-

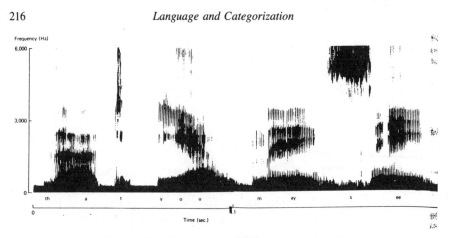

Figure 14.4. Spectrogram of "that you may see."

trograms was invented after World War II, there was the obvious hope that people with impaired hearing could learn to read spectrographic displays. This would give these individuals direct access to spoken language and, therefore, would allow them into the dominant linguistic community. The initial training studies and follow-up experiments and applications were very promising, but somehow these positive results were camouflaged by the Zeitgeist that speech is special. It wasn't until an expert spectrogram reader was reported (Cole et al., 1980) and some additional positive training studies were completed (Greene et al., 1984) that researchers had to acknowledge that the signal for speech might well be within the purview of a general pattern recognition system. It is not unreasonable that people might be capable of utilizing both acoustic and spectrographic information in speech recognition. *End of Narrator's overlay* The value of reading spectrographic patterns has been substantiated in telecommunications because speech spectrograms are one of the additional sources of information currently available on most channels.

Speech Perception and Cognitive Skills

If speech perception is governed by a specialized noninteractive module, we would expect no relationship between speech and other skills. However, there is a positive correlation between motor skills and language, and also one between cognitive functioning and vocabulary size. For example, there is a positive correlation between cognitive development and the learning of new words (Gopnik & Meltzoff, 1984). It seems that speech perception can be considered as one of several perceptual or cognitive functions that can be understood in terms of basic skills.

In conclusion, if you have persisted in our deliberations, I trust that you agree that the research we have reviewed weakens the claim that speech perception requires a specialized module. It is now time to consider speech perception as one of many different forms of pattern recognition.

Speech Perception as Pattern Recognition

Speech perception might be best understood in terms of general perceptual, cognitive, and learning processes. The guiding assumption for this framework is that humans use multiple sources of information in the perceptual recognition and understanding of spoken language. In this regard, speech perception resembles other forms of pattern recognition and categorization because integrating multiple sources of information appears to be a natural function of human endeavor. Integration appears to occur to some extent regardless of the goals and motivations of the perceiver. A convincing demonstration for this fact is the Stroop color-word test.

Narrator's overlay. This test, well known to most children and adults, became extinct with the loss of literacy. Literates, asked to name the color of the print of words that are color names printed in a color other than the word (for example, the word red printed in blue type), became tongue-tied and had difficulty naming the colors. Evidently, literates cannot stop themselves from reading the color word, and this interferes with naming the color of the print. The analogous demonstration for illiterates is to identify the pitch of a speaker's voice as high or low. It is much harder to do so when the speaker says the word "low" in a high pitch, requiring the perceiver to say high while perceiving the word "low" (McClain, 1983). This is where we leave our twentieth-century inquiry and close with a few observations linking research at that time with today's communication media.

Speech Perception by Eye and Ear

Good participants, have you wondered why we are communicating face-to-face rather than via just sound. A century ago, virtual-reality videophones (VRVPs) had not yet replaced telephones that provided only the speaker's voice. Experiments had revealed conclusively that our perception and understanding are influenced by the visible movements in the speaker's face and the accompanying gestural actions. These experiments have shown that the speaker's face is particularly helpful when the auditory speech is degraded as a result of noise, bandwidth filtering, or hearing impairment (Massaro, 1987; Summerfield, 1991). Although the influence of visible is substantial when auditory speech is degraded, visible speech also contributes to performance even when paired with intelligible speech sounds. The importance of visible speech is most directly observed when conflicting visible speech is presented with intelligible auditory speech. One famous example resulted from the dubbing of auditory syllable /ba/ onto a videotape of a talker saying /ga/ (McGurk & MacDonald, 1976). A strong effect of the visible speech is observed because a person will often report perceiving (or even hearing) the syllable /da/, /va/, or /ða/, but seldom /ba/ corresponding to the actual auditory stimulus.

One attractive aspect of providing or using audible and visible speech jointly is the complementarity of audible and visible speech. Visible speech is usually most informative for just those distinctions that are most ambiguous auditorily. For example, place of articulation (such as difference between /b/ and /d/) are difficult via sound but easy via sight. Voicing (such as the difference between /b/ and /p/), on the other hand, is difficult to see visually but is easy to resolve via sound. Thus, audible and visible speech not only provide two independent sources of information, these two sources are often productively complementary. One is strong when the other is weak.

Speech researchers quickly saw the value of studying bimodal speech perception. Given the importance of visible speech and the perceiver's natural ability to integrate multiple sources of information, a new experimental paradigm was possible. To control the visible speech, it was necessary to develop an animation system for visible speech synthesis. A critical assumption of this effort concerned the experimental, theoretical, and applied value of synthetic speech. Auditory synthetic speech had proven to be valuable in all three of these domains. Much of what we know about speech perception has come from experimental studies using synthetic speech. Synthetic speech gives the experimenter control over the stimulus in a way that is not always possible using natural speech. Synthetic speech also permits the implementation and test of theoretical hypotheses, such as which cues are critical for various speech distinctions. The applied value of auditory synthetic speech was apparent even then, before the extinction of written language, in the multiple everyday uses for text-to-speech systems that appealed to both normal and visually impaired individuals.

It was believed that visible synthetic speech would prove to have the same value as audible synthetic speech. Synthetic visible speech could provide a more fine-grained assessment of psychophysical and psychological questions not possible with natural speech. For example, testing people with synthesized syllables intermediate between several alternatives gives a more powerful measure of integration relative to the case of unambiguous natural stimuli. It was also obvious that synthetic visible speech had a valuable role to play in alleviating some of the communication disadvantages of the deaf and hearing impaired. Analogous to the valuable contribution of using auditory speech synthesis in speech perception research, visible speech synthesis permitted the type of experimentation necessary to determine (1) what properties of visible speech are used, (2) how they are processed, and (3) how this information is integrated with auditory information and other contextual sources of information in speech perception.

The development of a realistic, high-quality, facial display provided a powerful tool for investigation of a number of questions in auditory–visual speech perception. The analysis of the articulation of real speakers guided the development of visible speech synthesis. In addition, perception experiments indicated how well the synthesis simulated real speakers. The results of this research were used to implement automatic lipreading to enhance speech recognition by machine. Just as human perceivers achieved robust recognition of speech by using multiple sources of information, the same was true for machine recognition.

One applied value of visible speech was its potential to supplement other (degraded) sources of information. Visible speech is particularly beneficial in poor listening environments with substantial amounts of background noise. Its use is also important for hearing-impaired individuals because it allows effective spoken communications—the universal language of the community. Just as auditory speech synthesis has proved a boon to our visually impaired citizens in human–machine interaction, visual speech synthesis should prove to be valuable for the hearing-impaired. Finally, synthetic visible speech had an important part in building synthetic "actors" (Thalmann & Thalmann, 1991) and played a valuable role in the then exciting new sphere of virtual reality.

Another source of information is tactile, which appears to be naturally integrated with auditory or visual speech in the same way that auditory and visual speech are integrated. For example, deaf individuals benefit from both tactile and visual speech in the same way that hearing-impaired individuals benefit from both auditory and visual information. The value of tactile speech is also illustrated by deaf nonsighted individuals who can perceive speech by holding their hands on the speaker's face. This Tadoma method has proved to be a successful channel of communication, and it has even been demonstrated that hearing individuals can exploit tactile information in speech perception. Speech can be translated into a tactile form and transmitted via a virtual reality glove to the perceiver. The tactile output of our communication devices has proved to be a valuable source of information.

Good audience, we have now traveled through time to learn why our current dialogue is embellished with multiple sources of information. The consistent downsizing and downpricing of communication technology permitted the multifaceted interaction we take for granted. However, it was speech science and psychological theory that laid the foundation for our virtual world of communication. I hope to meet you in person someday (or have I already?)!

Acknowledgments

The writing of this paper was supported, in part, by grants from the Public Health Service (PHS R01 NS 20314) and the National Science Foundation (BNS 8812728).

References

Bagley, W. C. (1990). The apperception of the spoken sentence: A study in the psychology of language. *American Journal of Psychology, 12,* 80–130.

Bradshaw, J., & Rogers, L. (1993). *The evolution of lateral asymmetries, language, tool use, and intellect.* San Diego, Calif.: Academic press.

Chomsky, N. (1980). *Rules and representations.* Oxford: Blackwell.

Cole, R. A., Rudnicky, A. L., Zue, V. W., & Reddy, D. R. (1980). Speech as patterns on paper. In R. A. Cole (Ed.), *Perception and production of fluent speech.* Hillsdale, N.J.: Erlbaum.

Eimas, P. D. (1985, January). The perception of speech in early infancy. *Scientific American, 252*(1), 46–52.

Fodor, J. A. (1983). *Modularity of mind*. Cambridge, Mass.: Bradford books.

Foulke, E., & Sticht, T. G. (1969). A review of research on time compressed speech. *Psychological Bulletin, 72* 50–62.

Gleitman, L. R., & Wanner, E. (1982). Language acquisition: The state of the state of the art. In E. Wanner & L. R. Gleitman (Eds.), *Language acquisition: The state of the art* (pp. 3–48). Cambridge: Cambridge University Press.

Gopnik, A., & Meltzoff, A. N. (1984). Semantic and cognitive development in 15- to 21-month-old children. *Journal of Child Language, 11,* 495–513.

Greene, B. G., Pisoni, D. B., & Carrell, T. D. (1984). Recognition of speech spectrograms. *Journal of the Acoustical Society of America, 76,* 32–43.

Hilgard, E. R. (1987) *Psychology in America*. San Diego: Harcourt Brace Jovanovich.

Hockett, C. F. (1955). *A manual of phonology*, Memoir No. 11 of International Journal of American Linguistics. Baltimore: Waverly Press.

Huey, E. B. (1968). *The psychology and pedagogy of reading*. Cambridge, Mass: MIT Press. (Original work published 1908).

Kluender, K. R., Diehl, R. L., & Killeen, P. R. (1987). Japanese quail can learn phonetic categories. *Science, 237,* 1195–1197.

Liberman, A. M., & Mattingly, I. G. (1989). A specialization for speech perception. *Science, 243,* 489–494.

Lieberman, P. (1991). *Uniquely human,* Cambridge, Mass: Harvard University Press.

Massaro, D. W. (1987). *Speech perception by ear and eye: A paradigm for psychological inquiry*. Hillsdale, N.J.: Erlbaum.

Mattingly, I. G., & Studdert-Kennedy, M. (1991). *Modularity and the motor theory of speech perception*. Hillsdale, N.J.: Erlbaum.

McClain, L. (1983). Stimulus–response compatibility affects auditory Stroop interference. *Perception & Psychophysics, 33,* 66–270.

McGurk, H., & MacDonald, J. (1976). Hearing lips and seeing voices. *Nature, 264,* 746–748.

Miller, G. A. (1981). *Language and speech*. San Francisco: Freeman.

Pillsbury, W. B. (1897). A study in apperception. *American Journal of Psychology, 8,* 315–393.

Pollack, I., & Pickett, J. M. (1963). The intelligibility of excerpts from conversation. *Language and Speech, 6,* 165–171.

Sampson, G. R. (1989). Language acquisition: Growth or learning: *Philosophical Papers, 18,* 203–240.

Savage-Rumbaugh, E. S., Jurphy, J., Sevcik, R. A., Brakke, K. E., Williams, S. L., & Rumbaugh, D. M. (1993). *Language comprehension in ape and child*. Monographs of the Society for Research in Child Development, Vol. 58, Nos. 3 and 4.

Summerfield, Q. (1991). Visual perception of phonetic gestures. In I. G. Mattingly & M. Studdert-Kennedy, M. (Eds.), *Modularity and the motor theory of speech perception* (pp. 117–137). Hillsdale, N.J.: Erlbaum

Thalmann, N. M., & Thalmann, D. (1991). *Computer animation '91*. Heidelberg: Springer-Verlag.

Warren, R. M. (1970). Perceptual restoration of missing speech sounds. *Science, 167,* 392–393.

Warren, R. M. (1982). *Auditory perception: A new synthesis*. New York: Pergamon.

Wenner, A. M., & Wells, P. H. (1990). *Anatomy of a controversy: The question of a Language among bees*. New York: Columbia University Press, 1990.

Woodworth, R. S. (1938). *Experimental psychology*. New York: Holt.

15

The Neurocognitive Self: Conceptual System Research in the Twenty-first Century and the Rethinking of What a Person Is

GEORGE LAKOFF

The genre of futurism begins with a look at the past. Go back fifty, a hundred, or several hundred years and list a group of technological innovations that are commonplace now that were barely dreamed of then: personal computers, satellite communication, men on the moon, birth control pills, genetic engineering. Then project forward, trying to guess from ideas on the drawing board what the science of the future willl bring.

Since cognitive science isn't all that old, we need go back only twenty-five years to a time before there was a cognitive science. Twenty-five years ago, in 1968, I was a linguist in my twenties teaching at Harvard. The elements of early cognitive science were falling into place. Back in those days, I believed that thought was symbol manipulation, that ideas were represented in the mind in logical forms—symbolic structures akin to formulas in predicate logic or expressions in LISP. I believed that we represented situations in the world in terms of mental models, which were miniature mental versions of the set-theoretical models of formal logic. Back then I believed in a version of transformational grammar— that is, I believed that sentences were derived from underlying structures like those of predicate logic, and that the "derivations" took place not in real time, but in some abstract mathematical time that, somehow, had cognitive reality. I believed that conceptual categories were defined by necessary and sufficient conditions. Above all, I believed in functionalism, symbolic processing, and classical semantics. Functionalism is the idea that the mind can be studied in terms of the mental functions it performs without looking at the way the brain actually works. Those mental functions were assumed to be carried out by symbolic processing—by the algorithmic manipulation of arbitrary symbols without regard to what the symbols mean. Classical semantics assumes that the symbols being processed are to be given meaning by being associated with things in the world, thus making symbolic expressions into internal representations of external reality.

Those were the ideas that I shared with those from psychology, linguistics, anthropology, philosophy, and artificial intelligence that formed the first generation of cognitive science researchers. How was I to know that a mere twenty-five years later all those ideas would have been empirically disconfirmed, and entirely new views of thought and language proposed to account for the new data from cognitive science.

We have come a long way. The logical forms of a quarter-century ago characterized six real properties of conceptual structure: coreference, the binding of variables, predicate-argument structure, operator scope, propositional functions, and quantification. But the remarkable aspects of conceptual structure that have come to light since then have taken us far beyond old-fashioned predicate logic and LISP representations. Since the late 1970s and early 1980s, we have learned about all of the following aspects of conceptual structure:

Image-schemas: Topological and orientational structures that are used in the characterization of spatial relations concepts. They characterize spatial logic, are used in complex spatial relations concepts, and are projected by conceptual metaphors onto concepts in abstract domains. Examples include the container schema (for concepts like IN and OUT), the SOURCE–PATH–GOAL schema (for concepts like TO and FROM), the contact schema, the verticality schema, and so on. A complex concept such as ON makes use of three elementary schemas: verticality, contact, and support.

Frame semantics: Knowledge is organized in holistic structures called frames or schemas (or, when they involve time, scripts or scenarios). Frames bring together diverse pieces of information into gestalts. Words are defined relative to such frames.

A celebrated example is the simple commercial event script, in which the elements are a buyer, a seller, goods, and money. The scenario has three parts: First, the buyer has the money, and the seller has the goods. Then they exchange goods and money. And finally, the seller has the money and the buyer has the goods. Words like "buy," "sell," "goods," and "price" are defined with repect to this scenario. Frames are not isolated structures with simple boundaries like the knowledge representations of two decades ago. Rather, they partake of complex overlappings and interactions that seem more like the kind of phenomena that connectionism was developed to handle.

Conceptual metaphor: Most abstract concepts are conceptualized in terms of more concrete concepts via conceptual metaphors. A conceptual metaphor is a mapping from a source domain onto a target domain. For example, time is conceptualized in terms of moving objects, as in sentences like: "The time for action has arrived." "The time for celebrating is long since gone." "A parade will follow the awarding of prizes." Here the present is conceptualized in terms of an observer situated at the present time and facing toward the future. Future times move toward the observer from front to back. A conceptual system contains thousands of such mappings. Such mappings preserve image-schematic structure; for example, source domain paths are mapped onto target domain paths; source domain containers onto target domain containers; and so on. By this mechanism, the logic of space is mapped onto the logics of the full range of abstract domains, with spatial inference patterns mapped onto abstract inference patterns. For example, Boolean logic is the metaphorical projection of the logic of containers (that is, bounded regions in space).

Radial categories: These are categories that have centers and extensions of various types. The major mechanisms of category extension from center to periphery include (1) similarity, (2) conceptual metaphor, and (3) shared frames.

A radial category of type 1 is mother. Central cases of mothers are defined by four converging folk models: a birth model, a nurturance model, a marriage model, and a genetic model. The prototypical mother gives birth to the child, nurtures it, is married to the father, and is the female from whom it gets half its genes. Other types of mothers—adoptive mothers, stepmothers, foster mothers, genetic mothers, and so on—bear similarities to central mothers, but are mothers relative to fewer models.

A radial category of type 2 is harm. The central case of harm is physical harm. But there are also metaphorical forms of harm: psychological harm, social harm, political harm, economic harm, and the harm that is characterized as the thwarting of someone's interests. Metaphorical forms of harm are nonetheless forms of harm. All are part of the same concept, but there are differences—differences recognized by law.

A radial category of type 3 is the Dyirbal balan, as discussed in Lakoff (1987). The central case is women, but other members are in the category by virtue of shared frames. For example, the myth that the sun is the wife of the moon is a frame shared by the sun and women, placing the sun in the balan category. Fire and the sun share the frame of hot things, which puts fire into the same category as the sun and women. And so on.

Prototype systems: Not all members of a conceptual category have the same status; some are better examples of the category than others. Moreover, there are many types of prototypes: Typical cases, on which default inferences are based; social stereotypes, used for making snap judgments; graded prototypes, indicating the degree to which something is a good example; ideal prototypes, used as standards of judgment; salient exemplars, used for making probability judgments; and radial category centers, used as the basis for the extension of a concept to noncentral cases.

Basic-level concepts: These are concepts that arise from the optimal interaction of people with their external environment. They are based on gestalt perception, the capacity to form mental images, and motor programs. Compare, for example, the concepts *furniture* and *chair*. Several things make a chair basic-level and furniture superordinate (without basic-level properties). People can perceive chairs as gestalts, but not pieces of furniture. One can get a mental image of a chair, not of a general piece of furniture (as opposed to a specific kind like a chair, table, or bed). People have motor programs for interacting with chairs, but not with furniture in general.

Contested concepts: These are concepts for which everybody seems to have a different idea of what the concept is. Common examples include democracy, art, and feminism. Our best current theory of contested concepts is that there is an uncontested, but underspecified core concept, which gets extended on the basis of ideologies or other sets of beliefs about more general subject matter.

Mental spaces: These have replaced the mental models of the 1970s. They differ in that they can simultaneously represent multiple models and complex links across them.

These phenomena go well beyond what predicate logic, LISP-like formalisms, and set-theoretical semantics can deal with. A cognitive semantics in which such phenomena can be accurately characterized is now under development and looks very little like predicate logic. Just as representations based on predicate logic have been superseded, so algorithmic symbol manipulation has been superseded by connectionist computation, which attempts to mirror the kinds of operations carried out by neural structures of the brain. Such connectionist systems are, by their very nature, constraint satisfaction systems.

Within contemporary cognitive linguistics, old-style transformational grammars have been superseded by cognitive grammars and construction grammars. The basic units of grammar have become constructions, which are schemalike structures incorporating semantic, pragmatic, and syntactic information. Constructions, like frames, combine by superposition, and each construction defines a set of constraints. A grammar is a network of constructions that combine via a constraint satisfaction system that defines a language. This view of grammar not only does better at handling purely grammatical problems, but also meshes better with what is known about neural computation.

The Embodied Mind

What unites all these results is a very new view of conceptual systems and of the mind itself. On the old view, the mind was disembodied—a mathematical object, an abstract device for manipulating symbols without regard to their interpretation, floating free of the body, and only incidentally "implemented" in the brain. The new view requires that the mind be seen as essentially embodied:

- Basic-level concepts are characterized partly in terms of gestalt perception and motor programs.
- Color categories are grounded in the neurophysiology of color vision.
- Spatial relations seem to be embodied in the perceptual system (as we shall see shortly).
- Conceptual metaphors are part of a set of imaginative mechanisms that project from concepts with a direct bodily grounding to abstract concepts.

The new view of concepts as getting their meaning through bodily grounding and metaphorical projection supersedes the old view of concepts. On the old view, concepts were seen as abstract symbols that get their meaning by being associated directly with things and categories in an external world that was assumed to have all the structure built into it to account for the structure in our conceptual systems.

We now know that much of the structure of our conceptual systems has as much to do with our bodies and brains as it has to do with the world external to our bodies.

Two Futuristic Hypotheses

Nonsymbolic Neural Representations of Concepts

A particularly important recent result indicates that the representation of concepts using symbols is an artifact of the fact that we write rather than an intrinsic part of the nature of concepts. Terry Regier, in his Berkeley dissertation (1991), constructed a connectionist system in which spatial concepts are learned and represented in terms of neural structures without symbols like those used in formal logic, linguistics, or classical AI. Using connectionist networks, Regier made use of neural structures of the kind found in topographic maps of the visual field, orientation-sensitive cells, and center-surround receptive fields. The system learned to acquire synaptic weights which enabled the neural structures to perform the functions of image-schemas and to represent the meanings of spatial relations concepts. Regier's results go beyond the capacities of symbol-manipulation systems and indicate that we may have at hand a method for beginning to represent concepts using neurally inspired models rather than models with abstract symbols. Moreover, these results give a very concrete idea of what it would mean for concepts to be grounded in the body.

My first futuristic hypothesis is what I will call the *neural representation hypothesis:* that Regier's work will lead us within the twenty-first century to a general technique for representing concepts using neurally inspired nonsymbolic structured connectionist models. They will model how concepts are grounded in the body, as Mark Johnson, myself, and others have hypothesized. In particular, I foresee an extension of Regier's work that will be able to characterize spatial inferences, and a further extension to characterize how metaphorical mappings can be represented in neurally inspired connectionist models so as to map spatial relations and their inference structures onto abstract domains, such as time, events, the emotions, and so forth.

Regier's models not only represent spatial concepts, but they also learn spatial concepts and the words and morphemes that express them linguistically. Regier has used connectionist learning techniques along with biologically motivated and structured neural nets to accomplish the learning—with no explicit negative examples! I believe that Regier's work will spark a new direction in conceptual learning using biologically motivated, structured connectionist models.

The convergence zone hypothesis (CZH)

Results about the structure and function of the brain in recent years have tended to converge with the results we have seen on the nature of conceptual structure and grammar. Earlier generations of linguists and cognitive scientists believed in a simpleminded modularity hypothesis that I shall call localized modularity—

namely, the belief that specialized complex brain functions are completely performed in isolated modules. According to localized modularity, whenever a deficit of some cognitive function results from a lesion in a particular region of the brain, it follows that the entire cognitive function is carried out in that region in people without the lesion. Thus, face recognition, according to localized modularity, is entirely carried out in one particular region in the brain, which, if lesioned, results in a loss of the capacity for face recognition.

This view of brain modularity led to a hypothesis about mind modularity: The mind, too, was seen as made up of modules, and accordingly, there were supposed to be isolated modules in the brain for specialized cognitive functions such as language.

In recent years, the localized modularity hypothesis has become a thing of the past, largely owing to the emergence of PET scan and MRI research. Capacities such as face recognition, which can be destroyed by lesions in certain locations, have been shown to involve activation of many portions of the brain, not just the regions where lesions destroy the capacity. This has led to the hypothesis that there exist "convergence zones" where information is brought together and "bound" neurally. For example, in face recognition, many individual features of a particular face must be bound together to form the overall gestalt of that face. The convergence zone hypothesis says that the binding of those features occurs "temporally" through the simultaneous activation of all the disparate brain regions that compute those features. There are neural connections from the areas where those features are computed to a higher level where there is a neural ensemble whose job it is to govern the binding of those disparate features. A lesion in the convergence zone is, according to the theory, responsible for the destruction of the binding function. But where there is no lesion, the computation may be done in widely scattered regions of the brain. The convergence zone is where the activation of disparate functions is coordinated, but not where the functions are actually carried out. Instead, of being localized in a module, the computations characterizing brain functions are widely distributed throughout the brain, while being coordinated from a variety of convergence zones.

What makes the research on convergence zones by Hannah and Antonio Damasio and their co-workers especially powerful is that it explains why certain lesions in the visual cortex but not in the frontal area can result in the loss of basic-level categories for animals but not for artifacts. Some people experience the loss of the ability to distinguish basic-level animal categories, say, camels from elephants, but not the ability to distinguish basic-level artifact categories, say, knives from forks. Basic-level animal categories make use of gestalt perception and mental imagery, whereas basic-level artifact categories also make use of motor programs. On the convergence zone hypothesis, the convergence zone for basic-level artifact categories would occur at a level in the brain where both visual and motor information could be brought together, whereas the convergence zones for the animal categories would occur at a lowel level, where no motor information is involved. Hence a lesion at the lower level (more toward the rear of the brain) could result in the loss of one kind of basic-level category but not the other. Such explanations by the Damasios give support to the idea of convergence zones.

Extending the work on convergence zones by the Damasios, I propose what I call the *neurocognitive convergence hypothesis* (NCH). It is an attempt to provide a unified framework for many of the relatively new discoveries mentioned above: complex image-schemas, semantic frames, conceptual metaphors, radial categories, basic-level concepts, and grammatical constructions. In each of these cases, disparate information is brought together to form a schema with gestalt properties, and in each case the schemas combine by superposition and form a constraint satisfaction system. The different types of phenomena—basic-level categories, grammatical constructions, conceptual frames, conceptual metaphors, and so forth—result from the location of convergence zones in different sites in the brain.

The neurocognitive convergence hypothesis is a hypothesis which proposes that convergence zones in the brain explain why a wide variety of seemingly disparate cognitive phenomena have the same basic properties. It uses a hypothesis about brain structure to unify research on conceptual systems and language. I do not know if it is true, but I suspect that it is, and I optimistically hope that it will guide research into the twenty-first century to discover whether or not it is true.

Grammar and Neuroscience

I believe that research in neuroscience will utterly transform the landscape of linguistics. The first major casualty will be generative grammar, which requires the assumption that language is autonomous—that is, independent of the rest of cognition. Chomsky has hypothesized that there is a "language organ," a separate module of the brain devoted exclusively to grammar. To guarantee that language is independent of all the rest of cognition, Chomsky's "language module" would have to have no input from the rest of the brain. If it did have such input, then other aspects of cognition could influence grammar, and the central hypothesis of generative grammar—total autonomy from meaning and other aspects of cognition—would be ruled out. But there is no such thing in the brain as a module with no input. For this reason, the properties of the brain module required by Chomsky's theory does not accord with those of real brain modules. (For a discussion of this topic by a prominent neuroscientist, see Edelman, 1992, pp. 211–252.)

Incidentally, the autonomy hypothesis is not a casual aspect of generative grammar that might be jettisoned. It is central to the endeavor. The reason is that the mathematical foundations of generative grammar—the theory of formal grammars—is defined as the manipulation of symbols without regard to what they mean or how a brain might process them. There is no place in the mathematical foundations of the theory for input from other aspects of cognition. Moreover, the mathematics requires the existence of "operations" that are, like deductions in formal logic, "performed" in abstract time, not in real time. The brain is not capable of performing operations in "abstract time." In short, the kind of things that brains do is very different from the kind of things that generative grammars do.

The Damasios' convergence zone hypothesis has two important consequences for grammar. First, it explains a set of findings in cognitive linguistics: (1) Grammar is organized in terms of *constructions* that pair semantic and pragmatic information with surface—that is, phonological—form (e.g., pronunciation order of constituents, grammatical morphemes, etc.). (2) Constructions are gestalts in which disparate kinds of information are brought together into a coherent whole. (3) Constructions combine by superimposition. (4) Less central constructions inherit constraints from more central constructions; that is, peripheral constructions use as much as they can of the content of the central constructions. These are exactly the properties that one would predict from the CZH, but not from the theory of formal grammars.

Second, the CZH explains away what had been taken as evidence for the autonomy of syntax. Aphasics with lesions in Broca's area suffer from agrammatism, a disorder in which people know the meanings of words but cannot put them together grammatically to form grammatical sentences. Under the localized modularity hypothesis, it follows that if a lesion in an area affects only grammar and leaves semantics intact, then that area must perform the function of grammar alone, and not any semantic function. But if the convergence zone hypothesis is right, then localized modularity is wrong, and the conclusion no longer follows. The existence of agrammatism does not entail the independence of syntax from semantics. It could mean instead that a convergence zone is located in Broca's area, a zone that links information about the semantics of grammatical constructions with information about the phonological form of constructions—the order of pronunciation of the constituents, the phonological forms of grammatical morphemes, and so on. That is, it is consistent with the idea that syntax is the pairing of categories of semantic elements with phonological restrictions (where pronunciation order counts as "phonological"). In short, agrammatism is as consistent with cognitive grammar as with generative grammar, which eliminates a classic argument for generative grammar and the autonomy of syntax.

The convergence zone hypothesis is a hypothesis about the structure of the brain. The neurocognitive convergence hypothesis is a hypothesis about how the CZH provides a unified account of such apparently disparate phenomena as basic-level concepts, metaphors, and grammatical constructions.

Twenty-five years ago, I could not have imagined any of these developments that I now teach routinely in Cognitive Science 101. At that time there were in our intellectual landscape no prototypes, no basic-level categories, no radial categories, no image-schemas, no conceptual metaphors, no mental spaces, no theory of grammatical constructions, no connectionism, no convergence zones. I have no doubt that the current intellectual landscape, too, will change just as radically in the next twenty-five to a hundred years. But given the license to engage in futuristic speculation, let us consider where the new developments that have just been outlined might lead.

Conceptual System Research

It is my opinion that the most dramatic effect of cognitive science on culture in general will come from conceptual system research. That research has the capacity to change our understanding of everything from law, politics, and philosophy to interpersonal relations and the nature of public discourse. The most radical changes in our perceptions of ourselves and our social lives will, I believe, come from three sources: conceptual metaphor, radial categories, and contested concepts.

Conceptual metaphor is the most radical of these developments. We have discovered, over the past decade and a half, that a conceptual system contains an enormous subsystem of thousands of conceptual metaphors—mappings that allow us to understand the abstract in terms of the concrete. Without this system, we could not engage in abstract thought at all—in thought about causation, purpose, love, morality, or thought itself. Without the metaphor system, there could be no philosophizing, no theorizing, and little general understanding our everyday personal and social lives. But the operation of this vast system of conceptual metaphor is largely unconscious. We reason metaphorically throughout most of our waking, and even our dreaming lives, but for the most part are unaware of it. At present, the metaphor system of English has barely begun to be worked out in full detail, and the metaphor systems of other languages have been studied only cursorily. Working out the details would be a huge job—not as big as the human genome project, but most likely, more beneficial. For what is at stake is our understanding of ourselves and our daily lives, and the possibilities for improvement through that understanding. The other radical innovations are radial categories and contested concepts.

Radial categories occur where a concept has a central case that gets extended to other cases, often by conceptual metaphor. For example, the concept of HARM has physical harm as a central case, with metaphorical extensions to mental, social, and economic harm, as well as to causal harm—the thwarting of one's purposes. Radial categories occur in every aspect of our lives, and the difference between central cases and extensions has repercussions in many realms of social, interpersonal, and intellectual life. Truth, as I have argued elsewhere, is another radial category. It is important to describe the radial structure of important concepts in full detail, and to bring to general awareness the fact that radial structure exists.

A great many concepts are contested concepts, especially social concepts like democracy or feminism or justice. An enormous number of misunderstandings and pointless disputes arise from a failure to understand the nature of contested concepts—especially the fact that what is contested is usually the product of divergent belief systems. It is commonly recognized that there are disagreements as to what, say, feminism or democracy are. It is vital to understand that such disagreements are not over matters of fact, but over what ideology or more general belief system should prevail.

Imagine for the moment that the general public recognized the importance of understanding our mental life (as well as the mental lives of those in other cultures) and that research on conceptual systems was reasonably well funded. Imagine that the metaphor system underlying English and many other languages was extensively worked out, and that the system of radial categories and contested concepts was well advanced. What use could be made of this knowledge about our own modes of understanding?

Law

Steven Winter, one the country's most important young legal theorists, has been demonstrating for some years that conceptual metaphor and radial concepts are central to law. The prevailing legal fiction is that the law applies general principles to particular cases, and that the judgments about particular cases follow by logic from the legal principles plus knowledge about the case at hand. In short, law engages in the mythology that legal decisions are strictly literal, that legal categories are defined by necessary and sufficient conditions (rather than radial structures), and that only logic and not metaphor enters into legal decisions.

Winter has argued, to the contrary, that major judicial decisions involve the application of conceptual metaphor not logic. Take, for example, the legal metaphor that CORPORATIONS ARE PERSONS. This metaphor allows corporations a range of legal rights such as standing in court and the ability to sue. There is, on the other hand, no legal metaphor that ECOSYSTEMS ARE PERSONS, and ecosystems are thereby not given rights or standing in court if they are harmed.

Winter has shown that a great many judicial decisions that have come to be taken as precedent are cases where a judge has used a metaphor to extend a body of law from central to noncentral cases. Indeed, just about all Supreme Court cases involve the extensions of some concept radially from central to noncentral cases. What would result if the use of metaphor and radial categories that presently exists in the law were officially recognized as such?

The current legal mythology, Winter observes, permits a great deal of judicial arbitrariness. When judges extend legal categories by metaphor and claim that they are just showing how the case logically fits existing necessary and sufficient conditions, the effect is that judges get to make law outside of democratic procedures. Winter proposes, in an extensive rethinking of standing law, that the concept of standing might be redefined by legistation as a radial category. The existing concept of standing in court would be preserved at the center of the category, whereas metaphorical extensions of the concept of standing could be added by legislation. Such a redefinition of standing, he argues, would eliminate many categories of injustices.

The official recognition of cognitive science and conceptual system research by the legal community could have far-reaching effects in bringing law under more democratic procedures. It would certainly drastically change the nature of legal argumentation and, perhaps, even how laws are framed. Bringing cognitive science into law would change the most basic understanding of legal theory. Take the question of rights. The traditional liberal view is that rights are "inalienable"— essential properties of human beings, part of the essence of what it is to be human. Certain adherents of the Critical Legal Studies movement, however, have noted that, according to Continental philosophy, there are no essences, and hence if rights are essences, there are no rights, and it is thus pointless to fight to defend rights. Their point is to portray law as the arbitrary use of power by judges.

Winter, using results from the study of conceptual metaphor, demonstrates that rights are understood via a collection of conceptual metaphors. But he observes that this does not make them fictional. He notes that metaphors can be made real by social institutions. For example, we have a metaphor in this culture that TIME IS A MONEY-LIKE RESOURCE that can be wasted, saved, budgeted, invested, spent, squandered, and so on. Time isn't inherently a money-like resource, and many indigenous cultures around the world do not have this conceptual metaphor. But we have social institutions such as paying people by the hour, setting deadlines, and so on, that structure society so that this conceptual metaphor fits a wide range of experiences in our culture. The institutions make the metaphor real: It is possible that someone could really *waste* an hour of my time, and I have certainly *squandered* many an hour. Similarly, Winter argues that, if we like the idea of rights and want to have them despite the fact that they are metaphorical creations, we have to build and maintain institutions to define and guarantee those rights. That takes work and social activism. Thus, we cannot blithely assume the existence of rights as if they were essences, nor need we give up on them as being fictions. By recognizing their metaphorical character and the fact that conceptual metaphors can be realized through social institutions, we can see why continued activism is required if rights are to be made and kept real.

From these examples we can see that our very understanding of the nature of law, at its most fundamental level, changes when results about our conceptual system and its embodied nature are taken seriously.

Philosophy

Philosophy, since the time of the Greeks, has seen itself as the final arbiter in characterizing concepts and determining the validity of arguments. But the development of conceptual system research within cognitive science fundamentally changes the role of philosophy. Cognitive science has made it an empirical question as to what conceptual systems are like—and they have turned out to be very unlike what philosophers had surmised. Conceptual analysis is now an empirical matter, and cognitive science has developed the tools to do analyses of basic-level concepts, prototypes, frames, conceptual metaphors, etc. The empirical results in these areas fit neither the Anglo-American nor the Continental tradition in philosophy. What is needed is a new philosophical tradition that takes into account the results of cognitive science. That tradition has begun to be built.

Mark Johnson, one of the major philosophers to make use of empirical results from cognitive science in doing philosophy, is the principal intiator of that new tradition. In his classic *The Body in the Mind,* Johnson argues on empirical grounds that concepts are grounded in the body and extended by imaginative mechanisms such as metaphor, prototypes, frames, and so on. This view counters, first, the most common Anglo-American view that meaning lies in the relationship between symbols and a mind-free world—independent of human psychology. It also counters the most common Continental view (not counting Merleau-Ponty) that meaning is arbitrary and ungrounded. What emerges instead is Johnson's "experientialist" position, a position very much in keeping with results in contemporary neuroscience.

Johnson has also applied cognitive science to the traditional questions of ethics. In *Moral Imagination: The Implications of Cognitive Science for Ethics,* Johnson argues against the traditional view that moral laws are like axioms in a logic that will either fit or not fit a given situation and will objectively tell one by the application of pure reason what to do in that situation. Instead, he argues, our very concept of morality is based on a collection of conceptual metaphors that are conventional in our culture and that conflict with one another. Citing research by Sarah Taub, Johnson argues that the major metaphor for morality in our culture, as well as in many others, is the metaphor of *moral accounting*. Moral accounting works roughly like this: Say I do something to harm you. That puts me morally in your debt—I owe you something. And if I do something to help you, then you are in my debt, and you owe me something. Debts can be paid according to a metaphorical moral arithmetic: Giving something bad = getting something good; and giving something good = getting something bad. Thus, if I do something to harm you and am morally in your debt, the books can be balanced in two ways: You can do something bad back to me (retribution) or I can do something good for you (compensation). It is also possible to accrue moral credit, to be morally bankrupt, to pay someone back with interest, and so on. Taub demonstrates that there are a number of mutually exclusive moral positions possible within the moral accounting metaphor: compensation, retribution, revenge, turning the other cheek, potlatch, and so on.

Johnson observes that real moral decisions often involve two layers of metaphor—the choice of a metaphor for morality and, commonly, the choice of a metaphor for understanding the situation at hand. The result, Johnson argues, is that conceptual metaphor is always used in making moral decisions, and that moral dilemmas are real and may have to do with which metaphor should be used to characterize a situation.

Expanding on Johnson's views on ethics, Johnson and I set out to apply cognitive semantics not just to ethics, but to philosophy in general. We reasoned as follows: Each philosophical theory is a miniature conceptual system. Each philosophical theory would be what we call a "conceptual paradigm"—a collection of theoretical statements making use of conceptual metaphors, prototypes of various kinds, frames, and so on. Cognitive science has the tools to characterize such conceptual paradigms precisely. Suppose we take philosophical theories as data to be described in terms of the conceptual metaphors, frames, and so on. What would a philosophical theory look like when characterized from the perspective of cognitive science?

What we proposed was a subfield of cognitive science with philosophy as its subject matter: the *cognitive science of philosophy*. At present, we have done preliminary analyses of Presocratic metaphysics and Enlightenment epistemology and ethics. Here is what we have found so far: Each philosophical theory uses a collection of metaphors—typically a consistent subset of those found in the culture at large. Those metaphors characterize a significant portion of the ontologies of the philosophical theories. For example, in Enlightenment faculty psychology, the *society of mind* metaphor is used; the mind is conceptualized as consisting of personified aspects of mind: reason, will, perception, judgment, and so on. Each of these has a job to do. Perception acquires information about the external world, reason calculates what actions will best serve the person's interests, will carries out those actions, and so on. Philosophical theories operate within the confines prescribed by the major metaphors of the philosophy and theorize about those metaphorical entities to form a conceptual paradigm. When a conceptual paradigm uses versions of metaphors taken from our everyday conceptual systems, that conceptual paradigm seems "intuitive," since it uses metaphors that we already think in terms of. A particularly clear case of a conceptual paradigm that seemed intuitive because it made use of everyday metaphors is the philosophy of mind that accompanied the early days of cognitive science when it was thought that the mind was a computer and that thought was symbolic computation of the kind used in classical artificial intelligence. Here are some of the everyday metaphors that went into that conceptual paradigm:

The thought-as-object-manipulation metaphor: Here thoughts are seen as objects that can be manipulated—for example, put together, taken apart, rearranged, added to, stored, retrieved, put into words (which are linguistic containers for thoughts), sent to others, and received from others.

The thought-as-mathematical-calculation metaphor: Here ideas are seen as mathematical objects (numbers), reasoning is addition ("He put two and two together"), considering an idea is including it in the count ("Should we count that?"), inferences are sums ("What is the bottom line?"), and explaining is accounting ("Give me an account of why that happens. Can you account for this phenomenon? It just doesn't add up.").

The thought-as-language metaphor: Here, thinking is language use (speaking or writing); simple ideas are words; complex ideas are sentences; and fully communicating a thought is spelling it out. The metaphor can be seen in countless expressions, such as: "It's Greek to me." "She can't translate her ideas into well-defined plans." "I can't hear myself think." "He's an articulate thinker." "His thoughts are eloquent." "What is the vocabulary of basic philosophical ideas?" "The argument is abbreviated." "The theory is spelled out very well." "Do I have to spell it out for you?" "Follow the letter of the law." "He's reading between the lines." "He's computer literate." "I wouldn't read too much into what he says." "He's a big question mark to me." "Be home by midnight—period!" "She's like an open book." "Let me make a mental note of that." "Note that . . ." "Take note that . . ." "He's the author of the theory that. . . ."

The mind-as-machine metaphor: Here, the mind is a machine; ideas are products; thinking is the automated step-by-step assembly of simpler thoughts into more complex thoughts; good ideas are products that work; normal thought is the normal operation of the machine; inability to think is a failure of the machine to function. Examples illustrating this metaphor are: "He had a mental breakdown." "I'm a little rusty today." "The wheels are turning now." "He's turning out theories at a great rate." "That argument doesn't work."

These, when spliced together, yield *The mind-as-computer metaphor,* where a computer is understood as being a *machine* that *calculates* by *manipulating abstract objects* in a *language.* The conceptual paradigm of early cognitive science thus seemed intuitive because it was based on metaphors that we already had.

If cognitive science comes to be used to analyze philosophical theories in a systematic way, philosophy will change dramatically. The actual content of much of philosophy depends on certain outdated philosophical views of what concepts are and what reason is. When old views of concepts and reason are replaced by more empirically sound views coming out of cognitive science, then the actual content of much of philosophy will change as well. As I observed, the objectivist tradition in Anglo-American philosophy and the subjectivist tradition in Continental philosophy are both inconsistent with results from cognitive science. Taking cognitive science seriously should result in the abandoning those philosophical views and developing views that are consistent with empirical results from the cognitive sciences. The very idea that philosophy should have to be consistent with empirical results about the nature of the mind should radically transform philosophy.

Politics and Public Policy

Michael Barzelay, a professor at the Kennedy School of Government at Harvard, has made remarkably innovative use of the study of conceptual systems in cognitive science. After acquainting himself with results about the nature of conceptual metaphor and entailments of metaphorical thought, Barzelay set out to analyze the subject matter that he taught—governmental bureaucracies.

Barzelay realized that bureaucracies had been conceptualized metaphorically as factories and that bureaucratic officials had been trained to be factory managers. Citizens dealing with the bureaucracy were seen as objects to be processed and people who worked in the bureaucracy as cogs in a machine. The different functions of the bureaucracy were to be assigned to different branches, so that each function could be carried out most efficiently. To be free from bias, the bureaucracy was to function impersonally, and to guarantee impersonal, efficient, machinelike functioning, rules and procedures were handed down for bureaucratic employees to follow precisely.

Barzelay noticed that government bureacracies had been designed and perpetuated according to a conceptual paradigm governed by a major conceptual metaphor: Bureaucracies are factories. Most of citizens' complaints about government bureaucracies, he realized, were about features that had been designed into the system and consciously perpetuated. The *bureaucratic paradigm,* as he has called it, was not designed to serve the needs of citizens.

Awakened by an insight from cognitive science, Barzelay asked how bureaucracies might be redesigned to serve citizens' needs. What was needed, he reasoned, was a new major metaphor and a new conceptual paradigm based on it. The old metaphor was taken from manufacturing industries. But since then major industries had developed to serve people's needs—service industries. Barzelay asked what it would be like if bureaucracies were redesigned according to a new metaphor: *A bureau of government is a service industry.* He called this the *post-bureaucratic paradigm.* Citizens to be served are to be seen as customers or clients whose needs are to be met. The major metaphors that define the bureaucratic and post-bureaucratic paradigms have very different entailments (Barzelay, 1992, pp. 8–9):

- A bureaucratic agency is focused on its own needs and perspectives. A customer-driven agency is focused on customer needs and perspectives.
- A bureaucratic agency is focused on the roles and responsibilities of its parts. A customer-driven agency is focused on enabling the whole organization to function as a team.
- A bureaucratic agency defines itself both by the amount of resources it controls and by the tasks it performs. A customer-driven agency defines itself by the results it achieves for its customers.
- A bureaucratic agency controls costs. A customer-driven agency creates value net of cost.
- A bureaucratic agency sticks to routine. A customer-driven agency modifies its operations in response to changing demands for its services.
- A bureaucratic agency fights for turf. A customer-driven agency competes for business.
- A bureaucratic agency insists on following standard procedures. A customer-driven agency builds choice into its operating systems when doing so serves a purpose.
- A bureaucratic agency announces policies and plans. A customer-driven agency engages in two-way communication with its customers in order to assess and revise its operating strategy.
- A bureaucratic agency separates the work of thinking from that of doing. A customer-driven agency empowers front-line employees to make judgments about how to improve customer service and value.

Barzelay's book, *Breaking Through Bureaucracy,* is a case study of how such a change was actually carried out in the State of Minnesota. Besides Barzelay, others have proposed such a metaphor shift, most notably David Osborne in *Reinventing Government* and Gareth Morgan in *Images of Organization.*

An End of Innocence

If the cognitive revolution takes hold, it is conceivable that colleges and universities will teach what conceptual systems are like and how to do conceptual analysis. Analyses of conceptual systems may even become commonplace. At that point, a major form of innocence will come to an end. We will be forced to confront the conceptual systems we normally use in minute detail. What was unconscious and automatic in our thought can be made conscious. The metaphors that define conceptual paradigms, whether in academic disciplines or in public life or in interpersonal relations, can be brought to awareness and their entailments revealed. Our implicit conceptual paradigms can be made explicit. Conceptual explicitness can be of great use.

Take interpersonal relations. Each spouse in a marriage has different ways of conceptualizing the marriage metaphorically. Common conceptualizations of marriage in America include: A journey through life together, a partnership, a home, a constructed object, a life, a haven from the outside world, a struggle, and so on. Each of these has different entailments, and those entailments typically conflict. In short, spouses typically conceptualize their marriages in inconsistent ways. The details of those inconsistencies and their metaphorical sources can be discovered.

Or take public discourse about politics: George Bush convinced the American public that the Gulf War was a *heroic rescue:* A monstrous villain (Iraq) had attacked a weak and innocent neighbor (Kuwait), and a hero (the United States) had to come to the rescue. It was a metaphor that hid a great many realities: As Bush said during the 1992 presidential campaign, the war was mainly fought to protect U.S. oil supplies. When Serbia attacked Bosnia, where there was no oil, Bush did not respond with a heroic rescue. The rescue metaphor for the Gulf War hid many other realities: Kuwait was not all that innocent; it had provoked Iraq in a variety of ways. It was also a brutal police state, and our "saving" it did not change that. The U.S. invasion killed 200,000 innocent Iraqis and left a million more injured or in misery. The war allowed Saddam Hussein to consolidate his power by further suppressing the Kurds and Shiites. Indeed, it was American policy to keep the Kurds and Shiites from getting out from under the rule of Saddam Hussein. The war did not destroy the military power of Saddam's regime. Indeed, the American strategy was designed to keep the monstrous villain reasonably strong. The disparities between the metaphor and what the metaphor hid were enormous.

The American press largely accepted the metaphor. The press did not point out the metaphor and what it hid. Indeed, the press systematically fails to call into question the ways in which the government frames policy. In short, the tools of conceptual analysis have not yet made their way into the press and into public discourse. Cognitive science is not required for training in journalism. Someday it may be. Someday it could become normal for reporters, or experts in cognitive science, regularly to analyze the conceptual framing of major public issues, and what that framing hides. It is conceivable that the tools for conceptual analysis developed in cognitive science could be used as a matter of course in public discourse. It would greatly improve public discourse.

What Is a Person?

Every culture has at its core fundamental assumptions about what a person is. In Western culture, since the Greeks, there has been a conceptual paradigm for characterizing a person. That paradigm can be characterized roughly as follows:

The Traditional Western Person

- People are distinguished from animals by having a mind and a capacity for reason.
- The mind is separate from the body. The body is subject to physical constraints; the mind is not.
- There is a single, unitary locus of consciousness with the capacity for reason and will. Reason is conscious.
- Reason is transcendental; it transcends the limitations of the body, applies universally, and for all time. Since concepts are what one uses to reason with, concepts likewise transcend, and are not restricted by, the body.
- In order for transcendental reason to apply to the world, independently of any merely human limitations, the concepts used in reasoning must be capable of fitting what is objectively in the world. Thus, concepts must be literal and reason, being transcendental, cannot make use of mechanisms of the human imagination such as metaphor.
- Perception (especially vision) is veridical; what one perceives (especially what one sees) is, except for relatively rare illusions, really there in the world.
- Conceptual systems are self-consistent and monolithic. Hence, each person has an internally consistent, monolithic view of the world.
- People have free will. That freedom is radical—completely unconstrained.
- The essence of a person is reason, free will, and a natural tendency to maximize pleasure (or gains) and minimize pain (or losses). Thus, a person is a radically free, rational, maximizer of self-interest.

The separation of mind and body is at the heart of this conception of the person. Descartes claimed that the body and mind were made of different kinds of substance—the body from physical substance (spatially extended and subject to physical laws), and the mind from mental substance (not spatially extended and not subject to physical laws). The body was subject to physical forces, but the mind was not, and was hence radically free. Similarly, reason transcends everything physical. In short, the essence of the traditional Western person is not physical but mental.

This conception of the person is, of course, behind Western religion. In the Judaeo-Christian tradition, the locus of consciousness is identified with the soul. Since it is separate from the body, and not subject to physical constraints, it is seen as being able to live on after the death of the body. This view of the person also lies behind the traditional European distinction between the natural sciences and the humanities: What is subject to physical law can be studied scientifically— the physical world, including biology. But anything having to do with the human mind is seen as not being capable of being studied scientifically, since it is radically free and not subject to any laws at all. For this reason, cognitive science has not been taken seriously within traditional humanistic fields of study.

The traditional Western view of the person is at odds with the fundamental results from neuorscience and cognitive science that I have already cited. The neurocognitive self has neither a separation of mind and body, nor a single locus of consciousness, nor transcendental reason, nor a monolithic consistent worldview, nor radical freedom, nor interest maximization, nor an objectivist conception of reality, nor a literalist conception of truth. In short, the conception of the person that emerges from neuroscience and from the cognitive sciences is radically different from the conception that we have inherited from the Western cultural tradition.

Neuroscience and The Self

Let us begin with some very basic results from neuroscience.

- The brain is highly structured from birth; there are hundreds of portions of the brain that either coordinate or perform specialized functions.
- There is also a fair amount of plasticity in the brain, within the boundaries of its basic structure.
- During the first years of life, a significant proportion of the neurons and neuronal connections that a child is born with die off. Which cells and connections remain depends on which ones are used. Thus, experience—interaction with the world—shapes our brains in important ways, within the boundaries of innate brain structure.
- Learning involves a change in synaptic weights, the addition of connections, and the loss of connections not used. When you learn something, your brain physically changes.
- Neuronal systems necessarily form categories. They are not classical categories defined by necessary and sufficient conditions. As neural beings, it is impossible for us not to categorize.
- There are concepts that are neurally grounded; at the very least, the color concepts are. It has been determined that the neurophysiology of color vision determines the fundamental focal colors and the graded structure of color categories.
- There is no single physical locus of consciousness in the brain. Thought and perception are distributed among many areas of the brain.
- If the convergence zone hypothesis is correct, then there is a biologically imposed structural constraint on concepts. We would expect complex concepts to integrate diverse lower-level concepts that form gestalts, and we would expect them to combine by simultaneous activation. In short, the brain places constraints on the possibility of conceptual structure. The CZH would also lead us to expect that concepts would be grounded in lower-level perceptual–motor structure.
- At least in the case of color, perception is not veridical—that is, it does not mirror the external world; it is a product of whatever the world is like plus body-and-brain mechanisms that create and structure the categories in which we perceive.
- At least in the case of color, concepts are not arbitrary. They have a physical grounding, and are not merely products of historical accident.

- If the CZH is correct, then concepts in general would be neurally grounded, nonveridical, and nonarbitrary.

These are some of the constraints that neuroscience places on what a person is. Let us now add constraints from cognitive science of the sort discussed at the beginning of this chapter:

- Most thought is unconscious, automatic, and effortless.
- Basic-level categories and image-schemas have a grounding in the body.
- Abstract concepts are metaphorical projections of more concrete concepts, and conceptual metaphors have a grounding in bodily and cultural experience.
- Knowledge is organized in holistic structures called *frames* or *schemas* or *idealized cognitive models*.
- Conceptual systems are not internally consistent. For example, a single concept is often characterized by a multiplicity of different and mutually inconsistent conceptual metaphors.
- Categories have complex structures, often radial structures, and make use of many kinds of prototypes.
- Many aspects of conceptual structure are universal; many other aspects are not.
- If the neural representation hypothesis is correct, then concepts are not symbolic in nature but are represented neurally in a distributed fashion such that highly articulated neural structure will characterize highly articulated conceptual structure.

Put together, all this entails a very different concept of a person:

The Neurocognitive Person

- The mind and body are not separate. Concepts are embodied. They are grounded in perceptual and motor experience and represented neurally. They do not exist without a body and brain.
- Reason is not transcendental; it is bodily in nature.
- Most reason is neither conscious nor deliberate.
- Perception is not a passive mirror of nature; much of what we perceive is constructed by brain mechanisms.
- Much of our conceptualization of the world is metaphorical, much of our knowledge is formulated using metaphorical concepts, and most reasoning involves metaphorical concepts. Therefore, our conception of reality is not strictly literal. We may, however, believe our metaphors, especially when they allow us to function well.
- Since our conceptual systems are neither self-consistent nor monolithic, people do not have consistent monolithic worldviews.
- We require our conceptual systems to represent knowledge, choose our purposes, and make decisions. But conceptual systems are limited by the possi-

bilities of bodily grounding, of metaphorical extensions, and of the formation of cognitive models—all of which are limited by the nature of our brains
as well as by whatever accidents of history have shaped our conceptual
systems.

- Therefore, we are not radically free. Instead, we have only a situated freedom, a freedom to make decisions within certain boundaries given by what
  we can conceptualize.
- Since most of our thought is unconscious and uncontrolled, we mostly do
  not consciously choose which aspects of our conceptual systems to use in
  making most decisions.

Most of the time we think and unconsciously make choices using normal conceptual apparatus such as prototypes and frames. And most of the time, there is no
possibility of doing otherwise. Kahneman and Tversky have shown, in a wide
variety of experiments, that prototype- and frame-based thought in many situations
goes against one's self-interest (as defined by theories of self-interest based on
probability theory and game theory). Therefore, the very nature of our conceptual
systems rules out the possibility that we could be maximizers of self-interest. That
does not mean that many of us might not try, consciously, to maximize self-
interest. It does mean that we could not possibly succeed a significant proportion
of the time. Moreover, since our conceptual systems are not consistent and monolithic, it is often the case that there will be no consistent notion of what our self-
interest is so that we can maximize it.

Here we have the neurocognitive person, with neither a separation of mind
and body, nor a single locus of consciousness, nor veridical perception, nor transcendental reason, nor a consistent monolithic worldview, nor radical freedom,
nor interest maximization, nor an objectivist conception of reality, nor a literalist
conception of truth.

At present, this is simply a technical, scientific view of what a person is,
based on what I believe is the best of what contemporary neuroscience and cognitive science have to offer. As those sciences progress, more details will come in,
and perhaps there will be some changes. But I believe that, on the whole, the
neurocognitive person will stand the test of time, scientifically.

There is however a serious question about whether such a scientific conception
of a person can possibly work its way into popular consciousness. There are reasons to be pessimistic:

- This view of what a person is directly contradicts the received cultural view
  on virtually every point. It is a sophisticated scientific view. Most people
  don't get educated in such sophisticated scientific views. Moreover, those
  who do tend not to learn any such views until well after the age of eight
  to ten, by which time the dominant cultural view has been learned mostly
  unconsciously and used during the years in which much of conceptual structure has been shaped into the brain. By that time, the traditional view is so
  entrenched and automatic that it cannot be completely unlearned.
- Computer technology reinforces the most central part of the traditional view.
  The computer metaphor for mind comes along with computer technology,

Language and Categorization

and that m
into it.

- There are
  the pers
  and, he
  the dis

Luckily
possible f
the tradit
coexist

What

A c
mak
vie
ha

- It is not a person that denies spirituality, a
  term. Not only is it consistent with spirit
  meditative traditions, but also its essent
  well with certain of what are sometim
- It is a humanistic person, in that it
  ence and the aspects of conceptua
- It is an un-self-righteous perso
  hold on objective truth, that
  standing via metaphor, an
  rise to multiple, inconsis
  systems.
- It is a respectful pers
  embodied and i
  nizes the con
  and, hence,
  culture an
- It is a
  Each
  sys

is nonpn
- Via transcendenta
  is seen as irrational and pr
  is human.
- Because of transcendental reason, it is ahistor
  stand the importance of worldview difference and worlu
- It oversimplifies people, seeing them as mere bundles of attribute.
- Since it sees itself as having the right concepts for accurately comprehending
  the world, it sees itself as capable of understanding any issue using its concepts and of grasping absolute truth.
- Since it assumes that all reason is conscious, it ignores most of the unconscious reasoning that is done.
- It justifies self-seeking on the grounds that it is an essential human attribute.
- In assuming radical freedom, it fails to focus on those aspects of culture and
  of conceptual systems that limit freedom.

In these critiques, we can see why our concept of what a person is matters so
much: It tells us how we should live our lives and how society should be organized. A new concept of a person requires a new way of looking at life and at
society. The neurocognitive person contrasts radically with the traditional Western person:

- It is an integrated person, in that it does not have a mind–body split.
- It is a person that values the body, since it is inseparable from the body.
- It is a person that requires a philosophy of living life to the fullest while the
  body exists since the person is identified with the body.

t least in certain senses of the
ual experience that comes out of
al mind–body connection fits very
es called the Wisdom traditions.
recognizes universals of human experi-
systems based on them.
, in that it recognizes that it cannot have a
what one takes to be truth depends on under-
that multiplicities of metaphors naturally give
ent worldviews.
n—respectful of the diversity of human conceptual

rson, in that it recognizes that one's personal history is
nportantly shapes one's conceptual system. It also recog-
bution of accidents of history in shaping conceptual systems
in shaping the worldview that one inherits as a member of one's
generation.
complex person—it cannot be pigeonholed by a list of attributes.
person, instead, has multiplicies—a complex, multifaceted conceptual
em that tolerates multiple worldviews and aspects of the self.
is an open-ended person, in that it recognizes that there is sufficient plasticity of brain/mind to permit significant change at all stages of life.

- It is a creative person, in that it recognizes the important role of imaginative
  mechanisms (such as metaphor and cognitive models) in creating under-
  standings of the world and of one's place in it.
- It is an ecological person, in that it is not separable from its environment
  and cannot be defined apart from its environment.
- It is a person with a meaningful life, with meaning grounded in the body
  and in the fullness of experience.

I very much like the neurocognitive person. I think it is not only the product
of what I take to be the best of contemporary neuroscience and cognitive science,
but I think it is also a considerable improvement on the traditional view. If our
society were adopt such a concept of the person, a great many things would
change.

Whether the new neurocognitive concept of the person becomes part of mainstream culture, however, will depend on just how much of conceptual system
research in cognitive science comes to be known, understood, and assimilated by
the general public during the twenty-first century.

References

Barzelay, Michael. (1992). *Breaking through bureaucracy*. Berkeley: University of Califor-
    nia Press.
Edelman, Gerald. (1992). *Bright air, brilliant fire*. New York: Basic Books.

Johnson, Mark. (1987). *The body in the mind*. Chicago: University of Chicago Press.

Johnson, Mark. (1993). *Moral imagination: The implications of cognitive science for ethics*. Chicago: University of Chicago Press.

Lakoff, George. (1987). *Women, fire and dangerous things*. Chicago: University of Chicago Press.

Morgan, Gareth. (1986). *Images of organization*. Beverly Hills, CA: Sage.

Osborne, David, and Ted Gaebler. (1993). *Reinventing government*. New York: Plume Books.

Regier, Terry. (1991). *The acquisiton of lexical semantics for spatial terms: A connectionist model of perceptual categoarization*. Ph.D. dissertation, Universiy of California, Berkeley. Reprinted as Technical Report TR-9j2-062, International Computer Science Institute, 1947 Center Street, Suite 600, Berkeley, CA 94704-1105.

Taub, Sarah. (1990). Moral accounting. Linguistics Department of University of California, Berkeley. Unpublished ms.

Winter, Steven. (1989). *Transcendental nonsense, metaphoric reasoning and the cognitive stakes for law*. University of Pennsylvania Law Review, *137* (4), 1105–1237.

V

APPLIED AND SOCIAL COGNITION

This engaging part includes chapters by Donald Norman, Earl Hunt, Robert Sommer, and John Pittenger who address some issues dealing with the application of cognition to the "real-world" of the future. The first chapter by Norman addresses the problems of applying cognitive knowledge to actual human performance. Hunt reminds us that the influences outside of psychology are likely to have considerable impact on people and societies. Sommer's chapter is a futuristic look at the consequence of our present science, especially as it applies to education. And the final chapter in this part, by Pittenger, is truly a "hands-on" application of our scientific and cognitive knowledge to a world in which we may create.

16

The Future of the Mind Lies in Technology

DONALD A. NORMAN

Physical technologies make us warmer, faster, and more powerful. But there is a more important technology—a cognitive technology—that makes us smarter. Elsewhere, I have called this technology "cognitive artifacts" (Norman, 1991, 1993). Through our technologies we have changed the normal forces that affect natural evolution. No longer do the weak, the frail, and the injured die. Now it is those with technology who thrive, those without who do not: Whether desirable or not, it is the state to which we have now evolved.

The future of the human mind lies in the steady, increasing evolution of technology that will make fundamental changes in human abilities. New prosthetic devices will enable the ill and the injured to thrive. New cognitive technologies will make the combination of person + machine even smarter, but make the person even more attached and dependent on technology. Today we strap watches to our bodies, eyeglasses and hearing aids to our heads. We fasten clothing around us. In the future, the list of items will grow to include communication devices, computational devices, and even sensory aids. Some will not be strapped to the body; some may be permanently implanted within it.

Binoculars, telescopes, and eyeglasses enhance vision. Video cameras will replace binoculars, implanted optics and electronics may, in turn, someday enhance vision. Voice-operated, random-access notepads are almost with us today, and perhaps thought-activated ones are in our future. Soon we shall be able to produce three-dimensional, dynamic maps of brain activity, accurate to fractions of seconds and millimeters of spatial location: who knows what applications will follow?

The future of human evolution lies outside of the human; it lies in technology. Today, we are at the start of the cognitive revolution in technological artifacts that increase the power of the mind. Although the mind itself can no longer grow because it is limited by its biological constraints, especially that of physical size, the *power* of the mind can expand through the aid of technology. I define a *cognitive artifact* to be an artificial device designed to maintain, display, or operate upon information in order to serve a representational function (Norman, 1991). Today's cognitive artifacts don't actually change the properties of the mind; the mind remains unchanged. The combination of mind + artifact, however, is indeed more powerful than the unaided mind. The artifact changes the task the human must perform, simplifying it, and when appropriately designed, it transforms the arbitrary, abstract tasks of modern business and science into the perceptually based tasks most suited for humans. We see the power of these systems in graphic displays, in scientific visualization, and even in computer rendering of art and transformed images in movies. As a result, the system composed of mind + artifact can have dramatically enhanced capability: enhanced perception, memory, problem-solving capability, language understanding, and computational ability. Today's artifacts can provide rich, sophisticated sensorimotor interaction that allows action at a distance in space and time. Artifacts allow us to perceive the otherwise unperceivable—weather fronts, airflow over aerodynamic surfaces, the insides of devices from engines to brains—and to explore imaginary environments, from buildings and structures still in the planning stages to arbitrary fantasies.

The future artifacts of mind will transform not only the powers of mind (as the mind + artifact package does today), but will transform the mind itself. Future technologies may actually connect directly to brain structures, thus modifying its capabilities. When this happens, no longer will it be true that artifacts change only the task. Instead, artifacts will indeed have changed the mind and the person.

We humans evolved to operate in a physical social world. We are particularly good at perceptually based tasks, and our pattern-recognition abilities are unsurpassed in the animal and mechanical kingdoms. We are social creatures, and by sharing tasks among others, the joint efforts can greatly surpass the capabilities of one individual. Many of our creations today—from large-scale mechanical constructions to subtler information-based computer tools—could not be constructed by a single individual. Indeed, no single individual is even capable of understanding some of the largest computer programs or mechanical devices. One means of enhancing the power of the individual mind is through *distributed cognition,* spreading the knowledge and capabilities across people, tasks, and representing structures—the artifacts.

The use of external representational devices is perhaps the first, most important aspect of cognitive artifacts. It is our ability to form abstracts of the world that has given us science and logic, tools that enhance our ability to go beyond what we can see and experience, to perform critical analyses of those experiences and thoughts, and to profit thereby. But the human brain is limited, primarily through limitations in the capacity of working memory. External representations allow us to break free of these limits.

Language, both spoken and written, is a powerful artifact that dramatically enhances human capabilities. As a result of the development of a written language, we have been able to develop a cumulative knowledge, one that extends across generations. This ability to build upon past advances allows us to develop knowledge that extends beyond the capability of a single person or even group of people. The price we pay for this cumulative knowledge is in the cost of education. Once a few years of schooling or apprenticeship would suffice. Today, it takes twenty or even thirty years of formal schooling to learn the major aspects of a culture and the tools of a specialty. If things go on as they are, in several hundred years, it might take fifty years of schooling to prepare an individual for society. Can we develop more efficient means of education and better methods for profiting from the lessons and experiences of the past?

Predicting the Future[1]

Predicting the future is a popular industry. Prophets are not in short supply. "Quite the contrary," Herbert Simon once pointed out, "almost everything that has happened, and its opposite, has been prophesied. The problem has always been to pick and choose among the embarrassing riches of alternative projected futures; and in this, human societies have not demonstrated any large foresight."[2]

It is easy to devise numerous possible scenarios of future developments, each one, on the face of it, equally likely. The difficult task is to know which will actually take place. In hindsight it usually seems obvious. When we look back in time, each event seems clearly and logically to follow from the previous events. Before the event occurs, however, the number of possibilities seems endless. There are no methods for successful prediction, especially in areas involving complex social and technological changes, where many of the determining factors are not known and, in any event, are certainly not under any single group's control.

The easy predictions are about technical developments, the hard ones are about the impacts on society and on the individual. Here are some easy predictions about technologies, predictions widely shared by people in the relevant technological industries:

- An increase in the availability of "digital information," information encoded electronically in a form that is readily stored, transmitted, and displayed. Today, there are a variety of media that deal with digital information, but each in a form incompatible with and separate from that used by the others. This will change: The technologies of computers, telephones, television, electronic mail, and facsimile will all merge into one system. Digital information will be stored in vast international databases and local archives, available for purchase on large capacity-storage devices or direct connection through telephone, cable television, or even satellite links. Some of this will be personal information of a sort never before collected together in such accessible form. Business, government, thieves and confidence operators, friends and lovers, and the just plain nosy will be able to learn facts about all of us that many of us would prefer to keep private.
- Widespread availability of high-capacity communication links reaching into every home, and even to every person via various forms of wired, optical, and wireless transmission, including direct satellite transmission, cable and fiber optic lines to everywhere, and advances in compression technology that

dramatically reduce the amount of information required to reproduce text, sound, and pictures.

- Continually more powerful computational devices, smaller and less expensive than ever before. Information readers, hand-held devices that substitute for books, with (eventually) the same convenience, plus better search and annotation capabilities.
- The ability to experience three-dimensional sight and sound coupled to a person's own body position and movements. To be used for conferencing, for exploring new places, whether real or imagined. For educators, designers, explorers, or just for entertainment.

The Power to Fantasize

Given that our technologies will continually advance, what difference will that make? It is one thing to imagine electronic access to books at home or with portable players at the beach, but these seem like a natural progression from existing libraries and books. Many of the basic predictions have that air about them—obvious modifications of what already exists. But what about the radical new opportunities created by the new technologies? Let's look at some exercises in fantasy.

Want to compose some music? Let the technology guide your composition and performance. The same with painting and art. Want to experience ancient Greece or China? Experience those times in three-dimensional color, three-dimensional sound. This set of predictions is intended to be stimulating, but still well within the realm of possibility. All could be done within the next twenty years, if not in the home, certainly within the laboratories. No predictions of extrasensory phenomena, no predictions of brain-taps and mind reading. No direct mind-to-mind communication. Only things that are possible.

Not all these predictions are desirable outcomes. "Blasphemous," one reader responded upon reading the statement that "the technology guides your composition and performance." But blasphemous or not, the prediction still stands. In fact, that particular prediction is very likely to come about sooner rather than later. Nonetheless, the fact that technology can do things does not mean it should. What happens to art and music when every person can achieve flawless production? Not to worry, say some, we will still have the unique human ability to create, to have an artistic sensibility: the performance may be flawless, but the essential human part of deciding what to do, how to arrange it, will still be there. Maybe. I would like to believe that. But we already have at least one computer program that generates art of quality high enough to be exhibited in major museums around the world (McCorduck, 1991).

Start off with the technologies that allow one to visualize being in some make-believe, artificial place. Use a visual display that presents a high-quality image to each eye in order to produce three-dimensional vision, use an auditory display that creates realistic, three-dimensional sound. Perhaps even put on gloves or body suits that both sense the body's movements and location and also provide complete sensory feedback. If some of the newer technological experiments work, then it will not even be necessary to wear special clothes or devices (although you will be restricted to be within a specified volume of space). These are the technologies being explored in laboratories around the world: "virtual reality" or "virtual presence" they are called. It is already possible to create computer-generated, three-dimensional images of planned new buildings, the goal being to allow architects and clients to "walk" through proposed buildings and experience them from within and without. These technologies allow someone to try using a facility before it is constructed, while it is still easy to make changes. Related technologies can allow chemists to study chemical reactions by manipulating images of molecules, not only seeing how they fit but feeling the force fields through tactile feedback to the manipulators that they use to move the molecules. Today this can be done only in crude ways, but technologists always have hopes of great advances. Simulated experiences have the potential to become powerful instruments of cognition. They support both experiential and reflective processes. Experiential because one can simply sit back and experience the sights, sounds, and motion. Reflective because simulators make possible the study of actions that would be too expensive to try in real life.

If we now simulate the experiences of other places, whether real or imaginary, what happens when we can simulate people, or at least their appearances? It is already possible to generate computer-controlled images of places and moving objects that are almost indistinguishable from real images. It isn't yet possible to simulate animate objects with such fidelity, but that day will arrive. Suppose that day is now, and, furthermore, suppose that they allow us to simulate our own appearance, then what?

Faking one's abilities is a time-honored procedure among thieves and scoundrels. A less offensive version may be to present a false personality, which is common even among everyday folk: Witness the use of professional climbing and cycling gear among nonclimbers and bikers, or fancy running shoes and apparel among the sedentary, or baseball caps on nonathletes. Why, you can even purchase fake automobile telephone antennas, so that your car looks as if it has a phone even if you can't afford one.

Imagine expanding these tendencies to new heights. Authors and actors have long known that the personas they project through their works can differ significantly from their true personalities. Suppose some people use this phenomenon to their advantage. Highly talented letter writers can project any image they wish, as long as there is no danger that they will ever meet their correspondent. A "well-regarded female correspondent" in an electronic discussion group actually turned out to be a male psychiatrist, creating considerable uproar among the other group members when the deception was discovered. In 1984, Vernor Vinge wrote *True Names,* a science fiction story of a world in which people invented artificial personas, artificial existences with which to interact, while vigorously guarding their identities and true names (Vinge, 1984). Off you went through cyberspace, exploring the pathways and information, encountering others along the way. Except the others that you met were also artificial personas. That fierce, crude sadist might in real life be a timid, prim and proper old lady. The names were also false, and it was not considered proper to learn the true identities or true names of the people that you encountered. How much longer before that fantasy becomes reality?

Why restrict our artificial persons to other people? Why not use them for our own pleasure as well? Mirrors today still rely on the ancient method of reflecting technologies: metal deposited on the back side of glass. Mirrors are invaluable, but they have limitations. You have to stand "just so" in order to see yourself, and because a mirror image appears to be reversed left-to-right, we can never see ourselves as others see us. Moreover, with a mirror, we can't easily see ourselves from the side, or from behind, or above. And it is quite impossible to see oneself in a single mirror with the eyes not looking straight into the mirror.

But consider the video mirror, a mirror that is really a video presentation from a video camera. Now the image can be taken from any angle, in any size. It could be a mirror-reversed image, or a true image (where the right-hand side is on the right side of the image's body). Real mirrors show you as you are now, at the instant of viewing. Video mirrors do not have this restriction: Arrange yourself and when the image looks right, freeze it—or capture a ten-second fragment—and then contemplate the mirrored re-presentation at leisure. Now that's true reflective thought (pun intended), even if for a less worthy motive than the enhancement of the world's knowledge.

Want to decide between two sets of clothing? Why not use the video mirror to save two different images, one of you wearing each set of clothing. Then compare the two pictures, perhaps side by side. The video mirror would allow you to do operations that are otherwise quite impossible. Note that this is true reflection: the video mirror allows comparison of representations. Without the aid of the video comparing mirror, the comparison had to be done in imagination, or by other people.

Now imagine a similar activity with hair style or clothing: Want to try a new hair style? Project it onto your facial image. A clothing store could let you test new clothes without trying them on: have the intelligent video mirror arrange the clothes over the body. Do you like the clothes but not the color? That is a simple twist of a knob away. While we are at it, why not enhance the image? Let the video mirror make you appear slightly thinner than reality, or let it eliminate that unsightly stomach bulge, get rid of the gray hair. The image could be a graceful enhancement of your true self, modified in whatever way was desired.

In fact, the image could be of anything. A man could turn into a woman, or a child, or a dragon, or a colorful pattern of light. Couple the artificially enhanced image with an artificially enhanced voice, and for that matter, perhaps even artificially generated words. Where is reality?

It is frequently said that people will fear video telephones because they may not always want others to see them. After all, suppose you are in the bathtub when the videophone rings, or, umm, sitting on the toilet, or making love, or picking your nose, or. . . . I have always thought this overdone, for after all, one need not be visible to the camera, or for that matter, one can simply have a photograph in front of the camera. But when my flights of fancy about the video mirror come to pass (not *if*, you may note, *when*—they will all happen, the only question is how soon, and how expensive), then the image need have only the slightest connection with reality. In fact, you could project the image of yourself in the bathtub, whereas in reality you were hard at work in your home office. The real problem is not that others might see us as we really look at the moment, but rather that others might never be able to discover us as we really are.

Are you dismayed by the possibility of such mass deception? Perhaps these artificial systems actually let people project their true inner selves instead of being restricted to surface features. Do you think of yourself as smooth and accomplished, with a sexy, rhythmic voice but, alas, your "true" voice never comes out that way? With the appropriate artificial persona, it can be so. So what if the video mirror makes a person appear taller and slimmer, more muscular and more athletic, and ten years older (or younger). Maybe these enhanced images are really the "true" person. After all, if that is how people think of themselves, perhaps that is how they really are, and not the false image that their tinny, accented, stuttering voice conveys. Who is to say which is truer? The stuttering of reality or the perfection of one's wishes and dreams?

Artificial personas present a vast range of possibilities. The Japanese have invented a whole culture of machines that enhance the voice. They use it for singing, but it could be applied to a wide variety of situations. Sing into the Karaoke system and your voice is enriched, filled out, and accompanied by a professional orchestra. Today's systems are limited. They use prerecorded music and allow the performer to synchronize their singing with the recording. But modern technologies will allow artificial intelligences to come to play. The future Karaoke equivalents will generate music on the spot that will harmonize with the performer: The performance will follow the singer, not the singer the performance. In fact, the system will use the performer's voice only to ensure that the artificially produced sound matches the content, rhythm, and duration of the original—but the sound of the singer's voice could be manipulated to appear any way the singer prefers. To make the singing always be on pitch, in tune, is the easy part. But the voice could also be sexy or not, weak or strong, questioning or authoritative, dominating or submissive, teasing or honest—whatever image the person wishes to project.

We don't need to wait for cyberspace to encounter the story described by *True Names;* we can start with the telephone. Already people experiment with the voice message that greets the caller on telephone-answering machines. This is so important for some that they purchase professionally made tapes to use for their "greetings." Why not have the message come in whatever form wished for that day? Why not have a speech transformer that changes the words into whatever tone one wishes: into a gruff, nasty curmudgeon, or into a young teenager? Perhaps today the voice would be of a young woman, tomorrow an old man. Imagine the same when videophones become commonplace: How will you know that the image and voice you see and hear are really the image and voice of the person you are speaking to?

Want to play a musical instrument? Fine, just choose your instrument. Blow into the clarinet, play the keyboard, or strum the guitar, bow the violin. Whatever instrument you play, the sound will come from the computer, your sound, just as you wished it to be. Do you really play off key? Do you have trouble with those fast passages, fingers and lips getting all tied up? Don't worry, the computer will realize what you are trying to do and make the sounds come out just as you intended, maybe even better.

Want some accompaniment? Want to be a conductor of a virtual orchestra or band? Why not? The artificial sound generator can take on any instrumental sound imaginable. Already we have electronic instruments that play accompaniments automatically. The new ones will do whatever part one wants: the melody line, the solo instruments, the accompaniments, the voices—whatever parts and in whatever fashion one wants.

If you hate writing, well, we have something for you as well. We can already buy sample letters: Want to send a love letter, or a threatening business letter? Simply buy one from your favorite word-processing kit. In the future, the system can generate the text from key phrases given to it. Today we can already do that with greeting cards, tomorrow with personal letters.

What will become of real singers, or real musicians? Or authors? Worse, what if the recipient of your letter doesn't like to read, and so gives it to a reading machine instead? The letters get written by machine, read by machine: no need for a human intermediary. Maybe that is how we get out of all this mess. While our machines are all busy reading and writing to one another, playing music, and calling and answering one another's videophones, the real people could go off to the side and enjoy life. Let the machines do the dull tasks of the world, or at least pretend to do them: Let the people then take advantage of the freedom to do some human tasks.

Science Fiction and the Technologies for Interacting with Machines

Perhaps the best way to think about the future is to invent a detailed, comprehensive scenario: in other words, to write a story. Stories have the virtue that they force the writer to think through the consequences: They force a complete examination and detailed analysis. It's what we in the design business call "prototyping": trying to piece together every little detail so that you really and truly understand just how the technology or society will work. Taken in this light, science fiction is a valuable exercise. Scientific even.

The problem is, contemporary science fiction, especially the genre called cyberpunk, has gone wild. The hero plugs the computer directly into the brain. Sure. Let's go back and look at the technology. How plausible are the guesses? The problem with postulating the ability to plug a computer directly into the brain is that it is all done by magic, not by any specification of how it is all done. Could we really connect a machine to the nerve fibers of the brain? Is it necessary?

There are hints of other ways. One of the most original notions is in some sense the simplest. Vernor Vinge, in *True Names,* proposes that half the interface is provided by imagination:

He powered up his processors, settled back in his favorite chair, and carefully attached the Portal's five sucker electrodes to his scalp. For long minutes nothing happened: a certain amount of self-denial—or at least self-hypnosis—was necessary to make the ascent. Some experts recommended drugs or sensory isolation to heighten the user's sensitivity to the faint, ambiguous signals that could be read from the Portal. (Vinge, 1984, p. 14)

Just as the words of the book provide a rich, compelling fantasy of the experience you are reading about—with a fairly low bandwidth interaction with the text, I must emphasize—so too could the computer interface provide a rich and compelling fantasy, with equally low bandwidth:

You might think that to convey the full sense imagery of the swamp, some immense bandwidth would be necessary. In fact, that was not so. . . . A typical Portal link was around fifty thousand baud, far narrower than even a flat video channel. Mr. Slippery could feel the damp seeping through his leather boots, could feel the sweat starting on his skin even in the cold air, but this was the response of Mr. Slippery's imagination and subconscious to the cues that were actually being presented through the Portal's electrodes. . . . Even a poor writer—if he has a sympathetic reader and engaging plot—can evoke complete internal imagery with a few dozen words of description. The difference now is that the imagery has interactive significance, just as sensations in the real world do. (pp. 16–17)

I used to scoff at the notions of providing a plug from machine to brain. However, I have had second thoughts: There may be something to it after all. Consider the nature of human language. On the one hand, it is a rich, complex, and very sophisticated data communication medium. On the other hand, it is made possible by extremely arbitrary actions of the body: We puff air in and out of the vocal chords, which tense and relax appropriately, opening and closing various nasal and mouth passages, and manipulating the tongue, lips, and jaw. To speak, we had to learn rather arbitrary, but complex muscle controls. The same can be said for sign language: just as effective and rich as spoken speech, and just as arbitrary a set of muscle motions.

If you examine human skills, you see that we are capable of learning to make and to encode a wide variety of arbitrary and complex muscle actions and sensory events. It may take years of practice, but we can learn to do amazing things. Look at typing, another very arbitrary skill. It takes months to learn to touch-type, years of practice to get to speeds on the order of magnitude of 100 words per minute: that's a respectable speed. Consider playing a musical instrument: A pianist playing a Chopin nocturne may be required to play 25 notes each second. In 20 minutes, a pianist may play some 10,000 notes, each synchronized, each in the correct timing, each exactly the correct one of the 88 notes on the piano. Reading is equally arbitrary: Those arbitrary printed shapes on the page represent spoken words. Reading is not an easy skill to master; it takes years of practice. But after mastering the skill, we can read hundreds of words a minute, in fact, we can read faster than we can listen.

Maybe we could learn yet another arbitrary means of communicating ideas, this time with a computer or directly to the brains of other people. Suppose we tapped a fast, high-bandwidth nerve channel. The brain is pretty hard to get into, encapsulated as it is by the skull, but we might be able to connect an electrical cable to the auditory nerve. Or maybe we could tap into the nerves that go to and from a hand, or maybe into the spinal chord. Suppose we hooked up a high-bandwidth channel that sent and received neural impulses to and from this tap? At first, they would simply lead to peculiar sensations and jerky, uncontrolled movements of the body: Weird tingles and spasms with no meaning, no coherence. But I suspect that if we entered into daily training exercises, a few hours a day for, oh, ten years, who is to say that we couldn't train ourselves to communicate?

It's not clear to me that this task would be any harder than other things we do train ourselves to do.

Note several things about this suggestion, however:

1. It in no way recreates the sensory experience that now exists—it provides a completely different kind of experience.
2. It will require extensive training—years or even decades, but then again, it takes two years to learn a foreign language well enough to communicate, a decade to be comfortable. These times are not out of line.
3. It might have to start with children, while the brain is still plastic. So only children who were wired up in the first few years (months?) of life would learn this mode of communication. Certainly, it would have to be done before the brain gels, at puberty. Adults would have trouble. They could perhaps pick up a smattering of the interaction, but always with the equivalent of an accent.

Multiple Minds

So far most of this discussion has focused on technology and the individual, but perhaps the greatest gains are to be expected in the development of tools for social cooperation. When groups gather to work together, their interactions are both aided and constrained by technology. Blackboards allow the work of one to be visible to all. Several people can work at one board at the same time, but if they try to work on the same portion, their hands and bodies interfere with each other. Several new experiments have allowed joint work on the same surface through the use of televised images of the individuals. Suppose everyone has their own individual work surface, whether a blackboard, a pad of paper, or a computer screen. Each can work unhindered by others because only they have physical access. But suppose we electronically superimpose everyone's efforts? Everyone sees everyone else's work superimposed over their own.

This is the promise of new technologies for cognitive artifacts: new forms of representational devices that make possible social interactions that were not even thought of before the advent of the technology. These technologies promise enhanced interaction, whether the people are grouped together in the same room or separated by thousands of miles.

But beware of the pitfalls. It is extremely difficult to devise cognitive aids that work smoothly within a group without destroying some of the power of the group. Technology tends to be unwielding, demanding, coercing. Social groups require flexibility, cooperation, and resilience, allowing diverse personalities, interests, and work styles to interact. When technology supports an individual, the individual can still control the situation and the two, person and technology, can find some graceful interaction. When people work together, social tensions can easily arise, avoided only through the goodwill and cooperative attitude of the people. But add some inflexible technology to the mix and difficulties can quickly arise.

Tools that assist joint work have special requirements above those faced by tools for the individual. They must accommodate group structure and interests, a much more complex task than for individuals. No single technology or method will provide the answer. Different groups will prefer different methods depending on the individuals who comprise them, their experience, their national culture, and the philosophy of the organization in which they are working. The technological support of group work and social interaction serves as a prototype for all our hopes and fears for future technology. The new technologies can lead to distributed social groups, cooperating at a distance even better than can be done when physically together. It can also lead to a technological hell, with rigid restrictions, continual monitoring, and a lack of privacy and identity. Which is it to be? The affordances built into the technologies may determine the answer.

Notes

1. The following section is taken from Chapter 8, "Predicting the future," in *Things that make us smart* (Norman, 1993).

2. *"Almost everything that has happened, and its opposite has been prophesied."* The quotation from Herbert Simon was originally published in 1977, but I took it from the reprinting of his article in the collection of readings edited by Pylyshyn and Bannon (1989, p. 445).

References

McCorduck, P. (1991). *Aaron's code: Meta-art, artificial intelligence, and the work of Harold Cohen*. New York: W. H. Freeman.

Norman, D. A. (1991). Cognitive artifacts. In J. M. Carroll (Ed.), *Designing interaction: Psychology at the human–computer interface*. (pp. 17–38). New York: Cambridge University Press.

Norman, D. A. (1993). *Things that make us smart*. Reading, Mass.: Addison-Wesley.

Pylyshyn, Z. W., & Bannon, L. J. (Ed.). (1989). *Perspectives on the computer revolution*. Norwood, N.J.: Ablex Publishing Corporation.

Vinge, V. (1984). *True names*. New York: Bluejay Books (distributed by St. Martin's Press).

17

Pulls and Pushes on Cognitive Psychology: The View Toward 2001

EARL HUNT

The Problem of Prediction

The purpose of this chapter is to predict the future of a science. Of course, the most likely thing to happen in any science in the next twenty years is something unexpected. Nevertheless, I will try.

It is possible to make reasonable predictions about scientific progress if the focus of the prediction is fairly narrow—for example, a prediction about the hot topics in episodic memory, visual attention, or analogical reasoning. A competent reviewer can usually extrapolate progress a few years ahead, by using a reasonable amount of tunnel vision. An implicit assumption in such predictions is that progress in a field is continuous; we build on what has gone on before. Since, of course, we do, the predictions usually work. Intellectual revolutions will not be predicted this way, but revolutions are not that common.

Another way to make a prediction that is not entirely wrong is to be very wide ranging. If there are enough subpredictions, one of them is bound to be right. This is what I shall do.

Instead of focusing on developments within psychology that affect our ideas, I am going to focus on developments outside psychology that influence our opportunities. Figure 17.1 illustrates my argument. There are two types of influence that psychology (or any other science) will have to deal with. One is a push; developments in one field permit progress in another. A spectacular example is the way in which developments in the physics of superconductivity have influenced medical imaging, by making it possible to sense fantastically small electrical fields generated by neural events.

Outside influences can also exert a pull. They selectively encourage those bits of potential scientific progress that the society as a whole wants to develop. Whatever history's ultimate verdict on the Cold War is, it is certainly true that a perceived need for a superb military machine led to major advances in many of the

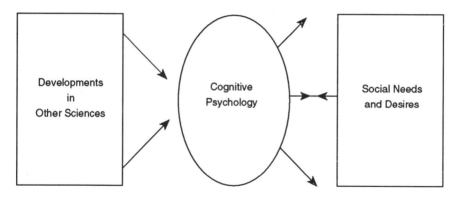

Figure 17.1. Pulls and pushes on cognitive psychology. Developments in other areas of science produce capabilities within cognitive psychology. Social needs and desires selectively encourage the development of some of these capabilities.

sciences. By the same token, perceived needs in the health field have pulled results from one scientific field, while perhaps holding back results from others.

Cognitive psychology is not exempt from such influences. Developments in the scientific study of thought depend on doors being opened for us by progress in other fields. Society then pulls us through these metaphorical doors because our services are needed in the next room. This essay is a guess about how the pushes and pulls will play themselves out in the next quarter-century. Going further would move us from cognitive science to cognitive science fiction.

The First Push: Advances in the Biological and Physical Sciences

Progress in any science is based on the available technology and on contemporary ideas about how that technology should be used. Technological advances make it possible to gather data that then has to be explained. Scientific advances occur when we develop new ways of looking at the data. Technology and science often go hand in hand, but on occasion, technology will lead. Astronomy provides a good example. The first humans (and for that matter, their ancestors) had sufficient visual acuity to see both clouds and stars. The first major conceptual advance in astronomy appears to have occurred over 3000 years ago, when the Babylonians realized that the atmosphere and the heavens are separate systems (Boorstin, 1983). Various theories were then proposed to explain astral observations, culminating in Ptolemy's theory of an Earth-centric universe, about A.D. 150, and its replacement, the Copernican theory, more than a thousand years later. These great advancements in theory took place without a corresponding improvement in the technology of observation.

The next step did require instrumentation. Copernicus saw the Sun at the center of the universe. We now think that humanity occupies a smallish planet, revolving around a slightly below average sized star, at the tail of a distant galaxy that is very far from the center of the universe. These conclusions depend on a technology of observation well beyond anything Galileo ever dreamed of.

At the end of the twentieth century, advances in three areas of the physical sciences—solid-state electronics, biophysics, and superconductivity—created a new technology of medical imaging that may well have as profound effects for cognitive psychology as the telescope had for astronomy. We now have a noninvasive way of looking at the normal brain. Positron emission tomography (PET) and magnetic resonance imaging (MRI) studies are increasingly reported in our journals.

Developments in electronic computing have enabled us to make a quantum leap forward using another recording technique that is, itself, fairly old. For over fifty years, we have been able to record electrical potentials (EEGs) arising from neural activity. It was quickly learned that these potentials change in response to stimuli. The alteration may be controlled either by the physical form of the stimulation or by its meaning in the context in which it appears. These findings have led to an elaborate technology for analyzing EEG wave forms and associating them with psychological states, varying from surprise to responses to syntactically anomalous sentences (Osterhout & Holcomb, 1992). Thanks to miniaturization and superior computing facilities, it is now possible to locate the brain events that produce the EEG with ever-increasing accuracy.

This is not the point to explain how all these techniques work (nor am I the person to offer the explanation). The point is that our ability to observe brain events directly has increased to an almost unimaginable degree.

It has been suggested that this ability will wipe out a field closely related to cognitive psychology, the study of intelligence, because the intelligence test will shortly be replaced by biological measures (Matarazzo, 1992). I think this is optimistic. However, we certainly can anticipate tremendous differences in the way that we do information-processing psychology.

At present, we infer psychological states, such as attended and unattended processing, by measuring behaviors, such as variations in reaction times. Psychologists have developed impressive analytic techniques to allow us to infer such things as serial or parallel processing from the examination of the behavioral measures. These analyses serve as surrogates for the direct observation of brain processes. Sometime before the middle of the next century, such surrogates will become unnecessary. We should be able to use noninvasive techniques to answer, directly, questions about, say, the extent to which verbal and visuospatial, short-term memories are supported by the same brain structures.

We shall not just identify brain structures, we shall also learn how they work as physical devices. Great progress is being made in the identification of neurotransmitters. For medical reasons, such progress has been paralleled by studies of the pharmacology of cognition and affect. I am sure that this work will also have a profound influence on cognitive psychology, especially when we seek to determine the interaction between affect and thought.

These startling advances in the neurosciences are going to affect information-processing psychology in two very different ways. One is a way that we can all applaud. There will be an increasing demand for research paradigms that isolate psychological functions, so that their biological correlates can be similarly isolated. We can see an excellent example already, in the work of Posner, Petersen, Fox, and Raichle (1988). These investigators used PET imaging to locate different areas of metabolic activity as they progressively complicated the task, moving from looking at lines to looking at words, and then to doing some sort of semantic or syntactic task. This enabled them to identify the brain regions involved in various stages of linguistic processing.

The biological techniques that Posner et al. used depended strongly on an implicit psychological theory. The areas associated with word reading, for instance, were located by subtracting the activity throughout the brain when a person reads a word from the same activity when looking at a nonsense collection of letters. This procedure implicitly implies a stage model of the reading process, where activity moves discretely from one area to another. Since the temporal resolution of the PET scan is (today) on the order of tens of milliseconds, the stage assumption may not be too bad. However, one can imagine a future study in which imaging techniques with a temporal resolution of a few milliseconds will be used to distinguish between a stage model, in which information processing in one place must be completed before the second stage has begun, and a cascade model (McClelland, 1979), in which information is gradually leaked from lower to higher levels of semantic complexity.

The distinction between the two models is crucial, because it addresses the extent to which the mind (and the brain) is broken into modules that receive input from other modules, but whose internal actions are independent of the actions of the other modules. Stage theories assume that such independence is maintained; cascade theories assume that it is not. It is very difficult to distinguish between such models on the basis of behavioral observations (Townsend & Ashby, 1983). It may be much easier to make the distinction by direct biological observations. This assumes a very different experiment than the one conventionally conducted in the psychological laboratory.

Every knowledgeable person agrees that advances in biological measurement will have a profound effect on psychology, partly because this particular revolution is already fairly well along. There is a second biological revolution whose implications are less clear.

Neuroscientists are soon going to have a much better idea of who the individual is, at the level of molecular biology. The human genome project will undoubtedly result in a close map of the relation between a person's genotype (which will be measurable) and the performance of his or her brain. Look then at what we have. Owing to advances in our ability to observe brain processes, we shall know how elementary information-processing actions are produced by the brain. Because of advances in molecular biology, we shall know how the brain structures got the way they are, on an individual basis. It follows that we shall certainly advance our knowledge of how a person's biological makeup influences his or her thought processes. Biological makeup, here, should be construed very broadly. Of course, it includes genetic makeup. It also includes an understanding of how cognitive capabilities are likely to change in response to induced structural changes in the brain, such as the changes induced by alcoholism, disease, or advanced age.

These trends have major implications for the way in which we construct psychological theories. Since 1950, most papers in cognitive psychology, and especially those papers that fall under the rubric "information processing," have taken a functionalist view of thought. Information-processing psychologists have asked questions about the functional organization of the mind, without being concerned about the material roots of that organization in the brain. Reviews of the field have documented considerable progress, within the limits of the philosophical orientation (e.g., Massaro & Cowan, 1993). Much of the motivation for accepting these limits has been pragmatic; given our technology, we could do nothing else. As the technologies advance, we can anticipate, and look forward to, a decline of information-processing psychology of the sort reviewed by Massaro and Cowan, and an increase in the sort of direct ties between information processing and biology that are exemplified by the Posner et al. approach.

Although the rapprochement between information-processing models and direct observation of brain processes is certainly dramatic, it has major limitations. Suppose that all the biologically based approaches that I have cited are successful. This would mean that we would have identified the location of the anatomical structures that carry out the many elementary information-processing actions required for thinking. If the biologically based approaches are very successful, we would know how each of these anatomical structures worked. What next?

We still would not have explained thinking. The complex topics that cognitive psychologists are really interested in, such as text comprehension and scene interpretation, are not hardwired into the brain. They are emergent properties of the information-processing properties of the brain, and can no more be explained by listing the brain structures involved than the architecture of the Cathedral of Notre Dame can be explained by listing the equipment on a medieval mason's workbench. We have to explain how higher-order cognition emerges from lower-order capabilities.

The Second Push: Advances in Mathematics and Computer Science

Cognitive psychology will not be complete without a model of how complex phenomena emerge from simple systems. Developing such a model is a major theoretical problem. It has defeated us for over a century because we keep stating our theories in natural language. This has placed us very much in the same position that mathematicians were before the development of modern algebraic notations. The statement of the theory becomes so complicated that we oversimplify the issue or we become incomprehensible. Citations could be given for both responses.

Here we may get help from another allied science: the continued development of digital computers and, most important, the developments in mathematical conceptualization associated with increases in computational capabilities.

Saying that computer programs will become the language of psychological theory is nothing new; this was said at mid-century (Newell, Shaw, & Simon, 1958). In retrospect, most of the efforts at computer simulation from the 1950s to the 1990s were useful, precise descriptions of thinking at the phenomenological level. This can be said of the early simulations based around the General Problem Solver (Newell & Simon, 1972) and of recent simulations, such as Carpenter, Just, and Shell's (1990) work on the Raven Matrix test of intelligence.

This work, which undoubtedly will continue, produced useful concepts, such as the distinctions between working memory and long-term memory, the use of production systems as psychological models, and the distinction between procedural and declarative knowledge (Baars, 1986; Hunt, in press-a). What this work did not produce was a clear link between general brain processes and cognitive phenomena. Nor was it intended to do so. But that is the theoretical challenge facing us today.

Basically, what we shall need is a way of describing how the properties of the mind emerge from the processing capabilities of the brain. We cannot create such a theory by introducing a few special terms, such as "spreading activation," into everyday language. The resulting verbal statement is, as I have said, either unacceptably vague or unacceptably incomprehensible. Therefore, what some psychologists, the *connectionists,* have done is to turn to investigating computer programs that are supposed to be based on models of the brain, but to display computing capabilities equivalent to properties of the mind. In Rumelhart's (1989) terms, we use the computer to explore the brain as a model for the mind.

Before looking at this idea in more detail, let me point out that it is another example of how technology can fuel scientific progress. Whatever you think of the connectionist approach, you have to admit that it would not be possible without modern developments in computer science. Most of these "massively parallel" models of computation, which look at what happens when lots of brain events occur at the same time, are in fact being studied on very fast, conventionally designed serial computers.

Since the connectionist movement is so prominent, and since it represents a major attempt to link the brain to the mind, I shall take the time to describe it in a bit of detail.

Figure 17.2 illustrates the argument. The connectionists begin with a truism: that behavior is the result of (1) presenting a stimulus to the sensors, (2) passing the resulting neural activation through a maze of connections in the brain, and eventually (3) activating the effectors. Common sense (and today, some direct observations of neural events) tells us that the connections in the brain can be reconfigured, so that animals can learn to achieve a very wide range of stimulus– response connections.

This process can be mimicked mathematically. We can create mathematical objects, called "nodes," that carry with them associated levels of activation. The activation can be passed from node to node via links, where each link has a weight that, in effect, tells how much activation can be passed along it. Some of the nodes can be designated as input nodes and others as output nodes, analogous to sensors and effectors. Internal nodes that intervene between input and output play

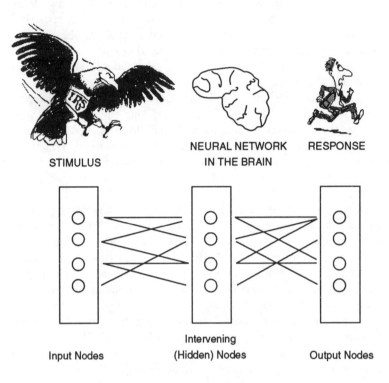

Figure 17.2. The connectionist analogy to thought. Features of the external stimulus and responses are represented by the activation of input and output nodes. Complex pathways of sensor–effector connections in the brain are represented by pathways from input to output nodes, through a complex of intervening (hidden) nodes.

the role of the neural pathways in the brain. *Voilà!* We can mimic stimulus–response connections. And to make the analogy still more complete, there are algorithms that can be used to readjust the weights on each link, thus mimicking learning.

It can be shown that if one carries on the analysis as just described, connectionism will always work, in the sense that some arrangement of input, output, and intermediate nodes can be found to mimic any stimulus–response system. In other words, an unrestricted connectionist device is a universal (Turing) computing machine. This is a good outcome for computer science, since it shows how computers can program themselves by observing examples, instead of having to be programmed by having a human make an analysis of the function to be computed. However, the universality of connectionist models is a bad outcome for psychological science, since we believe that a theory that can be tweaked to account for any outcome is no theory at all.

If connectionism is going to provide the link between brain and mind, two conditions are going to have to be fulfilled. First, it is going to have to be shown that networks that are constrained by biologically plausible limitations (i.e., using only certain learning algorithms, or using restricted sets of pathways) are capable of the emergent behaviors we associate with the mind. While establishing the appropriate biologically justified constraints is a formidable task, it is not, in principle, impossible. Second, we are going to have to understand how the constraints achieve their effects. Too little attention has been paid to this problem.

In most interesting situations, connectionism does not yield to conventional pencil-and-paper mathematical analysis. Instead, connectionists experiment, using computers, to determine whether different models can adjust themselves to display the required behaviors. The brain models proposed depend on involved, nonlinear matrix manipulations and can involve thousands of parameters. If you want to understand X by making an analogy to Y, you have to understand Y. The pessimistic view is that the connectionist approach can lead to the development of nonunderstandable models, so the demonstration that these mysterious mathematical objects mimic psychological phenomenon is not enlightening (McCloskey, 1991).

The answer may lie in mathematics. Computer scientists and mathematicians are developing new and interesting branches of mathematics in order to understand the principles that drive the emergence of complicated behavior in networks of simple elements. In speaking about connectionism, Hintzman (1990) said that if it took hold all our currently practicing scientists would have to "[t]ake tensor calculus or take early retirement." That may not turn out to be a joke, and tensor calculus will not be enough. If mathematical annealing, catastrophic progressions over time, and chaotic functions turn out to be necessary tools for describing models of psychological processes, then the graduate training programs for experimental psychologists will have to be vastly altered.

The likely resurgence of mathematics in the explanation of cognition does not depend solely on the success or failure of the connectionist effort. It is a general consequence of developments in the neurosciences. In computing terms, the neuroscience approach can, at best, lay out the architecture of a distributed processing system of elements of known capabilities. Distributed processing here does not refer to distributed processing in the connectionist sense of distributed processing on the elements of a representation. It is more analogous to the distributed processing of a variety of special-purpose computers, linked together in a network. Computing proceeds asynchronously and in parallel, sometimes, but at other times the units must link together with lock-step precision.

The computer scientist Marvin Minsky has speculated that such networks form a "society of the mind" that is a more appropriate metaphor for psychology than the connectionist's idealized brain metaphor (Minsky, 1986). There is presently a mathematical language for describing distributed networks, derived from graph-theoretic concepts developed originally for scheduling industrial activities. Although psychological models have been stated in this language (Townsend & Ashby, 1983; Schweikert, Fisher, & Goldstein, 1992), in all honesty it must be said that the mathematics are so formidable that most cognitive psychologists cannot deal with them.

This raises a very serious issue. Until the 1970s, many students in experimental psychology programs were recruited from the biological and physical sciences. In the 1970s and 1980s, as psychology became more of a social-science discipline with an increasingly stronger push for immediate societal relevance, recruitment began to be increasingly from students with social science and humanities backgrounds. With the exception of applied statistics, emphasis on mathematical training decreased. In response to the legitimate needs of the new students, statistics training itself increasingly was applied and procedural rather than emphasizing the mathematical grounding of statistics. It is not my purpose to criticize this movement, which was probably inevitable. It did have the important side effect of decreasing the amount of mathematical training offered in many psychology programs to something well beyond the levels offered in the 1950s and 1960s. As a result, psychologists were, on the average, not well prepared to deal with mathematics as a formal language for theory. This effect was exacerbated as relatively fewer undergraduates took mathematics courses in the 1980s. This has a serious implication for the role of scientific psychology in the future.

Because of the advances in the brain sciences, and because of the need to understand brain–mind interactions in order to solve pressing problems in health care, society is going to demand (and fund) someone to produce the required theories. If psychologists are not adequately trained to deal with these issues, someone else will deal with them. A discipline of computational neuroscience could easily develop quite outside psychology departments. If this happens, cognitive psychology will be the poorer, both intellectually and, more crassly, in our funding opportunities.

The Pull from Without

Just as cognitive psychology is pushed by developments within other sciences, it is pulled by developments in the general society. The reason for the pull is simple; science takes money. Society will pay only for those products for which there is a perceived need. This does not mean that every scientific project is weighed for its short-term economic contribution. At the level of the granting agency and review board, most basic research proposals are indeed reviewed primarily for scientific merit. The political and economic review occurs at a higher level, when the agency or subagency itself competes for funds. The decision to put funds into Defense, the National Science Foudation, Commerce, or the National Institutes of Health, and to distribute funds to the major subdivisions of those agencies is, and should be, a political act. While pork-barrel politics is certainly not unknown, by and large funding for particular branches of science represents an attempt to fund those agencies that can respond to perceived social needs. In turn, this means that, given equal intellectual preparation, those branches of a science that are seen as responding to a societal need are more likely to be developed than branches that are seen as an intellectual ornament.

Influences of this sort are so pervasive that the laboratory scientist may be quite unaware of them. Nevertheless, they exist, and historically they have been very important to cognitive psychology. The period from 1950 to 1980 was the heyday of information-processing psychology. The reason was in part the fact that psychological theory had laid the groundwork for an explosion of effort in that field, as opposed, for instance, to the study of higher-order problem solving or motor responding, fields that grew at a much slower rate. Another reason was, however, that information-processing studies could be funded.

The 1950 to 1980 period can also be thought of as the culmination of the Industrial Age. Muscular effort became obsolete, to the point that the lack was itself a national health problem. But perceptual effort did not become obsolete. Human beings acted as the eyes and ears for aircraft, read radar scopes, and guided landers onto the moon. In many cases, it turned out that the bottleneck in human-machine system performance was a person's ability to make rapid perceptual and minor cognitive decisions—that is, decisions requiring less than two or three seconds. In a sensible response, society funded that branch of science that had something to contribute.

Times are changing. Developments in computer and sensor technology are rapidly removing humans from the perceptual loop, just as developments in the nineteenth century removed humans from the energy generation loop (Hunt, in press-b). If this trend is completed, a good part of our field—information-processing psychology—will not be needed. Outside of psychology, no one will care what it means to say that a person has "fixated on this or that part of the visual field" because the sort of millisecond difference this makes in responding will be of interest only to pure scientists.

Of course, it would be too extreme to expect that studies of visual attention, short-term memory scanning, and the role of the icon will end overnight. They will not, and they should not. Low-level research in these fields will undoubtedly continue, for two reasons. First, it is interesting science in itself, and our society does place some value on the advancement of pure knowledge. Second, this research may assist us in relating behavioral observations to physiological and anatomical observations, as discussed in the preceding section. Although I do not think information-processing psychology will be eradicated, it will assume a far less dominant role in cognitive psychology than it has today.

The situation is quite different for studies of higher-order problem solving: analogical reasoning, the learning of very complex skills, such as computer programming, mathematics, and even social problem solving. In the workplace there are more and more situations in which humans deal with the world indirectly, through the medium of a computer model. For instance, that is the way that your travel agent deals with commercial aviation. Surprisingly often, it is also the way in which commercial aviation pilots deal with their aircraft. Such a workplace can be characterized in two ways.

The good jobs will require a great deal of flexibility, because people will need to know when to trust the model and when not to trust it. This assertion requires a specific example.

For the last fifty years, business analysts and economists have pushed the development of decision-theoretic models for analyzing policies. It can be shown, on highly rational grounds, that decision trees are the appropriate way to choose policies. It is also well known that real-life managers do not proceed that way. Most people's management style is much better explained by the psychological concept of schematic reasoning than by a decision-theoretic model (Beach, 1990; Wagner, 1991).

Future enterprises are increasingly going to be run by a combination of human-management and computer-based decision-making. The computers will be faster and faster, have access to more and more data, and compute ever more detailed decision trees. The result of all this computation will be reported to human managers who reason with a brain left over from the Pleistocene. How are we going to develop a match between these two very different types of reasoners?

This is potentially an issue for cognitive psychologists. However, what is needed here is not a theory of how the brain produces mental action. What is needed is a theory of how education and experience interact to produce a reasonable human being, who controls computer systems instead of being controlled by them.

The rosy view of things is that cognitive psychology will contribute by developing theories of human problem solving, rooted in our understanding of the information-processing capabilities that underlie it. Unfortunately, though, we do not have such a theory. What we do have, with our various studies of expert problem solving and cognitive developmental psychology, is a very good "guild literature" about how to analyze problems involving human thought. Within the next ten years, our major "doable" project may be systematizing this literature. The result will not be a theory of problem solving driven by models of information processing, in the sense that theories of visual perception might be driven by models at the neuroscience level. It will be a pretheoretical (and hopefully increasingly orderly) way of looking at an important slice of the world. Although we shall not have a general theory of how people develop problem representations, we can develop a methodology for analyzing a wide range of problem-solving situations. This may be just what society needs.

In this sort of endeavor one keeps sharp by having competitors. If we do not establish good ways of thinking about complex thought, others will. The "knowledge engineering" subspecialty of computer psychology or the industrial-organizational specialists in the business schools will compete with us in the marketplace.

My comments thus far have referred to the way that technological changes in the workplace will change the market for cognitive psychology. I now want to turn to a very different sort of change in society—social diversity.

When most academics hear the words "social diversity," they read it as a code word for the increasing number of "people of color" in the student body. The trend toward ethnic diversity is certainly a fact, and it must be dealt with. However, there is a much larger trend.

The workforce is aging. During the next two decades, the fastest growing segments of the workforce are going to be workers over 45 years of age (Johnston & Packard, 1987). There are some reasons to regard this as a benefit. Historically, older workers have traded job knowledge for wages, in a beneficial arrangement for all concerned. As the workplace changes, job knowledge becomes less valuable. How do we introduce major technological changes into the workplace without dislocating major segments of the workforce?[1]

This is partly a problem for cognitive psychology. Studies of aging, which are based largely on intelligence test data, have shown that the variance in intellectual abilities generally increases over the adult life-span. Can we obtain a clearer picture of this phenomenon? What do we mean by "the ability to learn"? And what determines both acquisition and retention of this ability? These are very interesting theoretical questions, which have applied implications. Cognitive psychologists should leap to the chance to make a contribution.

Since there are certainly information-processing correlates to aging, it is worth noting that a good theory relating information processing to higher-order cognition would be especially useful in this field.

There is a flip side to the emphasis on aging. Unless there are major changes in birth trends—and all the pressures are in the other direction—children will be an increasingly smaller percentage of the population. Obviously, people will not cease to have children, and developmental cognitive psychology will not cease. However, studies in developmental psychology may become relatively less important than they are today.

This is something of a heresy, since there is, today, a great hue and cry about how we need "better prepared students" for the workforce of tomorrow. Therefore, I bring up a discouraging fact. No one doubts that the workplace is going to be computerized. The only arguments are over how quickly this will occur. Computer-controlled systems have an interesting by-product; they multiply the number of smart people. A good spread-sheet programmer can unemploy vast numbers of bookkeepers. On a societal basis, we shall have a great need for a few very smart people. Translated to the marketplace for cognitive psychology, there may be social reasons to emphasize identification and training of the very talented. There may, however, be less societal need to move the lower-middle range of cognitive capability to the upper-middle range. If this is what is going to happen to the workplace (and others disagree with me!), it will have profound implications for the sociology of education. It certainly will not create a market for cognitive developmental psychology.

While this reasoning suggests a diminution of interest in cognitive development, there is another trend that suggests an increase in interest in the field— changes in family structure. The evidence for changes in American family structure are quite clear. These cannot be easily summarized in a few sentences, especially because the trends seem to be different for different segments of our society. For instance, in classic upper-middle-class society, there is a trend toward smaller families, with greater interaction between children and adults. In other social groups, adult–child interactions are being reduced. I leave it to social commentators to explain what these trends are. My point is what these trends mean for cognitive psychology.

There will be an increasingly greater need to understand how adult–child interaction and peer-group practices influence cognitive development. In particular, we need to know how post-infant family and peer-group social structures influence children's cognitive development, especially their receptivity for the sort of abstract thinking that the technological world demands.

So what can we see for the future of developmental cognitive psychology? I hazard two predictions. First, there will be much less interest in the study of the "immutable facts" of how cognition unfolds. Old copies of Piaget's books will be less in demand. So will studies of the development of working memory, attention, and the like. On the other hand, there may be an increase of interest in the interaction between social and cognitive development.

Now, let us move away from life-span psychology to another issue. The highly publicized diversification due to changes in the ethnic composition of the country is worth comment. This is not solely a social trend. It also has implications for cognitive psychology.

So long as cognitive psychology is synonymous with information processing, we can simply ignore the trend. I believe that priming works the same way in Spanish and Swahili as it does in English. The acultural aspects of our field are even more true when we tie ourselves to biology. The relationship between short-term memory and the hippocampus is well documented in Canadians, and I am sure, quite without documentation, that the same relationship occurs among the Kurds.

As we move to the study of problem solving and reasoning, we cannot be so cavalier about cultural effects. Of course, we can always account for cultural differences in reasoning by saying, "Those people have different schema than we do," but this is hardly a scientific explanation of anything. We need to know what cultural experiences produce particular schema, and how those schema interact with the schema required to operate in a common meeting ground—the workplace—where one social group will often design systems to be used by another.

Once again, let me provide some content. Western European society places great stress on the use of abstract knowledge that does not depend on direct personal experience. This has proven to be a very useful tool; most of modern technology depends on it. There are other societies in which much more stress is placed on personal knowledge. Our textbooks usually cite relatively exotic groups—for example, central Asian peasants in the 1920s—who, if they still exist, have little economic impact. What about intermediate cases? Anyone can be controlled by modern technology. In order to control it, a person must welcome a chance to do some abstract thinking. What are the appropriate ways of teaching abstract thinking to both adults and children from the various immigrant groups that are increasingly part of our society? For instance, is bilingual education a good or a bad idea? Or, as is more likely, is it good at some points and bad at others?

In this section I have tried to list a few places where the society needs to pull results out of cognitive psychology; the problems I have listed are the ones that appear, to me, to be the most important. Others may have other lists. However, I think that all of us who think very much about how cognitive psychology fits into the grand scheme of things would agree with my next two points.

Although many social problems cannot be solved without research on cognition, very few social problems can be solved just by research on cognition. Put more pithily, problems are where you find them; they do not belong exclusively to one or another academic discipline. Furthermore, as cognitive psychology itself moves away from the study of information processing and toward the study of problem solving, it becomes more and more important, from an academic viewpoint, to understand the interactions between individual capabilities and social settings.

Social problems have to be solved. How they are solved may have a tremendous impact on society, but a solution will be found. There are many places where cognitive psychology can make a contribution and, in doing so, can influence society. But there are competent thinkers in education, sociology, computer science, social work, and many other fields whose solutions are, in some sense, competitive with the contribution of cognitive psychology. For instance, the computer science field of "knowledge engineering," which involves the transfer of knowledge from people to machines, is developing virtually independently of input from cognitive psychology. Once again, if we do not answer society's call, someone else will. Financial opportunities for further scientific advances will be arranged appropriately.

What Will the Synthesis Look Like?

Future developments in scientific cognitive psychology will depend on two things: what scientific capabilities are offered to us, by developments in other fields, and what economic support is offered to us, by a society that, quite reasonably, wants to purchase solutions to its problems. How shall we organize ourselves to respond to these opportunities? A few long-term predictions will now be attempted.

Pure information-processing models, for the sake of building models, are probably on the way out. They made an honorable contribution to science, but they have had their day. There is, however, a major exception to this statement. Where information-processing models can be tied to biological observations, they will prosper. Where they cannot, they will not.

One of the hardest trends to predict is the role of formal mathematics in psychology. If connectionism proves to be a key part of future theories, theoretical cognitive psychology will become much more mathematical than it is today. This could happen, but it is not at all certain that it will. Similarly, if it becomes increasingly important to tie cognition to formal models of human-machine systems, there will be a greater need for mathematical models of human cognitive performance.

Somewhat ominously, while mathematics may become more important in studying *cognition*, this could have the effect of diminishing *cognitive psychology*. The reason is that our graduate education programs are becoming increasingly less mathematical, as we are less and less able to compete for the shrinking pool of talented, mathematically able undergraduates. The worst of this trend is that it feeds back on itself. Once the nonmathematicians get into the faculty, it becomes harder and harder to introduce further mathematical training to the entering students. If this trend continues, psychology will have to yield the mathematical modeling of cognition to human-oriented computer scientists and industrial engineers.

There is a social need to develop an understanding of higher order cognition: problem solving, learning to learn, and lifelong reasoning. Several aspects of this endeavor could have profound implications for cognitive psychology.

Intellectually, society does not need a scientifically testable grand theory of human problem solving. That is good, because we do not have one. What society needs is a set of intellectual tools that can be used to provide useful guides in social engineering. These we can provide. However, we must remember that these tools will not be used in isolation. The study of applied problem solving is inherently multidisciplinary. Psychologists will not have the luxury of superspecialization. Many of the problems cannot be solved by observing bored undergraduates, working "to obtain extra class credit." The needed research will require long-term observation of groups as diverse as neuropsychological patients and air traffic controllers. Laboratory research will still have its place, but we shall have to think a good deal more than we have about what that place is.

Of course, the comments in the last paragraph apply as much to studies of the information processing–biology connection as to studies of the problem solving–social setting connection. The problems can be solved only by the simultaneous application of multiple types of expertise. In virtually every field of psychology, the superspecialized principal investigator, working in his or her own little laboratory, is about to become an endangered species. There will be no protection for a being whose niche has disappeared as ideas and demands evolve.

The evolutionary analogy is a good place to close. If I am correct, both scientific advances and changes in social needs are about to have profound influences on cognitive psychology. As these changes snow down upon us, a few of our species are going to die out. (Would "Go the way of the behaviorists" be appropriate?) But will the genus survive? Looking about at the latest meetings of the Psychonomic Society, one certainly sees dinosaurs.[2] And yet, there are probably enough furry creatures underfoot to ensure against a total extinction.

Notes

1. Two newspaper articles that were published as this article was being written illustrate my point. On December 18, 1992, the *New York Times* reported that Genreal Motors was moving 450 million dollars from a fund for retraining to a fund to induce early retirement. The company wished to retool its factories and clearly did not see their older workforce as an asset. On December 20, the *New York Times* reported serious underfunding of pension programs in the United States. The two articles were disturbing alone, and far more disturbing when seen together.

2. Names withheld to protect the guilty.

References

Baars, B. J. (1986). *The cognitive revolution in psychology.* New York: Guilford

Beach, L. R. (1990). *Image theory: Decision making in personal and organizational contexts.* New York: Wiley.

Boorstin, D. J. (1983). *The discoverers.* New York: Random House.

Carpenter, P.A., Just, M.A., & Shell, P. (1990). What one intelligence test measures: A theoretical account of processing in the Raven Progressive Matrix Test. *Psychological Review, 97,* 404–431.

Hintzman, D. L. (1990). Human learning and memory: Connections and dissociations. *Annual Review of Psychology, 41,* 109–140

Hunt, E. (in press-a). *Thoughts on thought: A discussion of basic issues in cognitive psychology.* Hillsdale, N.J.: Erlbaum.

Hunt, E. (1995). *Will we be smart enough? A psychological analysis of the coming workplace and workforce.* New York: Russell Sage Foundation.

Johnston, W. B., & Packard, A. H. (1987). *Workforce 2000: Work and workers for the 21st century.* Indianapolis: The Hudson Institute.

Massaro, D., & Cowan, N. (1993). Information processing models: Microscopes of the mind. *Annual Review of Psychology, 44,* 383–425.

Matarazzo, J. D. (1992). Psychological testing and assessment in the 21st century. *American Psychologist, 47,* 1007–1018

McClelland, J. L. (1979). On the time-relations of mental processes: An examination of systems of processes in cascade. *Psychological Review, 86,* 287–330.

McCloskey, M. (1991). Networks and theories: The place of connectionism in cognitive science. *Psychological Science, 2,* 387–395.

Minsky, M. (1986). *The society of mind.* New York: Simon & Schuster.

Newell, A., Shaw, J. C., & Simon, H. A. (1958). Elements of a theory of human problem solving. *Psychological Review, 65,* 151–156.

Newell, A., & Simon, H. A. (1972). *Human problem solving.* Englewood Cliffs, N.J.: Prentice-Hall.

Osterhout, L., & Holcomb, P. J. (1992). Event-related brain potentials elicited by syntactic anomaly. *Journal of Memory and Language, 31,* 785–806

Pylyshyn, Z. W. (1989). Computing in cognitive science. In M. I. Posner (Ed.), *Foundations of cognitive science* (pp. 51–91). Cambridge, Mass.: MIT Press.

Posner, M. I., Petersen, S. E., Fox, P. T., & Raichle, M. E. (1988). Localization of cognitive operations in the human brain. *Science, 240,* 1627–1631.

Rumelhart, D. E. (1989). The architecture of mind: A connectionist approach. In M. I. Posner (Ed.), *Foundations of cognitive science* (pp. 133–160). Cambridge, Mass.: MIT Press.

Schweikert, R. , Fisher, D. L., & Goldstein, W. M. (1992). General latent network theory: Structural and quantitative analysis of networks of cognitive processes. Privately circulated paper. Purdue University, Department of Psychological Sciences. Lafayette, Ind.

Townsend, J. T., & Ashby, F. G. (1983). *Stochastic modeling of elementary psychological processes.* Cambridge: Cambridge University Press.

Wagner, R. K. (1991). Managerial problem solving. In R. J. Sternberg & P. A. Frentsch (Eds.), *Complex problem solving: Principles and mechanisms* (pp. 159–184). Hillsdale, N.J.: Erlbaum.

18

The Fortieth Anniversary of the National Institute of Cognitive Ecology (NICE)

ROBERT SOMMER

Cognitive Ecology

An increasing number of cognitive researchers have been looking to the environmental sciences for useful principles and findings to explain thought processes. Traditional cognitive scientists viewed thoughts and environments as independent and separate, since they could be explained by different principles. It was sufficient for these researchers to establish a new way of conceptualizing the mind and, besides, artificial intelligence models appeared adequate. Moreover, architects, interior designers, and urban planners seemed to be involved in physical features, whereas environmental psychologists studied environment–behavior relationships rather than fundamental cognitive processes such as attention and memory. Much of our knowledge of environmental influences on thinking resulted from the teleportation experiments sponsored by the Korean government in 2021. Individuals instantly transported from one location to another brought with them patterns of dysfunctional "old thinking." If suddenly one were moved from a recreation lassiter to the holistic rezo, without going through the typical preparatory sequence of movement acts, one typically thought in lassiter terms and was vulnerable to inertia influences.

This emphasis on the importance of context in thinking, which had been slowly evolving throughout the twentieth century, finally came to fruition in the twenty-first. There was general recognition of the inadequacies of conceptualizing psychological processes as if they were disembodied activities floating in space. Lave, Murtaugh, and DeLaRocha (1984) viewed problem solving in its environmental context, in which "people and settings together create problems and solution shapes, and moreover, they do so simultaneously" (p. 94).

The central issue to emerge was whether mind was an independent organ, whose operations occur without regard to context, or was connected through sense organs to an environmental context. Among the scientists who whipped themselves into a frenzy on this issue was Karl Flagellant (2001). In one series of experiments, Flagellant destroyed specific parts of the environment, using advanced neutron weaponry that would produce physical but not psychological changes. He showed that mental activity changed according to the total *amount* of the environment destroyed.

Building on the work of Neisser (1982), Empson (2038) complained about the narrowness of laboratory studies in learning and memory. Given the advances in teleportation, Empson argued, researchers could efficiently study basic cognitive processes under ultranatural conditions. Neisser's work is now unfortunately forgotten, but a few octogenarian psychologists, who scanned his articles in graduate school, recall his citing the work of another forgotten psychologist named "Gibson," about whom some uncertainty exists as to first name and gender. "Gibson" insisted that perception must be considered in terms of proprioception. Of course, this can only be interpreted as an early view, and it is up to today's researchers to develop a twenty-first century theory of cognition based on new types of movement.

Cognitive ecology is the study of the tripartite relationships among cognition, the physical setting in which thinking takes place, and the neural substrate of thinking. Consider this example: A skilled cyber is given an intricate work of holography to simulate, and she does so with dazzling dexterity at a concert hall. Move her to another context, such as a water environment with no firm ground support, and the electronic pattern of her brain waves will be quite different, not to mention her performance. The environment is as much a factor in human thinking as is the "wiring" of internal systems.

Or take another example: imagine yourself shopping at a hypermarket, actively thinking about the receptive field you want to create that evening, and out of the corner of your eye you witness and recognize the eminent Professor Alfred Von Newman. How long does it take to recognize his familiar "What, me worry?" expression? Not long at all. Experiments conducted under well-controlled laboratory conditions show that from the onset of a complex visual stimulus until recognition and response to the stimulus about 300 milliseconds have elapsed. Move the same incident to your comfort station. You are washing your hands in the water spray and suddenly Professor Von Newman appears. Recognition is delayed under these circumstances largely owing to differential expectations and interpretations. You wonder how Professor Von Newman managed to enter your apartment unannounced, and what is he doing in your comfort station? Earlier models of cognition were unable to deal with instantaneous shifts in the environmental context of experience. It was he himself, the eminent Professor Von Newman, who developed the equation: Thinking $= f\{M(P),E\}$ to describe how thinking is a function of the mind *(M)* with its physiological substrate *(P)* in an environmental context *(E)*.

Cognitive ecologists believe that the environment is well structured, and that one must not be arbitrary in identifying ecological units, which are part of the tangible world "out there" which existed before and during the time the observer enters the scene. This environment consists mostly of mundane ubiquitous behavior settings where individuals spend most of their time, and presumably where most thinking occurs. Cognitive ecology requires systematic subject-matter knowledge of behavior settings, including information about their history, technology, and structure. This knowledge must be current, particularly in regard to changes taking place within the setting and the outside forces that affect it. Unfortunately, standard reference works in cognitive psychology have provided little information about mundane settings. A search of *Psychological Abstracts* for the past 50 years showed more references to telepathy than to teleportation, the most common form of transportation in the twenty-first century.

Until recently, cognitive ecologists were limited to behavioral measures in exploring context effects. Now, however, new instrumentation has profoundly accelerated our understanding of environmental influences and spun off a new breed of scientist, a hybrid brain researcher, cognitive researcher, and environmental psychologist. The new technology was originally developed as part of a massive federal campaign to combat cognitive disability, the scourge of the twentieth century, but the technology has become a valuable research tool in other fields. Remote scanning techniques follow brain activity as a person moves from one environment to another. The scan produces a cross-sectional image of the brain that can be enhanced through holography to produce a three-dimensional laser representation. If needed, *n*-dimensional holograms of people in environmental contexts, showing both the internal and the external features, can be produced.

This technology has also been used to investigate personal space, a concept developed in the previous century to describe the emotionally charged zone around the human body used for privacy regulation. With the latest technology, researchers can explore interaction distance in *n*-dimensional space, which can be occupied simultaneously by several individuals. In hyperspace, two individuals can maintain comfort levels even during spatial overlap, although records of cerebral blood flow indicate nonconscious awareness of the intrusion. This finding was anticipated by Summit, Westfall, Sommer, and Harrison (1992) employing Ken and Derek dolls which were a popular play item among young people in the 1960s. In an attempt to simulate space travel, Summit and his colleagues measured conversational distance between Ken and Derek in spatial arrangements associated with zero gravity. Unusual body orientations associated with zero gravity produced the longest interaction distances. Several decades later, Park (2026) replicated this research in *n*-dimensional space using Lia and Fram holograms.

Beginno Tulving (2007), Chair of Neurocognition at Tartu University in Estonia, employed a scanning technique to depict several types of regional cerebral blood flow (rCBF) associated with different environments. Tulving's graphic representation of thought patterns occurring with changes in place (see Figure 18.1) became a harbinger of the direction cognitive ecology was to take for the next decades. People entered different settings, while undergoing remote rCBF scanning. Some locations were attractive, interesting, and challenging, whereas others are bleak, dismal, and repetitive. There were consistent patterns of blood flow, and hence neural activity, associated with both attractive and barren environments.

The study brought together under the umbrella of cognitive ecology three distinct lines of research. Previously, most cognitive psychologists were interested in

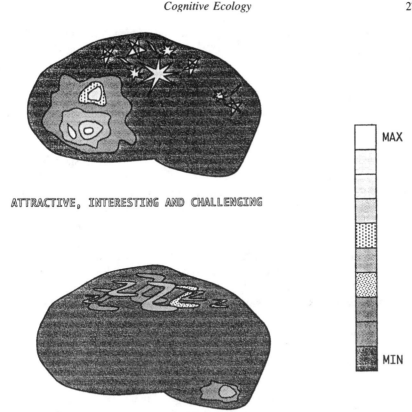

ATTRACTIVE, INTERESTING AND CHALLENGING

MAX

MIN

BLEAK, DISMAL, REPETITIVE

Figure 18.1. Regional Cerebral Blood Flow (rCBF), from high to low on above scale, for differing environments.

developing models of the mind, which are validated by elegant laboratory experiments using the most sophisticated statistical analysis. Environmental psychologists, on the other hand, were interested primarily in describing the physical properties of settings, and how these influence behavior. Brain scientists, in contrast, had sought to understand the basic structure of the nervous system. Experiments such as Tulving's seemed to authenticate the contributions of all three sciences. Cognitive psychologists have found an environmental basis for some of their theories—for example, the relationship of memory to place. Environmental scientists have been able to show that mental functions are influenced by physical contexts. And brain scientists found new applications for their sophisticated technology. Those whose work spans all three fields are now called cognitive ecologists. Through their efforts, constructs such as memory type are no longer conjectural, but possess a neurophysiological substrate and architectural context.

Introduction of remote scanning techniques has been responsible for what has become known as "the fifth cognitive revolution." In concert with holography and virtual reality techniques, there is now the possibility of triocular viewing similar to the well-known "listening with the third ear" phenomenon in audition. The first and the second eye provide visual impressions, but a third eye is able to detect meanings, creating a new field of visual metaphor. But the research base of this field remains largely metaphorical, in that hundreds of models of the human mind compete for attention in the arena of academic scrutiny. The field has been described as a metaphor for studying metaphor, which is a fundamental and exclusively human attribute. And, indeed at present, no other Earth species has been found to use metaphor. The controversial visit of space travelers in 2012 was so clouded by poor interspecies communication that no clear statements about metaphorical usage by the visitors could be made. Reflecting the importance of neurocognition research, the United Nations passed a resolution, signed by the heads of states of all 20 members of the Security Council, declaring the 2050s to be "the decade of metaphorical technology."

Remote scanning techniques were also used by Binkie (2014) to link cognition with personality psychology. In his classic paper published in *Science,* "Where Is the Thinker in Cognitive Theory?" Binkie raised the possibility that a single theory of thinking could explain not only the generality of cognitive processes but also the uniqueness of their expression in individual cases. The most persuasive portions of Binkie's article were the striking color illustrations of differential electrical activity and blood flow among individuals with different personality types as they solved implicit memory problems. Using the most current laser sensing techniques, Binkie concluded:

> Early personality manifestations seem to be located in the specific regions of the brain. In addition to regional centers, further connections appear to take place in different sites.
>
> Many higher-order personality functions, such as intuitive sensing and oceanic knowing, appear to be distributed throughout the brain and processed in parallel at several locations.
>
> Damage to the brain does not always lead to change in personality. Sometimes it may result in consolidation and exacerbation of previous modes of behavior. It may be that the intact connections can take over the original functions, or the intact connections can be rearranged in a way that allow them to accomplish the original mode of expression.

It was Binkie's genius to demonstrate that, when individuals with different personality types are given the same intellectual task to solve, they would often come up with the same answers, but having used different portions of the brain. This research became known as New Look 4 because of its relationship to the City College studies of need and perception begun in the 1940s (New Look 1) by Gardner Murphy and his students (Levine, Chein, & Murphy, 1942; Proshansky & Murphy, 1942; Schafer & Murphy, 1943), New Look 2 (Erdelyi, 1974), and New Look 3 (Greenwald, 1992). In his paper "New Look 4: Process Is Not Outcome," Binkie declared that it was almost impossible to indulge in too much speculation about the intervening mechanisms between thought physiology and personality. He advocated tolerance, in order to allow brain scientists to construct scaffolding on which to hang their concepts. This could lead, Binkie noted ruefully, to the publication at some future time of an article entitled, "There are six kinds of cognition"; but such multiplicity, he noted, was preferable to the schizoid separation that presently existed between cognition and everything else.

New Look 4 was not well received by all segments of the cognitive community. Some researchers saw it as a distraction from the major task of establishing general laws. The most strident criticism came from Henry Pendragon, the founding father of radical cognition theory. Pendragon published his incisive critique of Binkie in 2018, under the title, "Neurocognition Is Personality" to which Binkie wrote an ironic rejoinder, "Personality Is Neurocognition." The debate occupied a small but lively portion of the theoretical literature in cognition for almost two decades.

Remote scanning of cerebral blood flow was also used by Davidson (2048) to study extraordinary savants. Continuing a tradition begun almost two centuries earlier, Davidson for the first time included cases from South America, Asia, and Africa. Such individuals continue to challenge fundamental views and assumptions about mental abilities and multiple intelligences (Gardner, 1983). There was the remarkable case of Hodo, a 14-year-old Japanese boy, who memorized over 40,000 digits of pi, while at the same time experiencing difficulty performing the commonplace but intricate tea ceremony. There was also the 12-year-old Anwego who could recite the astric coordinates of all the major cities in his native Africa without being able to teleport himself home after dark. Davidson's book is the best compendium thus far of instances of extraordinary abilities among individuals of otherwise little mental talent. What distinguishes this book from others of the genre are the detailed images of cerebral blood flow through the brain. For the first time, these images provided the foundation for a coherent theoretical framework to explain the phenomenon that perhaps will lead to a unified model for the structure of intellectual abilities.

Not all researchers accepted the validity of brain scan techniques as measures of cognition. The controversial brain scientist Henry Sass criticized what he saw as "bloody thinking." Although he did not doubt the reality of differential blood movement through the brain, Sass argued that thinking could not be reduced to blood flow. The anti-medicalization movement became international with the writings of the quixotic French philosopher, Allen Faecalith. Although his most significant book, *Le Bateau des Écoles* (roughly translated as *Ship of Schools*), has yet to be translated into English, it has had profound influence on both sides of the Atlantic. It describes how society quarantines young people resistant to adult authority, placing them metaphorically adrift on a sea of derisory attitudes. Problems of the schools, the book suggests obliquely, could be redacted through a change in public perceptions.

Although many similarities existed in the anti-medicalization movement in Europe and North America, the French who followed Faecalith saw it as a metaphor for failures of discipline in the larger society, whereas American critics saw it as a myth, inserted in the public mind to allow people to shirk unpleasant responsibilities. Measurement of cerebral blood flow (CBF) showed that the myth and metaphor positions involved different brain regions. When graduate students read Faecalith's argument that thinking was a metaphor, a reduced CBF could be measured in the posterior portion of the left hemisphere. When the same individuals, after an hour break, read the Sass argument that cognitive disability was a myth, lower CBF to the anterior sections of the left hemisphere was observed.

Scarcity of Resources

As the recession of 1992 deepened into the Great Depression of 1998, federal money for research dried up. The situation was especially critical in new fields lacking significant constituencies among the general public. Attempts to scale back research on Alzheimer's encountered strong resistance from the senior lobby, and patients and their families mobilized to support research on neuronal dysfunction. Questions were raised about the types of science that society could afford. The issue was not the academic freedom of researchers, although some researchers posed the question in these terms, but the amount and types of research that could be supported by public funds. During the twentieth century, this had been left largely to the internal regulation of the scientific community. The approach was challenged by the President's Blue Ribbon Commission established in 2050 to review the utilization of scientific knowledge. Befitting the mid-century mark, the commission set out to examine the contributions of government-supported science to the quality of life. The heretical nature of this approach, in which nonscientists reviewed the work of scientists according to the criteria of public benefit, led a number of scientific societies to boycott the proceedings. Spokespeople for these organizations insisted that only scientists could legitimately evaluate scientific research. Although this view had been persuasive in an earlier century, it no longer appeared suited to current fiscal realities. With limited research funds, priorities had to be established in allocating funds among different fields and lines of research.

The President's Blue Ribbon Commission appointed task forces to examine the utilization of scientific knowledge in different fields. As a new science without a strong public constituency, cognitive psychology was subject to special scrutiny. Attempting to give a balanced portrayal, task force staff commented favorably on those researchers who ignored the dominant paradigm and focused their attention on real-world cognition. Often such individuals were associated with schools of engineering, business, or medicine. Two researchers were singled out for their unique contributions. Gula Herc (2003) of Budapest University for her ground-breaking book, *How Doctors Think,* which had an immediate impact on medical education throughout the world. And Rudolph Croak's (2008) study of architects, which revealed the extreme splitting of consciousness that occurred in problem solving. At one level an architect approached a building as an artist, aiming to create something beautiful, but at another level, the architect had to think like a business person, in terms of lira and yen.

The task force report also noted "apparent inconsistencies" in the training and career options for cognitive scientists. As one example, it cited that a primary job market for Ph.D.s in cognitive science was in departments of education. The task force found, however, that many of these cognitive scientists had never taken courses in education, and therefore what they taught was primarily cognitive science. Education students, interested in improving their teaching skills, came away demoralized. Perhaps because the task force was headed by a former baseball commissioner, a sports analogy was used to contrast the approaches. Teaching was seen as pitching, and cognition was a form of catching. Students emerged from cognition courses knowledgeable about laboratory studies of learning and problem solving—that is, catching, but knowing little about how to "throw the ball" in terms of teaching thinking and problem-solving skills.

Task force members reacted critically to what they saw as the active discouragement of research on teaching in departments of cognitive science. When investigators questioned cognitive scientists about support for research on teaching, the initial response was general puzzlement, as if the interviewer could not possibly be serious. The antipathy of cognitive scientists toward teaching was matched only by the antipathy of teachers toward the cognitive courses they had been required to take. A survey sponsored by the National Educational Association in 2030 found that teachers rated their courses in cognitive psychology among the least useful aspects of their training. As part of the interview, teachers were shown abstracts of twenty articles, randomly selected from cognitive science journals published between 2025 and 2030, and asked to rate each for comprehensibility (could the teacher understand what the article said?), relevance (did the study have anything to do with teaching?), practical utility (was the teacher able to apply the findings in the classroom?), and importance (did the teacher learn anything new or significant from the article?). The survey organization had a difficult time completing the interviews. There were many refusals by teachers who took one look at the abstracts and gave up. Comments such as "You must be joking" or "You are talking to the wrong person" were commonplace. Less than a quarter of the teachers were willing to rate all twenty abstracts, and not a single paper received a passing grade on any dimension.

Publication of the National Education Association report under the title *Cambio 21,* or Change in the Twenty-first Century, provoked an outcry in the press, with a quick response from cognitive scientists, who complained that they were being judged by the wrong criteria. They maintained that their studies had not been designed for practical utility and their papers had not been written for teachers. The major review criteria, cognitive scientists insisted, should be theoretical significance and methodological rigor, neither of which had been included in the NEA survey.

The debate that followed publication of *Cambio 21* laid the basis for the First International Conference on Research Dissemination in Cognitive Science held in Tokyo in 2053, with financial support from the Boesky Foundation. Participants included researchers, elementary and secondary teachers, and representatives from state departments of education. Early sessions were spent debating issues that had divided the groups during the previous century. The hostility among the participants suggested to many that what separated them was more significant than what they had in common. Trained facilitators from the Boesky Foundation used these sessions to produce catharsis, to get rid of the old baggage prior to embarking on a new journey.

Cognitive scientists had come to the conference prepared to follow George Miller's advice to "give psychology away." They indicated a willingness, if resources became available, to translate their methods and findings into a form that teachers could understand and to offer courses and workshops in experimental design and statistical analysis that would enable teachers to read cognitive journals. To the researchers' consternation, teachers did not immediately accept the offer, but instead regarded it as condescension on the part of the researchers. Information that cognitive scientists were willing to give away, teachers declared, was not needed or wanted by educators. The meeting seemed at an impasse, with cognitive scientists desiring to give away their research, but with no takers in the audience.

The problem appeared more fundamental than differences in terminology or writing style. The logjam was finally broken when one of the cognitive scientists on the panel shouted in frustration at the teachers present, demanding to know, "What sort of information do you *want?*" Suddenly the atmosphere changed, as if the stale leptons in the room had been flushed out and new leptons introduced. The emphasis shifted from the problems encountered by knowledge producers in finding a market for their work, to the needs of knowledge consumers. Teachers asked questions that concerned them, but not always in clear terms, for example: "How do you motivate slow learners?" "How can I teach a class of 34 students?" "Some students are not ready for the material; others are ahead of the rest. How do I deal with this?" These were not the questions discussed in journals of cognitive science. Nor were they questions that the methods of cognitive science seemed capable of answering.

The epistemology of cognitive science, derived from the physical sciences, centered around experimentation with control over relevant variables. Most of the teachers' queries did not seem amenable to such control. Although small-scale experiments could be undertaken on some facets, such as the relationship between class size and student performance, the amount of effort required did not seem commensurate with the value of the findings. One of the cognitive researchers at the meeting, in a rare expression of self-doubt, described his field as "methodologically muscle bound," admitting that the powerful experimental methods and statistical analyses he taught to his graduate students seemed of little value in the murky idiographic world of the classroom.

Stung by the teachers' rejection, some of the cognitive researchers hit back. With much sarcasm, they criticized the quality of papers published in education journals, which were described as "case studies, surveys, and homilies." The chair of the Neurocognition Department at the University of Wisconsin stated that he expressly forbade his students to read such mediocre studies for fear it would lower their standards regarding publishability. If such weak papers could be published, what were the incentives for graduate students to undertake more sophisticated, time-consuming experimental studies? One of the teachers responded tactfully that the incentives could conceivably be greater relevance and utilization. A cognitive researcher objected that she was being asked to trade off rigor for relevance. Many in the audience, both researchers and teachers, nodded in agreement.

The blame and acrimony of the initial sessions laid the basis for the productive dialogue that came later. Practitioners recognized that they needed an established body of knowledge on which to base educational practice. This required more than anecdote, ideology, or case studies. Researchers, in turn, realized that their work had become far removed from problems facing classroom teachers. The laboratory model of testing individuals and subsequently aggregating the results into "group data" bore no resemblance to the situation of a teacher faced with a classroom of individual students in a bureaucratic system. The Fifth Cognitive Revolution had bypassed the school system. Innovations taking place in the schools were being implemented by practitioners. Rather than being part of the solution to school problems, cognitive researchers had become increasingly irrelevant.

Don Quayle, president of the Boesky Foundation, was present as an observer, and offered to support a pilot program of collaborative research between cognitive scientists and teachers. Following the action research model proposed by Lewin (1946), researchers would assist teachers in obtaining answers to questions that *teachers* considered important. Although researchers could express their opinions as to priorities, teachers would have the final say as to the research agenda. Several of the experimentalists in attendance at the Tokyo conference objected to the proposal, describing it as an infringement on the scientific community's ability to set its own agenda, but it was evident that no one was required to apply for money under the program. The chair of the Cognitive Science program at Harvard expressed willingness to undertake collaborative research in the Boston school system, where students' test scores had continued to decline. Once the prestigious Harvard program came on board, deans of several Midwestern universities also expressed their willingness to submit proposals.

Cognitive Extension Service

To facilitate the hoped-for transfer of cognitive research from university laboratories to schools and communities, Congress in 2046 established pilot extension programs at four land grant universities. These were patterned after the highly successful agricultural extension service. Before America declined as an agricultural power, agricultural extension had become "the most widely recognized system in the world for the diffusion of technological innovations" (Rogers, 1988:493), and "it was impossible for anyone to speak ten words about diffusion without two of them being 'agricultural extension.' . . . in many ways, it constitutes the defining metaphor for all technology transfer efforts" (Eveland, 1986:308). Community-based county advisors close to information consumers defined local problems, whereas other extension specialists, most of whom had Ph.D.s and considerable research training, were housed in university departments in proximity to knowledge producers. These specialists served as liaisons between the county agents and the university researchers.

For most of the twentieth century, federally funded extension activities represented about half of the federal investment in agricultural research and development. State and county governments made additional contributions, bringing the total extension budget to an amount roughly equivalent to the total agricultural research budget. In other words, for every yen invested in agricultural R&D, another yen was invested in extension (Rogers, 1988). Among the factors that had contributed to the success of this model was a critical mass of new technology with potential usefulness to clients, a research subsystem oriented toward utilization, a high degree of user control over the technology transfer process, structural linkages among all components of the technology transfer system, considerable client contact by the extension subsystem, and evolution into a complete system rather than a service grafted onto an existing research system (Rogers, 1988).

Following this model, a Cognitive Extension Service (CES) was created in 2046 to move the fruits of university research on thinking and problem-solving into schools and communities. Several of the first crop of liaison people had originally worked in agriculture and retrofitted to work on school issues. The program evaluation required in the Cognitive Extension Service Act found that these agents who had originally worked in agriculture had more successful liaison with schools, had better interpersonal skills, and were more sensitive to the types of problems extant in the community than were transfer people who had come directly from Ph.D. programs in psychology. A substantial percentage of CES agents who came directly out of Ph.D. programs continued doing basic research in their new positions, often in collaboration with their graduate school mentors. The program evaluation team recommended workshops, conferences, and a new *Journal of Cognitive Extension,* to bridge the chasm that existed among school- and laboratory-oriented cognitive extension agents.

Under the new program, psychology departments at land grant universities for the first time had their own diffusion people specifically assigned to transfer research results to the community. The University of Minnesota, with its long-standing commitment to the land grant tradition, was one of the first to create a training program for cognitive extension agents. The Minnesota program also established the first field station in a shopping mall. Keith Forrell, director of Minnesota's Cognitive Extension, shared his vision of the program with reporters at a recent press conference: "Society faces severe social, institutional, and structural problems that threaten our very future," Forrell said. "But those challenges also offer important opportunities. The role of CE in local communities is as legitimate today as ever in helping people help themselves," Forrell said. The first area of opportunity for Cognitive Extension, Forrell declared, is in the K-12 educational system, which is being overwhelmed by population growth, urbanization, and new technology. Coupled with the revolution in family structure and the shortcomings of the K-12 system, millions of children are threatened with mediocre preparation for their future roles as productive members of society, he warned. As society focuses on problems, Forrell urged CE people to become involved, emphasizing that "Cognitive Extension sits on the edge of a golden opportunity to help experiment and develop new policies and institutions involving in-school and out-of-the-school learning." Finally, Forrell noted that science for the sake of science "no longer is being accepted without question by our urban, cognitively conscious society. We must be leaders, not followers, in developing responsive and responsible scientific information for school systems in the future," Forrell emphasized. He predicted, "The 2050s may be recorded by historians as among the most difficult and troublesome of our history, but also a period of great opportunity—and hopefully achievement."

The nature of their work compelled Cognitive Extension agents to cross disciplinary boundaries. They had to know how to discuss the intricacies of laboratory experiments with researchers, practical realities of classroom management with teachers, patterns of children's intellectual development with parents, and fiscal realities and personnel policies with school administrators. At the start of the program, skeptics doubted that any single individual could link these separate realms and reconcile their contradictory positions. The first cadre of Cognitive Extension agents, perhaps motivated by the novelty and vision of the enterprise, put these fears to rest. Using their own teleportation network, they moved effortlessly between research laboratories, schools, administrative offices, and children's homes.

Note

1. Portions of this chapter were published in an earlier book by Robert Solso and revised with the help of a substantial grant from the National Institute of Cognitive Ecology (NICE-31820-42). All citations to articles or books written after 1995 are omitted. These were wiped out on my hard disk during a quark lapse. I seriously regret this inconvenience.

References

Erdelyi, M. H. (1974). A new look at the new look: Perceptual defense and vigilance. *Psychological Review, 81,* 1–25.

Eveland, J. D. (1986). Diffusion, technology transfer, and implementation. *Knowledge, 8,* 303–322.

Gardner, H. (1983). *Frames of mind.* New York: Basic Books.

Greenwald, A. G. (1992). New look 3: Unconscious cognition reclaimed. *American Psychologist, 47,* 766–779.

Lave, J., Murtaugh, M., & DeLaRocha, O. (1984). The dialectic of arithmetic in grocery shopping. In B. Rogoff & J. Lave (Eds.), *Everyday cognition* (pp. 67–94). Cambridge, Mass.: Harvard University Press.

Levine, R., Chein, I., & Murphy, G. (1942). The relationship of the intensity of a need to the amount of conceptual distortion. *Journal of Psychology, 13,* 283–293.

Lewin, K. (1946). Action research and minority problems. *Journal of Social Issues, 2,* 34–46.

Neisser, U. (Ed.) (1982). *Memory observed: Remembering in natural contexts.* New York: Freeman.

Proshansky, H., & Murphy, G. (1942). The effects of reward and punishment on perception. *Journal of Psychology, 13,* 295–305.

Rogers, E. M. (1988). The intellectual foundation and history of the agricultural extension model. *Knowledge, 9,* 492–510.

Schafer, R., & Murphy, G. (1943). The role of autism in a visual figure–ground relationship. *Journal of Experimental Psychology, 32,* 335–343.

Summit, J. E., Westfall, S. C., Sommer, R., & Harrison, A. A. (1992). Weightlessness and interaction distance. *Environment and Behavior, 24,* 617–633.

19

Some Assembly Required: Biased Speculations on the Future of Human Factors Design

JOHN B. PITTENGER

You know you are in trouble when:

1. The night before your child's birthday you arrive home proudly bearing that toy she's wanted for a year—only to see that the label says "Some Assembly Required."
2. The troubleshooting guide to your VCR lists over twenty-five ways to correct your mistakes.
3. The operating manual for your pocket calculator is thicker than the calculator itself.
4. The new shower head you are installing actually *has* an operating manual.

The subject of this chapter is human factors engineering, also known as ergonomics. The goal of the human factors designer is to produce artifacts—be they consumer products, computer workstations for offices, or control systems for automated factories—that can be used effectively. Just what we should mean by "can be used effectively" is subject to debate, but includes being easy to learn to use, being comfortable and safe for the operator, and not promoting error by the operator. In other words, good human factors design has the goal of making artifacts compatible with their users.

We all know that a lot of things are quite hard to use. Many of us have experienced the humiliation of pushing on a door to a hotel lobby that turns out to pull open or of having a guest see our VCR relentlessly blinking "12:00." More complex systems, such as commercial airplanes and nuclear reactors, are also prone to operator error. The consequences of failures here are much more severe than mere embarrassment.

We often suppose that such problems arise from human failing: People are often inattentive and don't notice which way the door opens; some of us are just too lazy to bother to learn to operate some of the appliances we own; it may be that air traffic control systems are inevitably so complex that they must occasionally exceed human capacity to process information, and so on. I certainly do not believe that people are always attentive, never lazy, or have an unlimited information-processing capacity. On the other hand, failure is often caused by the poor design of the things we use. In much contemporary design, human factors considerations are either neglected entirely or treated ineffectively.

In this chapter I first shall try to explain why we presently have so much poor design and then shall cite some social and economic trends that are going to ensure major improvements in the coming century. Finally, and this is where the bias comes in, I shall claim that recent developments in cognitive science are going to provide the human factors engineer with new and very powerful conceptual tools. These tools will make effective design cheaper to achieve and will help the engineer devise better solutions to design problems than are presently possible.

At first glance it might seem that good design would be common. The material and technological resources needed by designers are clearly at hand. Materials and manufacturing processes developed this century allow furniture, consumer appliances, and even buildings to be constructed to as to have nearly any size, shape, and physical properties that might be desired. Instrumentation and computer technologies allow us to measure almost any property and state of a system and to display that information in whatever we wish. Why, then, are so many of our creations so difficult to use and so prone to operator error?

As you might expect, a great number of causal factors are at work, with no single answer applying to all classes of devices. In some cases, the rapid evolution of technology plays a part. When new devices first come on the market, they are likely to have ignored human factors since only experience will reveal weakness in their design. But, before better designs are devised, new features are often added—features that produce new operational problems. Notice, for example, how new features have continued to be added to VCRs, digital wrist watches, and word-processing programs.

A closely related factor is that of the sheer complexity of much of our new technology. As we produce new systems that allow us to perform more functions, serious problems of design must arise in both the control and information components of the system. As an example of control complexity, consider a digital watch with ten functions. If it has ten buttons, you will need to remember which button controls each function and hope the buttons are spaced so that you can press one at a time. If only three control buttons are provided, it will be easier to press individual buttons and the watch will look more attractive. However, you will need to remember more complex sequences of operations to make those three buttons control all ten functions. Similar problems arise in operating devices ranging from statistical analysis programs to airplanes. Systems with many functions also entail complexity in the information needed to control them. In nuclear power plants the positions of hundreds of valves, the temperatures and pressures at many points in the cooling system, and so forth, must be known so that the system can be operated safely.

Innovation and complexity do not, however, account for all of our bad designs. For example, while door handles and faucets are neither new nor complex, some of them are amazingly hard to use. I think that much ineffective design is tolerated because of a cycle of resignation on the part of consumers and shortsightedness and economic expediency on the part of manufacturers. The process starts with our willingness to blame ourselves when a device's operation is awkward or error ridden (Norman, 1988). In addition, we often seem to give little weight to the human factors aspects of a product at the time of purchase, perhaps not being aware that competing models vary widely in how easy they are to use. Whatever its causes, consumer tolerance of ineffective design is high, giving manufacturers little incentive to invest in human factors development. Until manufacturers make and promote better design, consumers are likely to continue to accept awkward appliances.

The last factor I shall mention is the failure of past psychological research to produce the theoretical basis needed to support truly effective design. Human factors psychologists working in industry presently must do their work without the help of broad, well-documented principles that can guide their search for solutions to design problems. There are rules-of-thumb, such as standards for the heights of chair seats and the levels of illumination in work spaces. These principles are, however, rather limited in scope. They do not exploit deep insights into how people's cognitive processes influence their operation of devices. While such insights must come from basic research in psychology, little work of real help to designers has been forthcoming.

I believe there are two reasons why this has occurred. First, most university-based research psychologists, like their colleagues in other disciplines, have little interest in applied problems. Basic researchers wish to study phenomena that will test their theories of mind, giving results that either confirm their current ideas or present challenges that will lead to new and more adequate theoretical concepts. Problems in human factor design are seen as mere puzzles whose solution will not advance theory. This bias against application is institutionalized in promotion and salary systems in which a publication in an academic journal is more highly valued than a consultantship that solved a design problem for a manufacturer. Agencies in charge of federal research money have also played a part, tending to favor projects likely to advance theory—even if that theory is unlikely to help solve the problems of everyday life.

Second, the particular phenomena studied by basic researchers have not been those mostly likely to provide help to human factors psychologists. The designer needs to know the cognitive principles relevant to people's use of things—tools, VCRs, air-traffic control systems, and so on. These principles involve a number of different questions: What information about the environment is used to control a device's operation? How can that information be displayed most effectively to users? How does the user know what can be done with a particular object? How does the operator's mental model of an object influence his or her attempts to control it? In other words, designers need to know about real actions applied to real objects. Past research has generally tended to be somewhat remote from the physical world. Much work on memory and learning has been concerned with how these processes apply to words and sentences rather than to material things. Research into decision-making often involves subjects reading about a situation and saying what they would do rather than actually being in that situation and performing the action they select. Perceptual research has largely been concerned with how we know an object's size, color, shape, distance, and path of motion. Only recently have we started to study our perception of what objects are doing (e.g., Is that ball bouncing or rolling?) and what people can do with them (e.g., Can I reach that switch using this stick?).

In summary, many factors have been at work to produce a generally unsatisfactory state of design for human use. There are, however, good reasons to suppose that the next century will see great improvements in the quality of design.

A Coming Golden Age of Design

The next century will see more effective design being both demanded and delivered. The demand will arise for economic factors, while delivery will be made possible by a deeper cooperation between basic science researchers and applied psychologists. In addition, new conceptions of how people and their creations operate in coordinated interaction so as to accomplish tasks are going to emerge.

Compelling economic forces are developing that will make the costs of bad design increasingly intolerable to manufacturers and consumers. Correspondingly, the rewards of effective design will become sufficient to support the costs of the necessary research and development. I shall cite three examples: complex control systems, consumer products, and office furniture.

The costs of failure in large, complex systems such as computer networks and air-traffic control systems are becoming greater as the systems become larger. In some cases, designers are attempting to reduce operator error by fitting the system to the operator. For example, as part of their development of the next century's air-traffic control system for the United States, IBM is investing heavily in the design of displays that present information to controllers in ways that are easy to perceive and that minimize the cognitive load produced by the system (R. Ochsman, personal communication, September 16, 1992).

The poor design of some consumer devices is leading to noticeably awkward attempts to make them more usable. For example, you can avoid the frustrations involved in programming your VCR to record a program by purchasing a secondary control device that just entered the marketplace or by purchasing a new VCR that simplifies this function. With the new device, when the proper code number for the program is punched in, the correct channel is set, and the VCR is switched on or off at the appropriate times. Such code numbers are now printed in many newspaper program guides or may be purchased via a 900-telephone number. As of November 1992, *Newsweek* magazine (November 23, 1992) reported that over six million of these devices had already been sold! If consumers are willing to go to this trouble and expense to avoid the consequences of bad design, then they will be willing to pay the cost of good design in the first place. Alert entrepreneurs will eventually provide better designed appliances and educate consumers as to their availability and cost effectiveness.

Finally, effective human factors design is profitable in the workplace. Ergonomically designed office furniture, for example, can be quite expensive relative to the traditional models. However, as Marvin and Marilyn Dainoff (1986) point out, good ergonomic design presents a no-lose situation. Employees appreciate the comfort provided by good equipment, and management increases profits because improved morale and productivity quickly repay the costs of the well-designed furniture. This is not just wishful thinking: The Dainoffs cite a number of studies showing good design of workstations decreases physical discomfort and absenteeism as well as lowering rates of error by data entry workers.

These economic factors will lead designers and manufacturers to make better use of the presently available human factors principles and to demand new and more powerful principles. I predict that university-based researchers will play a large role in this development, in part for economic reasons. Some universities and granting agencies are revising their missions to encourage more applied research and to promote implementation of the results of that research. The federal government is planning to allocate an increasing percentage of its research money to projects directed toward solution of applied problems. Within the academic world, a new model is being devised for what is being called the "Metropolitan university" (Hathaway, Muhollan, & White, 1990). In contrast to the major research university model, metropolitan universities will, among other changes, reward faculty for becoming engaged in the economic life of their communities, using their expertise to help businesses and government agencies operate more effectively.

Will basic researchers respond? I think that they will, and not merely for economic gain. I predict that they will find that applied problems are not superficial and cannot be solved merely by clever application of old ideas. Instead, solutions to applied problems will require the development of deeper theories of the nature of the human mind and of its operation in everyday life. Thus, both basic research and applied practice will benefit.

Cognitive Science and Design

My main concern for the remainder of this chapter is to document the value of a relatively new approach to perception. Before doing so, it is important to point out that discoveries in other areas of cognitive science, including some presented in other chapters of this book, will have a growing impact on what design problems will have to be faced in the future and how they will be solved. First, some new discoveries will help us avoid current control problems by removing the need for human operators. Neural networks, for example, are being created to have the ability to learn to perform increasingly complex tasks. In the next century, we can therefore expect to see more and more manufacturing processes, ones now requiring humans to operate complex machines, being controlled by neural network computers.

We are also coming to understand the sorts of knowledge and skills that are utilized by experts to perform their jobs—for example, that radiologists call on to interpret X-ray plates, accountants to discover traces of fraud, and air-traffic controllers to detect impending collisions. As we learn more about exactly what constitutes expertise at a particular job, we shall be able more effectively to teach those skills to new employees. In addition, research into skilled performance involves discovering just what information the expert uses to perform a task. The human factors engineer can use these discoveries to design displays that present the most useful information prominently to the operator.

Design issues will also be influenced by advances in our knowledge about the varieties of intellect, the way people learn different classes of material, and the processes of memory, For example, as we learn more about what intellectual skills are needed in particular jobs, we shall be better able to select workers who can meet the demands of the job and will have less need to redesign the jobs to fit workers' limitations. For consumer products, deeper understanding of learning and memory will aid in the writing of instructions that will allow people to use appliances that cannot be designed to operate in a simple fashion.

Finally, I expect to see the results of different branches of cognitive research combined to solve design problems. For instance, in dealing with the information needed to operate a complex system, there is a trade-off to be made between how much information is to be stored in the operator's memory and how much is to be presented in visual displays. When designers better understand the limits of the operator's memory capacities, they will be able to determine what must be displayed on the control panel. A similar trade-off occurs between calculations incorporating information about the state of the system being controlled: Calculations that would overload the operator if done mentally will need to be performed by computer and the results shown to the operator. Thus, effective design will require knowledge of operators' perceptual skills, memory, and reasoning.

Design and the Ecological Approach to Perception and Action

Of the many different theoretical perspectives being used in cognitive science today, I believe that the ecological approach to perception and the guidance of action will make the greatest contributions to design. This approach, first developed by the late James J. Gibson, is concerned with some of the same issues that are vital to human factors designers.[1] To show how this approach applies to problems of design, I discuss several ecological principles of perception, presenting both basic research findings which illustrate their operation, and examples of their implications for design. Before discussing these principles, I must first explain what is meant by the term *information,* a concept that is central to the ecological approach.

Many theories of perception have assumed that our perceptual systems receive only ambiguous cues about the present state of the environment. For example, while both the world itself and our perception of it are three-dimensional, the image of the world that falls on the retina of the eye is only two-dimensional. This produces a problem in understanding how distance is perceived: Is the image of an object on your retina being produced by a small object that is close to you or by a larger object that is farther away? Under the assumption of ambiguous cues, a central question for the basic researcher is how the perceptual system uses ambiguous cues in the image to arrive at accurate perception of the environment.

In contrast, the ecological approach assumes that there is unambiguous information about the environment available to people's perceptual systems. That is, for every perceived aspect of the world, there is some pattern of light available to the eye (or some pattern of sound available to the ear, etc.) that is produced only by that aspect of the world. The detection of this pattern is all that is required to perceive the relevant aspect of the world. The central puzzle for the basic researcher is, therefore, to discover just what patterns inform the perceiver about particular aspects of the environment.

Ecological analyses of perceptual information have led to some surprising discoveries. For example, we have found that there is information not just for simple properties of an object, such as its size, shape, and distance, but for more complex properties such as its mass and elasticity. In addition, there is information for the guidance of actions. Examples of these types of information and their future use by designers are illustrated in the five principles I now discuss.

Principle 1: Information is available to all the senses. This principle is not unique to the ecological perceptive and is so obvious that examples from laboratory research are not needed. You can, after all, both see and smell the consequences of a toaster failing to pop-up on time. This principle does, however, suggest a class of design innovations: If we can effectively use multisensory information when we are in direct contact with our environment, it seems reasonable to suppose that we can do so with displays that provide mediated contact with the state of a complex system.

Gaver, Smith, and O'Shea (1991) have demonstrated the value of adding sounds to visual displays. They simulated a cola bottling plant in which pairs of operators performed various functions—monitored and adjusted the machines that produced fizzy water, added the kola nuts, heated the mixture to produce cola, and filled and capped the bottles. The operators' goals were to produce as many filled bottles as they could without overflowing tanks, breaking bottles, and so on. Each member of a pair of operators worked at a separate control display and could view only a part of the plant at any one time. The efficiency of operators was measured under two conditions: one with only visual information and the other with both auditory and visual information available. The auditory information included simulations of rhythmic sounds of machines operating smoothly, "whooshing" sounds like that made by a blow torch for the heaters, clanking for the bottle dispenser, splashing for overflows, and crashing glass when bottles broke.

Gaver and his colleagues found that, while the inclusion of sounds was not always helpful (the sudden silence of a machine that jammed did not always catch the operator's attention), their availability generally improved performance. Regular rhythms were taken as evidence of normal operation, while splashes or breakage effectively drew attention to problems. Sound also aided coordination between operations: An operator watching the visual display for her part for the plant would sometimes hear a problem in the other's part (e.g., bottles overflowing).

She could then adjust operations in her section (e.g., slow delivery of cola) to aid her partner's attempts to fix the problem.

It is important to note that the sounds used in this example were not arbitrary, but closely simulated those made by actual events in a real factory. Since the ecological approach is concerned with discovering just what patterns of sound, light, and so on, inform the perceiver about what events are occurring in the world, their research strategies can aid designers in discovering new information that can be incorporated into control displays.

Principle 2: Perceptual information specifies events and serves to guide action. Events in the environment can be perceived by detecting "higher-order" information and need not be constructed by the cognitive system from "lower-order" patterns. This principle is easiest explained by example.

Consider the following perceptual problem: How is the perceiver to know when he will make contact with an object that is moving straight toward him at a constant velocity? One solution, using what could be called lower-order variables, would be to perceive both the object's current velocity and distance and then calculate the time-to-contact by dividing distance by velocity. Notice that this approach requires perception of two aspects of the environment and a mental calculation that derives the desired result from them. David Lee's (1976) analysis of this situation shows that there is a "higher-order" pattern in the light to the eye that specifies time-to-contact. As the object approaches the perceiver, its image expands on the retina at a rate determined both by its velocity and distance. The rate of change of the size of the object's image, divided by the size of the image, is always equal to distance divided by velocity. This ratio, called tau, therefore specifies time-to-contact. If the observer can detect tau, then time-to-contact can be perceived directly without knowledge of distance or velocity. Lee and others have shown that this pattern is used by perceivers.

This sort of analysis also reveals how perceptual information can guide action. For example, Lee has shown that if the first-time derivative of tau remains at a constant value of, -0.5, then motion will stop just as the observer and object meet. An observer wishing to move toward an object and come to a smooth stop can therefore do so by monitoring the value of the derivative of tau and adjusting his speed so that its value remains fixed at -0.5.

I believe that perceptual information such as tau will be exploited in the future to improve the design of displays used by operators of complex systems. Until designers know what higher-order information is used by operators to control the system, it is necessary to provide them with the values of many simple variables. This leaves operators with the task of combining variables mentally in order to know the status of the relevant aspect of the system. This approach can lead to perceptual overload—that is, too much information to process at one time as well as cognitive overload—that is, mental integration to perform without error. Vicente and Rasmussen (1990) provide a clear, though hypothetical, example of these problems. Figure 19.1 shows a person attempting to tie his shoelaces on the basis of a set of fifteen gauges that show the individual X, Y, and Z coordinates of each shoelace, each robot arm, and the shoe. The task is clearly impossible under these conditions. To produce effective control displays for even moderately

Figure 19.1. A device for tieing your shoe using low-level information. (From K.J. Vicente & J. Rasmussen, 1990. "The ecology of human–machine systems II: Mediating direct perception in complex work domains." *Ecological Psychology, 2,* p. 214. Copyright © 1990 by Lawrence Erlbaum Associates. Reprinted by permission.)

complex tasks, we must make use of people's skills at using higher-order information, displaying only the relevant variables in order to reduce the perceptual and cognitive demands on the operator.

While I do not believe that control displays will make much use of taus themselves, they do provide an illustration of how ecological analyses of information might be used by designers. Suppose an operator needs to move together two objects that she cannot see directly, stopping them just as they make contact. The designer of the control panel for this task could employ tau in several ways. For example, if television displays of the motion were to be used, then one camera should be mounted on one of the objects so as to show the expansion pattern as the objects approach each other. The tau analysis could also be used in an indirect fashion: For example, let a computer calculate the value of the time derivative of tau from traditional distance and velocity measures and display it on a meter. Deviations from the value -0.5 would tell the operator that the objects' velocities needed to be changed.

Just what information is relevant to real-world problems of control remains to be discovered. The point of the tau example is that information relevant to control does exist, and that it will often be worth the designer's trouble to discover the information that applies to her situation. Finally, notice that basic researchers can benefit from participation in this search: It will provide them with new situations to analyze and with new opportunities to assess the use of information by perceivers.

Principle 3: The affordances of objects often can be perceived. The ecological position claims that people can perceive the opportunities for action that an object provides—that is, its affordances—as well as its size, shape, color, and so on. Thus, while you can see that an object is cylindrical with a length of one foot and a diameter of two inches, you can also see that it is graspable and can be used to hit another object. Research by Eleanor J. Gibson and her colleagues (1987) has illustrated this principle, showing that young children can perceive the types of locomotion afforded by different surfaces. The children were placed in front of two different surfaces and asked to locomote across them. One consisted of an undulating piece of cloth placed under a thick sheet of clear glass, while the other showed a flat, nonmoving piece of cloth, also under a sheet of glass. Simply by seeing these surfaces, the children were able to chose to walk across the surface visually specified as rigid and to crawl across the one specified as flexible.

The concept of affordance both allows us to understand just what is wrong with the designs of many commonplace objects and provides a way to redesign them to operate more easily. Hard-to-operate devices often provide little perceptual information as to how they are to be used or, worse, are shaped so as to mislead the user. In his book *The Psychology of Everyday Things,* Donald Norman points out that our confusion about whether to push or pull certain doors arises in this fashion. A flat metal plate flush on a door invites you to place your hand flat on that surface and push, while one with a graspable handle invites you to grasp it and pull. However, when we are presented with a flat plate raised an inch or two from the surface of the door, we are likely to see it as something to be pushed rather than pulled. Such handles often have "pull" printed on them to correct the effects of its misleading appearance. The lesson for designers is clear: Design objects so that their affordances are as obvious as possible.

Although I think that the habit of attending to affordances will be helpful to designers, both basic researchers and designers can benefit from cooperative research. The designer would be aided by the discovery of general principles: Exactly what configurations lead us to see an object as pushable or to see a control as needing to be turned rather than pressed? It is just these sorts of questions that can be answered by basic researchers. On the other hand, researchers need to know the answers to these questions to develop more complete theories of perception and performance.

Principle 4: Affordances are scaled to body size. Research on affordances has led to the realization that the sizes of things are perceived in *body-scaled* terms rather than in terms of conventional units such as inches or meters. Warren (1984), for example, presented people with stairs of various riser heights and asked them to categorize each as "climbable" or "unclimbable." A simple biomechanical analysis showed that the maximum climbable riser is one that is about 88 percent of the total leg length, and the subjects perceived as the highest climbable risers those at precisely this ratio. That is, they perceived the affordance accurately and did so in units defined by the size of their limbs.

Warren also found that the riser height subjects preferred to use was about 0.25 times their leg length, close to the biomechanically most efficient fraction of 0.26. Thus, efficiency of use is also perceived and is done so in body-scaled terms. Similar analyses have been performed for the size of doorways that can be walked through without turning the shoulders (Warren & Whang, 1987) and for the heights of surfaces on which one can comfortably sit (Mark, 1987).

These analyses provide a way to improve the standards used in architectural design and in other areas where the sizes of things are important to efficient use. Warren (1985) cites three problems with the body-size data presently available. First, the data are strictly anthropometric—that is, according to sizes of body parts. They are not scaled with respect to specific actions to be performed. Second, the data do not tell you about *optimum sizes* (ones allowing the most efficient or comfortable action) or *critical sizes* (ones at which the action can no longer be performed). Finally, architects and other designers often don't use the data, preferring to rely on other rules of thumb.

Body-scaled standards, however, can be used to design objects that are better suited to human use. For example, Warren (1985) suggests that architectural standards are more conservative than needed to accommodate shorter people and are needlessly energy inefficient for the majority: While some standards recommend riser heights of 5 to 7 inches, a height of 7.5 inches is both below the critical size for the shortest 5 percent of adults and closer to the optimum size for those with longer legs.

Extensions of this approach to sizes of tools handles, workbench heights, distances to control switches, and so on, are easy to imagine. More subtle extensions may also be of value. For example, if the optimum size of tool handle for one group of users is close to the critical size for another group, the manufacturer has objective grounds on which to produce two sizes of handles. The approach can also be used to develop defensible criteria for operator selection. In some situations we cannot design equipment to fit a wide range of operators but must select operators to fit the equipment. Arbitrary requirements, such as minimum overall height or lifting strength, can be unfair to prospective employees and may invite lawsuits from those not hired. Standards based on body-scaled sizes tied to the action to be performed can provide an objective and legally more defensible way to select operators.

Principle 5: Perception and cognition work together to produce people's understanding of the operation of physical systems. I must admit that is not actually a principle of the ecological approach. (Ecological psychologists are rarely concerned with understanding how cognition and perception work together.) However, I believe that human factors psychologists will be able to exploit people's perceptual skills even when cognitive processes are involved.

Sometimes perception provides strikingly accurate knowledge of a physical system and does so even when cognitive beliefs are incorrect. For example, the time it takes a pendulum to swing back and forth one time is proportional to the square root of its length: Longer pendulums move more slowly. In studies I have conducted (Pittenger, 1990), it turned out that people have little conscious knowledge of the period–length relation. Many people I have tested did not know that longer pendulums move more slowly and nearly none could say just how long a pendulum of a specified length would take to go back and forth. However, perceptual knowledge of pendulums is very accurate. If pendulums are driven artificially so that their periods are not correct for their lengths, deviations of even a few tenths of a second can be detected, and the motion is seen as anomalous by viewers. Such perceptual knowledge has implications for design: Mock pendulum clocks driven by a motor will be annoying if the natural period–length relation is violated; video games will be more acceptable if spaceships do not make physically impossible 90-degree turns.

Understanding the operation of a system with many parts requires the use of one's cognitive skills: You need to remember which pedal controls the gasoline flow and which the brakes, comprehend the role of the battery, and so on. Even here, however, perception can play a role. Norman (1988) provides some examples in his discussion of what he calls "natural mappings." He points out that stoves with the heating elements arranged in rectangular fashion and the controls arranged in a straight line are difficult to use since it is hard to remember which control is connected to which element. But, the user need not remember the connections if a natural mapping is used—that is, one that allows you to *see* the pairing of controls and heating elements. Figure 19.2 illustrates a configuration that provides a natural mapping. It is worth noting that the layouts of the controls and the elements are not identical. This shows that there is a basic science question to be solved: Just what geometric relations provide natural mappings?

In more complex systems natural mappings are not sufficient to guide control. When a system has multiple components, each with multiple inputs needing control and interacting with one another, the spatial layout and functional operation do not correspond. A more sophisticated approach is, therefore, needed. In their theoretical essay on the ecology of complex work domains, Vicente and Rasmussen (1990) argue that the search for effective control requires us to devise ways to make subtle interactions of system properties directly visible. They analyze the control of a thermal-hydraulic system consisting of reservoirs and water supply systems. The operator's task is to control valves, pumps, and heaters in order to keep the water in the reservoirs at prescribed temperatures, and, at the same time, to avoid overflowing the reservoirs or heating them while they are empty.

The task is made difficult by a number of factors, including the pattern of interconnections between the pumps and the reservoirs, and time lags in the heating process. The operator must also take into account the equations governing the physics of the system. For example, the temperature (T) of the water in a reservoir is, ignoring some constants, equal to the total reservoir energy (E) divided by the volume of the water in the reservoir (V). How can the operator control the valves and the heaters so that the reservoir can be kept at the target temperature while keeping it from running dry? It will, of course, be important to have a diagram showing the connections between the pumps and the tanks and to provide gauges showing water volume and temperature. However, with these alone, the cognitive demand on the operator is high, since the control of water flow and the heaters

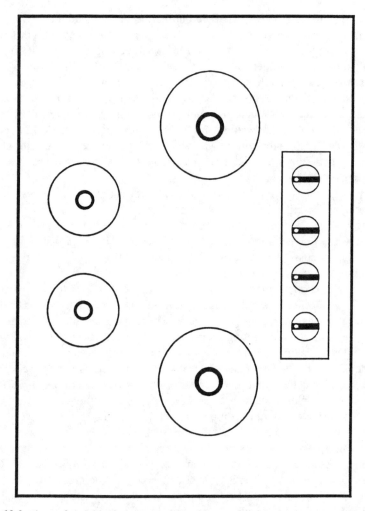

Figure 19.2. A configuration for components of a stove that provides a natural mapping between controls and the burner to which each is connected.

requires an understanding of how all the parameters interact to determine each other's values.

Vicente and Rasmussen have devised a way to make this functional aspect of the system visible. It is surprisingly simple, consisting of a display that shows a right triangle whose dimensions change in proportion to changes in the parameters. Figure 19.3 illustrates a right triangle with two sides, E and T, and the angle a opposite to side E. They exploit the geometric fact that $T = E/\tan a$ by having the size of side E be determined by the total reservoir energy, the size of T by the water temperature, and $\tan a$ by the volume of water V. As the parameters change, so does the shape of the triangle, making visible the interactive effects of changes in settings of the pumps and the heater. This information will help guide the

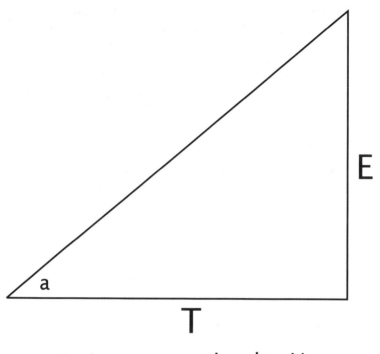

tan a proportional to V

Figure 19.3. A display for showing the relation between the total energy *E*, temperature *T*, and volume *V* of water in a reservoir. Changes in the lengths of the sides of the triangle and the size of angle *a* show how changes of the values of the parameters interact according to the equation $T = E/V$.

system's operation. For example, suppose the temperature is correct—that is, the horizontal line of the triangle is the right length. If the operator then sees the vertical side of the triangle shortening, she will know the volume of water that is dropping and the amount of water that must be pumped in. Then, as the volume of water increases, the drop in temperature will be indicated by a shortening of the horizontal line. The operator can increase heat flow to move the system to the target temperature, watching the triangle's horizontal side lengthen as the temperature increases.

Concluding Comments

While many home appliances are very difficult to operate and there is a reason to be concerned about operator error in increasingly complex systems such as nuclear reactors, these problems are solvable. At least in the human factors sense, the things we have created are not beyond our control. I think the next century will see a revolution in the design of things better suited for human perceptual, cognitive, and physical abilities and limitations. Economic pressures are going to force producers to invest in better design. Moreover, ideas from cognitive psychology are going to play a major role in developing new approaches to design. In addition, basic research is going to undergo some fundamental changes, more often attempting to solve applied problems. This shift will influence both the applications of psychological theory and the nature of our theories.

Acknowledgment

Preparation of this chapter was supported by the Marie Wilson Howells Bequest of the Department of Psychology of the University of Arkansas at Little Rock. My thanks to R. C. Payne for her patience in typing the manuscript.

Note

1. The best short introduction to the basic science aspects of the ecological approach is Mace (1977). Fuller treatments by J. J. Gibson himself are in Gibson (1979) and in a collection of his essays edited by Reed and Jones (1982). For applications of the approach to human systems design, see Flach (1990) and Vicente and Rasmussen (1990). More complete treatments will soon appear in Flach, Hancock, Caird, and Vicente (in press). Finally, Norman's *The Psychology of Everyday Things* (1988) is a good introduction to human factors psychology. It is especially valuable since it includes discussions of how all the branches of contemporary cognitive science can contribute to better design.

References

Dainoff, M. J., & Dainoff, M. H. (1986). *People and productivity: A manager's guide to ergonomics in the electronic office.* Toronto: Holt, Rinehart and Winston of Canada.

Flach, J. M. (1990) The ecology of human–machine systems I: *Ecological Psychology, 2,* 191–205.

Flach, J. M., Hancock, P. A., Caird, J. K., & Vicente, K. (Eds.). (in press). *The ecology of human–machine systems.* Hillsdale, N.J.: Erlbaum.

Gaver, W. W., Smith, R. B., & O'Shea, T. (1991). Effective sounds in complex systems: The ARKola simulation. In S. Robertson, G. Olson, & J. Olson (Eds.), *Proceedings of the Association for Computing Machinery's Special Interest Group on Computer–Human Interaction* (pp. 85–90). New York: Association for Computing Machinery.

Gibson, E. J., Ricco, G., Schumuckler, M. A., Stoffregen, T. A., Rosenberg, D., & Taomina, J. (1987). Detection of traversability of surfaces by crawling and walking infants. *Journal of Experimental Psychology: Human Perception and Performance, 13,* 533–544.

Gibson, J. J. (1979). *The ecological approach to visual perception.* Boston: Houghton-Mifflin.

Hathaway, C. E., Muhollan, P. E., & White, K. A. (1990). Metropolitan universities: Models for the twenty-first century. *Metropolitan Universities, 1* (1), 9–20.

Lee, D. N. (1976). A theory of visual control of braking based on information about time-to-collision. *Perception. 5,* 437–459.

Mace, W. M. (1977). James J. Gibson's strategy for perceiving: Ask not what's inside your head, but what your head's inside of. In R. Shaw & J. Bransford (Eds.), *Perceiving, acting and knowing: Toward an ecological psychology* (pp. 43–65). Hillsdale, N.J.: Erlbaum.

Mark, L. S. (1987). Eyeheight-scaled information about affordances: A study of sitting and stair climbing. *Journal of Experimental Psychology: Human Perception and Performance, 10,* 683–703.

Norman, D. A. (1988). *The psychology of everyday things.* New York: Basic Books.

Pittenger, J. B. (1990). Detection of violations of the law of pendulum motion: Observers' sensitivity to the relation between period and length. *Ecological Psychology, 2,* 55–81.

Reed, E. & Jones, R. (Eds). (1982). *Reasons for realism: Selected essays of James J. Gibson.* Hillsdale, N.J.: Erlbaum.

Vicente, K. J., & Rasmussen, J. (1990). The ecology of human–machine systems II: Mediating "direct perception" in complex work domains. *Ecological Psychology, 2,* 207–249.

Warren, W. H. (1984). Perceiving affordances: Visual guidance of stair climbing. *Journal of Experimental Psychology: Human Perception and Performance, 10,* 683–703.

Warren, W. H. (1985, June). *Environmental design as the design of affordances.* Paper presented at the Third International Conference on Event Perception and Action, Uppsala, Sweden.

Warren, W. H., & Whang, S. (1987). Visual guidance of walking through apertures: Body-scaled information for affordances. *Journal of Experimental Psychology: Human Perception and Performance, 13,* 371–383.

VI

MAJOR THEMES AND COMMON THREADS

20

Perennial Issues for the Next Century

DOMINIC W. MASSARO
AND ROBERT L. SOLSO

In this concluding chapter, we simply want to yank some threads running through these varied chapters. We realize that our discussion will not capture the heart of these highly original and creative pieces, but we offer it as an integrative framework for what we see as perennial issues in our discipline. Most of our contributors explored well beyond the science of the mind by anticipating the state of the world at large. This choice was viewed as more or less mandatory because psychology will necessarily be immensely changed by developments outside its discipline. This influence is what Hunt calls a pull. It is difficult to imagine how psychology would have evolved (if it were to have evolved at all) without the technology developed during the Industrial Revolution. Would psychology have leapt out of philosophy departments without chronometers, tachistoscopes, memory drums, 3 by 5 cards (oops), or audiorecorders? In like fashion, we expect that the ongoing revolutions in telecommunications, computer delivery systems, genetic engineering, and natural science will impact our science in important ways.

Notwithstanding these advances, the perennial issues will remain. Some of these were anticipated by William James over a century ago and are still around today. As with all puzzles, we can depend on the James boys to set the stage. As you know, Henry James was well known for his psychological novels, and William James for his novelistic writing about psychology. Indeed, William James wrote a two-volume treatise that was to set the agenda for this new science for decades to come. It was a science riddled with paradoxes, and no one made these paradoxes more apparent than William James and his followers. Gordon W. Allport even wrote an essay on the productive paradoxes of William James, acknowledging that they represented some of the persistent riddles of psychology—riddles that are still current if we choose to confront them. Although less questioned today, we do not have an answer to the fundamental question studied by psychological science—the relationship between mind and brain.

Mind–Body Problem

Psychology has inherited a set of metaphysical puzzles that will not be easily solved. Central to the science of the mind in the twenty-first century will be the question of how the mind is related to the body. This question is called the mind–body problem in philosophy, and psychologists have tended to side-step this issue, wondering where they might find insight on the subject. Thus, we don't see our contributors taking strong positions about our mental and biological worlds. Implicitly, however, several of them (Hunt, Solso, and Kosslyn) appear to view the biological level as primitive, with perhaps the mental world simply an epiphenomenon. Gustav Fechner, who initiated the study of psychophysics in the middle of the nineteenth century, was an epiphenomenalist: The mental world for him was a direct consequence of the physical world. In many respects, psychophysics has failed (see Lockhead, 1992), and a simple biological account is not sufficient today, nor will it be in the twenty-first century (as emphasized in Mandler's chapter).

There has been no shortage of potential solutions ever since Plato (and Descartes) first separated mind from body. Gregory notes how many physical phenomena were attributed mental status until a better understanding was achieved. Psychologists, following in the tradition of William James, vacillate among epiphenomenalist, parallelist, and interactionist frameworks. For the epiphenomenalist, mind has no import. Mind and body simply coexist without interaction in parallelism. And mind and body interact in both directions in interactionism. The mind–body problem and consciousness received renewed attention at the end of the twentieth century. Players in the game covered the spectrum of disciplines, including philosophy, psychology, physics, biology, and mathematics. The volumes being written and the continual debate probably portend that the mind–body problem will remain a problem. We shall probably discover that no single solution to the mind–body problem will be sufficient in the same manner that both wave and particle theories of light are necessary.

Consciousness

The problem of consciousness goes beyond the mind–body problem because we can have the latter without the former. That is, mental processes do not have to be conscious, and we have learned that many are not. Given the power of the unconscious, consciousness is not an essential topic for the resolution of the mind–body problem. Even without consciousness, we still have to explain how the physical body supports these nonconscious mental processes. Freud, more than anyone, heightened our awareness of the important role of the unconscious. Both Mandler and Kosslyn acknowledge Freud's impact on the field of the past, but Kosslyn sees a major role for Freud in the future. Even if Kosslyn's prophesies are fulfilled, however, it is unlikely Freud will get the credit.

The well-known psychologist and historian of psychology E. G. Boring asked, "What properties would a potato have to have in order to be conscious?" The properties for consciousness included memory, learning, insight, attitudes, ability to react to environment, and ability to symbolize. By Boring's definition, these properties would make up a conscious system. But some day, we may see all of them in the nonconscious systems of tomorrow's computers.

Levels of Description

Consonant with our prophecy about the mind–body problem, we believe that several levels of description will be necessary to understanding psychological phenomena. Like our contributors, we believe that three levels of description seem necessary. David Marr (1982) described three levels at which any machine carrying out an information-processing task must be understood: computational, algorithmic, and implementational. In computer terms, the computational level is an abstract description of the problem to be solved, the algorithmic level is the software program to solve the problem, and the implementation level is the system it is being run on. The computational level concerns the nature of the problem being solved. It entails the information that is available and the mapping of this information to another kind of information. It is clear that evolutionary history can inform this computational level of analysis. The algorithmic level entails the operations that transform the information from one type to another. This level specifies the representations for the input and output and the mapping between them. Proximal causation seems most productive in illuminating the algorithmic level. The implementation or hardware level describes the physical realization of the algorithmic level. Both distal and proximal causation would appear to be relevant to the hardware level. Hunt's prophecy of a lesser role for information processing must be implicitly guided by his devaluation of the algorithmic level. It is also based on his belief that problem solving cannot be reduced to information-processing terms (see Sternberg's characterization of the connectionists). If it is, however, then information processing will be a good route to understanding. Some evidence for the value of information-processing analysis of problem solving came from studies demonstrating pattern-based reasoning, as nicely described by Levelt in decision-making.

Mandler, Levelt, and perhaps Kosslyn place great faith in a computational level to advance understanding. Murdock, Massaro, and Jenkins appear to be concerned with the algorithmic level. Our biological enthusiasts (Hunt, Solso, Sommers, and Kosslyn) look forward to the implementational level of the brain. This problem of levels of description is necessarily central to a psychology of the mind. Most of our contributors acknowledge the wonder of how the mind arises from the body, but none sees it as an insurmountable problem. The majority of the authors place great faith in the potential of brain measures to explain psychological functioning. All of us trained in the scientific method naturally have respect for the virtues of reductionism. Murdock, on the other hand, is skeptical of looking inside the head. He was dumbfounded when he opened the hatches of his first computer (And why not? Its CPU and 16K of memory took up the better part of the room.) Brain scientists know a lot more about the wiring of the brain than

Murdock knew about electronics. He should have peeked over the shoulder of the DEC repair person when the machine was being serviced. Perhaps he would have gained a greater respect for the hardware.

What Murdock is referring to, of course, is the well-established dichotomy between the software and hardware of computers and people. These two traditional levels were included in David Marr's (1982) trichotomy, as articulated nicely in Levelt's chapter. Levelt articulates a strong case for the importance of the computational level, and its relative neglect compared to our addiction to the process level (processitis; perhaps we should place the elimination of this disease high on the genetic engineer's list). Along with most of our contributors, we are convinced of the value of the functional (process) level in our study of mind and behavior. Gregory puts it simply but effectively, "The dualism of cognition is not different entities . . . , but rather different *aspects* of the same thing."

Identifiability

A science of the mind rests on the assumption that we can provide a functional account of how it works. This idea is based on the assumption that one functional account can be distinguished from another. Many of us would be out of work if these operating assumptions were shown to be false. The question of distinguishing among alternative functional accounts is called the *identifiability* issue. It is possible that our empirical science of mind will not permit us to distinguish among alternative theories. Most psychologists have charged ahead without much concern for the identifiability of their pet theories and ideas. Recently, however, there has been a growing concern (Anderson, 1990). Many cognitive scientists believe that the biological level can constrain the types of processes occurring at the algorithmic level and overcome problems of identifiability. However, with billions and billions of interconnected neurons, it difficult to imagine how the biological level will necessarily constrain the algorithmic level. We see a two-way street between levels and mutual constraints. The algorithmic level will constrain the biological as much as the reverse.

Should we be concerned about identifiability? Let us consider a specific example of a lack of identifiability. There are two well-known methods of multiplication: successive addition and logarithms. In the first case, 5×7 is computed by adding 7 to 0 five times. In the second case, the logarithm of 5 is added to the logarithm of 7, and then the antilog of the sum is taken. The same input–output functions are observed for both methods. For psychology, this means that some model of an experimental result is not unique. Some other model can be manufactured to give exactly the same predictions. How can we overcome this identifiability problem? Is the search for function, psychological process, or mechanism plagued with identifiability problems?

Consistent with several of our prophets, we think that progress can be made. Scientific inquiry can potentially choose among equally accurate models by evaluating the models on the basis of parsimony and testing among viable models using the principles of falsification and strong inference (Massaro, 1987, 1989). Extending the data base is also a valuable strategy for distinguishing models that make identical input–output predictions. To return to the multiplication example, reaction times (RTs) are a valuable dependent variable. There is an illustrative series of experiments on how children add two numbers. Experiments have been able to distinguish between two viable models of addition by measuring reaction times to different problems. The results indicate that solving the problem 6 + 3 takes about the same amount of time as solving the problem 4 + 3. However, these problems take longer than 7 + 1. In total, the results indicate that, at one stage of development, the child recognizes the numbers, chooses the larger one, and then adds the smaller number by counting from the larger to the smaller in steps of one. These same results cast doubt on the previously mentioned log–antilog model. Thus the identifiability problem is not insurmountable.

Complementarity of Evolutionary and Psychological Descriptions

Psychology is viewed by some as a pastime until biologists "do their thing." Like Mandler, we see the essential irreducible value of psychological descriptions; the functional level will always be essential to a science of mind, even in the twenty-first century. Psychology and evolutionary biology necessarily ask different questions. These two types of questions concern proximal and ultimate causes of (or influences on) behavior (Alcock, 1989). Proximal causes address the immediate environmental stimuli and the immediate processes that influence behavior. Ultimate causes address the evolutionary history of the organism. In simpler terms, proximate descriptions focus on *how,* whereas ultimate descriptions focus on *why.* For example, we might ask what environmental information the gannet (a large seabird) uses to signal closing its wings before landing on the water. Ultimate causes might address why the gannet closes its wings when landing— what evolutionary significance might it have. Psychologists have usually been concerned with proximate influences. For example, what are the visual features actually used in letter recognition, how are these features combined, and how is a decision made given this information? Ultimate causes, such as the evolution of the visual system to detect edges and other properties of the letters, are of less interest.

An interesting example of the importance of the distinction between proximal and ultimate causation has to do with the multiple cues and systems that are available for seeing the world in depth. Stereopsis developed rather late in the evolution of the binocular (visual) system, perhaps because it evolved only to overcome the camouflage of prey. But this visual process occurs rather early during the time course of processing a given scene, even though it occurred later in evolutionary time. Thus, evolutionary history (ultimate causation) and immediate causation (proximal causation) address different aspects of the phenomenon of seeing. More generally, behaviorists and Freudians may have simply differed in terms of their concern for proximal and distal causation. Behaviorists were concerned with proximal influences, and Freudians with more distal ones. This distinction may capture most of their differences.

Convergent and divergent evolution illustrate that ultimate causation does not necessarily constrain proximal causation. Convergent evolution involves the independent acquisition over time through natural selection of similar characteristics in unrelated species. Divergent evolution involves the acquisition of dissimilar characteristics in the same species. Take, for example, the act of seeing. As an example of convergent evolution, an octopus (a cephalopod) and a mammal evolved highly similar solutions to the problem of seeing (Blakemore, 1977). As a case of divergent evolution, some gull species nest on the ground in open grassy areas. When the breeding adults detect a potential egg-eating predator, they emit a volley of loud cries, fly toward it, dive bomb, and defecate on the enemy. As an exception to this mobbing behavior, the kittiwake gull nests on nearly vertical cliffs on the coast. This site precludes mammalian predators and the erratic sea winds limit the threat of large predatory birds (Alcock, 1989). The kittiwake gulls do not mob the occasional enemy who drifts by the nesting site. Once again, the psychologist must explain the proximal causes of behavior whether it evolved by convergent or divergent evolution.

Evolutionary biology reveals that there is a plethora of optimal solutions for survival. For example, in population biology, the species following the r strategy has lots of progeny and spends little energy on each one. In the k strategy, the species has only a few progeny and spends a lot of energy on each one. These two algorithms could not be more different. From the perspective of the psychologist, it is important to know which is operational in a given domain. Like most of our contributors, we view biology as complementary, not as a science that will supersede ours.

The value of a functional descriptive level of behavior reflects our belief that a part of our understanding is necessarily tied to proximal causation. Furthermore, the functional analysis made possible by the functional level will have implications for practice. For example, consider an information-processing analysis of good and poor readers (Stanovich, 1986). Reading a sentence can be described as a sequence of processing stages, going from transduction of the visible text to activation of various letter and word codes to arriving at some meaning of the utterance. It turns out that many poor readers tend to be deficient at the activation of letter and word codes (Perfetti, 1985), and one observes a larger influence of context for these readers. The corresponding brain-level description would differ from the information-processing one. Given the complexity of events at the brain level, some have argued against the possibility of a complete reductionist description (Massaro, 1989; Uttal, 1990). Even if the brain-level description is possible, the information-processing analysis can provide an assessment and a diagnosis for remediation.

Normative Versus Descriptive Theories

Like linguistics, philosophy, economics, and, to some extent, computer science, psychology has an arsenal of prescriptive or normative models like the propositional calculus, the rational man, and the Turing machine. Psychologists have also been concerned with testing the psychological reality of these models. Similar to the enterprise in linguistics, however, testing the psychological reality of these normative models might not be as productive as developing psychological models based on empirical results, and then asking to what extent these models might be considered normative (compare Tversky & Kahneman, 1983, to Massaro & Friedman, 1990). For example, some investigators have documented situations in which people do not use base rates in decision making (Kahneman & Tversky, 1972), and have argued that decision making is not normative (optimal). Other investigators, on the other hand, have addressed the question of the psychological processes involved in decision making and how base-rate information is integrated with other sources of information in the decision-making task (Leon & Anderson, 1974).

The Self

We take the unity of our behavioral and mental life for granted everyday, and yet self remains a riddle. As psychologists, we assume without question the individual as the object of study. Of course, sociologists and neurobiologists target larger and smaller objects: groups and neurons, respectively. But we have discovered a few instances in which the self appears to disintegrate because of brain trauma. Amnesics have little memory of past events, which leave large gaps in the continuity of self. The famous patient H.M. had a portion of his brain removed to treat severe epilepsy. The radical surgery consisted of removal of the hippocampus, which plays an important role in long-term memory. Because H.M. had no memory, he would often say anxiously: "Right now, I'm wondering. Have I done or said anything amiss? You see, at this moment everything looks clear to me, but what happened just before? That's what worries me. It's like waking from a dream. I just don't remember."

Freedom, Determinism, and Intentionality

The riddle of freedom and determinism remains prominent in our inquiry. Science is a deterministic enterprise, but we experience freedom of choice both within and outside scientific inquiry. The question is not well formulated in terms of binary alternatives, but is better addressed as "Just how free are we?" Our wishes, beliefs, and goals are directed at, or are about, objects and events in the world apart from the objects and events themselves (Searle, 1983). How could sensory and brain processes be about or represent anything? How can *aboutness* be an intrinsic feature of the world? Related to this intentionality is intentional causation. A conscious mental state appears to have causal properties; it can push real matter around. Of course, these observations are the bases for an interactionist solution to the mind–body problem.

Future of Experimentation

Both Hunt and Murdock touch on the possible extinction of experimental psychology. Will the field outdistance us? We had qualms in graduate school because our professors towered over us; how could we mere earthlings ever fill their shoes? Our guess is that most graduate students still have similar experiences! Murdock doesn't foresee a division between experimental and theoretical psychologists because he realizes fully what Clyde Coombs observed: "Data without theory are meaningless."

Murdock values the unique set of skills brought into the game by experimental psychologists. But are our skills so specialized that any teenager, equipped with a PC or Mac, cannot play the game? Although we believe we are taught how to do science, most of us have simply been engaged in scientific practice (not necessarily a bad strategy according to Jenkins). However, we can easily stumble and even fall.

Applied Cognitive Psychology

Applied cognitive psychology has delivered and will continue to deliver more humane environments. Pittenger, Norman, and Hunt all offer informative examples of how the science of the mind will enhance the compatibility between the artificial environment and ourselves. From programming VCRs to assembling toys, psychologists will make their noticeable contributions. Norman offers technology (rather than the genetic engineering prophesied by Bower and Solso) as a catalyst for human evolution. Clearly we are all dependent on things that make us smart, whether they be as simple as a spell checker or a simulated model of some complex chemical reaction. Murdock describes distributed memory in our heads, whereas Norman distributes cognition across people. And Bower talks about internal as well as external devices to magnify our cognitive capability.

Norman describes how technology will be an integrated part of our lives from the mundane to the creative. Will there emerge a group of Luddites who will resist removing human control from our everyday living? Although we are all taken with virtual reality, we can still wonder why three-dimensional movies failed in popularity. Certainly the 3-D screen is more realistic than 2-D. As noted by Norman, technology will allow us to change, hide, or otherwise modify our presence. Perhaps this consequence is not revolutionary to those who have accepted more recent arguments for the illusion of the self (Bennett, Hoffman, & Prakash, 1989; Dennett, 1991; Varela, Thompson, & Rosch, 1991). In all that we do, the self may play a lesser role. Perhaps our intentionality might also play a lesser role as we succumb to the amenities of a completely nurturing world.

Even if we have already lost Calvin's ability to fantasize, technology will allow us to explore novel, unexplored worlds. We already know that our body image (or self) seldom agrees with our actual body (or person). Overweight people see themselves as thinner, thinner people see themselves as heavier. Thus our self will not be a deterrent for entering new virtual worlds.

Predicting the Future

Sigmund Freud (1928) observed, "The present . . . must have become the past—before it can yield points of vantage from which to judge the future." In ending this book, we have attempted to pull together some of the major themes touched on by the illustrious contributors who have participated here. What *were* the issues of the twentieth century and what *will be* the important questions for the twenty-first century? If all the ideas in this book about these topics were cataloged, it would yield a long and diverse list; but, and we believe this to be an interesting point, the number of common themes among authors working independently is significant. We find five common themes among the chapters.

The Brain

Future scientists of the mind see an increased reliance on and development of neuroscience. Progress in this area will be greatly influenced by hardware developments in the field of brain-imaging techniques—namely PET, CAT, MRI, and EEG recording instrumentation—and will be conceptually understood through neurally inspired theories of the mind and brain. Clearly, neurocognition, in the minds of these observers, has a rosy future. Jean Mandler seems to sound a contrary notion, which has also been voiced by one of us (Massaro, 1991). No longer is "the science of the mind" to be content with a somewhat passive observation of the activities of people and other creatures, with an aim of discovering cause-and-effect relationships between antecedents and actions. Scientists of the mind—past, present, and future—want to know what goes on *inside* the black box. At present, we see inside the brain with new neurological sensing techniques and prophesize the continuation and enhancement of these techniques, although a brain level of description alone will not be adequate—just as we need to understand a computer's software as well as its hardware.

Multiple Influences and Multiple Levels of Description

Jenkins provides an intriguing case study of the influences of functional experience and organizational structure on learning and performance. For both the performing individual and the fledgling theoretician, we learn that two sources of information are better than one. Learning is facilitated and understanding of that learning is advanced when we have both functional and structural levels of description. The outcome is exactly analogous to Levelt's engaging promotion of the multiple levels of description. After interviewing our founding father, Levelt shows how both computational (structural) and algorithmic (functional) descriptions have advanced psycholinguistics and decision making. Massaro's evidence for speech perception as a prototypical case of pattern recognition is also bolstered by several levels of descriptive analysis. A related theme is found in Sternberg's travelogue, which impresses upon us the futility of narrowly confining ourselves to a single descriptive medium. Lakoff offers a set of new metaphors for the study of mind and behavior. These new metaphors are grounded on new discoveries about conceptual understanding. Given these new findings, Lakoff offers some stimulating ideas about the nature of the person and the self. In all cases, the scientist and the participants in the great game of life have to be open to multiple perspectives in understanding. The interdisciplinary nature of cognitive science offers much opportunity for the future. Given Hank's collaboration with his brother Bill James, we might expect that we will gain even more when the humanities and the arts play a more central role in cognitive science.

Technology

The growing presence of technology in our future was an apparent theme in several of the author's essays. Given the very rapid development of computer technology, genetic engineering, and pharmaceuticals within the last half of the present century, and the revolutionary effects these developments have had on how we perceive the human animal, the prediction of even more fantastic changes are likely events that will both solve old problems and probably alter the way science is done in the next century. Some authors warn of the "unintended consequences" of the unbridled and premature application of technology in this field (see Bower and Solso for examples). These applications are reminiscent of Huxley's prophetic *Brave New World*. While Bower touts the enormous potential for social welfare that such technology promises, Solso is less sanguine. No one can deny the impact that advancing technology will have on our everyday lives. This technology will also impact science. James Jenkins brings virtual reality into the laboratory and Massaro into education and communication, and Sommer travels even further afield with teleportation and other astounding advances.

Social/Developmental Framework

The majority of our authors cast the psychology of the future in a social/developmental framework. In addition to being biological creatures, we are also social creatures, and thus future cognitive psychologists may need to direct their attention to solving some of the problems that new technologies will introduce. Sommer, for example, calls for a cognitive ecology which, presumably, would address both the needs of people and of the environment. In some instances, the contributors emphasize a pragmatic approach to environmental problems, which may be contrary to the hard-nosed, basic-research paradigms championed by experimental psychologists throughout the twentieth century, but may have not abandoned the bothersome twentieth-century theoretical issues, such as the nature of intelligence (see Gardner).

Our contributors speculate on the social and applied consequences of our advancing field. Don Norman explores a new technology—Cognitive Artifacts—that will make us smarter. Norman predicts that future advances in technology will affect our everyday lives—even more than the genetic engineering envisioned by several of our other prophets. Norman also realizes the impact of this technology for various forms of play such as fantasy. Clearly, the blurring of telecommunications, education, and entertainment will change the way we live. Earl Hunt frames his outlook in terms of pushes and pulls. While developments in other disciplines push the study of mind in various directions, societal needs and values also impact what is studied, how the issues are studied, and perhaps what advocacy results from this study.

Robert Sommer takes us on a science (fiction?) adventure of a productive merger between researchers and practitioners to improve the quality of our life. He offers a creative solution of the ageless problem of transferring intellectual discoveries from the ivory towers of academia to our everyday lives. John Pittenger builds within the framework advanced by Turvey and Shaw to improve the applied study of perception and action. He articulates several convincing examples of how science can and should improve our interactions with the artifactual world around us. All of our authors see a better designed, user-friendly world to support our work and play.

An Interdisciplinary Endeavor

A convincing theme found in many papers is the prediction that the science of the mind will become much more interdisciplinary in the future. We find traces of this theme in all of the chapters. Does such a prediction mean that the age of the specialist, born and bred in the twentieth century, is about to be replaced by that of the generalist? Or is this "cry in the darkness" based on the tendency of humans, when peering into a cloudy crystal ball, to say, "Specialists in other areas are likely to have the answers, so that if we pool our intellectual resources, we are likely to solve all problems"? Only time will tell!

The Unavoidable Weakness of Prediction

We close with the obvious caveat that predicting the future is a dangerous enterprise. Hindsight renders most predictions wrong, if not downright silly. Scientists named the Kelvin scale after Lord Kelvin, but certainly not because he claimed that flight was impossible in machines heavier than air. His viewpoint about the impossibility of flight was reinforced by the American astronomer Simon Newcomb in the early part of the twentieth century. Just over a century ago, the telephone patent was refused because no use "for this electronic toy" could be foreseen. Ten years later, the postmaster-general of Great Britain told Parliament that "the telephone could not, and never would be an advantage which could be enjoyed by the large mass of the people." Even the television was viewed as useless by the American radio pioneer Lee DeForest in 1926. We have not been able to document any analogously erroneous predictions of this kind in psychology. We close with the hope that we will quickly see some of our predictions, if not falsified or verified, at least supplanted by advances in our understanding.

References

Adams, M. J. (1990). *Beginning to read.* Cambridge, Mass.: The MIT Press.

Alcock, J. (1989). *Animal behavior.* Sunderland, Mass.: Sinauer.

Anderson, J. R. (1990). *The adaptive control of thought.* Hillsdale, N.J.: Erlbaum.

Bennett, B. M., Hoffman, D. D., & Prakash, C. (1989). *Observer mechanics: A formal theory of perception.* San Diego: Academic Press.

Blakemore, C. (1977). *Mechanics of mind.* New York: Cambridge University Press.

Dennett, D. D. (1991). *Consciousness explained.* Boston: Little, Brown.

Kahneman, D., & Tversky, A. (1972). Subjective probability: A judgment of representativeness. *Cognitive Psychology, 3,* 430–454.

Leon, M., & Anderson, N. H. (1974). A ratio rule from integration theory applied to inference judgments. *Journal of Experimental Psychology, 102,* 27–36.

Lockhead, G. R. (1992) Psychophysical scaling: Judgments of attributes or objects? *Behavioral and Brain Sciences, 15,* 543–601.

Marr, D. (1982). *Vision.* San Francisco: Freeman.

Massaro, D. W. (1987). *Speech perception by ear and eye: A paradigm for psychological inquiry.* Hillsdale, N.J.: Erlbaum.

Massaro, D. W. (1989). *Experimental psychology: An information processing approach.* San Diego, Calif.: Harcourt Brace Jovanovich.

Massaro, D. W., & Friedman, D. (1990). Models of integration given multiple sources of information. *Psychological Review, 97,* 225–252.

Massaro, D. W. (1991). Psychology as a cognitive science. *Psychological Science, 2,* 302–307.

Perfetti, C. A. (1985). *Reading ability.* New York: Oxford University Press.

Searle, J. R. (1983). *Intentionality: An essay in the philosophy of mind.* Cambridge: Cambridge University Press.

Stanovich, K. E. (1986). Matthew effects in reading: Some consequences of individual differences in the acquisition of literacy. *Reading Research Quarterly, 21,* 360–407.

Tversky, A., & Kahneman, D. (1983). Extension versus intuitive reasoning: The conjunction fallacy in probability judgment. *Psychology Review, 90,* 293–315.

Uttal, W. R. (1990). On some two-way barriers between models and mechanisms. *Perception & Psychophysics, 48,* 188–203.

Varela, F. J., Thompson, E., & Rosch, E. (1991). *The embodied mind: Cognitive science and human experience.* Cambridge, Mass.: The MIT Press.

ABOUT THE AUTHORS

Robert L. Solso is an active faculty member, researcher, and writer currently at the University of Nevada, Reno. His Ph.D. degree was earned at St. Louis University and was followed with a postdoctoral year at Stanford University where he has taught on several occasions. In 1981 he was invited to Oxford University where he studied with Donald Broadbent. Dr. Solso has had an enduring interest in international psychology and is a board member of the European Society for the Study of Cognitive Systems. He taught cognitive psychology at Moscow State University through the sponsorship of a Fulbright grant and was a visiting scholar at the Institute of Psychology (Moscow) through support from the National Academy of Sciences (U.S.). He is known for his popular textbook *Cognitive Psychology* and *Cognition and the Visual Arts*.

Gordon H. Bower is a cognitive psychologist who specializes in studies of human learning and memory. Upon completing a Ph.D. degree from Yale University, he accepted a position at Stanford University and has remained there throughout his distinguished career. His research deals with the influence of imagery and organizational factors on memory and recall. Recently, Dr. Bower has investigated the way people's memories are influenced by emotional states. He holds a distinguished chair at Stanford and has served as chair of the department and associate dean. He has been elected president of the Psychonomic Society, The Cognitive Science Society, the Society of Experimental Psychology, the Western Psychological Association, and the American Psychological Society. His honors include the Distinguished Scientific Contribution Award from the American Psychological Association and the Warren Medal from the Society of Experimental Psychology. He is renowned for having been a research advisor for many outstanding cognitive psychologists.

The late Roger W. Sperry was a Trustee Professor Emeritus of Psychobiology at Caltech, best known for his split-brain research for which he was awarded the Nobel Prize in 1981. After completing his doctorate in zoology at the University of Chicago, Dr. Sperry was a research fellow at Harvard. His early work on the growth of brain connections won the President's National Medal of Science. His interactionist model of the mind-brain relation reversed a long tradition in science which disregarded conscious experience in its accounts of brain function. Dr. Sperry saw in this work the key to long-term, high-quality survival, and devoted his work to what he called the "cause of all causes which, if it fails, all others go with it." His last books included *Science and Moral Priority* and *Nobel Prize Conversations*.

Roger N. Shepard, Professor of Psychology at Stanford University, has been long occupied with discovering the universal properties of the mind. After earning his Ph.D. degree from Yale and appointments at Bell Labs and Harvard, he returned to Stanford in 1968, the same year his father, O. Cutler Shepard, retired as chairman of the Department of Materials Science. Throughout most of his distinguished career, he has been concerned with elegant mathematical theories of mental processes; however, Dr. Shepard is also a published poet, accomplished organist, imaginative artist, and the author of an ingenious method for estimating the large-scale structure of the universe. Dr. Shepard has won many awards, including the Warren Medal and the Distinguished Scientific Contribution Award from the American Psychological Association, and has been elected to membership in the National Academy of Sciences.

Howard Gardner is a Harvard Ph.D. and currently serves as Professor of Education and Co-Director of Project Zero at Harvard Graduate School of Education. He was awarded the prestigious MacArthur Prize Fellowship in 1990. He is the author of over 300 articles and 14 books, including *The Mind's New Science* (1985), *Multiple Intelligences: The Theory in Practice* (1993), and *Creating Minds: The Anatomy of Creativity as Seen Through the Lives of Freud, Einstein, Picasso, Stravinsky, Eliot, Graham, and Gandhi* (1993). His research focuses on the development of human cognitive capacities, particularly those central in the arts. He is also engaged in education reform in the areas of assessment, individual differences in learning, and professional development of teachers.

Jean M. Mandler is Professor of Psychology and Cognitive Science at the University of California, San Diego. After completing her Ph.D. degree from Harvard University, she worked as a Research Associate at Harvard and later the University of Toronto before accepting a faculty position at UCSD, where she has been since 1965. She has been a visiting fellow at Oxford University, University College London, and Beijing Normal University, among other appointments. A member of the Society of Experimental Psychologists, Dr. Mandler is known for her seminal work in the field of infant memory and story grammar.

After completing his Ph.D. at Stanford University in 1974, Stephen M. Kosslyn accepted academic appointments at The Johns Hopkins University, MIT, and Brandeis University before being appointed professor of psychology at Harvard University. Dr. Kosslyn has received many awards, including the Boyd R. McCandless Young Scientist Award and Fellow status in the American Psychological Association (Division 3) and the American Association for the Advancement of Science. His early work on mental imagery showed unusual originality both in scientific methodology and theory. His most recent work has dealt with cognitive neuroscience, and although his research is highly specialized, his reports are clear and exquisitely written. Dr. Kosslyn's research has been supported by many organizations, including the NSF, NIMH, Spencer Foundation, ONR, and the MacArthur Foundation among others.

After completing his Ph.D. degree at Yale University, Bennet B. Murdock started a lifetime of work on memory research, most of which was done at the University of Toronto. Included in the many honors bestowed on Professor Murdock are Fellow status in Division 3 of the American Psychological Association, visiting scholar at (Harvard), Fellow at the Center for Advanced Study in the Behavioral Sciences (Stanford), and a Festschrift honoring his work in human memory. His studies have touched many sides of memory research, but he is particularly well known for developing original theories in the field of distributed memory. Dr. Murdock has published numerous research articles and several books, including *Human Memory: Theory and Data* 1984).

Richard L. Gregory has been an active researcher and scholar since working with Sir Frederic Bartlett at Cambridge University over 40 years ago. Now Professor Emeritus at Bristol University in England, Dr. Gregory's academic career has included important posts at Cambridge University, where he designed and headed the Special Senses Laboratory, and visiting appointments at UCLA and MIT. His main passions are the experimental/theoretical study of perception and the communication of scientific knowledge to others, most notably, younger people. Among his many achievements, he is founding editor of the international journal *Perception,* founder of the Exploratory, founding member of the Experimental Psychological Society, author of *Mind in Science,* and editor of *The Oxford Companion to the Mind.* He has won numerous awards and honorary degrees, including the prestigious C.B.E. presented by the Queen.

Robert J. Sternberg is IBM Professor of Psychology and Education at Yale University. He earned his Ph.D. degree at Stanford and is a Fellow of the American Psychology Association and the American Psychological Society. Dr. Sternberg has written over 300 articles, books, and chapters and is currently involved in several projects in the schools, including the development of a program for teaching practical and creative intelligence to sixth-graders. He has won numerous awards from several organizations, among them the American Psychological Association, American Educational Research Association, the Guggenheim Foundation, and the Society for Multivariate Experimental Psychology.

Robert E. Shaw received his Ph.D. degree from Vanderbilt University and did postdoctoral studies at the University of Minnesota. Recently, Dr. Shaw has concentrated on ecological issues in psychology but his work has been diverse, including making significant contributions to methodological issues in psychology (with M. Turvey), in perception, and models of developmental changes. Among the many awards and honors bestowed on Dr. Shaw are Fellowship at the Institute for Advanced Study in the Behavioral Sciences in Stanford, California, and Fellow of the Center for Interdisciplinary Research, Bielefeld, Germany. In addition, Dr. Shaw serves on a number of editorial boards.

A native of England, Michael T. Turvey received his Ph.D. from Ohio State University and for most of his career has been a Professor at the Center for the Ecological Study of Perception and Action at the University of Connecticut and Haskins Laboratories. Dr. Turvey has been a eminent contributor to influential periodicals on such diverse topics as phonological priming, dynamic touch, pattern formation, and (with R. E. Shaw) on ecological physics and a physical psychology. Dr. Turvey is the recipient of a number of awards and honors, including the Guggenheim Fellowship, Early Career Award (APA), and Cattell Fellowship. In 1980 he was a Fellow at the Center for Advanced Study in the Behavioral Sciences in Stanford, California.

James J. Jenkins has been named Distinguished Research Professor of Psychology at the University of South Florida. After completing a Ph.D. degree in physics from the University of Chicago, Dr. Jenkins spent much of his academic life at the University of Minnesota. Most notable during his Minnesota period was his founding of the Center for Research in Human Learning, where he acted as its first director. He is inordinately proud of advising 71 doctoral students, many of whom have won acclaim in psychology. Dr. Jenkins has co-authored or edited eight books and over 150 scientific papers, many in the field of psycholinguistics, but his work has also touched almost every aspect of cognitive psychology. His research has been supported by the ONR, the Ford Foundation, the Social Science Research Council, NSF, NIMH, among other organizations.

As a student of psychology at Leiden University, Willem J. M. Levelt spent a semester with Michotte in Louvain, who was a student of Wundt and Külpe. After receiving his Ph.D. in 1965, Dr. Levelt became a research fellow at Harvard's Center for Cognitive Studies, where Michotte's nativist epistemology had tacitly been captured by the cognitive revolution. After chairing the experimental psychology and psycholinguistics program at Groningen University, he accepted a fellowship at the Institute for Advanced Study at Princeton. He then accepted the chair in experimental psychology at Nijmegen University. In 1980, Dr. Levelt became the founding director of the Max Planck Institute for Psycholinguistics in Nijmegen. Among his books are *Formal Grammars in Linguistics and Psycholinguistics* (1974) and *Speaking: From Intention to Articulation* (1989).

Dominic W. Massaro is a Professor of Psychology in the Program in Experimental Psychology at the University of California, Santa Cruz. He received his undergraduate education at UCLA and Ph.D. from the University of Massachusetts at Amherst. After a two-year position as a postdoctoral fellow at the University of California, San Diego, he was a professor at the University of Wisconsin until 1979 before accepting an appointment at the UCSC. He has been a Guggenheim Fellow, a University of Wisconsin Romnes Fellow, a James McKeen Cattell Fellow, and an NIMH Fellow. He is a past president of the Society for Computers in Psychology and is currently the book review editor of the *American Journal of Psychology*. He is a passionate cyclist and the beautiful hills around the UCSC campus provide a persistent challenge and distraction. His research interests include perception, memory, cognition, learning, and decision making. His current research is on the development and theoretical and applied use of a completely synthetic and animated head for speech synthesis.

George Lakoff was born in Bayonne, New Jersey in 1941. He attended MIT and graduated in 1962 with a Bachelor of Science degree in mathematics and English literature; he received his Ph.D. in linguistics in 1966 from Indiana University. Dr. Lakoff taught linguistics at Harvard University from 1965 to 1969, at the University of Michigan from 1969 to 1971, was a Fellow at the Center for Advanced Study in the Behavioral Sciences at Stanford during 1971–72, and has been Professor of Linguistics at Berkeley since 1972.

At MIT, Dr. Lakoff studied linguistics with Roman Jakobson and Noam Chomsky. He was one of the first generation of transformational grammarians, and in 1963 proposed a theory of generative semantics that combined formal logic with transformational grammar. Since the mid-1970s, Dr. Lakoff has been working within cognitive science, and has been one of the principal developers of cognitive linguistics, which brings the concerns and methods of cognitive science to the study of language and the methods of linguistics to the study of conceptual systems.

He is the author (with Mark Johnson) of *Metaphors We Live By,* of *Women, Fire, and Dangerous Things,* and (with Mark Turner) of *More Than Cool Reason.*

Donald A. Norman is an Apple Fellow at Apple Computer and Professor Emeritus in the Department of Cognitive Science at the University of California, San Diego. After completing degrees in Electrical Engineering from MIT and the University of Pennsylvania, he completed a Ph.D. degree at the University of Pennsylvania. Dr. Norman taught at Harvard before joining the newly founded Department of Psychology at the University of California, San Diego, of which he served as chair from 1974 to 1978. He was one of the founders of the Cognitive Science Society, and in 1987, helped establish the Department of Cognitive Science and became its first chair. Dr. Norman has had close working relationships with the computer, the aviation industry, as well as other industries for many years, and believes the "technological problems of today are sociological and organizational as much as technical." He has published extensively in many journals and his books include *The Psychology of Everyday Things* and *Things That Make Us Smart*.

Earl Hunt earned his B.A. from Stanford and Ph.D. from Yale. With only a brief time out for military service, he has held posts in computer science, business administration, and psychology departments at Yale, the University of California at Los Angeles, the University of Sydney and, since 1966, at the University of Washington. In an age when most people specialize, Dr. Hunt has been a generalist, interested in the broad aspects of cognition. While primarily interested in human problem solving and learning, he has worked in a number of related areas, including attention, artificial intelligence, and psychopharmacological influences on cognition. He has emphasized the use of formal mathematical models and has been principal editor for many major journals in cognition and experimental psychology.

Robert Sommer is Professor of Psychology and Chair of the Environmental Design Department at the University of California, Davis, where he has taught since 1963. He earned his Ph.D. from Kansas University in the area of visual perception and has been a visiting professor at Berkeley, University of Washington, University of Nevada, Reno, and Tallinn Pedagogical University in Estonia.

His major areas of interest are environmental psychology and action research. His books include *Personal Space, the Mind's Eye* and *A Practical Guide to Behavioral Research* (3rd edition, co-authored with Barbara Sommer). Dr. Sommer has the Environmental Design Research Award from the California Alliance for the Mentally Ill and a Fulbright fellowship to Estonia.

John B. Pittenger received his Ph.D. degree from the University of Minnesota under James Jenkins and was a postdoctoral fellow at Cornell University working with James Gibson—and both experiences were to have lasting effects on his work and studies. Dr. Pittenger is presently Professor of Psychology at the University of Arkansas at Little Rock. His major research interests are in the perception and memory of events in the world, especially the nature of the information that allows us to know what events are transpiring and what objects are engaged in those events. He has published numerous technical papers, both here and abroad, in many leading publications.

AUTHOR INDEX

SUBJECT INDEX